Inhabiting the Sacred
in Everyday Life

INHABITING THE SACRED IN EVERYDAY LIFE

How to Design a Place that Touches Your Heart,
Stirs You to Consecrate and Cultivate It as Home,
Dwell Intentionally within It,
Slay Monsters for It, and
Let It Loose in Your Democracy

RANDOLPH T. HESTER, JR. AND AMBER D. NELSON
WITH A FOREWORD BY FREDERICK R. STEINER

GTF
GEORGE F. THOMPSON
PUBLISHING

CONTENTS

This book is dedicated to Atticus Sessions Hester who told Grandy,
"My house loves me." Atticus, you show me the sacred with
everyday observation, dazzle me with complex insights,
challenge me with single-minded determination,
reflect me with self-motivation,
and give me hope by your willful being.

—Grandy Hester

This book is also dedicated to Adolfo "Fito" Ignacio Celedón Bravo,
who fought injustice until his last breath.
Mi Amor, your passion for life, love, and adventure was infectious
and is a continual example for my life's purpose
that I strive to pass on to the family I am creating
based on your teachings.

—Amber Nelson

FOREWORD

Frederick R. Steiner

To paraphrase Winston Churchill: First, we shape our surroundings; then our surroundings shape us. To paraphrase this message further: First, we shape places; then, with care and love, those places become sacred to us.

Randy Hester and Amber Nelson map out a clear process for such shaping of places. They guide us on a heartfelt journey of learning how to read landscapes, as J. B. Jackson taught us, and then how to use community-based knowledge to reveal and create "sacred" places for a community. Bottom line: Hester and Nelson urge each of us to forge "deep" and "thick" (that is, "profound" and "meaningful") relationships with the totality of our surroundings—both natural and cultural—and to engage in a democratic process by which citizens influence the shape and design of their neighborhoods, towns, and cities.

For example, it is early April as I write this, and I am thinking of my former home in Austin, Texas, where I was Dean of the School of Architecture at the University of Texas for fifteen years. By now, the leaves of the majestic live oaks would have fallen and the bluebonnets in the fields outside the Austin city limits would be in bloom and attracting scores of bumblebees. Even within the city, the Carolina wrens (*Thryothorus ludovicianus*) would have multiplied, as would the squirrels, raccoons, and opossums. A bluebird might compete with the squirrels for the peanuts I would toss around the thick trunk of one of the live oaks in our backyard. A pair of cardinals would search for food, the male's red always impressive. Weird, bungee-jumping creatures would hang from the branches of the live oaks. And tons of yellow-green pollen from those oaks would be blanketing the sidewalks and cars—products of rampant tree sex.

Thanks to Hester and Nelson, I even ponder the sacredness of the male Carolina wren that was always hopping around the backyard. Unlike other wren species in its genus, only the male sings its distinctive loud song, sometimes nearly 3,000 times in a single day. Austin is near the western limits of its year-round range. The small jumps of this handsome brown bird are always ordered and purposeful, and its routine and intention always settled my soul while stimulating my thoughts.

Now I live and work as Dean of the School of Design at the University of Pennsylvania in Philadelphia where, again in April, change is in the air, change is all around. Although the nights can still be brisk, every day the temperature inches upward; every day more plants bloom in explosions of color as an emergent green canopy expands across the city. This is my third time to live in Philadelphia, and it feels like home. I have returned north like so many birds filling the newly green branches, taking on mates and building nests. The squirrels race across the power lines that criss-cross my neighborhood.

Philadelphia must be ground zero for squirrels in North America. I monitor their activity from my front porch. Watching people on the sidewalk, I am happy that West Philadelphia has remained refreshingly diverse. The University of Pennsylvania has taken many measures to make the neighborhood safer and family friendly; I witness the success of those efforts. Good design and planning can do much to reveal and restore places.

Hester and Nelson write with considerable experience, understanding, and wisdom as landscape designers. They draw on established methods, especially from landscape architecture and urban design, but they infuse them with fresh insights and passion. We learn to recognize how our everyday landscapes convey deep biophysical and spiritual structures. In sharing many stories and examples, the authors make a compelling case for identifying, valuing, and taking better care of the everyday places where we live, work, and play through thoughtful practice and an active citizenry.

As the world's population continues to grow and becomes increasingly urban, the insights provided by Hester and Nelson are invaluable. They show how we can inhabit our neighborhoods, towns, and cities more thoughtfully, gracefully, and actively. And they demonstrate how we can live better with one another and with other species by awakening to a place that touches our heart. Their guidance is ultimately grounded in a respect and love for other people and their environments.

INHABITING THE SACRED
IN EVERYDAY LIFE

INTRODUCTION
Why Inhabiting the Sacred Matters

We hunger for settings that fill our lives with meaning, but a growing number of citizens in advanced urban societies have become numbed by places that are little more than efficient machines for economic investment and status. They may be able to afford ever-larger homes and pleasurable land-scapes, yet these places remain fundamentally unfulfilling. Research supports such discontentment, and a deep subconscious dissatisfaction shadows us.[1] Relationships with place, essential to a robust life and, indeed, our survival, are being lost.[2] Too few of our public and private spaces encourage vigorous con-templation or democratically induced human development. External forces beyond our control, such as global capitalism and remote technologies, contribute to a diminishing sense of interconnectedness to a place. Without control over our environment—whether at home or in our community—many of us are driven by fear, seeking security in gated communities but seldom finding it. Some of us become immo-bilized by the complexity of our problems, while others seek superficial thrills to subdue instability or obsess over personal social rank.

Meaningful relationships with a place are also suppressed by increased cultural sophistication. The general trend of social evolution has been a change from natural, naive, and simple creatures con-nected directly with the nearby environment to artificial, worldly, and refined motilities disconnected from place. Simply put, our reliance on what is nearby is diminishing daily. As we rely less on local resources and primal instincts for survival, essential human functions are corrupted, including both sen-sual pleasure and reciprocal relationships with others in the human and nonhuman world.[3] Furthermore, our way of knowing is reduced to rational thought alone, rendering one sensually and ecologically illiterate.[4] As this dependence on sensing what is nearby withers, so, too, does our identity with and commitment to familiar places such as home and neighborhood.[5] Loss of belonging undermines our personal and societal humanity.

Although it is easy to blame external forces, the problem begins with personal choices such as the mindless pursuit of consumption and status, of individual comfort and mobility, each of which can preclude knowing a place intimately enough for it to nourish and keep us well.[6] Loss of a deep attach-ment to our home and habitat threatens individual health and psyches and compounds to endanger communities and the basis of democracy itself.[7]

To offset this catastrophic trend, places that touch our hearts and give meaningful form to everyday environments—in our homes, places of work, neighborhoods, public landscapes, towns, and cities—must be cared for and created (Fig. 1). These places that arouse emotions symbolize deeply held values

Cherry Blossom viewing Botanical Garden 4 8 2001

FIG. 1. To recapture relationships essential to our well-being, we must
know places intimately; then those places reciprocate our caring,
filling us with simple pleasures such as being covered in a blanket of
cherry blossoms.

and ennobling purposes.[8] They provide a strong basis to confront dissatisfactions and treat personal and community maladies as opportunities for positive change Each of us can create such places for our own welfare and for the public good in concert with others in our home communities.

Living according to purposeful values makes us fully human by providing meaning to life. When given physical form by way of architecture and landscape design, these values are concretized as a "sacred" space or place.[9] This is not the standard use of "sacred," which is a loaded and multi-dimensional word that evokes powerful but often misguided or misunderstood reactions. Originally derived from the Latin words *sacer*, meaning "holy," and *sancire*, meaning "to consecrate," historical uses of "sacred" associate it with religious architecture. For example, as John Ayto writes in *Dictionary of Word Origins*, "In sacred architecture, humans attempt to bring themselves closer to the divine by creating a special space to hold this powerful and precious contact."[10] This type of architecture was closely aligned to a society's political situation, and, today, it is often built to embody a model of ethics and morality of a society.[11] More contemporaneously in the wake of the modern environmental movement, scholars sometimes use the phrase "a sacred place" to mean "a place with spirit" or *genus loci*: powerful places that are attractive due to their outstanding landscape qualities, making them prime targets for tourism and, after that, overdevelopment.[12]

These architectural claims to the sacred—that is, to the holy and the pristinely wild—justify elitist commodity-making and support a view of architecture as a monument and landscape as an aesthetic space with meaning mainly to fellow designers and art theoreticians. These views conspire with public insecurity, making the home a disposable consumer item and the civic environment a source of fear. It is, therefore, critical in our evolution as a species to expand the meaning of the sacred to include the places that people inhabit every day. While, as authors, we do not exclude standard definitions, the term "sacred" is herein broadened to describe the ability of a place to satisfy fundamental human needs. Sacred places possess such significance that they enable people to be moved by the ordinary and to live according to their most deeply held values in daily life. We refer to this continual act of intentional living as *inhabiting the sacred* (Fig. 2). Having sacred places in daily life has multiple benefits. Superficial motivations in everyday routines may distract us from simple observances that can provide purpose and joy, but creating and inhabiting a sacred place in our common environments call attention to the most crucial and pleasurable aspects of life. Here's a story of how an awakening can shape our space.

Ward, a colleague of ours, had become extremely unhappy in his cottage on Cape Cod and had decided to sell it. Before he accepted bids, Ward did a drawing exercise on sacred place that we introduce in the chapter entitled "Step 1: Awakening." In each of his drawings was a prominent sun, a reminder of his childhood in North Dakota, where he would lie in the sun after the last snow had melted and then gaze far away into the big open sky. The light made the place special; it was this sunlight he wanted to invite into his home. The dark interior simply did not accommodate his radiant worldview. Ward realized he could solve the problem inexpensively by adding windows in key locations and extending the

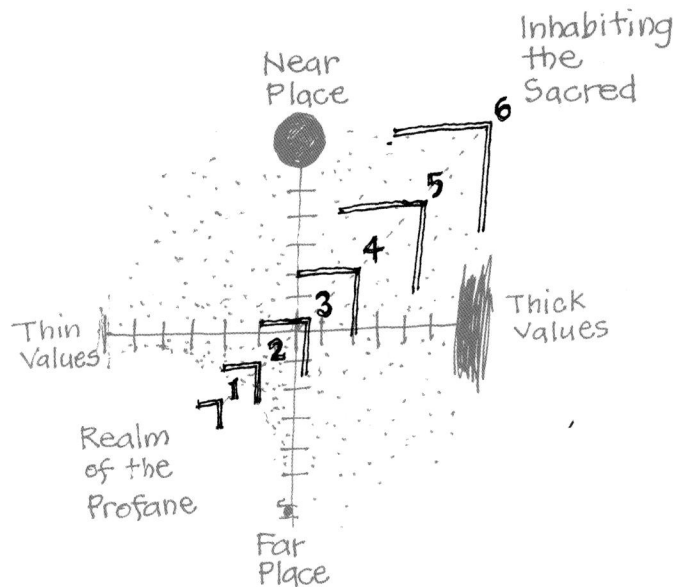

Fig. 2. Uncovering deeply held values about a place requires an
intentional design process and a focus on the environment nearby.

kitchen to receive full southern exposure. He decided not to sell the cottage. Instead, he did the renovation plans himself and has joyfully inhabited the sacred place he made more than thirty years ago.[13] As Ward cared for the house, the house became a more optimistic place, its drabness replaced with dazzling sunlight that made it irresistibly cheerful. Instilled with Ward's optimism, in ways both symbolic and built, the cottage in return cared for him.

Sacred places nurture their inhabitants, and they, likewise, are nurtured in a cycle of mutually beneficial give-and-take. In this reciprocity, places are not inert but active players. This is described beautifully in Kenneth Grahame's enduring 1908 children's novel, *The Wind in the Willows*, as Mole and Rat were returning to the river after a great adventure when Mole caught the smell of his long-abandoned home. This scent stopped him in his tracks. Although a terrible snowstorm was about to overtake them, he could not continue and "cried freely and helplessly and openly" to go back to find his home. Mole's former happiness at Mole End was matched by its reciprocal happiness with him: "And the home had been happy with him too, evidently and was missing him, and wanted him back, and was telling him so, through his nose, sorrowfully, reproachfully, but with no bitterness or anger; only with plaintive reminder that it was there, and wanted him."[14]

Making a place sacred enriches not only the home, but, when applied collectively, entire neighborhoods, towns, cities, watersheds, and ecosystems. Even the most neglected and fearful space can be made more habitable by calling up what is sacred to a community. In many cases, identifying and incorporating through design what people share as most valued in their public landscapes creates civic pride and a safer environment, increases acts of voluntary care and stewardship, strengthens the local participation in a ground-up democracy, beautifies and heals an area, and offers a greater sense of belonging.[15]

Inhabiting the sacred will welcome us all to healthier home places and simultaneously revitalize our nation's; home and nation depend upon the other. Only healthy individuals can create a healthy democracy; only a healthy democracy can create healthy communities. Democracy is as strong or hollow as its citizens. Presently, most Americans vote occasionally, consume voraciously, expect public subsidies for their private lives, complain about those they elect, and feel debilitated to make real change. In only the narrowest sense are they free. In a deep, ever-evolving, and healthy democracy, everyone needs to be free by being informed, affective, and fearless, to participate actively in civic life every day. Citizens would soon reclaim self-governance, take responsibility for it, make it transparent, and disperse its power. Inhabiting the sacred deputizes all of us to center our lives; it is a tangible way to regain control over our civil rights and responsibilities at home and in the community.[16]

Inhabiting the sacred, like caring for democracy, is not always easy, so this book serves as a guide through the most difficult moments with a series of steps and tested techniques. This is neither an essay of unachievable theory of the ideal nor a self-improvement manual that promises the world in convenient sound-bites. There is theory but only when it informs action; there are also "how-to" suggestions, because inhabiting the sacred often requires taking paths untraveled or oppositional to prevailing cultural trends. As a result, we see that big changes by ordinary people are not only plausible, but are already being realized. These are the places that enhance the quality of life.

So how do we achieve these ends? After more than five decades of collective professional work, testing many approaches, trying them as instructional tools, and reflecting on our own experiences, we conclude that six steps and associated techniques directly accomplish the above goals: (1) Awakening, (2) Evidencing, (3) Transforming, (4) Organizing, (5) Manifesting, and (6) Inhabiting the Sacred. Although we have already published much about ways to overcome detachment from place, for the first time we provide a practical road map for individuals to take control of the design of their environments, to live intentionally, and to reap the benefits of deep relationships with the landscapes they inhabit. We unite meaning and architectural precision so that any layperson or designer can preserve, reclaim, or create new places of deep value with distinct spatial form.

It is important to note that every successful domestic or public process is organic. Although we have experimented with design and planning methods in our careers, we know that solutions can never be predicted in perfect order. Nonetheless, the six steps should help any person or community to visualize the likely opportunities and challenges. Therefore, use this book as you would a map; locate yourself and your situation within your community, keep what is helpful now close to your heart and mind, and store the other array of tools until they are needed.

Inhabiting the sacred is important not only for concerned citizens, but also for professional architects, landscape architects, urban designers, city planners, civil and transportation engineers, private developers, and policy makers. Therefore we provide techniques and examples for how laypeople can develop the capacity to express precise spatial qualities and dimensions in order to inhabit the sacred; likewise, professionals learn how to gain trust and instill the motivation and means of capturing the public's deepest values regarding their home and community.

The challenges facing the architect, landscape designer, and planner in the twenty-first century are many. All now confront rapidly changing environmental, economic, and social conditions that the world has never before seen, and all are asked, in their own ways, to create sustainable solutions. All must mitigate conflict between invested citizens and stakeholders, often with differing ecological, economic, and philosophical worldviews. Simultaneously, all must grapple with new tools of design technology that provide unprecedented power and reach but, when used inappropriately, can separate the designer from a place and stifle creativity. Furthermore, the timelines for projects are growing shorter, demanding more in less time. In order to accommodate this reality, professional training in design and planning and a normal way of thinking must be supplemented with additional procedures such as community outreach, collaboration, and creative conflict. New terms need to be adopted into the professional nomenclature, including "sacredness" and "attachment to place." Workflow should incorporate both intuitive and precise tools in order to practice and enhance fundamental skills. Nothing can prepare the designer adequately for this radically uncertain future, but there are ways of training the design professional to be grounded, flexible, and visionary.

Understanding that the layperson and the professional have distinct points of view, we address both readerships in Part I by telling two stories that are different in scale, timeline, and interpersonal dynamic but comparable in objective and outcome. In "The Story of Manteo," Randy focuses on the empowered public working in tandem with the design professional to inhabit their sacred; in "The Story of Fito's Place," Amber focuses on a personal journey to awaken to and inhabit a sacred place in Berkeley, California, and then apply it to professional practice.

The story of Manteo may sound familiar, because much has been written about the distinctive process that Randy encouraged by which the once-dying city in coastal North Carolina recovered by identifying its sacred structure and using it as an inspiration to forge a healthy future. The success of Manteo and other community-design projects are encapsulated in the six steps: awakening, evidencing, transforming, organizing, manifesting and inhabiting the sacred. We summarize what each step has achieved in Manteo and then expand upon them in the rest of the book.

Amber follows the Manteo example with an intimate example from her own life. She explains how she made sacredness out of unspeakable tragedy. In September 2010, she lost the love of her life, Fito, to senseless violence and led an effort to create a public place at the corner where he was killed. Although the process of creation was completely organic at the time, we later found that, even then, the six steps were followed. Her anguish over this place was largely replaced by loving support by those in her neighborhood. These are valuable lessons that instruct us about the power of sacred place and the plausibility of one individual making a positive impact on the community that surrounds her.

In Part II, we describe the six steps toward inhabiting the sacred in sufficient detail for any layperson, city council member, or professional planner and designer to identify, enhance, protect, remake, and create their sacred landscapes. We explain each step, introduce useful techniques, and illustrate use of the step with case stories.

The first step, *Awakening*, is about personal sacred places. Without an understanding of personal values, it is impossible to ask a diverse population to agree on collective values. We provide instructions that allow an individual to explore and analyze his or her most-valued places and compare them to frequent outcomes of this exercise. Specifically, the reader is asked to explore you and your home's histories and consider changes that can be made in the everyday environment to concretize your most-cherished values, fundamental needs, and desire for pleasure and nourishment. The result is a personalized manifesto for intentional living.

The second step, *Evidencing*, explains how to document attachments to an existing place and legitimize subconscious places of the heart through precedents, surveys, testimony, and citizen science. These techniques for gathering evidence lead to a collective awareness of sentiment embedded in a community's sacred places.

The third step, *Transforming*, shows ways to evaluate existing plans for development that lack the means of inhabiting the sacred and to develop meaningful alternatives. We describe the essential aspects of public assembly, visualization, and comparison of the costs and benefits—not always financial—between various possible futures and finally the sacrifices required to attain a higher civic purpose.

The fourth step, *Organizing*, provides a step-by-step approach to mobilizing a community and turning grassroots democracy into an effective process of strengthening local power. This step addresses differences in the politics of preserving an existing sacred place, reclaiming a lost sacred place, and creating a new sacred place from the ground up.

The fifth step, *Manifesting*, explains how to plan and design sacred space. Sacredness is linked directly to humankind's most fundamental needs for security, new experience, reciprocal response, and belonging. We call these needs the four wishes and we describe them in detail, along with the four monsters, which detract us from the four wishes. Understanding the wishes and monsters and utilizing the design theory and techniques we outline in this chapter may facilitate the creation of places of great significance.

The sixth step, *Inhabiting the Sacred*, is the culminating plateau and the beginning point for further rewards in personal and community life. We discuss five basic ways of inhabiting the sacred—constructing, dwelling, stewarding, ritual visiting, and advocating—and the chapter concludes with an illustration of how one person's labor of love allowed him and his whole community to inhabit the sacred.[17]

In the Epilogue, we reflect on the fullness of inhabiting the sacred in even the most mundane activities of daily life. We summarize the advantages in terms of deep meaningfulness and simple aesthetic joys. While we have articulated one way to intentionally create valued, healthy, and beautiful places, we realize we have merely broadcast seeds that others will cultivate and reap the harvest. We look forward to those harvests.

PART I

Two Approaches to
Inhabiting the Sacred

RANDY'S STORY OF MANTEO

Steps toward Inhabiting the Sacred

When bridges opened access to the Outer Banks of North Carolina and its renowned beaches during the 1950s, highways bypassed the city of Manteo on Roanoke Island. Once the only safe harbor, Manteo had been the most important city of the area's barrier islands, but automobile transportation rendered the harbor unnecessary. Manteo plummeted from being the region's primary trade center to that of a near ghost town. Its businesses closed and tax base shrank, causing its tax rate to soar and seasonal unemployment to exceed twenty-two percent.[1] The commercial center and waterfront, with half its buildings vacant, lacked maintenance and use. The port was unrecognizable as the bustling wharf that locals remembered, but the decline had been so gradual it was difficult for citizens to grasp the decline as a threat (Fig. 3).

Most residents accepted the lost economy, because they felt powerless to reverse it, but newly elected Mayor John Wilson in 1980 decided to do something. He and other community leaders loved Manteo and wanted to recapture the spirit of this place they had experienced as children playing on the bustling docks. A young architect and Manteo native, Mayor Wilson saw the city through the eyes of a professional designer and local insider. He hired my design team to develop a comprehensive design for the city. We had never heard people speak of a place with such affection, but we agreed that Manteo's citizens needed much more than a nostalgic attachment to their city. To save Manteo, citizens needed a 180-degree economic turnaround.

On the day I first met with Mayor Wilson, the hardware store moved from downtown to a nearby coastal resort. It was the latest of many losses of Manteo's essential businesses. Only after our design team began to describe the dramatic changes necessary for economic recovery did residents realize the extent to which their community was in a financial freefall. Plans we presented for economic rebirth became the unwelcome messenger about their community's decline. Suddenly, they felt threatened and angry. The scope of the proposed plans forced people to think about the social patterns and places that mattered most to them.

At the time, the process of inhabiting the sacred occurred organically, though we have since recognized the process to consist of six steps:

1. *Awakening* to the special aspects of the city's everyday places.
2. *Evidencing* citizens' subconscious attachments to place.
3. *Transforming* values embedded in places through sacrifice.

4. *Organizing* an action plan for intentional civic living.

5. *Manifesting* places of certainty, new experience, reciprocal response, and belonging.

6. *Inhabiting* the sacred.

These steps form the structure of this book, but here we recount the story of how Manteo, faced with a terrifying future of decline, reversed that trend and, along the way, discovered a unique civic identity and used it as a guide to inhabit the sacred in daily life.

Step 1: Awakening to the Sacred

Mayor Wilson had a vision but was unsure how to proceed in a democratic way. Billie Harper, one of the designers, suggested interviewing city leaders (Fig. 4). This process of listening to influential citizens uncovered places that were special in their daily lives, but they wanted to know how other citizens felt, so a survey was conducted to discern community-wide goals. Citizens were randomly interviewed in their homes, and the survey focused on broad community concerns. In the process, many of the same points the mayor and leaders had articulated resurfaced, and affection for their home place was mentioned frequently. When asked what they liked most about Manteo, fifty-one percent of those surveyed noted friendly neighbors and listed informal friendliness in an open-ended question, a somewhat higher but not dramatically higher response than we found in other North Carolina cities. Being able to walk almost everywhere in town garnered twenty-two percent, an unusually high response. Places in the center of Manteo such as the waterfront, the village, and specific shops were described as being especially important, because they represented home or provided roots.

Residents were clear about a few critical community needs. They wanted jobs but wanted the character of the town preserved. Our design team knew that neighborhoods could be protected by zoning, facilities could be located compactly to reinforce walking, and a historic district could save venerable architecture. These were included as part of the plans to be presented, but people wanted something else. They were unable to verbalize this "something else" until the evening of the community meeting, when we presented the design proposals.

The awakening began when the community reacted with alarm to our concepts for economic recovery. A few were adamant that the proposals would ruin the character of the town; others remarked that economic growth was not worth it, if what was special about the place was destroyed. When we pointed out the high unemployment and taxes, residents still stood their ground. The few outspoken voices caused all of us to reconsider their everyday places. After our proposals received a strong though civil rejection, we doubled our efforts to find out precisely what cultural patterns and landscape features were essential to the city's life. What we did not understand at the time was that we were witnessing the beginning of a process to discover the city's sacred places. We were shaken from normalcy's slumber by a few wise residents.

Fig. 3. The derelict wharf in Manteo reflected a local unemployment rate of twenty-two percent that dampened the spirits of residents and prompted a few community leaders to call for a plan to revive the city.

Fig. 4. The process of place-making in Manteo began by listening to leaders in the community who were frequently at odds with each other. This helped to reveal deeply shared values about the center of town, surrounding wetlands, and front porches that made Manteo unique. Those shared values overcame previously held disagreements.

Step 2: Evidencing Attachment to Place

Although it was clear from the survey and community meetings that residents held special places in Manteo in their hearts, it was less clear which spots were important and why. In order to use beloved places for design inspiration, our design team had to gather more evidence.

Mapping of behavior proved to be an important tool. For several weeks, we sat in various locations and recorded what people did and where. The resulting maps showed the social ecology of everyday life, the "activity settings" for the daily patterns of Manteo's townspeople. While people had listed some of these behaviors as important in the survey, most had not been mentioned, and none had been described in form-describing detail. For example, some people told us it was important to be able to walk to the post office, but the behavior maps revealed a complex pattern of "newsing at the post office." Not only did people walk from distant neighborhoods or drive and park in the gravel lot across from the postal building, but the whole area, including the street, was a social space for residents to stop and talk, check out the water, gossip and discuss private and civic matters. There was a considerable amount of lingering, a form of adult hanging out, in groups from two to five people. These social exchanges were encouraged by the availability of protected niches: the post office's foyer, the street corner, the open door of a parked vehicle. People often met at the post office, seemingly by chance, then walked to the Duchess Restaurant or Fearing's Drugstore for coffee, iced tea, or lemonade. Going to the post office served many essential purposes besides getting the mail; it provided a setting that encouraged a sense of a caring community. Both social setting and proximity mattered in daily life. Minute temporal and spatial structure such as the size of the foyer or width of the street enhanced public interaction.

Newsing at the post office was only one of these ritualistic daily activities. Hanging out at the docks, public debates at the Duchess, and checking out the water (tides, shoreline, fishing catches, weather, and civic matters) were also community hotspots (Fig. 5). Lifestyle and setting were inextricably intertwined. Daily ritual had specificity to places, and the cultural dependence on places seemed more widespread than people had reported in the survey. This meant that changes in land use had the potential of significant, disruptive impact on the community (Fig. 6).

Our design team still did not know which places were most essential to the life of Manteo. So, on the basis of the behavioral mapping and discussions with the mayor, we made a list of the places we thought were important and asked community leaders and other residents to refine this list.

At first, even local leaders took their sacred places for granted. These places were not distant enough in time or separate enough from the toils of life to be seen consciously as special. Their value resided in the community's subconscious until the list was circulated around town. Slowly, both residents and the design team realized that residents' strongest attachments were to places with unremarkable aesthetic appeal; initially, this aesthetic seemed to be the simple distinction between vernacular and high-style architecture. The "good design" that local people observed in the media was one of mass consumption,

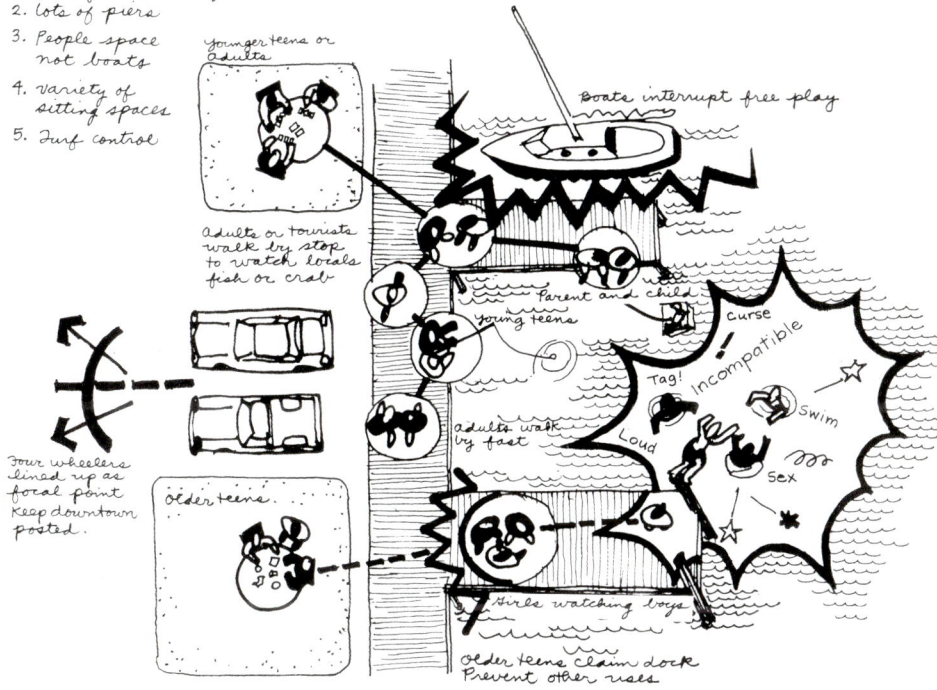

Conclusions:
1. Variety in water edge
2. Lots of piers
3. People space not boats
4. Variety of sitting spaces
5. Turf control

younger teens or adults

boats interrupt free play

adults or tourists walk by stop to watch locals fish or crab

Parent and child

young teens

curse

incompatible

Tag!

Swim

Loud

Sex

Four wheelers lined up as focal point Keep downtown posted.

Older teens.

adults walk by fast

Girls watching boys

Older teens claim dock Prevent other uses

FIG. 5. Drawing daily activities uncovered the importance of detailed design in rituals like hanging out at the docks.

FIG. 6. The design for the new boardwalk in Manteo accommodated each traditional activity pattern. Even amidst thousands of visitors, places were created for teenagers to hang out at the docks.

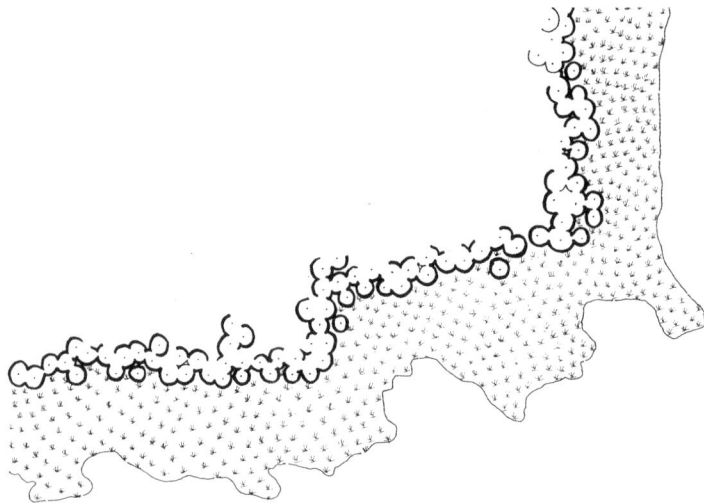

Marshland and Symbolic Property,
Natural Visual Backdrop

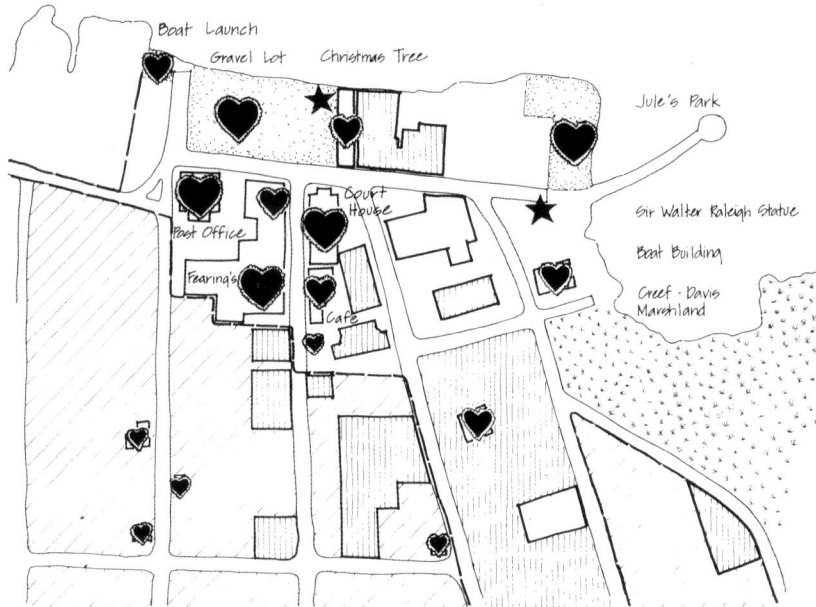

Boat Launch
Gravel Lot   Christmas Tree
Jule's Park
Sir Walter Raleigh Statue
Court House
Boat Building
Post Office
Creef · Davis Marshland
Fearing's
Cafe

LEGEND
♥ SACRED PLACES
★ SACRED LANDMARKS
▢ SACRED OPEN SPACE
∴ SACRED MARSHLAND
▢ OTHER IMPORTANT PLACES
// SACRED NEIGHBORHOODS

Fig. 7. When a member of the Town Board reviewed this drawing of places that residents insisted on preserving, he called it "The Sacred Structure of Manteo." This map was the single most important part of the community inventory, inspiring the revitalization of the downtown.

low density, upper-middle-class suburbs with residential areas neatly segregated from modern shopping facilities to which everyone drove. Not a single sacred place in Manteo matched this image.

Manteo had always disappointed visitors expecting Colonial Williamsburg's quaintness, making locals feel that their homey places reflected badly on their community. This silent shame needed to be converted into pride through a process of legitimization before a real economic plan could be conceived. We organized a series of community workshops that allowed residents to share their love for these places that satisfied their daily needs and reflected their values. In Manteo, there is a tradition of using workshops to supplement public hearings, and this proved to be an effective way for citizens to plan their city's future. The workshops allowed face-to-face exchanges of ideas between the community and designers. As outside experts, our design team acknowledged the import of these places by making loving public presentations of the daily patterns we had recorded, pointing out that we were learning from them what made Manteo unique. Had these places remained illegitimate, townspeople would have only told us about the places that tourists valued, and we would have never arrived at the design that revived Manteo.

Next, we presented a collective picture of the valued places to the community in a map that came to be called *The Sacred Structure of Manteo* (Fig. 7), after Jule Burrus, a member of the Town Board, saw how many of the places ranked higher than local churches and the cemetery. Although every person used and valued some of the places, few people knew them all intimately. No one had comprehended how much others valued the same places they did, nor could they visualize the patterns of sacred places until it was presented as a list with a map and a catchy title. The Sacred Structure map was a land-use map of everyday life that provided indisputable evidence of Manteo's most essential form. Many residents acknowledged that they suddenly saw relationships in the map they never knew before. It unified the separate special spots into an interconnected whole. The map's visual accessibility made it a part of the local vocabulary and could then be debated at the Duchess Restaurant and Betty's Country Kitchen along with such typical topics as job opportunities and property-tax benefits of tourism. The subconscious values embedded in the special places had become part of the collective consciousness. Hard evidence had legitimized these everyday sacred places.

Step 3: Transforming through Sacrifice

We agreed with public officials that historic tourism and boat building seemed the most viable economic development strategy among the alternatives being considered, but some redevelopment would still be necessary. To preserve Manteo's Sacred Structure, we developed a newspaper questionnaire to get residents to rank these places in order of significance. The local newspapers ran the survey as a public service. In it we asked residents to state which places they thought could be changed to accommodate tourism and which places they were unwilling to sacrifice in order to attract tourist dollars.

A series of specific trade-offs were posed, such as whether it was more important to leave the Christmas tree in the gravel lot downtown or to use the space for public parking. Responses to these questions provided a precise measure of the intensity of attachment to places in addition to the economic benefits and challenges of tourism. These additional responses allowed us to compare the relative importance of places stated in the newspaper survey compared to the earlier survey and mapping of behavior. Ones that ranked high in all three methods were deemed most sacred and became the top priority for preservation.

We created a ranked and weighted list of significant places from the responses. Because local people considered the cemetery and school inviolable, these places served as cutoff points for the list of places that should not be negatively affected by new development. Any place that ranked higher than the cemetery and school was to be preserved. The Sacred Structure included the marshes surrounding town, Jule's Park (Fig. 8), which was constructed by volunteers from the rubble of a demolished school, a drugstore and soda fountain that still squeezed fresh lemonade, the post office, the churches, the Christmas Shop, the front porches, the town's boat launch, the old wooden boatwright shops, the statue of Sir Walter Raleigh (Fig. 9), the Duchess and Country Kitchen Restaurants, the town hall, the locally made street signs, the town's cemetery, the gravel parking lot where the Christmas tree was located and where biannual community celebrations and daily teen "hanging at the docks" occurred, the park's lightposts placed in Jule's Park and along the waterfront in memory of loved ones, the old school, the local department store, and two historic sites. Two neighborhoods also received high rankings: one was the predominantly white neighborhood adjacent to City Center, home to long-time families, and the other was the predominantly African-American district, where a Freedman's Colony had been established during the Civil War and the homes of many celebrated local craftsmen and most-famous heroes of an all-black Coast Guard station remained. These neighborhoods contained not only historic houses, but also centuries of memories.

The places were drawn on a map that was called "The Sacred Structure of Manteo." The map simply showed the places colored with varying tonal intensities, based on the rankings from the newspaper survey. It looked similar to other inventory maps such as flood zones, building conditions, and property values, except it represented an affective attachment to place instead of topographic contours, deteriorated foundations, and real-estate prices. The official nature of the map allowed it to stand as a powerful addition to the inventory prepared as part of the planning process. It stated loudly and clearly that residents wanted these places protected.

The map was highly publicized in the newspaper and became a heavily debated topic. One editor at the paper expressed his concern that the identification of these sites in the survey meant that the design team was considering change for the places. In a prominent editorial, he listed places that must not be profaned for tourists, stating they were "perfect jewels" just the way they are.[2] His "perfect jewels" referred directly to Jule's Park but also included many of the other most-valued places. Frequently

Fig. 8. Jule's Park was designed to be a flexible multi-use place that could accommodate many special activities, from Easter Sunrise Service to demonstrations of early canoe-making techniques.

Fig. 9. The statue of Sir Walter Raleigh was erected to celebrate the unique local identity, becoming the setting for picture taking when friends or relatives visited as well as street festivals, art fairs, and fund-raising events.

Fig. 10. After a series of intense workshops, residents chose a plan for
revitalizing Manteo that preserved their sacred places but initiated
actions to boost a new economy.

during the planning process that followed, the editor retold me the story of Jule's Park to remind me
that local people were willing to sacrifice financial gain to save their beloved places. The rubble recalled
childhood memories and symbolized the local value of building from ruins. Each time, the editor gestured
with a pointed index finger and concluded ever so slowly, "More valuable than dollars."

Many other residents followed suit by responding to the newspaper survey. At a community
meeting, they evaluated a series of plans the design team developed and finally chose a plan most
inspired by their sacred places (Fig. 10). One resident recalled, "We were working in small groups,
negotiating to choose a plan that preserved our most-valued places; it was like we had assembled for
a solemn ceremony." By the time the design plan for the city was complete, residents had agreed upon
which places to preserve in their entirety, despite any new development. This process of separating the
most-important places from the less-valued ones consecrated the places and legitimized the residents'
affection for the unspectacular though nonetheless sacred cornerstones of their hometown.

Preserving these places required sacrifice. To help people choose a course of action, we presented
a projection of public and private costs and benefits of each alternative plan. Economic development
would suffer to the extent some residents might judge any potential project to be incompatible with the
Sacred Structure. In the first five years after the plan was implemented, preserving the sacred places cost
the town more than $500,000 in annual retail sales alone. People were aware of this real cost before-
hand, because the cost-benefit analysis had accurately predicted it. This sacrifice further consecrated the
places. The newspaper editor confirmed this sentiment each time he said that these places had a higher
value for Manteo than the calculated dollars.

Step 4: Organizing an Action Plan for Intentional Living

Despite local importance, only two places among the Sacred Structure were protected by official historic-preservation legislation, and only a few others could be protected by existing zoning law. This meant that the standard planning mechanisms for preserving local cultural heritage entirely ignored many of the places most critical to the present lifestyles and memories of Manteo. Decades of national advances in local land-use controls had completely missed this essential aspect of community life. The community had to organize an action plan to guide development, change zoning ordinances, and more. Residents who were not normally active had to learn to utilize political action to succeed in saving Manteo's character while improving its economy. An informal coalition coalesced around Mayor Wilson. For complex reasons, he drew admiration from old-time families, business owners, supporters of history and the arts, environmentalists, the African-American community, and newcomers alike. These diverse interests had never before rallied around a single person or cause, but they did for Mayor Wilson. The normally disparate voices of the coalition united in their endorsement of his ideas. He, in turn, mentored many political novices in the exercise of power for the public good (Fig. 11).

The loose coalition focused, first, on preservation through changes in the zoning law. They supported legislation to make the entire downtown subject to conditional-use permits. One condition was that any new development must demonstrate to the Planning Board no negative impact on the Sacred Structure. The coalition also lobbied the Town Board to adopt *The Guide for Development* that our design team wrote in 1980. It has provided guidelines for conceptual design and site plan approval and detailed architectural standards ever since.

Citizens have also used the Sacred Structure as the basis for negotiation with outside developers who proposed inappropriately scaled projects. This prevented wholesale redevelopment of the waterfront and led to smaller-scale projects that local developers have been able to undertake, simultaneously strengthening the local economy and maintaining a human scale in the new buildings.

The Sacred Structure provides the basis for ongoing evaluation by citizens of zoning and development proposals. In one debate over the development of a new marina, residents used the statistics gathered in the survey on goals in which sixty-five percent of townspeople preferred improved boat ramps and docks for locals, even if it meant less revenue from a marina for tourists. As a result, the Manteo waterfront became an unusual mixture of local and visitor facilities attractive to both populations (Fig. 12). The improved boat ramp still occupies a central location downtown and creates an essential point of everyday life.

Most importantly, the Sacred Structure serves as political common ground. The 1980 plan for the town consisted of forty-eight specific actions, all but one of which was implemented but not without considerable political disagreement. Over the years, control of the Town Board seesawed between

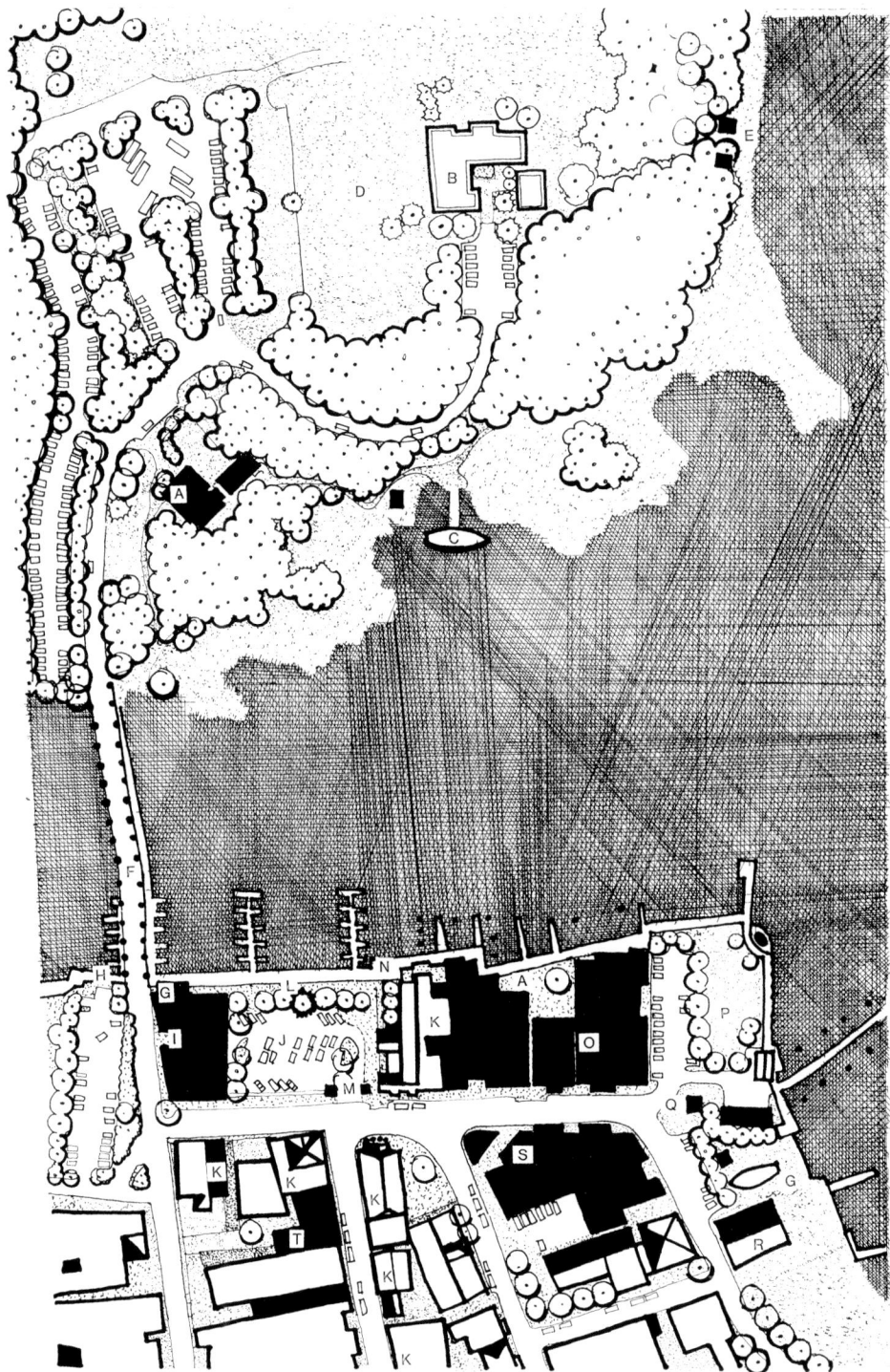

Fig. 11. The plan for Manteo called for a new visitor center and festival park to house a replica ship of the early colonists and a revived wooden boat-building industry, connected by a trail along the waterfront that is designed as a front porch.

Fig. 12. The waterfront has long served both local needs and visitors' entertainment. Integrated into the heart of the promenade, the boat ramp supports fishermen and recreationists.

supporters of the visionary plan and those who questioned it as too bold and beyond the capability of a small city. At one point, opponents dismissed the planning staff hired to secure funding and oversee zoning and permits to implement the original plan. Projects were delayed, and ugly conflicts of interest created dissent. Mayor Wilson, whose foresight and energy gave form to the original big dream of economic rebirth, resigned in 1984, only to be elected to the Town Board, then reelected mayor in 2003 on the platform of undertaking another visionary community effort. Town leaders realized they needed a plan to address emerging issues, so we created a new set of design guidelines called the *Manteo Way of Building*. This guide more pointedly and comprehensively preserves and inspires the future character of the city, as it lays out a plan for redevelopment of the suburban strip into an everyday downtown. It describes precise patterns for new buildings, streets, and open space grounded in the geometries proven to be sacred to the community today. As a result of this recent planning, much of the surrounding wetlands and flood-prone uplands that create the boundary for Manteo have been purchased and restored through the extraordinary organizing and fundraising of a local nonprofit group (Fig. 13). Another local group has conserved key farmland along the main road into Manteo, which the State of North Carolina designated as a Historic Corridor, providing additional protection for the surrounding woodlands. All parties supported the preservation, in perpetuity, parts of the Sacred Structure and the new development inspired by it. Throughout this political roller coaster ride, the Sacred Structure remained a constant point of agreement during acrimonious political periods.

Fig. 13. Restoration of wetlands and rain gardens constructed by community volunteers have improved Manteo's water quality, essential for oystering and fishery industries.

Step 5: Manifesting Meaningful Form

Manteo's Sacred Structure, for the most part, consists of humble places, "holes-in-the-wall," that are settings for daily routines. They cultivate security and mutual caring. Because most of the sacred places were clustered within walking distance, they formed a center, the focal point of everyday life that contributed to a shared sense of community. The post office, town launch, and Duchess Restaurant were part of this center. At the Duchess Restaurant, for example, was a separate locals-only wing with counter, stools, and booths. In the corner was a large, somewhat circular table called the "round table." Here, starting in the early morning and changing in shifts throughout the day, locals discussed major issues, tried to understand differences, and reason out solutions to propose to the Town Board. Many people participated and listened intently to each other's opinions, exhibiting a sense of shared civic responsibility in daily life.

Another special place, equally humble, is the setting for teenagers "hanging out at the docks." The teens appropriated the area where much of the waterfront can be patrolled from one spot directly on Shallowbag Bay, with views of the water and every main route into downtown. Teens had learned to swim there as long as anyone could remember. They do what youth do, pushing the limits of acceptable behavior in terms of noise, language, sexual activity, and interracial mixing. The docks are a setting for rebellion against parental restraint and gentle insurrection against local authority. For teens, this is a place of security, new experience, heightened sensuality, and belonging, satisfying all fundamental needs we discuss later in this book. Despite frequent conflict, hanging out at the docks connects generations. The bay is a place of adventure and danger. It offers a setting of present activity for the current generation of teens and past memory for their parents and grandparents. It also forms a powerful natural boundary for Manteo's residents, delineating the inside from the outside, the near from the far.

Memories are also embedded in the many wooden-boat-building shops that once housed a thriving economy, then became a source of public embarrassment and have been recently revitalized. The Creef-Davis Shop was one of the most famous. For several hundred years, beginning with George Washington Creef's Shallowbag shad boat, each generation of this family invented and produced a new wooden boat, employing people throughout the area, but, by 1980, these boatwrights were among the unemployed. For all its past accomplishments, the Creef-Davis Shop, empty and decaying, was only an eyesore occupying a key waterfront location. The family gave the property to the city, which restored the building as a maritime museum and boat-building center (Fig. 14). It informs citizens of the power of the family's public generosity.

Places in Manteo represent shared identity and remind residents that the Sacred Structure reflects values such as responsibility to democracy, fellow neighbors, and the dream of racial equality. In particular, Jule's Park, which we speak about at length at the end of the book, symbolizes the belief in civic volunteerism and Phoenix-like recovery from misfortune. The shared value of grassroots democracy is invested not just in the round table at the Duchess Restaurant, but also in Town Hall. It is symbolically owned by most residents who consider the local government truly theirs. The sentiment of keepers of unmet dreams was first encapsulated in the beloved yet homely wooden statue of Sir Walter Raleigh, whose lost colony had founded the first English settlement on Roanoke Island in July 1584, and more recently in a statue recalling the Black Life-Saving Unit. Front porches are essential for climatic comfort but also represent informal friendliness and neighborly helpfulness (Fig. 15). So important are these porches that a federal grant for low-income housing was nearly lost when Mayor Wilson refused to build the apartments unless they included porches, which were considered by the standards an "extravagance" for the underprivileged. The mayor insisted that the poor most needed the natural cooling and spaces for social interaction; finally, the federal government relented, and the front porches are now intensively enjoyed.

The Sacred Structure directed and infused life into the final chosen plan. Of the seven plans our design team proposed for the village center, residents chose one with somewhat less economic potential, because that plan preserved more of the Sacred Structure and interrupted fewer of the residents' accustomed patterns, rituals, and symbols. That plan also captured the hearts of the community, because it created a new economy inspired by Manteo's history.

Through this plan, Manteo reinvented the traditional wooden-boat-building industry where each boat is crafted by skilled hands that now teach younger hands centuries-old secrets of the trade. Traditional boatwrights constructed a ship reminiscent of the vessel Sir Walter Raleigh's lost colonists arrived in. It serves as a floating classroom for schools along the navigable waters of the state and

Fig. 14. The generous donation of the Creef-Davis Shop provided a place to restart wooden boat-building industries, now a thriving local economy.

Fig. 15. The civic front porch is an essential part of everyday life in Manteo and a point of orientation between security and danger, home and wild seas.

attracts enough tourists to allow the town to supplement public services for its residents. Other boat-wrights began producing a range of crafts, from dinghies to large pleasure boats, and they form the backbone of Manteo's industrial economy today (Fig. 16). As the city expanded its wooden crafts industry, it also replenished its local economy, village charm, and confidence. It expanded its identity to become a center for the performing arts. Today, Manteo hosts not only the Lost Colony Outdoor Drama, but also musical performances in Festival Park (Fig. 17). For residents attracted to industrial work, boat building remains the premier performance art.

People in Manteo also consciously make places to dwell, to linger, to strengthen their community and to participate actively in the politics of the city. To some extent, these have been codified in land-use and building codes that state Manteo's intention to preserve the valued sites. These codes provide performance criteria for development consistent with the height, bulk, scale, and public character of the village and emphasize to builders the importance of constructing new projects within the existing community framework. As a result, new development has, for the most part, fit in with and actually enhanced valued ways of dwelling. For example, most of the new tourist facilities were located on previously unused Ice Box Island to prevent filling marshes. This action also retained the natural boundary people cherish. In other cases, the codes showed developers how to in-fill around and enhance the sacred places rather than raze buildings for larger-scale commercial projects. This has created more places to meet friends, linger, and discuss civic matters. The codes also facilitate walking instead of driving, a key aspect of dwelling in Manteo.

One of the most-distinctive projects the community has undertaken is the linear waterfront porch, consisting of several parks, an urban promenade, exhibit spaces for boat building and performing arts, and a boardwalk that leads from the city center through natural areas to nearby neighborhoods. The Sacred Structure inspired the idea that places for tourists and locals could be mixed together along the waterfront to create an urban promenade shared by visitors and residents alike. Consistent with the residents' love of their front porches, the promenade was conceived as a public front porch, where the community could have fun and informally convey to younger generations and visitors the lessons and joys of Manteo. Boat-building shops and a native canoe-burning exhibit invite all to "Come, sit on our front porch and let us tell you of the dreams we keep." The waterfront porch combines everyday living and learning (Fig. 18).

These are no mere places. They provide the settings for everyday life. Together, they create a center, a natural boundary, and a unique physical identity. They also remind people of their obligations to the community, intergenerational ties, harmonious and conflicted shared history, and noble civic aspirations. These places combine to express Manteo's uniqueness and structure the residents' internal images of their city (Fig. 19). They are familiar and homey, yet each is heroically inspiring and eloquent in its context. They make manifest the deepest needs and highest aspirations of the community, none of which could have been possible to achieve from an outside-in or top-down or single-purpose approach to revitalization and redevelopment.

Fig. 16. Boat building expanded to include replicas of traditional fishing boats, life-saving vessels, and museum-quality pleasure craft.

Fig. 17. Festival Park is the setting for a variety of outdoor performances, from informal events to major music concerts.

Fig. 18. The revitalization plan called for hands-on exhibits and demonstrations of traditional ways of life integrated into the fabric of the boardwalk.

Fig. 19. An abundance of short piers and entrances to shops, crafted to encourage hanging out and socializing, punctuate the walkway along Manteo's waterfront.

Step 6: Inhabiting the Sacred

The process of uncovering the residents' most-cherished places and the values embedded within them allowed them to inhabit the sacred in multiple ways. They have made it a tradition to construct their city with their own hands. They dwell there willfully. They steward the place. They invite ritual visiting. They serve as advocates for a more-meaningful public life.

In constructing the new Manteo, the unseemly appearance of some of the sacred places animated the new development's visual quality. It feels and is homemade. It is understated and invites social interaction and empowers personal participation. It has an unfinished aesthetic that makes it open to community change. Local people continue to add new touches. The feeling conveyed is a homey and unpretentious atmosphere that already existed on individual front porches. As a result, the development is intimate, small in scale, and inspired by local people.

It is hard to imagine now that the waterfront porch almost did not happen this way. The first phase of construction was a multi-million-dollar project to build the promenade. Days before it was to go out to bid, Mayor Wilson realized that no local contractors were bonded sufficiently to receive the contract. He agreed to serve informally as supervising contractor in order to keep the work local. The city divided the project into dozens of small contracts, which were undertaken by local businesses and volunteer civic groups. As a result, the pieces of the promenade along the water are not quite as polished as they might have been, but the community's identity, bolstered by the effort, has more than compensated (Fig. 20). A local manufacturer of yard furniture crafted all the public furnishings. The promenade feels like a part of home. It truly serves as the civic front porch. Making it together was a key step to the community collectively inhabiting the sacred. Residents continue to do much of the labor on community projects, and constructing projects is now part of Manteo's identity.

Certainly, the waterfront porch is the quintessential dwelling place, providing not just places for teens to hang out, but lingering spots for people of all ages and persuasions. There are places for impromptu performances and boat building, quiet spots for lovers, docks from which to fish and crab, and remote locations to view wildlife (Fig. 21). Many of these are recent additions to the Sacred Structure of Manteo, carefully conceived and executed to enhance everyday life.

The Manteo tradition of volunteerism and community stewardship seems unlimited. Jule's Park is only one example. The plan, based on the Sacred Structure, made these values more visible in the public landscape, stimulating more actions than ever before. Residents refer to the volunteer-made waterfront porch. They also recall the generous gifts of valuable waterfront property such as the Creef-Davis Boat Building shop and surrounding marshland as well as the discounted sale of the Meekins property on Ice Box Island, which made the community's recovery possible without taxing poor and middle-class citizens. Others note the long and continuous service of people such as Bill Parker, Chairman of the Planning Board, who donated thousands of hours to revise and steward new projects so they embody

Fig. 20. The waterfront promenade was designed for celebrations of historic events and for everyday enjoyment of the bay and surrounding wetlands. It was built entirely by local contractors and volunteers.

Fig. 21. The civic front porch connects to nearby neighborhoods to encourage walking and to quiet spots to take a contemplative rest.

Fig. 22. The Little Farm and Festival Park provide hands-on learning where children of all ages can make furniture, plow with an ox, and practice other necessities of living intentionally.

Fig. 23. For the most part, new development in Manteo has been harmonious with the old two-to-four-story buildings, maintaining the homey scale that people value while increasing density to sustainable levels.

qualities consistent with the Sacred Structure. Parker and other community members created assertive nonprofit organizations to preserve key historic areas and open space. Other residents recall the unusual labor of state employees to create a processional entry into Manteo that maintains the forests to form a natural boundary east of the city. A landscape architect in the state bureaucracy worked for years to plant hundreds of native live oaks all along the corridor, creating a five-mile long alleé that juxtaposes ordered nature with native wilderness. This heightens the drama of arriving in Manteo and clearly defines a sense of being inside and outside the built and natural environments that residents say is important to their identity. A recent labor of love by Mayor Wilson and Bill Parker is the recreation of a subsistence farm from the ruins of an early homestead. It allows people to experience the dreams and hardships of island life during previous centuries. The Little Farm also offers dozens of practical lessons for anyone who wants to live intentionally and sustainably (Fig. 22). Above and beyond the Little Farm, Mayor Wilson has dedicated most of his life to stewarding Manteo, allowing himself and others to inhabit the sacred in innumerable ways.

All of these actions have made Manteo a place people return to whether native, new resident or visitor, who sense it is a special place. Manteo lures them back in powerful and often unconscious ways. People make ritual visits to relive or learn from its history, to make their own boat, or simply to enjoy the city's civic front porch. They come for festivals that celebrate the beginning and end of tourist season. They come for Christmas and Easter celebrations or simply to be in the lively downtown.

Manteo has become a poster child of economic recovery and has enjoyed much publicity over its success. Each time it wins an award or receives national notice, Manteo advocates the cause of inhabiting the sacred in everyday life. Most celebrated is the waterfront designed as a public front porch. Much of the attention focuses on the use of the Sacred Structure as both a means to preserve the local culture and to inspire harmonious new development (Fig. 23). The inclusion of the Sacred Structure created a process distinct from most planning and design schemes. The process has inspired scores of other cities throughout the United States and Asia to implement an approach that develops from residents' noble values and emotional attachments to a place.

Manteo's Success

Within ten years of implementing the plan, Manteo was thriving economically. Unemployment was reduced from twenty-two percent to a mid-single digit. The tax base was healthfully expanded. Property taxes are now appropriately average compared with other cities statewide. What began as a conscious, public financial sacrifice when townspeople chose the plan to protect their sacred places turned out to enrich the community's economic value in the long run.

The village center is bustling in ways that gladden the hearts of the dreamers who envisioned its transformation. There is both upscale and blue-collar pedestrian street life. Blacks as well as whites are walking and talking; tourists as well as locals are shopping; older couples on their daily exercise routes as well as teenagers on bikes are passing through town. Most new neighborhoods are dense, compact, and connected. Older ones are being in-filled and lovingly repaired. Poorer neighborhoods are receiving significant public investments to redress past neglect. In recent years, the community has researched the African-American role in the U.S. Coast Guard. There was a station on Pea Island manned exclusively by African Americans, many from Manteo, who were famed for their life-saving exploits. Now, the most prominent statue in town (Fig. 9) depicts their heroism. It is the centerpiece of a park commemorating black history.

Of course, no city or town is without problems. To address theirs and identify changing issues, Manteo makes an annual survey to determine residents' satisfaction with their city. During the 1980s, local concerns focused on unemployment, the rundown waterfront, declining business, and poor maintenance of streets and sidewalks. As the economy improved, these issues were replaced by traffic congestion and lack of parking. Today, people worry that the city is becoming too commercialized. Others worry about the quality of Manteo's drinking water and offshore pollution, so the city recently created rain gardens with native wetland plants to capture urban runoff and clean the pollution before it reaches the bay. These actions will eventually lead to restored habitats and healthier seafood harvests. Some local officials think the biggest problem is rising housing costs. The second-home market is exceedingly profitable, pricing younger local residents out of the market. This presents a most-challenging issue, because Manteo has made an extraordinary effort to produce affordable housing, consistently keeping ten percent of the housing stock for low- and moderate-income residents.

The other serious issue is the decline of the aging commercial strip. To revitalize that area as a more urban, mixed-use district will require connecting the strip to the now-thriving village shopping area to create a single town center. *The Manteo Way of Building* provides guidelines to achieve this, but implementation will take years and require creative partnerships unavailable at present.

Manteo has taught me many lessons. Among them is the realization that community design is not about making monuments to the designer. Rather, design is about the more important goal of empowering citizens to reform their community and even society. This requires me to walk in their shoes and for them to walk in mine. We must transact as equals and teach each other. I must engender enough trust that the community will expose to me their most-profound hopes and fears. I can neither hide behind nor use my expertise in design and planning to intimidate, but I must use my design and planning skills to give their values form, I must challenge what I consider bad ideas, and I must make my thinking about design transparent so that citizens can make well-informed decisions about the design of their city. If the architect, landscape designer, and planner truly share in the process, stewards will take over and achieve successes the designer can only dream of. To do this, I had to change my motivation as a designer. I also had to learn techniques to engage the public and to develop a language for and with people about the civic landscape.

This book provides our best effort to provide these methods and vocabulary. We have learned through a wide array of professional experiences such as Randy's involvement in Manteo that these steps comprise the essential progression toward inhabiting the sacred. It was not until Amber's creation of Fito's Place, however, that we learned how instinctual the design and planning process can be. This discovery further validates the steps and their use in design and planning at city, neighborhood, and residential scales. In the next story, Amber explains how she subconsciously followed the steps to inhabiting the sacred in everyday life, with lasting results for a neighborhood in Berkeley, California.

AMBER'S STORY OF FITO'S PLACE

Subconscious Steps toward Inhabiting the Sacred

Most designers can trace their careers back to the first vivid moment when a place set off a spark that touched their fundamental essence. This is the moment when they realize the importance of design. For this instant, nothing exists but the budding designer and the place. They experience their deepest needs being met by physical space. They may not know it, but they are learning to inhabit the sacred. Each designer has a distinct path that leads them to continue the search of inhabiting the sacred in their design careers. In this chapter, I will explain mine.

Interest and Thought

For me, this moment occurred when my father moved into a house on a military base in Florida with an extraordinary tree in the backyard. Its massive branches began low and horizontal, spread wide and continued high. Its roots came up out of the ground and weaved mazes in the grass around it. It was the perfect climbing tree. We had an immediate affinity for each other. I named it the "Everything Tree" and spent hours each day climbing and swinging, dreaming about the things I could build within its large and generous limbs. I was nine years old and had never heard of architecture before. For the time being, I was thrilled simply to exist with the Everything Tree and our fantasies.

The love affair had only begun when Hurricane Andrew devastated much of Florida in the summer of 1993 and destroyed my Everything Tree. Amazingly, however, as the tree uprooted, its reaching branches held fast to the roof and kept our belongings inside relatively intact, while neighbors' homes were stripped down to the structure, losing everything. I felt it had sacrificed itself for our family to show gratitude for the love we had showed it. Afterwards, the man versus nature conflict occupied a lot of my creative energy. I remember making paper models of the Everything Tree and writing poetry about rainstorms. Through art I explored my miraculous experience with the tree. I had never heard of landscape architecture either.

Education and Design

By high school, I desperately wanted to take advanced art classes, but the only one available to me was mechanical drafting followed by architectural drafting. I was, nonetheless, thrilled about the precision of drafting. It counter-balanced intuitive expressions such as music, dance, sketching, and poetry that I pursued outside of school. My passions for precise drafting and intuitive arts led me to study architecture.

In my first job out of college at a luxury handbag company's architecture department, I served only the business of architecture and profit-driven aims of the free market. I began to question American society's norms for success. I realized I had been blissfully ignorant of how my First World actions were having disastrous effects on the many billions of people who reside elsewhere. I quit my job and moved from Manhattan to Lima, Peru. There, I discovered people with few material possessions, rich with dignity and genuine respect for each other and Pachamama (Mother Nature). I fell in love with a Chilean activist-actor, a man larger than life, passionate beyond reason, loving past words. He had also recently quit his lucrative job as an engineer to pursue more life-affirming work. His name is Adolfo Ignacio Celedón Bravo, or Fito for short.

I came home to the U.S. determined to learn to make places that dignify culture and nature, so I pursued a dual master's degree in architecture and landscape architecture. Graduate school gave me precise and intuitive tools to exercise conceptual form-making, but still I felt a gap between theory and practice in my profession. It was in Randy's "Landscape as Sacred Place" class where I was able to reconcile my frustrations with design by learning to collaborate with the community in the design process. I gained a vocabulary and purpose for my creative work in a way I had not known since the Everything Tree and Pachamama. Thereafter, we began this book.

Practice: Fito's Place

On September 12, 2010, about a year into writing *Inhabiting the Sacred*, my fiancé and I were attacked just blocks from our home in Berkeley. Fito did not survive his injuries. This event had catastrophic effects on many: our families, our friends, our neighborhood, and me. In an impulsive blur, I gathered our community and painted the IMAGINE mandala, Yoko Ono's tribute to John Lennon, where Fito fell and, soon after, gathered some friends, turned the soil of a derelict public strip of land adjacent to the site, planted some cabbage and kale, and returned each day to maintain it. In this way, public sacred place was created, and I was only one of many who inhabited it .

Unfortunately, this awakening was stirred by tragedy rather than an effort of goodwill or a deliberate attempt to inhabit the sacred. Only now, upon reflecting on the process of how Fito's Place came to be, can I see how, even in moments of intense grief, my earlier conceptual teachings of inhabiting the sacred helped guide me from a place of debilitating loss to enabling action. At the time the project began,

I was acting neither as designer nor as activist but simply as a broken-hearted woman, but elements of design, activism, and mourning subconsciously worked within me. I had absorbed lessons from Randy's class and during the semester when I taught with him and was in the throes of writing this book, so these elements, too, were silently active. The concept of Fito's Place was not premeditated or planned; it evolved slowly into the neighborhood landmark it is today. To illustrate the story along the trajectory of this book, I refer to the six design steps for inhabiting the sacred:

Step 1: Awakening

Fito's death was the violent act of awakening to a new reality that no one should witness. I felt an intense need to relate this nightmare with the rest of my world, which previously had been promising and optimistic. Before the flowers were cleared from the street, I was already determined that this senseless crime could not be forgotten soon by the community. I think—again, everything at this time was subconscious, instinctual—I was searching for a way to evidence what happened here. We gathered for vigils and were a constant presence at the corner, but, eventually, we would need to return to work, the flowers would get swept up, and life would resume.

Step 2: Evidencing

The decision to paint the IMAGINE mandala on the place where Fito died came to me, as if by a divine order. I emailed my friends with the idea, and, five hours later, we had a crowd of twenty people, a laser-cut stencil replica of the original mosaic, and two colors of spray paint. Everyone took turns painting, but I had the distinct honor of painting the word IMAGINE in the center. Then, we placed the flowers from the street corner over the painting in a mandala pattern. We encircled the painting and sat in revered silence of the evidence we had created (Fig. 24).

The act of converting the invisible pain of grief into a visible marker of crime and hope by painting the IMAGINE on the crosswalk of the street was an act of validation. It at once legitimized a sentiment shared by the community and raised awareness to people previously unaware. People continually inquire about what happened here. They are thankful for the attention paid to the spot, and, as one person said recently, "I had no idea this happened, but now every time I come by I will be careful not to drive over this sacred spot in the road."

Step 3: Transforming

Just steps away from the spot where Fito fell is a taco stand. The owner was sympathetic and offered us a place to put the collectibles that had been accumulating at the corner. He showed me a long strip of compacted mud and weeds and suggested that he would be open to a plaque or planting in Fito's Honor (Fig. 25). Immediately, the light bulb switched on, and I explained to him that I was

Fig. 24. A violent act that took the life of Fito prompted the spontaneous creation of a place to give evidence to his loss, celebrate his life,
and heal Fito's family and friends and Amber herself.

a landscape architect and would love to steward this strip for him. He allowed use of this strip for a
garden, but, wary of potential negative effects of the crime on his business, he had several requests: take
everything off the chain-link fence, plant nothing that grew higher than two feet, and place no fliers
about the crime around the entry of his restaurant (this latter request was unspoken but understood
without words). We had begun a transformation of place through sacrifice: the restaurant owner's willingness to risk losing business to allow a memorial, my promise to work at no cost in order to have a
place to grieve, and, of course, to honor Fito's ultimate sacrifice as well.

Step 4: Organizing

I visited the strip several times with the intention of organizing a plan for it. I knew I wanted a
place for people to sit amongst plants with a view of the painting on the street. I discussed my ideas
with my friends and the owner of the taco stand, so we would be in agreement as to what should be
done here. I also had considerable work to do before the soil would support anything besides the
most-resilient weeds, so first priority was to devise a soil-amendment and planting plan.

Fig. 25. When an adjacent property owner offered to post a plaque to honor Fito in this derelict strip of land, Amber's grief intermixed with her skill as a landscape architect, and it was agreed that she would convert the strip into a garden.

Fig. 26. Amber intentionally organized friends, residents, and business owners to amend the soil based on a rough plan she had envisioned, but the resulting garden was a collaborative project by the community.

[Left] Fig. 27. A tree stump made as a place to sit and contemplate soon became an altar for flowers and other gifts for Fito as well as for anonymous others in the community.

[Right] Fig. 28. Posters attached to the utility pole provided evidence of the tragedy, asked for justice for Fito, and attracted neighbors to help make Fito's Place. Notice the IMAGINE mural in the crosswalk to the left of the post on the crosswalk.

Step 5: Manifesting

On December 12, three months after Fito left us, we acknowledged the day with a gathering to prepare the soil. Ten hours later, my friends and I had not only turned the soil but also de-littered it (not an easy task—we even found a huge sheet of steel a foot beneath the top soil), mixed in compost, and planted about a dozen tiny cabbages, kale, and purple aeonium along with vetch and clover seeds as nitrogen-fixing cover crops. Friends brought plants to contribute as well. At the day's close, we had planted a garden! We had unintentionally taken the initial step in manifesting. Design decisions from this point were made on-site, in real-time and with our own hands (Fig. 26).

The garden is only one aspect of Fito's Place; the IMAGINE painting is an important second component. The garden and painting work together because stewarding the garden daily gave me an opportunity to also visit IMAGINE each time. Another important feature is a tree trunk at the garden's center. We had originally planned to carve it into a seat, but it evolved into something of a soapbox, where fresh flowers and holiday offerings are placed and pictures of Fito are hung (Fig. 27). A fourth component is a utility post positioned between the garden and IMAGINE (Fig. 28). Since the homicide case was (and is) still unsolved, we had posted fliers around Berkeley, asking the community to give any information they have to the police. But they were routinely almost immediately torn-down. The only place they were respected and still persist is on this post at Fito's Place. It has become the community's message board, the outlet for communication where people can read about the crime, about Fito's amazing life, and the inexplicable pain of losing him. Together, the garden, picture trunk, IMAGINE, and community post make up Fito's Place. Only half of these elements were planned to function as they do today, and it is only a result of the daily visits, daily maintenance, and collaboration with the community that they have become so.

Step 6: Inhabiting the Sacred

My daily visits became a routine of inhabiting the sacred. I looked over all the plants, gave thanks and praise to the ones in bloom or surviving especially well, and encouraged the ones struggling. I removed the litter that was regularly blown or tossed in. Finally, I gathered the fallen flowers and leaves the plants had dropped (Fig. 29). With them I constructed the day's mandala on the IMAGINE. Some days, the mandala was little more than a few decaying leaves arranged in a spiral, while on other days, an elaborate pattern emerged. Sometimes, the wind blew the flowers away before I finished arranging them, but sometimes they persisted for weeks, getting ever-more smashed into the paint by turning automobiles and blessing the concrete with love where hate, for an all-encompassing instant, once reigned.

People in the neighborhood also inhabit Fito's Place. Nearly every day a neighbor visited me and the place when I was there. Numerous times, I observed how people encounter it for the first time and connect the dots between the garden and IMAGINE. Usually, it begins at the garden, as they pass by and are touched by the profuse growth and diversity of plants. Then, they reach the trunk and see the pictures and read "*Justicia para Fito*" (Justice for Fito). They turn around to see the post, which has the same phrase and more information, including a description of the crime and its precise location. They realize they are standing near the same corner and walk to it, finding IMAGINE with its ephemeral mandala. Usually, they ask for confirmation that this is the place that was spoken about in the flier and if I am Fito's fiancé. They usually offer a hug and thoughts about death. They are compassionate and open, telling me their own experiences and promising they will respect and care for this place in support of me and Fito: "I never met this gentleman, but every time I walk by here, I feel that he was a wonderful person" (Fig. 30). Recently, I met a carpenter who was sitting on the trunk and eating his lunch. We introduced ourselves, and he explained that he is from another city, working a few blocks away, and comes here every day on his breaks, because it is a peaceful and beautiful place to rest. He said it had taken him several days before he made the connection but now thinks a lot about Fito while he dwells in this place.

Fig. 29. So many people contributed to the garden that it was soon growing profusely, with new details added continuously by Amber and neighbors.

Fig. 30. Captivating beauty reminds Amber and passersby of Fito's passion for performance art to bend the world toward tenderness and justice.

Besides the dwelling of many regular and casual visitors, some neighbors share in stewardship responsibilities over the garden. One man, who lives across the street, was the first to offer support by donating a watering can, complete with a home-made spout. He found solar lights, each one distinct, and installed them for an illumined presence at night. Despite his criminal record, he scolds people for disrespecting the garden if they urinate, litter, or steal plants. His experience with the garden has fostered a new interest in plants, and he gives me updates about his new acquisitions and strategy for keeping the cactus and fern both happy in the same pot. Likewise a middle-aged neighbor is a constant presence each day there is major work to be done and a solid source of gardening knowledge (Fig. 31). He watered when I was away and shares my joy when a plant thrives or flowers beautifully. We became acquainted shortly after the garden's inauguration, because he was being evicted forcibly from his home and garden he had made sacred. He needed a loving home for the plants he tended for nine years, and I needed loving plants for Fito's garden. Today, in large part because of him, the garden is thriving with lush greenery. We joke that Fito's Place—with dozens of species of plants plus the worms, ants, crickets, bees, butterflies, and beetles—is the most-biodiverse garden in Berkeley.

Ritual visits are made by many, from the commuters, who pass it daily and take note of the new mandala, to out-of-towners, who make a point to come here during each visit to Berkeley. For friends of Fito, his birthday and date of passing (which are the same day) and *Dia de los Muertos* (Day of the Dead) in November are especially important. Compassionate members of the community who did not know Fito personally visit on their own days of remembrances. I saw evidence of their ritual visits when gifts appeared on the tree trunk: Christmas decorations, a rock painted with glitter, hand-embroidered cloth, collage art, hand-made and costume jewelry, a passport, a diploma and ashes, packaged and fresh food, a record, money, many cut flowers, and dozens of potted plants.

The owner of the apartment building on the block significantly advocates for Fito's Place. Besides providing water to irrigate the garden and picking out litter, he is a longtime resident with unique historical knowledge of the area. Once, he brought me photos of the garden before it was Fito's. First, it was Box Spring Park, named for the mattress where a homeless man slept in the dirt. Then, it was replanted by himself and some neighbors and featured a flower arrangement that spelled "OBAMA" during his first presidential campaign. Eventually, that, too, fell into disrepair, and, shortly thereafter, I began its current phase as Fito's Place. This neighbor took a class about healing gardens and used Fito's Place as an example for his final presentation. In this way, he advocates for this sacred place and enriches its meaning by providing historical tales about it.

The community at large has also embraced the roll of stewardship of this spot. As if painted by Fito himself, a powerful mural of upraised fists of resistance now adorns the wall opposite the garden, extending the reach and increasing the potency of the place to the entire block. Additionally, in April 2016, Fito's Place was chosen to be the meeting point for a walking tour of the neighborhood. Even without knowing the full history, the leader of the tour chose this place because it is a pleasant place to

Fig. 31. As the garden grew wilder than Fito, Amber sustained
it with gentle maintenance befitting sacredness: she nurturing it,
it nurturing her.

Fig. 32. Fito's Place has not been abandoned as so many spontaneous
memorials are; rather it thrives and inspires innovative community
improvements, from urban greening to a mural calling out the principles
Fito lived by.

gather, no longer the uninviting Box Spring Park from a decade ago. Randy, who visited recently, said that he could feel the sacredness now more than ever, and it is thanks to the community who inhabits this special spot (Fig. 32).

Lessons of Fito's Place

We seldom have a comprehensive method of judging implementation of initial aspirations for the design of a place. In Fito's Place, success can be determined by the ratio of positive to negative feedback of the neighborhood and visitors and by contributions from the community around it. By this measure, it is clearly a powerful and positive addition to the neighborhood. My daily visits enabled me to experience not only my own needs being met, but the larger community's as well. Nonetheless, as a public space situated between a liquor store, an unkempt parking lot, and a Bay Area Rapid Transit (BART) station, Fito's Place still collects discarded alcohol bottles and cigarette butts (though much less than before) and occasionally evokes conflict. Once an aggressive woman screamed uncontrollably at us for "remembering my dead boyfriend for too long." Fito's Place had touched a deep pain for her own unacknowledged loses and made her publicly confront taboos around the mourning process. She later acknowledged that she was sorry for her outburst. She had clearly rethought her actions. In moments such as these, I am most convinced of the public good that sacred places serve. Fito's Pace serves a unique need for the public to ponder critical human issues such as death, justice and hope after crippling loss.

For me, Fito's Place works as a learning laboratory for many lessons I was never taught in design school. For instance, sacred place need not depend on drastic changes in the architecture of a place but, instead, in the details. No matter how humble, a well-cared-for place evokes subtle beauty and changes people's behavior and attitudes. Creating quality environments available to anyone at any time is essential.

The universe within which the design profession operates is actually larger than is commonly practiced. Designers conventionally see the destination of their work as a Construction Document or a Post-Occupancy Evaluation at best, but there is untapped potential to awaken communities to values of place that combat fear, pseudo-adventuring, rootlessness, and untethered status seeking. Energy saved from these vices can be spent in quality ways instead.[1]

Fito's Place is one demonstration of how a public sacred space on a small scale has the power to reconnect and capture the maximum benefits of opposing forces. It is, as are all sacred places, a connection between architecture and landscape, past and present, public and private, macro and micro, near and far, dependency and autonomy, precision and intuition, community and self, life and death, being human as an organism and human as a machine, this and that, you and me.

PART II

PRESERVING, RECLAIMING, AND CREATING SACRED SPACES IN EVERYDAY LIFE

Step 1: Awakening
New Thoughts and Feelings about the Everyday Landscape

Step 2: Evidencing
Sentiments for Community Place

Step 3: Transforming
Values of Place through Sacrifice

Step 4: Organizing
an Action Plan towards Intentional Living

Step 5: Manifesting
Four Wishes through Planning and Design

Step 6: Inhabiting the Sacred
in the Everyday Landscape

NEW THOUGHTS AND FEELINGS
ABOUT THE EVERYDAY LANDSCAPE

To discover deep relationships with a place, people need to locate themselves in the world by taking time to reflect upon personal values, history, and points of contentment or unhappiness. In this process, they will awaken the ability to sense the environment and assess it from a deeply embedded yet previously undiscovered subconscious. With this new awareness, they can pinpoint the source of pleasure or dissatisfaction with their present environment. They can then "introduce" their sacred places to their current home, so there is a clearly defined point of departure for improvement and sustenance.

In this chapter, we begin the steps toward inhabiting the sacred by allowing the reader to uncover and record personally sacred places. Once individual values about place are identified, we use them as a basis for understanding community-wide values about place and, ultimately, as evidence in how to make changes in the design of one's home, neighborhood, town, and city.

A Journey to the Personally Sacred

Begin the sacred-place exercise by reading the following instructions or, better yet, have someone you trust read them to you. We also recommend that everyone in your household do this exercise. Take turns with a partner exploring and reading. If you feel uncomfortable doing the exercise with another, read the instructions to yourself slowly and deliberately. Set aside an hour to record three or four places at each sitting, eventually completing drawings of ten sacred places. You may want to do more. That is fine, but be sure to record at least ten different places.

At a minimum, get a pen and some paper to write and draw on. If you have favorite materials for drawing and writing, be sure to bring them and spread them out in front of you. Even if you do not think of yourself as an artist, it is always good to have a variety of materials at your disposal. You will be amazed at what you are able to draw. Find a quiet place to sit, where you will not be distracted or interrupted. Be sure you are sitting comfortably in a relaxed position. Have your partner read this passage deliberately with frequent pauses, so you can contemplate the directions and let the words sink in deeply. Note that there are two sets of instructions: The phrases presented in CAPS are to be read aloud, and the words in *italics* are notes to the reader to aid with timing and mood.

The Sacred-Place Exercise

CLOSE YOUR EYES AND CONCENTRATE ON YOUR BREATHING.

Reader, allow your partner to take a few full breaths between each statement. It will help if your words are controlled, soft, and slow.

TUNE OTHER THINGS OUT AND CONCENTRATE ON YOUR BREATHING UNTIL YOU FEEL YOURSELF IN TUNE WITH THE RHYTHM OF INHALING AND EXHALING.

Reader, you should pause and take a few deep breaths yourself. Be sure to be quiet, except for your breathing.

TAKE YOUR TIME AND RELAX YOUR MUSCLES.

Reader, take several more breaths.

VISUALIZE THE FLOW OF AIR, AS YOU PULL THE OXYGEN THROUGH YOUR NOSE AND DEEP INTO YOUR LUNGS.

Reader, your partner will need time to internalize this instruction and then actually follow it. There is a longer pause here, requiring three breaths.

FEEL IT AND SEE IT OCCUPYING YOUR WHOLE CORE.

Reader, take three breaths.

WITH A CONTROLLED EXHALE, RELEASE THE AIR AND WATCH IT, THROUGH YOUR MIND'S EYE, INTER-MINGLE WITH THE AIR OUTSIDE. THEN PULL IN ANOTHER DEEP BREATH.

Reader, take three breaths.

CONTINUE TO CONCENTRATE ON YOUR BREATHING UNTIL YOU FEEL WHATEVER TENSIONS IN YOUR BODY DISSIPATE WITH EACH EXHALE.

Reader, there is a long pause here of about one minute.

WHEN YOU FEEL THE TENSION GONE FROM YOUR BODY, GIVE ME A SLIGHT NOD, AND WE WILL GO TO THE NEXT STEP.

Reader, wait for some acknowledgment, but if there is none after about a minute, proceed.

LET YOUR MIND'S EYE SEARCH FOR THE PLACES THAT ARE MOST SACRED TO YOU PERSONALLY. SACRED PLACES ARE PLACES YOU KNOW AND THAT MAKE YOU FEEL SPECIAL OR EXCEPTIONALLY WELL WHEN YOU ARE THERE.

Reader, there is a short pause here, one breath.

At first, let these special places go by, as if they are individual images on a film clip going by slowly enough that you can see each frame. Let them move in and out of your imagination at will.

Reader, take one breath.

They can be places from your past, present, or future. There may be a lot of them or a few.

Reader, take one breath.

Let yourself see all the places several times.

Reader, take one breath.

Allow your mind's eye to settle on the place that seems most sacred. Do not worry if there are several and it is hard to distinguish. You can visit all of these soon enough. Simply focus on one place for now.

Reader, take one breath.

Linger on that one place in your imagination. Picture yourself completely in that place. Appreciate it. What senses does it most awaken?

Reader, proceed slowly. Extend the silences to allow time for contemplation and investigation.

Explore it. What do you see?

Reader, take a thirty-second pause.

How does it smell?

Reader, take a thirty-second pause.

What do you hear?

Reader, take a thirty-second pause.

If you reach out, what do you touch? Feel the textures of the place.

Reader, take a thirty-second pause.

What is the temperature? Is it warm or cool?

Reader, take one breath.

WHAT IS THE QUALITY OF LIGHT? GET A GOOD SENSE OF THE LIGHT. WHERE DOES IT ORIGINATE? HOW DOES IT FALL? WHAT DOES IT HIGHLIGHT?

Reader, take a thirty-second pause.

IS THE SPACE OPEN OR ENCLOSED? DOES SOMETHING FORM WALLS AROUND YOU? ON HOW MANY SIDES? IS THERE SOMETHING FORMING A ROOF OVERHEAD? HOW FAR IS IT FROM YOUR REACH?

Reader, take a thirty-second pause.

HOW BIG IS THE SPACE? MEASURE IT BY COMPARING ITS DIMENSIONS TO SOMETHING YOU KNOW WELL. LOOK AT THE DETAILS OF THE PLACE. ARE THERE SPECIFIC THINGS THAT SEEM ESPECIALLY IMPORTANT?

Reader, take a long pause of about one minute.

NOW TAKE NOTE OF WHAT YOU ARE DOING IN THE SPACE.

Reader, take one breath.

IS THERE ANYONE ELSE WITH YOU IN THE PLACE? WHO? WHAT ARE THEY DOING?

Reader, take one breath.

IS THERE SOME PARTICULAR ACTIVITY THAT DEFINES THE PLACE?

Reader, take one breath.

NOW ALLOW YOURSELF TO JUST BE IN THIS SPECIAL PLACE. SOAK IN THE ESSENCE.

Reader, take a long pause of about one minute.

HOW DO YOU FEEL BEING HERE? ARE YOU EXPERIENCING PARTICULAR EMOTIONS? ALLOW THAT FEELING OR THOSE FEELINGS TO SOAK IN.

Reader, take a breath.

YOU CAN STAY AT THIS PLACE AS LONG AS YOU LIKE.

Reader, pause for a minute or longer.

WHEN YOU HAVE A GOOD SENSE OF THE PLACE, BE SURE TO CONCENTRATE ON THE WHOLE OF IT FOR A FEW MOMENTS. GET A CLEAR IMAGE IN YOUR MIND'S EYE THAT CONVEYS THAT SPACE TO YOU. ALLOW

ONE IMAGE TO SETTLE INTO YOUR CONSCIOUSNESS, AN IMAGE THAT WILL EXPRESS PHYSICAL ASPECTS, THE ESSENTIAL QUALITY, AND MEANING OF THIS PLACE TO YOU. EXAMINE EACH ASPECT OF THE IMAGE, EVEN THE EDGES AND CORNERS OF THE FRAME.

Reader, pause for a minute.

WHEN YOU HAVE A CLEAR IMAGE ETCHED IN YOUR MIND AND ARE READY TO RETURN FROM THIS SPECIAL PLACE, THINK ABOUT HOW TO DESCRIBE IT: WHAT MEDIA (PENCIL, CRAYONS, PAINT, COLLAGE, MODELS) BEST CAPTURES THE ESSENCE OF THIS PLACE? AGAIN, CONCENTRATE ON YOUR BREATHING. BE AWARE OF THE RHYTHM, AS YOU BREATH IN AND OUT.

Reader, take a breath.

WHEN YOU ARE READY, OPEN YOUR EYES. VISUALIZE THE IMAGE THAT EXPRESSES THE PHYSICAL ASPECTS, THE ESSENTIAL QUALITY, AND MEANING OF THIS PLACE.

NOW, ON YOUR PAPER, MAKE A PICTURE OF YOUR SACRED PLACE. IT DOES NOT NEED TO BE FANCY. SIMPLY CREATE THE IMAGE THAT YOU RECALL FROM A MOMENT AGO. IF IT SEEMS DIFFICULT, CLOSE YOUR EYES AGAIN AND GET THE IMAGE CLEAR. YOU MIGHT BE ABLE TO TRACE THE IMAGE THAT WAY. THIS IS A PICTURE FOR YOU AND YOU ALONE, SO DO NOT WORRY WHAT IT LOOKS LIKE. IF YOU CANNOT GET ALL THE ASPECTS OF THE PLACE IN ONE IMAGE, YOU CAN ADD NOTES OR OTHER SKETCHES TO DESCRIBE QUALITIES THAT WERE HARD TO JOT DOWN AT FIRST. IN ANY CASE, DRAW, WRITE, CONSTRUCT, OR MAKE POEMS UNTIL YOU HAVE RECORDED EVERYTHING, PHYSICAL AND EMOTIONAL, THAT YOU FELT AND SAW.

Reader, you may quietly leave the person alone to work on his or her drawing, or, perhaps, you would like to draw a sacred place of your own.

ONCE THE DRAWING IS FINISHED, TAKE A SHORT BREAK. THEN REVERSE ROLES AND REPEAT THE EXERCISE FOR THE OTHER PERSON, STARTING WITH THE BREATHING. YOU MIGHT FEEL EXHAUSTED AFTER DRAWING THREE OR FOUR PLACES IN ONE SITTING, SO PERIODICALLY CONTINUE THIS EXERCISE UNTIL EACH OF YOU HAVE DRAWN TEN DIFFERENT SPECIAL PLACES. . AT SOME POINT, YOU MAY FEEL FLOODED WITH PLACES AND WANT TO DRAW THEM ALL AT ONCE INSTEAD OF ONE AT A TIME. THIS DOES NOT WORK AS WELL, PRIMARILY BECAUSE THE BREATHING AND RHYTHM OF THE SPOKEN DIRECTIONS HELP YOU RELAX AND STAY IN A DREAM-LIKE STATE. GIVING THE INSTRUCTIONS IN A REASSURING VOICE PARTICULARLY ENHANCES THE DREAM-LIKE STATE, ENABLING THE SUBCONSCIOUS TO COME INTO THE MIND'S EYE, ACTIVATING THE RIGHT AND LEFT SIDES OF THE BRAIN, BOTH SENSE AND SENSIBILITIES, AND GIVING YOU INFORMATION YOU MAY NOT ACCESS IN YOUR CONSCIOUS LIFE. IT IS ALSO A JOY TO DO!

Themes and Hidden Messages

The next step is to analyze your drawings and notes. If you have drawings, photographs, or mementos of special places that you have from the past, you may want to locate and include them in the following analysis. After spreading the mementos and the drawings you have completed of your ten sacred places in front of you, look at them carefully. As you study the pictures and words, do you see any recurring themes? Record your overall impressions, observations, and discoveries. For example, is there a spatial quality, period of life, people, or special events that stand out in more than one drawing? Write and diagram half a dozen observations.

Analyze your sacred places in various systematic ways. Start by listing the physical characteristics of the places such as enclosed, quiet, windy, colorful, or other factors that recur. Then count to see which characteristics do occur in the most places. You might count settings such as a kitchen, garden, mall, city center, urban or rural area. Write down feelings you associate with each place such as comforting, energetic, fearful, or loving and then see if you can match feelings with physical qualities. Are there any physical and emotional partners, such as kitchen and comfort? You might do the same trying to match spatial characteristics and activities that are especially important to you. We have found it particularly useful to write the spatial descriptions for activities or feelings as precisely as one can. In some cases, spatial specificity may not matter, but, in others, a matter of inches, foot candles, shades of color, or degrees of Fahrenheit can distinguish the sacred from the profane.

Now consider in detail what these places say about you, your identity, your worldview, your emotional needs and desires, your most deeply held values. What do these places mean to you? What do they symbolize? What are their hidden messages about you? Make a list of these things. Think about this last list for a few days. Reflect on what you wrote.

Compare Your Places with Those of Others

Let us turn our attention to frequent responses of other people to the same questions about their sacred places. This analysis will likely provide additional insights into your own places. We will offer general conclusions based on more than four decades of work during which we asked people about their most valued or sacred places, observed behavior and drew sketches of those places, and presented content analysis of the results. The U.S. Forest Service, the Environmental Protection Agency, and the California Department of Forestry supported the formal research. Other data came from surveys done by Community Development by Design as part of planning projects, during which the firm was designing cities, neighborhoods, and parks.[1] The respondents represent individuals from diverse regions, economic conditions, and ethnicities. These places and associated values are highly variable from one person to another, yet some are shared with other people. Some people are much more place-dependent.[2] They have long and sustained relationships and form stronger bonds with places.

There is an important debate about what this means. People who have maintained a continuous physical connection with their most formative sacred places often believe that their commitment to the places and the values they symbolize is due to this sustained kinship with the places. To them, anything less creates rootlessness, unstable worldviews, and poor stewardship. Others who are more mobile and have less-lasting co-dependence with places may contend that they, too, have abiding values rooted in place, but they do not need to be tied to a singular place to be healthy individuals or stewards of the land.

Randy and I have debated this duality at length throughout the writing of this book. Both of us have powerful relationships with places, but Randy recently moved from Berkeley back to the North Carolina farmland of his youth, the center of his world. Amber has lived a mobile life and cannot identify wholly with any one culture or place so single-mindedly as Randy does. Although we come from opposite ends of this spectrum, our imbedded values are still rooted in place. We agree that being deeply attached to place is essential for healthy human development, local empowerment, a sense of community, a place-based economy, and ecological sustainability. We expect that the following generalizations will prompt personal reflection as well as debate between those in your household:

Childhood

Although sacred places can be from any period of life, the majority of the ones people remember are from childhood. Only a few are imagined places of the future. Many represent peak experiences and important passages of life, both in childhood and as adults. They almost always stimulate memory of several senses simultaneously, like taste and touch or smell and hearing. Childhood places are particularly formative. These places are often associated with family and friends. They concretize how family is supposed to dwell and what activities are highest priority. Settings for celebrations, daily rituals, and quiet time with relatives when the family is the single, undistracted focus are often remembered by both children and parents.

Childhood places that provide centering and testing of boundaries figure prominently (Fig. 33). Private space and places that were symbolically owned are remembered with great pleasure and inner pride. Places of fear, danger, exploration, challenge, hardship, construction, and creativity seem especially formative. Capabilities and passions of adult life can often be traced directly back to childhood places of intense personal experience where we learned firsthand by doing.[3]

Fig. 33. Sacred places are often settings where a child tested limits, confronted fear, and explored the landscape free from adult supervision.

Outdoors

Settings designated personally sacred are overwhelmingly out of doors, from remote wilderness to a hummingbird nest outside an apartment or a balcony of potted plants. Natural settings and ones with abandoned, incomplete, and leftover remnants of natural processes or human habitation are especially important to adolescents. Vegetation, water, sunlight, mountains, hilltops and raised, enclosed spaces within larger open spaces often make up special places for both children and adults. We estimate that each of these is included in more than a third of all responses to inquiries we have made about personally sacred places.

One such place, Grassy Creek, has remained sacred to Randy since childhood, when he built dams, searched for wildflowers and traces of American Indian dwellings, and hunted along its serpentine route to Hyco River. Steep slopes on one side alternate with broad floodplains on the other to provide an endless diversity of wonders to explore. Surviving seasonal rapids and copperhead moccasins enhanced self-reliance. Today, as an older adult, he traces his childhood routes with similar pursuits. His wife, Marcia, calls these treks "aimless wandering," in which the outdoors restores him and always provides something unexpected. It is likely that some of your places contain these elements, too (Fig. 34).

Home Place

When Glinda, the good witch in *The Wizard of Oz* (1900), told Dorothy to click her heels and repeat "There's no place like home," she spoke to a subconscious landscape in everyone's heart.[4] Home is sacred. It orders our lives and worldviews. The idea of home, the emotion of home, and the physical place of home are all important. The kitchen and bedroom as places of creation and nourishment are particularly sacred. Small, enclosed spaces such as rooms, boxes, and attics are also described as sacred. Such places help us define intimacy. Yards and gardens adjacent to home are often mentioned. For children, these outdoor places close to home provide initial nature experiences, settings to play with domestic and small wild animals and territory that can be appropriated for personal space, projects, and experiments, which all contribute to establishing an enduring identity. For adults, home likewise marks identity. Randy's wife, Marcia, considers her kitchen overlooking her garden from which she feeds family and friends as most sacred. She identifies as an intentional farm-to-fork master.

The meaning of homeplace varies dramatically from person to person. This is shaped by the form of the house or dwelling and by the neighborhood and access to nature in one's town or city. It is also influenced by gender, family situation, social class, and many other cultural and environmental factors. Still, for all its variability, home centers us (Fig. 35).

Moral Place

For some people, places reflect moral instruction from parents, mentors, peers, and self-discovery. The instruction may be traditional family sayings, religious and civic verses, or lessons learned by observing unspoken behavior of those one admires. For most people, these lessons were transformed from abstraction into concrete reality in the form of places. The value and the image of the place are intermixed; we do not separate place from lesson. These places communicate morals just like stories do.

Amber's grandparents lived far away from her childhood home. Each summer, she and her brother looked forward to visiting them during vacation. They knew they would get one special night when Grandma and Papa took them to a "nice restaurant," the Concord Grill, which was actually a bowling alley that served the best open-faced turkey sandwiches loaded with gravy and cranberry sauce. Papa would explain to them in the parking lot that he expected them to act appropriately for the place

Fig. 34. Natural landscapes with water and topographic complexity such as Grassy Creek provide settings for imaginative play, mental restoration, spiritual communion, and surprising interactions with wildlife.

Fig. 35. Enclosed spaces with overlooking views such as attics and lofts
provide the security of home and a sense of intimacy and control.

they were about to eat or else! Through trial and error at the Concord Grill, Amber and Vince learned
how to be respectful of people in public, and still they never forget the Concord Grill when the subject
of table manners comes up (Fig. 36).

Growth

Many of our most meaningful spaces are settings where transformations have occurred (Fig.
37). Places mark growth. As an example, a student described a playfield in his neighborhood and the
moments when adolescence changed his previous childhood world. Early one fall, a pal hit a home run
over the massive pine tree down the right field line; never had any of them been able to hit so high
and far. Childhood space was broken. A few days later, they were forming teams when his best friend's
twin sister showed up. She was a capable fielder, a good hitter, and the fastest runner of the group, a
desirable teammate. That day, she announced that she wasn't interested in playing baseball anymore.
Adolescent-gendered space was born. These two events became one with the field, symbolizing a rup-
ture in youthful boundaries. Many rites of passage are similarly concretized: falling in love, graduation,
independence from parents, marriage, overcoming hardship, and other accomplishments. Key changes

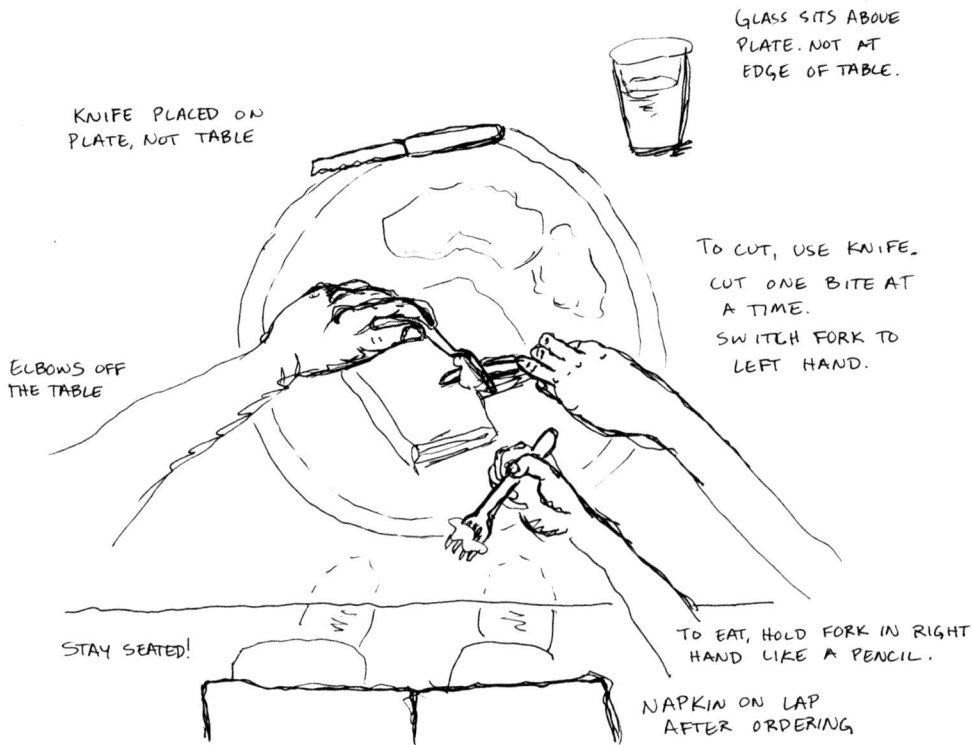

Fig. 36. Places remind us of moral lessons as profound as respect for others and as practical as where elbows and knives belong at the dinner table. Amber still visualizes the Concord Grill at every meal.

Fig. 37. Growth is marked in place whether a childhood accomplishment like learning how to catch minnows by herding them into shallow water or the recognition by adults that they have done a good job of parenting.

in self-awareness throughout life are marked in special places. Sudden consciousness of impermanence, uncertainty, life and death, decay, seasonal change or ephemeral sightings of wildlife are likewise associated with places of growth (Fig. 38).

Ritual and Spatial Sequence

For most people, ritual behavior is embedded in special places. Whether daily, seasonal, or annual, there is a habitual pattern to ritualistic behavior: a precise, sequential way in which the rite is performed and particular spatial qualities are present for the event to be satisfactory. The Japanese tea ceremony is one such ritual, in which every spatial detail is attended, including sprinkling water on the leaves along the entry path to give the impression of dew.

Daily patterns, from practicing piano to private time commuting from work, may not be so aesthetically sensitive, but we all have mundane but essential routines (Fig. 39). When he lived in Berkeley, Randy always checked the road sign in his backyard that pointed east to Hester's Store to remind him of his place, his origins. It was a violation of the new day to forget. Then he made Marcia coffee. Amber always greets the moon in Spanish or in English, saying goodnight to Fito. Sacred places are often family trips or vacation spots to which the family returns each year. For some, these are the only times when there are no distractions and the family shares a special time and place.

Participation

Other places are sacred because of our participation in making them. They may express our identity, control, creativity, or accomplishment. Many people consecrate the memory of forts and treehouses they built, the first room they decorated, or the first apartment they furnished. Few Americans today build their own houses, but the reports from those who do indicate they are profoundly more meaningful than purchased homes. Even remodeling or small home improvements engender special meaning (Fig. 40). As an example, after Amber's friend, Emily, and her husband had professionals paint their home on the outside and rework the landscape, she observed, "I don't take care of it, because I didn't make it." The next year, after she and her mom had repainted several rooms, she proudly told us, "We worked, worked, worked! Now it feels like home—it's *my* space."

You may have observed similar qualities in your own sacred places. Check to see which of your places are childhood, outdoors, lessons, transformations, rituals, and participation. Note how yours coincide or vary. Each time we do these exercises we uncover nuances we had not precisely identified previously. For example, Amber recently did the sacred-place exercise to introduce undergraduate students to the notion of inhabiting the sacred and apply their observations to their living spaces. Although most of their insights fit the categories above, some provided additional details that we had not previously

Fig. 38. Amber associates her independence from her parents with this particular spot in Lima, Peru. She often recalls the setting to reinforce her resolve to think for herself.

Fig. 39. Settings for daily rituals become sacred, because a commonplace activity such as practicing the piano represents special time shared between parent and child. Note the precise drawing of distractions from the ostensible purpose.

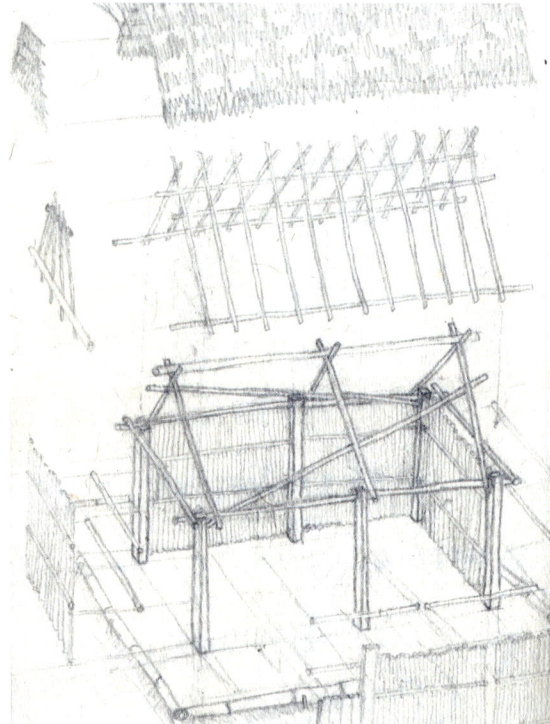

Fig. 40. Places people make themselves hold deep
meaning. Building one's own home or simply improving and maintaining it make it special, because that
expresses both mastery and personal identity.

considered in such detail. They noted places that a person spends long spans of time, places where food
is eaten or shared, and places that allow for relaxation or seclusion from the daily routine. So do not be
surprised if your places provide some unexpected discoveries.

Places and Emotional Partners

Places evoke strong emotional responses. There is the wonderful line from John Fowles's *The Collector*
(1963), in which the female prisoner exclaims, "But I couldn't possibly fall in love with you in this room,
I couldn't fall in love with anyone here. Ever."[5] Places have this power to stir our emotions positively
and negatively. Big, open landscapes make some people feel vulnerable while making others feel free;
others feel claustrophobic in a dense forest whereas others are jubilant beneath a forest canopy. We
found in one study that spacious wilderness areas valued by upper- middle class people might be feared
by lower-income urbanites. The urbanites felt they would be vulnerable to gunfire in such places.[6] Likewise, the edge of heights or corners may evoke fear. American streets are often associated with fear and

Fig. 41. Emotions are intertwined with places. Kitchens usually evoke
warmth, parental caring, love, sharing, hospitality, and family pleasures.

loneliness. Fog mystifies us. Barren landscapes depress us. Dark places make us feel all of these at once. Rain and certain trees—the aptly named weeping willow among them—evoke sadness.

In contrast, enclosed spaces generally evoke intimacy and privacy and make us feel relaxed, safe, and secure. Kitchens partner with love, hospitality, and joy (Fig. 41). Warm spaces evoke feelings of nurturing. Gardens are similarly associated with healing and spirituality for some and pleasure and seduction for others. Smells, colors, and sounds delight and arouse us. Likewise, cities can invite sensual exploration, excite the intellect, and provoke civic deeds.

The landscape settings that are most positively valued—water, sunlight, vegetation, hilltops, and mountain tops—are associated with many different emotions. Besides our home, we seem to have the most reciprocal relationships with these places. They are the most able of all environments to interact with us, reflecting a range of emotions and, therefore, evoking a great variety of feelings. Water is especially reciprocating. It is associated with joy and loneliness, power and nurturing, spirituality and sensuality, relaxation and creativity. Depending on its application, it can evoke vitality, awe, or mystery among many other emotional partners .

Vegetation stimulates many of the same feelings: nurturing, sensuality, awe, relaxation, health, and spirituality. For many people, it prompts sadness or accomplishment. Sunlight partners with joy, creativity, sensuality, nurturing, health, relaxation, and contentment. Hilltops and mountain tops with views are co-mingled with power, awe, and fear. They also prompt philosophical musings. Mountain tops with views to water are especially power- and awe-inducing.

Think about your places and what feelings you associate with them. Which of the generalizations match your own experience? Which of your places evoke distinctive emotional responses?

Awakenings of Self-discovery

After studying their sacred places, people describe various awakenings of self-discovery that have positive effects on their well-being. Here are the summaries:

Enjoying the Discovery

The process of discovering the sacred is personally satisfying. Many admit that, at first, they are skeptical. Randy remembers the blank stares when he announced to a religious community in rural Union County, Pennsylvania, that he wanted them to map their sacred places as part of a land-use planning process. Initially, people thought he was asking about the location of their churches, but after he explained the concept of everyday sacred places, a kind dairy farmer urged others to try it. Skepticism was quickly replaced by pleasure. People enjoyed exploring themselves and their special places.

Empowering the Center

Many people derive personal empowerment from calling up their sacred places. They say that these spaces center them, give them a clarity that allows them to embrace the uncertainty of the world around them and shape it. One participant in a workshop on sacred place described this beautifully: "Grounding empowers us to venture forth; otherwise we are free-falling toward somewhere that some-one else tells us is progress."[7]

Numerous therapies use metaphors of place or teach people to have a special, empowering place within themselves. Psychology aids sports teams from gymnastics to football to enhance or overcome homefield advantage. A few years ago, Tony Stewart, the bad boy of stock-car racing with an uncon-trollable temper, moved back home to his childhood neighborhood. That season, he went from reckless to the season champion, crediting "home" for having calmed him.[8]

Discovering Sensual Intelligence

People report that exploring their sacred places gives them expanded consciousness. It accesses ways of thinking they did not know they had. This is called sensual intelligence—a way of thinking that combines detached analytical reasoning with direct sensory experience. The key seems to be integrating opposing ways of knowing: the rational and emotional, the conscious and unconscious, and the spiritual and sensual (Fig. 42).

For many, the new discovery is simply that they can draw. Even accomplished artists are surprised that their drawings are alive yet spatially precise. This is partly due to the process employed in the tech-nique. Entering a dream-like state enables us to discover underused creativity and long-term memory. Even distant events in powerful places can be recalled, because they are likely etched in spatial memory, thereby making it easy to draw them evocatively and accurately.

Accessing the Sacred

Another insight is how attainable inhabiting the sacred can be in one's personal life. Typical responses include "It doesn't take much to make me happy" and "The sacred is inexpensive, whereas

Fig. 42. Places with primal elements of uncontrolled water, intense sunlight, sounds, and textures stimulate creative problem solving, because such environments supplement rational thinking with sensual arousal and intelligence.

the profane is really costly, but it requires critical thinking and decisions about status seeking." One participant in a workshop said that all she needed for a most meaningful life could be summed up like a short-order cook as follows: (1) adequate shelter, a homeplace surprisingly small, three-story minimum with an attic, a sunny, enclosed kitchen, and an empty space for creative endeavors; (2) trees and other vegetation, still or moving water, however miniature, inside and around the homeplace; (3) a city with lots of rituals and settings to compete, accomplish, share, cooperate, and be recognized; (4) wild nature within walking distance to test boundaries, connect to one's ecosystem, see wildlife, imagine and construct, be in danger and be fearful at night; (5) a hillock with a philosopher's view and a lover's aedicula, all sunny side up. She also offered a P.S. that she needed a library, a soapbox for debates, a place to grow food, and a junk pile. Her point was that fulfilling lives require much less materially than we have come to expect.

Enhancing Health and Well-being

Exploring and inhabiting the sacred enhances health and well-being. In one study we did in the working-class neighborhoods of Fort Bragg, California, ninety-six percent of the people interviewed through a geographic random sample reported that going to their most valued places made them feel better if they were in a bad mood.[9]

Sometimes, sacred places stir painful memories, especially when the home environment was or is oppressive, abusive, or belittling. Growing up homeless or in the old-fashioned "broken home" prompts not just a bad memory, but lasting trauma. A person may recall being alienated from the very place most considered to be a safe haven. A debilitating adult relationship or situation can extend this trauma throughout life. Amber's friend, Emily, realized that she needed to live in the "here and now," because "The past is painful, and the future is scary."

The sacred-place exercise may have no impact on such pain, but it can be a catalyst for healthy change. In several cases, the exercise freed the person to make a new home reflective of her values rather than those of an old demon or an overly dominant partner. The change may also occur outside the home. One medical doctor became a high school football coach; his most valued place was, not surprisingly, a football field rather than his medical office. Others have redirected their energy to fulfill their most profound values—building houses for Habitat for Humanity, volunteering to save endangered species, and coordinating environmental stewardship projects. But most people make small changes, like our colleague who enlarged a few windows to bring nurturing sunlight into his home. Others have reported that simple acts such as installing a swing, making a flower garden, or using wallpaper like that in a grandmother's kitchen enhanced their well-being and health.

Inspiring Creativity

Another realization that people gain from this exercise is that we are captives to the settings we hold most dear. We are inspired and enraptured by them, and they, in turn, incite creativity to create places like them. This awareness is especially critical for designers and planners. Landscape architect Will Hooker had grown up in an enchanting landscape tucked into a distant corner of a large woodlot near his home: "a waterhole banked by moss-covered mounds, hemlocks and yellow birch trees festooned with golden ruffles." He and his friends sensed that this was a special spot, christened it "Peaceful Valley," and consecrated it with an adolescent pledge: "to use it only for quiet, peaceful, loving thoughts." In a conversation one day, Will suddenly blurted out a personal realization," As a designer, I've been trying continuously to recreate that space."[10] The next day, he showed Randy drawings for a central-city plaza he was designing. The plaza had the form of a bog with downed trees for walkways, saplings to swing from, hemlocks and yellow birch, and a swampy waterhole surrounded by mounds of moss. Will laughed and explained that he now understood why his clients did not like the plan and why he was unwilling to change it. His sacred place was inappropriate in this context, even though his childhood memories had served as inspiration to create extraordinary reciprocal landscapes elsewhere. Lesson learned.

Living Intentionally

After doing the exercise, people report that they need to concretize their values in their everyday lives. They realize there is room for healthy change in their private and public lives. Most are simple things such as rearranging family portraits on the mantle or creating a more obvious shrine for personal treasures instead of hiding them. Others are more dramatic actions counter to prevailing culture. Things like living in a smaller home and bicycling instead of driving to work serve to refocus life on the personal level and to resist a consumer-driven lifestyle on a larger cultural level. The home needs to be a symbol of both oneself and the principles by which one wants to live. Most respondents say they need to be reminded of their values through space or objects in home and at work. These then provide a strong point of orientation and a rudder to guide oneself in daily actions. This becomes intentional living.

Techniques for Place-Based Action

While the momentum of the awakenings inspires you, return to the analysis of your sacred places. Think about what actions this list stirs you to take. The list may suggest changes in a daily routine, rearranging priorities, modifying your living environments, and adjusting the ways you inhabit them. Sacred places may, at first, seem like simple memories having little to do with the places we presently live, but, over time, you realize that each lesson from these places leads to potential changes in present dwellings and daily lives.

Professional architects, landscape architects, and planners are struck by how much the exercise of discovering our sacred places has transformed the way we later designed and inhabited our homes and communities. In doing this exercise for ourselves, we realized that both of us were living away from the places we held most special and were prompted to create techniques to reroot ourselves:

First, we wanted to know better the places where we were now living. We realized that we lacked both knowledge and intimacy with our new places. This lack made us somewhat uncentered and kept us from participating actively in our communities. So we created a timeline technique called "You and Your Home's History."

Second, the sacred-place exercise made us aware that some nagging unhappiness with our present homes and communities could be identified precisely just as our colleague Ward did in his cottage. The "Home for Better or for Worse" technique allowed us to identify aspects of our present living environments that were already fulfilling and those that were unsatisfactory.

Third, the findings from these techniques compelled us to write personal manifestos for everyday living. Focused on our relationships with our homes and neighborhoods, this technique centered us in place and turned rather neglected everyday places into special settings for more intentional living.

You and Your Home's History

Getting to know your place and your relationship with it can start with a timeline beginning with the present and moving backwards through time. Make two timelines: one of your home and one of yourself. Record the time you and your present home have shared together. This is your common ground. Next, populate the line with your previous homes and your family lineage and notate where these places are located (Fig. 43).

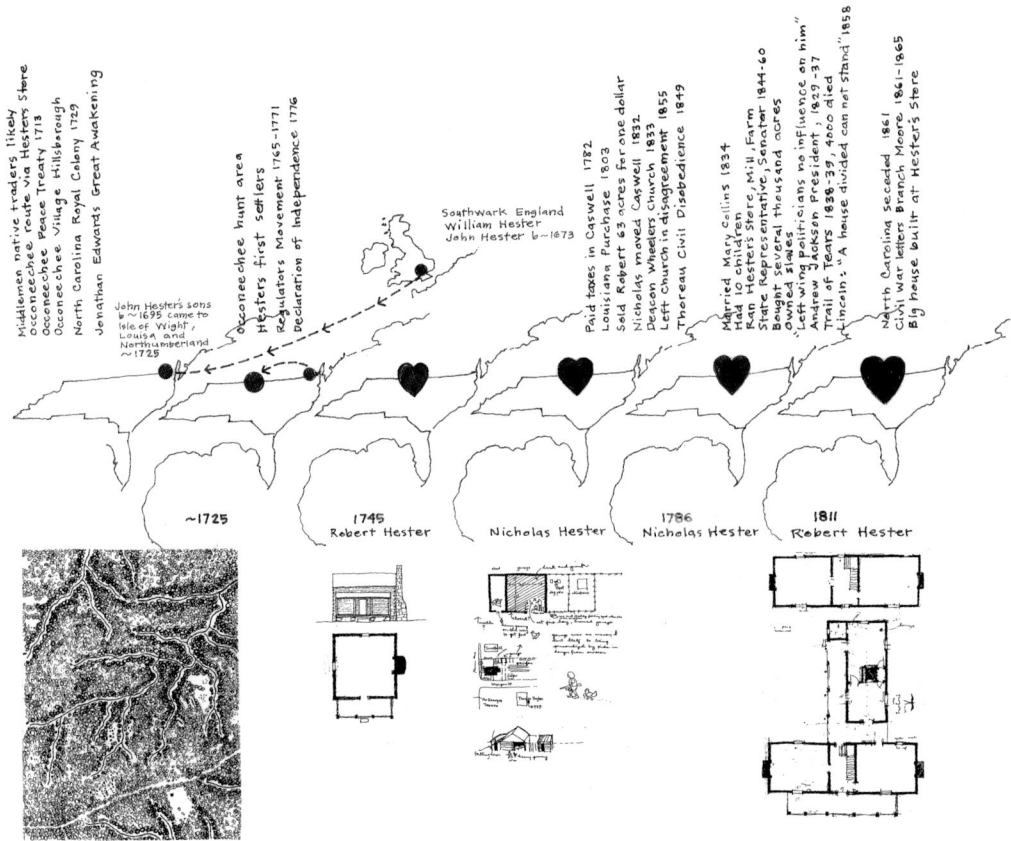

Fig. 43 (left and right). Randy's timeline is tied to the land and the various houses on his family's land. This has been a continuous relationship for ten generations, except during the 1940s, when his immediate family rented housing and day labored on others' farms. Every house since 1745 has been built by the family from timber on the land, increasing affection for both.

Making your home's timeline may require more research. Try to discover all previous users of the land and what they did here, both at your exact location and its immediate context.[11] What did they build and when? How did climate or available materials influence the things they made? What plant communities and wildlife existed in each phase? What major events triggered drastic or slow changes in your home or area? Usually, the local library or historical society has information on the natural history of places—its climate, vegetative mosaic, and native animals among other things such as seasonal rainfall, geology, and soil. Also, you may find books on the cultural history from first peoples to European settlers and more recent immigrants. Old maps provide excellent records of land use through time. The planning department in your town or city should have maps of more recent developments, neighborhoods, and subdivisions. Remember, fiction and fables are often as revealing as non-fiction. Do not discount old-timers as a rich source of this information. Many more details can be discovered by consulting other resources in your community such as the local college, the Local

Married Ella Thompson
Lived in Cabin across the road
Raised family in Big House
Ran Hester's Store
Made trips to Danville for merchandise
Camp at Hell's Half Acre
Bowes House built 1890s
US enters WWI 1917

Married Ada Jacobs
Had 7 children
Ran Hester's Store, Farmed
Built Nate, Saralynn's House 1905
Superintendant Sunday School
Salem Church
John Scopes Evolution Trial 1925
Great Depression 1929-1940s
Randy helped build Jr. Bullocks
Travel once to Florida

World War II 1939-45 Boise, Idaho
Married Virginia Green, school teacher
First generation not to inherit land
USDA Tobacco grader, farmer
Grew tobacco in Venezuela w brother
Bought land at Hester's Store
Bought First house in town 1954
Bought Homeplace and 400 acres 1960
Grew vegetables to give away
First generation to travel outside area

Grew up in Clayton's apartment 1954
Farmed Hester's Store 1954-1967
Letter from Birmingham Jail 1963
Shotgun house Chavis Heights 1970
Raleigh City Council 1975-78
Neighborhood Space 1975
Married Marcia McNally 1983
400# house, Berkeley 1981-2010
Circle of Love 1986
Lives in renovated homeplace

Grew up in Raleigh, Berkeley
Houston, Paris, New York, Boston
and Durham for education
Married Saralyn Parker 2009
Renovated Great grandparents
House at Hester's Store
Artist and Divinity school student
Built barn for art studio
Preaches occasionally Salem Church

Lives in house great great grand-
parents built at Hester's Store.
Tenth generation of Hesters here
"Why did God make Katama?" 2012
"My house loves me" 2013
"Bob the builder could use this
book" 2013

1853
George Coggins Hester

1888
Howard Hester

1913
Randolph Hester

1944
Randy Hester

1976
Nate Hester

2009
Atticus Hester

1760 1850 1900 1920 1940 1950 1960 1970 1980 2000

1890
2010

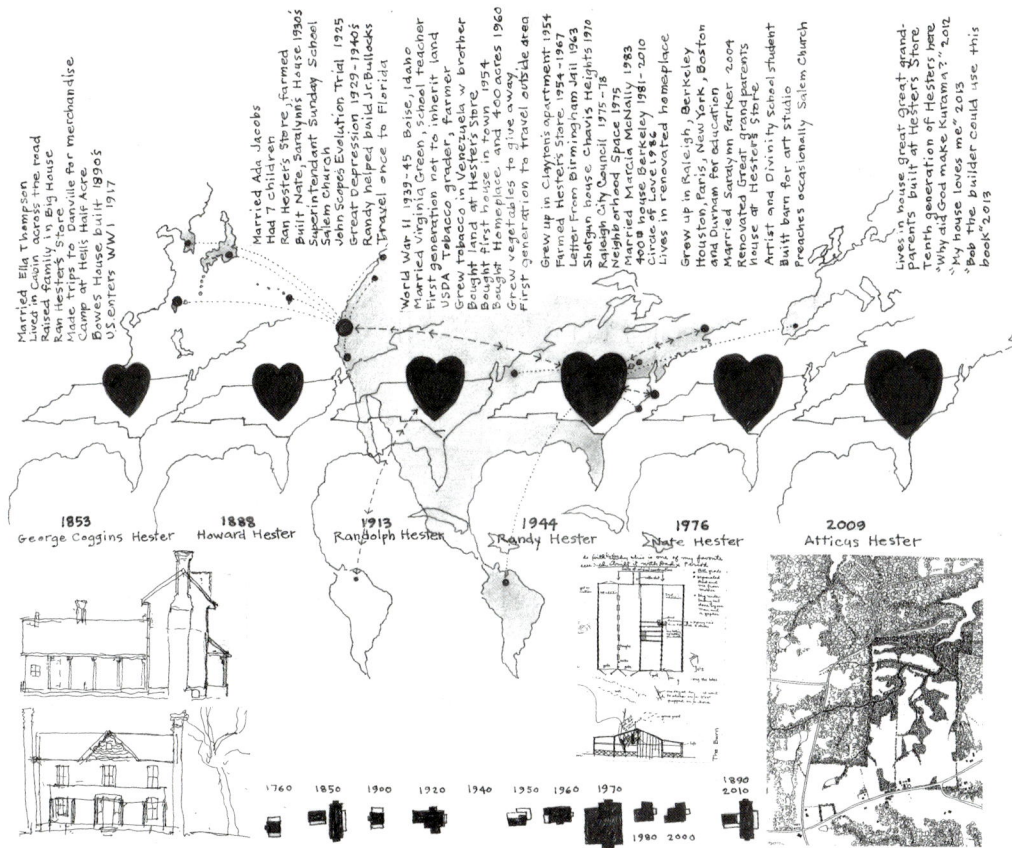

Agricultural Extension Office, appraisers, realtors, and developers, United States Geological Survey, and Google Maps (Fig. 44).[12]

Home for Better and Worse

With the timelines complete, make some evaluation of the aspects of your home and community that are satisfactory and those that are not—from both your perspective and that of your house. Begin by comparing your present home with the qualities of the places most sacred to you. Make two lists, one of things that are most satisfactory and/or sacred about your present living environment and another list of things that are unsatisfactory. Be sure to include qualities that you identified in your sacred places that are lacking presently (Fig. 45).

Now it is your home's turn to judge you for better and worse. Sit someplace in your home and pretend you are your home. Maybe let the living room sofa or kitchen table or screened-in porch speak to you for the whole house and your immediate neighborhood. Project carefully what they might say and how they might feel about you. How do your habits in the house make your house feel? Does it feel cared for or neglected? Where do you go in your neighborhood? Do parts of your neighborhood feel

December
US built + Emily
I house built we moved in
no occupan
Jan & June 18 06
Decade Dec 06 ogh house
1.41 old house
Dec 07 yr ogh house
Feb 08 new addition
Sept 08
Re-landscaped
Fenced, added
plants, and
color to our
home

May 18 05
engaged
living @
Tipton
MARRIED
Apartment
Craig
left
mom

our
first
home!

1 yr
Dec 08 ogh house
life in
home

June 18 09
3 yrs married

March
painted
kitchen
Aug-nov 07 mom moves
July 09 mom moves
Dec 09
4 yrs
old house

It's feels like
home now.
Decorated
my spaces!!!

Fig. 44. The realtor provided the history of this house: Built six
months before Emily and her husband bought it. Emily marked
incremental improvements, including re-landscaping, painting,
and decorating her spaces.

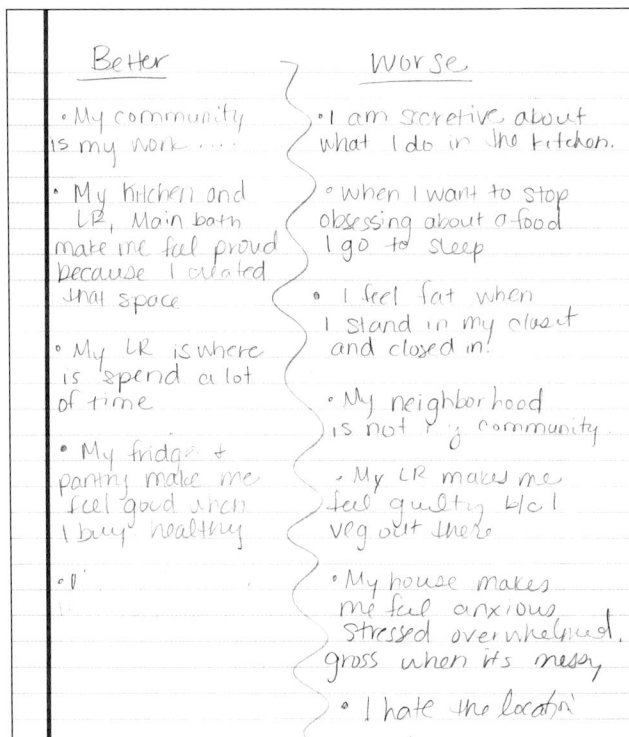

Better	Worse
• My community is my work....	• I am secretive about what I do in the kitchen.
• My kitchen and LR, Main bath make me feel proud because I created that space	• when I want to stop obsessing about a food I go to sleep
• My LR is where I spend a lot of time	• I feel fat when I stand in my closet and closed in!
• My fridge + pantry make me feel good when I buy healthy	• My neighborhood is not my community
• I	• My LR makes me feel guilty b/c I veg out there
	• My house makes me feel anxious, stressed overwhelmed, gross when it's messy
	• I hate the location

Fig. 45. Listing good and bad things about your relationship with your
house makes you aware of things you love (I am proud of my kitchen)
and things that must change (I hate the location).

maintained while others feel abandoned? Do you make your house and neighborhood happy or sad? If you are thinking that your house does not express emotions, consider this: As Randy and his three-year-old grandson, Atticus, recently drove away from Atticus's home, Atticus looked out the window and said with a smile, "My house loves me." So, be honest, how does your house feel about you?

Make two new lists. In one, list the things your home and community find satisfactory, healthy, or terrific about you. Make another list they find unsatisfactory about you and how you act regarding them.

Reflect on these four lists. Go back and look at your drawings of the ten sacred places. Do any actions to improve your daily life, your personal environment, or community emerge from this reflection?

When Amber was working with undergraduate students in Berkeley to improve their everyday environments, she focused on their sleeping places (usually, a dorm room or an apartment) and had them compare it to their idea of homeplace. Like this exercise, they made four lists: one about their satisfaction of their current living situation and another about their dissatisfactions plus two more about their home's contentment or discontentment with them as occupants. By addressing both points of view, the students had the opportunity to reflect on both the place and themselves.

For many, this was their first home away from the home of their parents. Not surprisingly then, a majority focused on organization and cleanliness. They were often frustrated about sharing space with roommates who did not contribute to a healthy living environment or were too busy to find time for housework. They were also concerned about new situations of public space, such as shared bathrooms or windows facing public corridors. A few students had appreciation or discontentment with architectural features of their place: for one, a window ledge scaled to human proportion was perfect to perch and do homework on while feeling both in and out of doors; for another, a seismic retrofit caused a room's otherwise large and pleasant window to be covered with a steel cross-bar. How does your life-cycle stage influence your satisfaction?

Manifest My Place: Live Intentionally

To act on what you have learned from these exercises requires listing desired changes and then making a formal declaration to yourself. This declaration states the underlying principles and outlines a plan of action needed to achieve the changes. This is the definition-of-a-place manifesto. To inhabit the sacred requires visualizing that sacred and committing to making places of value in your daily life. This usually entails changing our environment *and* ourselves. A place-based manifesto helps stay on that path, because, when posted in a prominent place, it reminds us every day of our best intentions.

To develop your place-based manifesto, start by reviewing all you have learned from the previous exercises. Let your mind wander through the drawings, timelines, and lists of things you observed about yourself and your places. Think particularly about what you need to do in order to make your everyday environment more satisfying and nurturing. Remember that these actions can be changes in your daily life and in the places you inhabit.

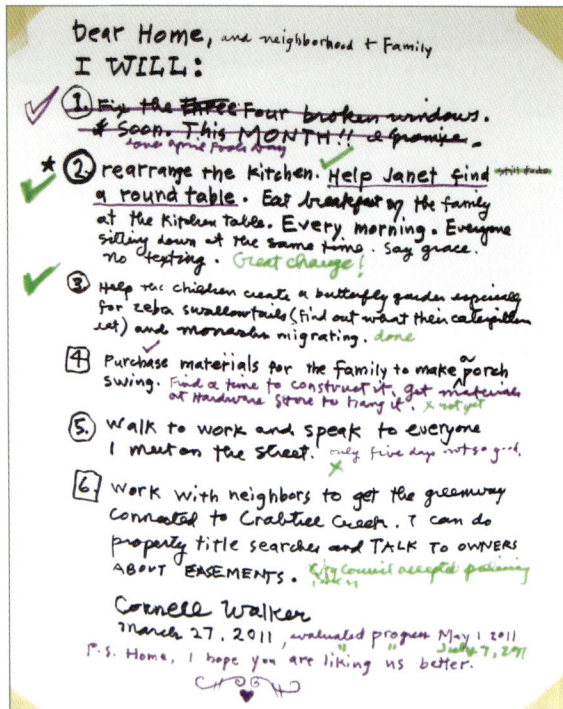

Fig. 46. In your manifesto, describe things you want to change regarding your house and community and what roles you must play to accomplish these changes. This is a lot like dog training: It is more about training the owner, less the dog.

Make a list of whatever actions come into your mind: big ones, little ones, mundane ones, and dramatic ones. You are not committing to these yet, so write down everything that occurs to you.

Now give yourself some time to reflect. Contemplate. Add, delete, refine, or change your list as you wish. Begin to organize the actions in a way that makes sense to you. Then rank ones that are most important to you. We suggest that five to ten actions make a manageable manifesto. For example, Amber's friend, Emily, resolved to (1) spend more time being creative in her home, (2) create more positive space for her and her husband, even if it meant accommodating each other's wishes in "her" space, and (3) connect and get involved with their local community, starting with getting to know the neighbors.

Take a few days to write the place-based manifesto in a form you are willing to tack up in a prominent spot. It is your guide, your action plan, your inspiration manifested into words on a page. Write it when you are feeling passionate, alive with the world, creative. Use words that are saturated with emotion. Hand-write it so it is more personal, and do not worry about spelling or grammar (Fig. 46). Most important, this manifesto will later remind you of the motivation, determination, and dedication you had at the time of writing to make positive changes in your lifestyle and physical surroundings.

Remember, when defining changes in your space, that space is not always physical but usually encompasses the mental and spiritual strata as well. Manifestos should be done individually for each person in the household to create a powerful collective shift of consciousness. Once everyone's place-based manifestos have been written, someone can either summarize them or everyone can read their own to each other to identify which changes can be shared responsibilities and which must be done individually. Put them in a place where you will see them often.

Start Living Your Manifesto

To put into practice what Amber was teaching her students about inhabiting the sacred, she encouraged them to write home-making manifestos, aiming to make their dorm-space feel more like home-space. Besides the common promise to maintain a cleaner home, there was also desire to organize better. Many wanted to put more effort into decorating with new and old personal objects or art to feel more ownership over an otherwise generic space. Some attended to quality day-and night-lighting for a warm and enchanting mood. One student resolved to make his bed into a swing so he could rock himself to sleep.

In addition to making their spaces more meaningful, the manifestos stirred other discussions. Many students talked about their passion for sustainable architecture. They were excited to learn ways of fixing the environmental problems facing them in their future. One talked about the power of architecture to cause a person to slow down and notice their environment, another about its power to create positive change in a crime-ridden area, and another the ability to heal people. A few discussed the architect's role to create space for other people's memories and to create a sense of magic and enchantment. One woman was concerned about places in the Third World, prompting a great conversation about First World design influencing rather than oppressing Third World values. Another student was interested in the maintenance of place and the education of a place's user to clean and respect that place.

Amber could see that the students had absorbed many of the fundamental concepts about inhabiting the sacred. Given this opportunity to reflect on their own history, students gained confidence in speaking about architecture, a crucial skill needed for the design profession. In addition, the conversations gave them a grounding in which to place their academic knowledge relative to the rest of their young adult lives. Most importantly, this early encouragement of intuitive observation about their world and lessons about inhabiting the sacred will be picked up in powerful ways later in their careers.

The awareness and habitation of sacred place is personally empowering, enriching, and, in some cases, life changing. For most of us, the threats and dissatisfactions that separate us from dwelling more meaningfully affect both private and public domains. To inhabit the sacred requires personal action as well as civic action. As we awaken to dissatisfactions, we seek evidence to pinpoint the malady and secure a proper treatment. As we awaken to threats, we are impelled to find scientific explanations of the causes of the crisis and the opportunities presented for collective action. How can professional designers better help people to meet their deep and abiding needs, and how can citizens be more articulate about the subconscious landscapes in their hearts? The next step towards inhabiting the sacred addresses these lingering questions and shows how to gather evidence about your community's feelings for places in order to initiate a collective awareness.

OUR SENTIMENTS FOR COMMUNITY-BASED PLACES

EVEN WHEN PEOPLE ARE AWAKENED to the vital importance of place in everyday life, most communities have difficulty truly acknowledging the significance. Partly because attachment to place is subconsciously held within each individual, it is seldom a part of conscious awareness at the community level. It is not shared, because we are unaware of it, and when we do become aware of it, it feels awkward.

The very notion that our emotions are tied to places is alien in our modern-day culture. America has even been described as a nation freed from place, of communities without propinquity.[1] The word "topophilia," meaning a "love of place," is absent in most dictionaries and is even rarer in daily conversation.[2] We lack a vocabulary to express sentiment for place. Furthermore, it is not socially acceptable to love places equally as we do people, pets, or pursuits. Affection for place may also be suppressed, because it frequently conflicts with other values such as monetary success, progress, or fashion. Additionally, sentiment for community-based places is infrequently a consideration in architectural design, city planning, and zoning.[3]

Evidencing is a necessary step for overcoming such barriers and incorporating sentiment for place into one's personal and community lives. Evidencing provides information to support the value of sentiment for a place. It does so in traditional ways, as in presenting material data and testimony, and in nontraditional ways, as in tapping the emotional domain and raising the subconscious to a conscious level. When successful, evidencing both legitimizes sentiment for a place and provides a collective awareness of the shared values embedded within that place.

We have found that when a community is clear about why attachment to place is important, its citizenry is able to speak together to defend, reclaim, or create public space that reflects such sentiment. There are many benefits to this united-we-stand approach. First, it establishes a common ground between neighbors who most often have reason to collide over differences. Second, it dedicates them to aims that have their best interests in mind. Thus, it motivates them to participate in democracy. Finally, it allows citizens a place at the table of negotiations when an outside force with a large budget or political strong-arm tries to impose narrow interests and single-purpose thinking onto them.

The complete process of evidencing has several subtle steps. After people become awakened to their personal place values, they must overcome the discomfort of speaking about them to their neighbors. The community will need a time and place to discuss, share, and debate their sacred places to arrive at a consensus of places that the community values. And, with the help of a professional or skilled community member, these sentiments must transition from ideas, words, and lists to concrete proof in the form of statistical data and provocative maps. These are the products of the evidencing process that a community creates to continue the journey of inhabiting the sacred.

Legitimizing Sentiment for Place

In consumer societies, space is viewed primarily as exchangeable real estate. Profit from this land is expected; affect toward the place is unexpected. Attachment to a place is often devalued and derided by consumers; therefore, topophilia often lacks legal standing in public policy. The powerful forces of public opinion and government further delegitimize feelings for place, but sentiment for place can be legitimized through intentional action. Usually, this begins with a small group of people who try to get others to embrace the value of attachment to a place and to participate in the creation of community-based evidence about places of emotional value (Fig. 47).

The initial efforts are usually met with skepticism, but a few people will be awakened through discussions with neighbors and join the effort. Theory about innovation considers these people "early adaptors" who require little evidence before trying something new, be it a technological advance, a dietary change, or, in this case, a new way to consider private property. As the movement grows, some cautious members will be convinced, but others will continue to reject the idea of producing evidence about the importance of place.[4] Paramount to the acceptance of the value of sacred places is material evidence that supports its usefulness. Studies show how the recognition of topophilia has successfully informed community development in other places and had a powerful legitimizing force.[5] For example, Manteo has continually played this role as a precedent for utilizing the sacred structure as a planning mechanism. The awards Manteo has won and the widespread publication of its positive effects on economic development and the quality of life are strong arguments to legitimize attachment to a place. The Manteo case resonates most strongly when there is a direct connection between certain places in Manteo and the city considering mapping its sacred places, such as the everyday use of front porches, "newsing at the post office," or a long history of industrial identity.

In most communities, scientifically gathered data on the values of a place is acceptable evidence.[6] Surveys that ask residents to rank their most-valued places and maps that explain behaviors occurring in those places appeal to communities accustomed to decision-making based on standardized logic, scientific rigor, and cautious reasoning (Fig. 48). In other communities, the most compelling evidence is supportive testimonial from local leaders, masses of organized citizens, and outside experts such as planners, politicians, or designers. In Manteo, Randy filled this role of the outside expert when he approved of protecting the humble and homey sacred places that are not attractive when measured by the aesthetic standards of his profession. He realized that his support for these sacred places mattered to the citizens. He voiced it clearly, thereby legitimizing the sacred structure.

Frequently, citizen science, gathered by residents, is the most powerful evidence. Roots of this technique derive from the century-old volunteer collection of weather data and the Audubon Christmas Bird Count. Citizen science as a hands-on participatory effort both educates volunteers and encourages them to possess the results.[7] They, in turn, legitimize the sacred places by elevating them from the

Fig. 47. To expand the numbers from a small group who believe certain places are sacred into a city-wide movement, Chao Yu uses a "Big Map," upon which people first mark where their homes are located and then add places they love.

Fig. 48. Scientifically gathered data are acceptable evidence in cities where decisions are carefully reasoned. These data sets may be compiled by experts or "citizen scientists."

qualitative and murky subconscious to a quantitative level. This allows sentiments of place to compete with more frequently measured aspects of community form like predictions of economic growth and traffic counts. In a recent case, citizens using dosimeters to measure radiation found alarmingly high radiation levels in their neighborhoods near the nuclear power plant in Fukushima Daiichi, Japan. This data, even though it was for only a few neighborhoods, contradicted government assurances of their safety. Their crude mapping was further legitimized by independent U.S. and Japanese radiation experts. This evidence, in turn, prompted the mayor to order the creation of a comprehensive radiation map of his entire city. He felt strict research, carefully plotted, was the only evidence that would restore credibility and reasoned decision-making. Citizen mapping mattered.[8]

Sharing a Collective Awareness of Sentiments for a Place

Values about a place have legitimacy only when a significant number of people in a community, often a majority, acknowledge their importance. This is complicated by several factors. Most people come to the public discussion primarily considering their own interests and narrow public values. In the same way that people have a private self and a public self, public values represent both private and public interests, and common ground must be found in order to establish a working majority. This is easier if there are many generations of like-minded people, because they share private values derived from childhood and adolescence as well as attitudes about public space developed in present-day adult life. In more diverse communities, the search for shared values about place requires finding the common ground across social class and cultural identity.[9] People of differing backgrounds know they hold divergent beliefs and are surprised that they hold dear many of the same public values because of a desire to share aspects of public life with others. The public common ground is likely to focus on places of social and civic engagement that evoke some positive memories of previously experienced sacred places.[10]

Typically, most valued public places in any community are evenly divided between parks and indoor spots. Almost always there is natural geography; in Berkeley, California, the waterfront of San Francisco Bay to the west and the hills to the east form the most sacred heart and soul for residents collectively. In addition to water and mountains, natural vegetation and farmland often define the edges of communities and are seen as sacred. Places that mark prominent moments in history, transformations, achievements, rituals, and principles are hallowed public common ground.[11] Places that invite widespread public participation are highly valued just as handmade private environments are in one's personal geography.[12] Together, these elements create a gestalt, an image of natural, cultural, and psychological phenomena expressing the essence of place-based community life that supersedes individual expectations (Fig. 49).

This gestalt is an integrated structure with properties not derivable from the mere sum of its parts. This image allows a community to visualize and then share a collective awareness of their collective attachments to their place.[13] This awareness provides insight, expands the depth of a community's

Fig. 49. Nearby residents place flower pots in the middle of a channel-
ized stream, creating a distinctive gestalt in the Japanese community
of Takesegawa.

knowledge and experience, and suggests and even authorizes action. Once placed on a map, sentiment
for place has standing, a geometry, and a place at the table of community decision-making. The collective awareness of place-attachment helps a community recognize a common identity that is deeply
grounded in the surrounding landscape (Fig. 50). Citizens also gain an appreciation for local residents
who have native wisdom, the intimate and integrated knowledge about the place that comes from long-
term and careful observation of everyday life and ecological processes.

   Once sentiment for a place is legitimized, communities generally enjoy uncovering their common ground, even when there are contested differences by age, gender, class, religion, and ethnicity.
Most are surprised at the particular places they agree have value and the extent to which they do
so. The process usually enhances pride, solidifies local identity, and encourages cooperative problem
solving. There is therapeutic value in explicating a genuine identity based on what is particular and
unique about a place, its people, and their common traits. These common traits may be distinctive
social values, history, architecture, or even childhood and adult memories. This identity reframes
problems such as functionality, economics, dominance, and control, exposes illegitimate demands,
and diminishes self-interests that too often dictate public design and planning. Sacredness serves as
a commonality among competing politics and increases empathy when divisions over identity, equity,
and values are present.

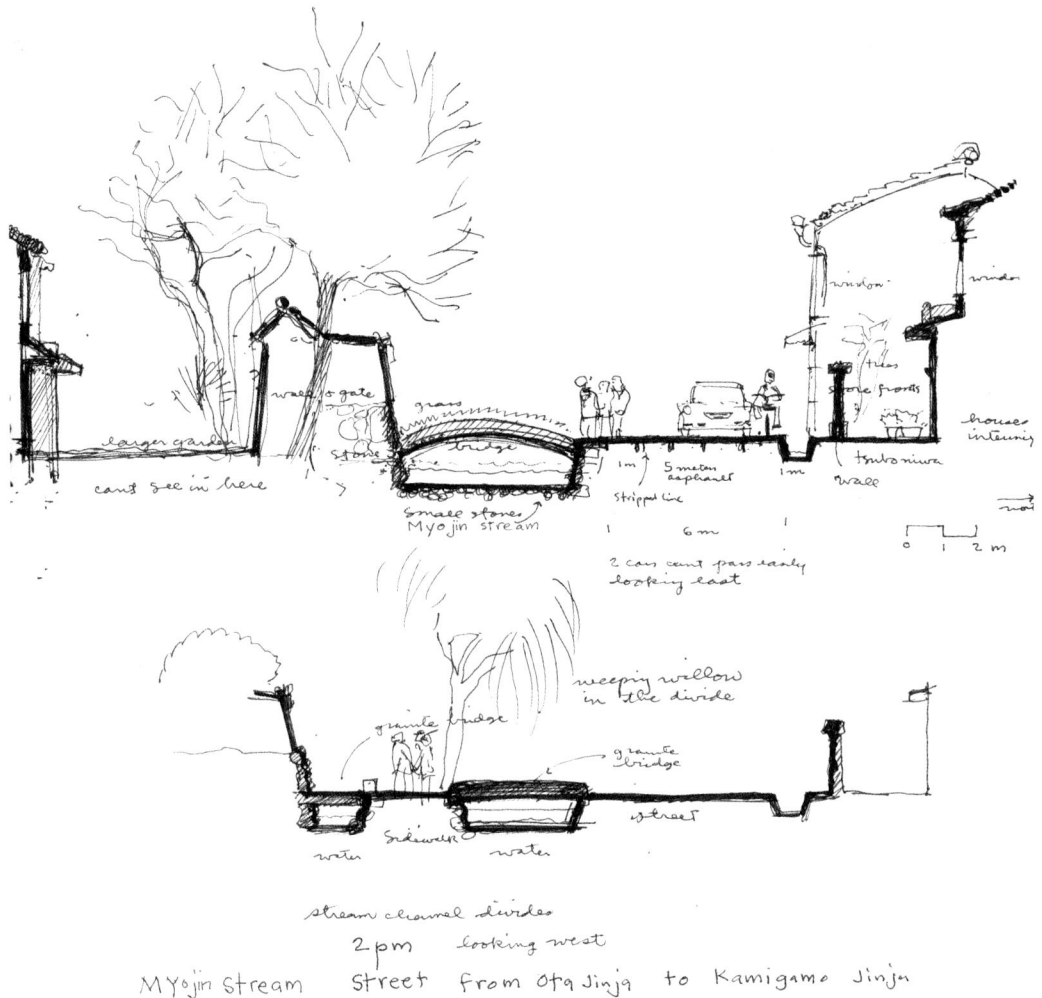

Fig. 50. In Kyoto, Japan, the sacred walkway to Oto Jinga is characterized by an ancient canal parallel to narrowing and widening streets that
creates rhythmic patterns of water, shade, and sun. Only when drawn in
section did some residents acknowledge the evidence that this nuance of
built form provided their neighborhood a unique identity.

In unusually distressed communities, the process may be painful but often is cathartic. Even in
communities with collapsing economies, as was once the case in Manteo, collective nostalgia may serve
as a stabilizing force during the crisis. In such cases, the public process provides an empowering direction for individuals who have a feeling of helplessness. It strengthens a community's resolve that "we are
all in this together." Place-based values inspire and offer clarity amidst confusion. Seeing the problem
in terms of valued assets, even if they are only memories, strengthens group identity, the capacity to act,
and ultimately the willingness to make change.

Evidencing the sacred in the public arena also gives credence to community members who may integrate abstract and phenomenological experience in unusual ways. Some are natively wise from years of residency; some may be newcomers; some may be eccentric; and then there are those in the counter-culture who may challenge the consumer values and speak from the heart about places that matter most to them in the community. No matter who the advocate may be, their evidence may be unconventional, unpleasant, or shocking.[14] Their demeanor or living style may make difficult for them to articulate this knowledge in effective ways to the public, but, when included, they offer unique insights. Their wisdom assumes a legitimate democratic role in the community's debate. This frees other members of the community to think about their own most meaningful relationships with place and create a forum for considering deep values instead of considering short-term interests.

In Mount Vernon, Washington, for example, Zell Young had grown up along the Skagit River. He knew the river ecologically and poetically, but he was considered weird by city leaders. He lived in a junkyard in the floodplain, rode a bicycle, and spent most days on the river. In discussions about what was most valued about the Skagit, Young imparted his wisdom and love for the place to a few receptive community members. His ideas introduced a hyper-awareness and new ways to think about the river that instilled the soul of the place into the city's plan for the river. He advocated keeping large parts of the river naturally wild, when most leaders wanted higher dikes. The wild areas reduced flooding in the city, provided children access to nature, and gave Mount Vernon distinctive beauty.

Techniques for Evidencing

A number of techniques are particularly useful in legitimizing sacred places and creating a collective civic awareness. Here, we describe two—Scavenger Hunt and Scripted Walking Tour—in sufficient detail that one can follow the examples and modify them to suit the situation in one's own community.

Scavenger Hunt

The Scavenger Hunt can be used in almost any context to uncover sacred places locally and provide the qualitative evidence needed to make a community-based plan. It works in many different settings: urban or rural, neighborhood or metropolitan, and affluent or poor. This technique was developed for the U.S. Environmental Protection Agency (EPA) in an effort to upgrade water quality in Chesapeake Bay by improving land-use practices in the upper reaches of its watershed. The EPA project focused on rivers in Virginia, Pennsylvania, and Maryland that feed the bay, from the Susquehanna in the north to the James in the south. The strategy aimed to increase citizen stewardship of the land

and water by employing wise land-use practices based on native knowledge and reconnecting people to those practices through a heightened awareness of reciprocal sacredness with their landscapes.

Marcia McNally and Randy did the Scavenger Hunt during weekend workshops in cities and rural areas in various parts of the vast watershed. When they arrived in each city, local people guided them around their communities. Because most communities had severe budget constraints, they had limited time to uncover their special places. To overcome the deficiency in time, a weekend workshop was helpful. Within a few days, citizens collected a lot of evidence about their most valued places, which promoted collective awareness and interest in inhabiting the sacred.

In this case in Rockbridge County, Virginia, the citizens had spent several months preparing for the workshop, so the tour and other activities were thoughtfully planned. Marcia prepared a list of tips for the weekend workshops and sent them to the organizing committee. It included tasks for the community as well as things she had to coordinate with the local organizers. These tips are included here, because they highlight basic things often overlooked:

Weekend Workshop Tips

- Give workshop attendees homework to do beforehand so as to familiarize them with the materials to be covered.

- Visit all the areas in your project site so you are prepared to talk details with residents of those areas.

- Have the locals show you around to see the area from their local perspective.

- Gain confidence in your attendees by showing successful precedents of similar projects, preferably your own work.

- Hold the event in a venue that is big enough not to exclude anyone.

- If the workshop accommodates more people than your team can handle alone, train enthusiastic local leaders to help (teams of twelve or less work best) and give these leaders identical details and easy-to-follow instructions.

- Make scripts for your exercises and incorporate input from community leaders and professionals in the field about the issues at hand.

- Plan how the findings will be presented and later used so that the information is useful. This means you need to organize every detail, such as colors on a map, numbers of sacred places to identify, and other important factors

Marcia and the committee used the tips to plan the workshop. So when Randy and Marcia arrived in Rockbridge County, the organizing committee had orchestrated a tour of the places most representative of their town for the visiting research team and other community members. They had also spent time organizing their own thoughts about what they valued most in the community. Some had already made lists. They had scheduled each venue for meetings according to Marcia's agenda and had gotten other citizens and the local media involved in tasks such as preparing food and publicity. The event was held in a large meeting hall in Lexington to accommodate several hundred local residents.

Typically on the first night, Randy and Marcia would provide some context and present the story of how Manteo preserved its Sacred Structure while increasing job opportunities. In Lexington, Randy showed slides of the process and results in Manteo. Then, he and Marcia introduced the participants to the agenda for the next day. They explained that the scavenger hunt would help residents prioritize, find, photograph, and map places that they consider most sacred in Rockbridge County.

The next day, Marcia and Randy conducted a day-long Sacred Places Scavenger Hunt to identify the most valued aspects of the local community. This technique condenses the approach used in Manteo, which occurred during several months, allowing the community to create maps of sacred places in only two days. The great advantage of the scavenger hunt is that the steps are simple and people in the community can be trained quickly to lead small groups with confidence. Because so many people had signed up to participate, Marcia recruited group leaders from the community and prepared these instructions for them. She did a brief "training session" with the group leaders in the morning before the workshop started. She gave each group leader the script to guide them during the process, answer questions other participants were likely to ask, and keep the group on schedule. Because the schedule allowed less than two hours to photograph throughout the county, Marcia and the local organizers calculated that only about fifteen places could be recorded by each group. In a small neighborhood, more places can be photographed. A part of the script created for Rockbridge County, Virginia, follows. You may find this script useful when you try this technique in your own work.

Instructions for Group Leaders

Scavenger Hunt for Sacred Places

When the participants are convened, Marcia will give a general introduction to what will happen during the day, and all the participants will introduce themselves. She will briefly explain the process and tell participants the workshop will end about 2:00 p.m. Marcia's introduction and assignments will take about fifteen minutes total (9:15–9:30 a.m.). Then, Marcia will assign people to groups of six to eight people and shares the following with the leaders of each group:

YOU ARE RESPONSIBLE FOR GETTING YOUR GROUP TO PRODUCE THE FOLLOWING:

- A LIST OF WHAT CONSTITUTES THE SACRED PLACES IN ROCKBRIDGE COUNTY

- UP TO FIFTEEN PHOTOGRAPHS OF DESIGNATED SACRED PLACES (THIS NUMBER CAN EXPAND, GIVEN ENOUGH TIME.)

- A MAP DEPICTING THE SACRED PLACES WITH PHOTOGRAPHS ATTACHED AND A BRIEF PRESENTATION OF THE RESULTING MAP

TASK 1. EXPLAIN TO YOUR GROUP THAT YOU WILL WORK TOGETHER FOR A LITTLE MORE THAN AN HOUR TO GENERATE A LIST OF MOST SACRED PLACES IN ROCKBRIDGE COUNTY BUT THAT TASK 1 WILL TAKE ONLY ABOUT FIFTEEN MINUTES (9:30–9:45 A.M.). TELL THEM THAT, AS A GROUP LEADER, YOU WILL INSTRUCT THEM TO CREATE A LIST OF THE SACRED PLACES, FACILITATE THE GROUP PROCESS, AND RECORD THE TEAM'S DISCUSSION. THEN, POSE THE FOLLOWING QUESTION AND ASK PARTICIPANTS TO WRITE DOWN ANSWERS INDIVIDUALLY. TELL THEM TO TAKE NO MORE THAN FIFTEEN MINUTES TO DO THIS:

Knowing what you know about the area, people, daily activities, community rituals, what do you think makes up the sacred places of Rockbridge County? On the sheet provided, be sure to write a brief explanation of why.

THEN, GIVE YOUR GROUP ABOUT FIFTEEN MINUTES TO WORK INDEPENDENTLY. IF EVERYONE FINISHES MAKING INDIVIDUAL LISTS SOONER, GO DIRECTLY TO TASK 2.

TASK 2. WHEN THE FIFTEEN MINUTES ARE UP, GO AROUND THE TABLE AND ASK PEOPLE TO SHARE WHAT IS ON THEIR LIST (ONE ITEM PER TURN). YOU SHOULD WRITE EACH PLACE AS THE PERSON TALKS ABOUT IT. KEEP TAKING TURNS. MAKE A LIST OF ALL THE PLACES MENTIONED. WHEN THE TIME IS NEARLY UP, GIVE EACH PERSON A TURN TO TELL YOU ANY PLACES NOT YET LISTED. GET AS FAR AS YOU CAN IN THIRTY MINUTES (9:45–10:15 A.M.). YOU SHOULD BE ABLE TO GET EVERY PLACE ON THE MASTER LIST IN THIS TIME.

TASK 3. THIS TASK SHOULD TAKE ABOUT FIFTEEN MINUTES (10:15–10:30 A.M.) ASK THE GROUP TO REVIEW THE MASTER LIST. TELL EACH MEMBER TO CHOOSE AND WRITE DOWN THE SEVEN PLACES THAT ARE MOST IMPORTANT TO EACH OF THEM. DISCOURAGE TALKING WHILE THEY WORK ALONE TO DO THIS. THEN, REVIEW THE LIST AND ASK PEOPLE TO VOTE ON THE SEVEN THAT ARE MOST IMPORTANT TO EACH PERSON. HAVE THEM DO THIS BY RAISING THEIR HANDS AS YOU READ EACH PLACE. BY 10:30 A.M., IDENTIFY THE TOP FIFTEEN PLACES THAT NEED TO BE PHOTOGRAPHED. IF THERE ARE FEWER, THAT IS FINE, BUT EXPECT THERE TO BE A LONGER LIST THAT NEEDS TO BE PRIORITIZED. IF SOMEONE ASKS WHY ONLY SEVEN OR FIFTEEN, EXPLAIN THAT RANDY AND MARCIA HAVE CALCULATED THAT ABOUT FIFTEEN PLACES CAN BE LOCATED AND PHOTOGRAPHED IN THE TWO hours available today. They work backwards from that number, knowing that, from past experience, the master list will extend to between forty and fifty places, if each person offers about seven places. To arrive at a priority list of fifteen will require making critical choices, producing a robust variety and deeply valued places.

Task 4. Tell your group that lunch will be served at 1:00 p.m. Form a team and send them out to photograph the fifteen places. Tell the photographers they need to be back no later than 1:00 p.m. Note: If the places are far apart, you may need to allow as much as three or four hours. Community leaders in Rockbridge County calculated that fifteen places could be photographed in two hours. Their estimates were close; each team of photographers returned by 1:15 p.m.

Task 5. After the photography team departs, assign one team member to give Marcia your list of sacred places. She will be at a station with blank paper on the wall. She will be responsible for making an aggregate list.

Task 6. The rest of the group needs to work on the map. Tell your group they will need to finish the map by 1:00 p.m. The map should be a clear, labeled depiction of the team's assessment of the sacred places. The map-makers should use dots to locate the elements of the sacred places:

- Red = the built environment

- Dark green = natural feature

- Light green = farm

- Blue = water

- Yellow = a view (it needs two lines connected to create a "v" to indicate the direction of the view.)

If the element is not a specific site but an area, use red, blue, or green crayons to color the area; if the element is a scenic drive, make a line.

Each dot, colored area, or line should be labeled and numbered according to the list of sacred places developed by your team.

Be sure the top choice is labeled 1. And so on.

When the photographers return, put the photos on the map and number them to correspond to the places.

Task 7. At about 12:45 p.m., you need to assign two speakers to work on a presentation of the map to the other teams. They should be prepared to present the map in only five minutes (beginning at 1:00 p.m.).

Task 8. To maximize limited time, sandwiches will be served for lunch during the presentation. Each group presents its map of sacred places to everyone else. This will take about an hour. If people ask, tell them the presentations will go until just a little after 2:00 p.m.

Tasks 1–2 of the script explain how to make a collective list of sacred places by making individual lists of sacred places and then sharing these with the others in the group, creating an unranked group list. This is the basic process for incorporating both individual and group ideas, both of which were essential to a useful outcome. Some people are shy and never voice their opinions, even in a small group if they have not already worked alone and written an individual list. In this process, each person got an equal opportunity to list sacred places.

In Task 3, the group leaders were instructed to have each small group vote on the fifteen most sacred places, each person voting on his or her seven favorites. In Task 4, in order to formalize the claims and gain collective awareness about those fifteen places, the group leaders created a team to photograph the places in their community. This is the most fun, for it encourages local people to sense the places firsthand and discuss why these places are valued (Figs. 51 and 52). In Task 5, another member compiled the small group list of most valued places for Marcia, who created one aggregated ranked list by adding up the results from all the small groups. That list became substantial evidence in planning the future of the county.

In Tasks 6–8, other members of the small group drew a map of their sacred places and prepared a presentation. When the team returned with photographs, they were taped to the map. The maps with photographs were then taped on the walls, and each group explained their conclusions. Because all the map's colors were pre-determined, they could easily be read and cross-referenced by everyone attending; differences and similarities of sacred spots were instantly clear.

Marcia's aggregated list of Most Sacred Places in concert with these maps and lists resulted in a collective awareness that had not existed previously. The list provided a statistical tally, whereas the map showed patterns of how each sacred place related to the other. These patterns also suggested new geometries of land use (Fig. 53).

This concluded the scavenger hunt, but additional exercises were used to help prepare the participants to incorporate the maps of sacred places into the community's existing plans and legal documents. In a creative extension of this method, our colleagues in Setagaya, Japan, installed large red picture frames at each sacred place, both to increase community awareness and as a means of evidencing the

Fig. 51. Every group involved in the Rockbridge County Scavenger Hunt photographed different streams and rivers (such as the Maury River, shown here at Goshen Pass) as central to their sacred structure. This provided a county-wide framework for land-use planning.

Fig. 52. Uncluttered views over open agricultural lands to nearby Blue Ridge and Allegheny Mountains were among the most cherished aspects of the community. This evidence challenged county policies that allowed these views to disappear so new subdivisions could be built.

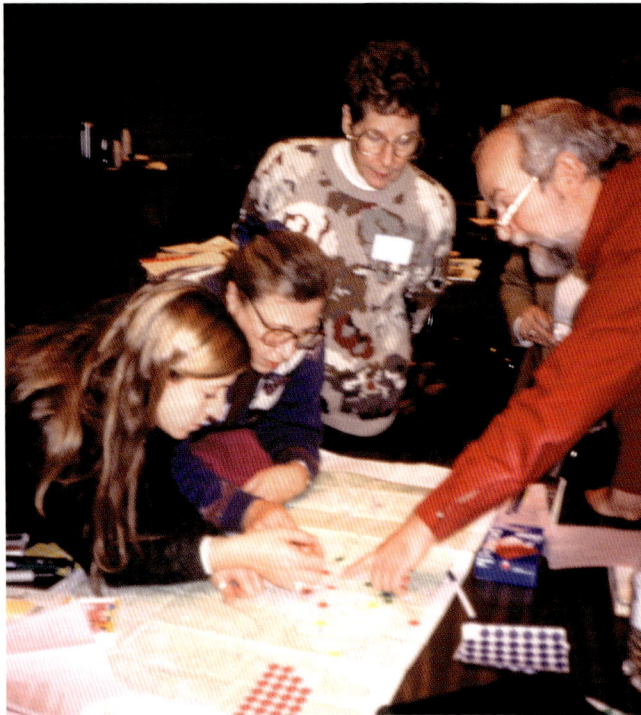

Fig. 53. Working in small groups residents located their sacred spots on a map, then color-coded buildings, farmland, streams, rivers, and other natural features. This revealed interconnected regional patterns the community had never considered before that required new policies to protect both the watershed and their collective identity.

hallowed spots. In general, results are more thorough using multiple techniques—interviews, observation of behavior, and newspaper surveys—but the Sacred Places Scavenger Hunt produces many of the same results in much less time.

There are two drawbacks to the scavenger hunt. First, it takes several weeks of preparation to create the specific tools, ready the presentation, and attend to the logistics. It can only be straightforward and successful if attention is paid to every detail in advance. Second, communities that undertake an effort to map sacred places are already concerned that special places are threatened, but they may not know what to do or how to prevent loss. This requires that a group of local people understands how to use the evidence to insert the sacred structure into community planning, zoning ordinances, and building codes. It may take several years to revise those plans, ordinances, and codes. A group must stick with it for this extended time frame in order to institutionalize the sacred structure and develop design and planning guidelines to use sacred places as inspiration for new development (Fig. 54). A weekend workshop does not guarantee such long-term attention.

After lunch, the group leaders in Rockbridge County reconvened their small groups for a few additional exercises, all important to evidencing but even more essential in consecrating the sacred places. These exercises included envisioning the future Rockbridge County by considering the sacred places and the best things about the county compared to things that worried people about their

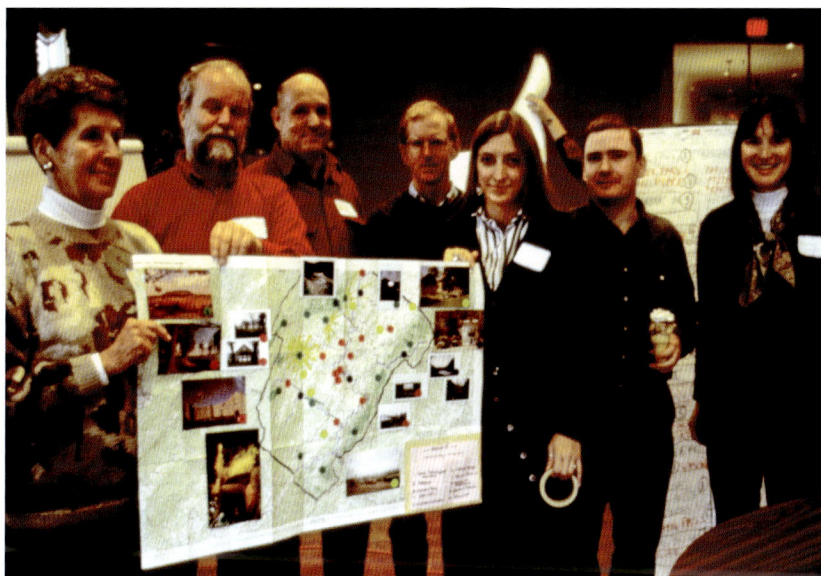

Fig. 54. A group formed to shepherd the Sacred Places Map into
Rockridge County's long-range planning.

community. Marcia also presented a brief lesson in how to ask these questions of other people in the community and how to listen fully to people who might have different opinions. Then, she helped them consider what people and groups were most important to creating the kind of future they envisioned. She concluded by having them form a steering committee to develop a strategy to create a plan for their county, utilizing the sacred places.

Envisioning, listening, and developing a strategy are means of consecrating the sacred places. The strategy also focuses on actions useful for incorporating the sacred places in local community planning. Because Marcia and Randy's involvement was limited, it was essential to form a group with specific objectives about how to proceed. The nature of the groups and the strategies employed were different in each of the three demonstration communities the EPA had chosen: Rockbridge County in Virginia, exurban Baltimore in Maryland, and Union County in Pennsylvania. Still, many important changes occurred as a result of the Scavenger Hunt and resulting maps of sacred places. This success is strong evidence of the utility of the technique in legitimizing the places and creating collective awareness. In Rockbridge and Union counties, the groups incorporated the Sacred Structure into their long-range plans. In another community, the sacred places provided the basis for a water-shed-open-space plan. Others modified land-use ordinances, undertook special projects to create a community center where none existed, protected agricultural lands, and formulated mechanisms for protecting streams.

Scripted Walking Tour

A few years ago, a team assembled by the Spanish Speaking Unity Council was designing Union Point Park, a new open space on former industrial land along the waterfront in Oakland, California. The surrounding neighborhoods are ethnically diverse—long-time African and European Americans, second-generation Vietnamese, and Mexican-American and Central-American immigrants. To gain a sense of the uniqueness of the area, professional designers attended meetings in each enclave and conducted surveys in each language. Out of these investigations, a list of desired program elements resulted: facilities for competing cultural celebrations, a place for teen employment, informal soccer and picnic areas for large groups, walking trails, and extensive planting of barren areas.

In addition to the surveys that established the multicultural program, the designers planned events to bring residents to the site precisely to establish a sensual relationship between people and the potential park, which, at that time, was a narrow strip of vacant land surrounded by industrial warehouses. It was, however, located on the Oakland Estuary, a big-harbor backwater with spectacular views and water covered with resting birds, both resident species and migrants along the Pacific Coast Flyway. Hundreds of residents went on scripted tours conducted in multiple languages.

After going on the field tour, each participant filled out a questionnaire that asked about appropriate activities for the park. Surprisingly, for every language group the single highest priority was to create places for bird watching. This had been only a minor consideration previously, yet after experiencing the place firsthand, learning the names of a few resident and seasonal birds, and sensing the relationship between wildlife, water, and vegetation, the participants saw an exciting opportunity unique to that site. No longer was the highest priority a subcultural construct with competing ethnic priorities but the desire for an encounter with wild birds, a value that transcended cultural differences.

The scripted tour is particularly effective at awakening all the senses to a setting. In the following example, we demonstrate how the method can serve other purposes of evidencing with only slight modification.

This tour took place in Yountville, California, as part of developing the urban design plan. Different than the weekend workshop conducted in Rockbridge County, the designers in our firm, Community Development by Design, had worked for many years on a variety of projects in the town and knew the people and place well. At each stop, the designers gave a brief summary of what they had learned from listening to local people, from their analysis of the town, and a few related stories of local history and ecology. The script was prepared in advance and personalized to anticipated participants, including newcomers, parents with babies in strollers, teenagers, and lifelong residents.

At the beginning of the tour, residents received a feedback form to fill out during the walk (Fig. 55). The first stop, a diner in an old building on the tree-lined Main Street, focused on sacred places in Yountville. Here, the tour leaders invited people to linger. This allowed stragglers to catch up and

Fig. 55. On the Yountville Scripted Walking Tour, the designers planned a series of stops where critical urban design issues were discussed. Then, participants gave individual written feedback about the experience of the place and their solutions to the problems.

for participants to help themselves to free coffee from the urn on the diner's front porch. This setting represented a hometown idiosyncrasy, the spot to experience an insider's sense of place. We expected the diner to rank high as a sacred place. Here, the designers included a list of places in town and asked people to rank those that were most special. The results were surprising and revealing: The most sacred aspect of Yountville was the overall atmosphere rather than individual spots .

The diner where the tour began was at the bottom of the list, as only two percent of the participants considered it most hallowed. In contrast, views to vineyards (eighty-four percent), pleasant places to walk in and around town (fifty-seven percent), and the human scale of buildings (forty-eight percent) were most sacred (Fig. 56).

As in so many other cities, natural boundaries, particularness, and the center of town made up the most sacred qualities. Trees and vineyards formed a clear boundary for the town and were ranked as the most special places of Yountville. In total, the importance of trees (eighty-nine percent) exceeded any other factor: big trees in town (thirty-three percent), Pistache trees in fall (twenty-nine percent), and narrow tree-lined streets (twenty-seven percent). Vineyards and trees contributed to Yountville's uniqueness directly and indirectly made it a pleasant place to walk (fifty-seven percent). It was unusual for walking to be so highly valued. That is most particular to Yountville. People also noted that the scale of buildings (forty-six percent) was special.

Rankings of Yountville's Most Special Places

Local Characteristics	Percent of Total
Churches	0%
Cemetary	2%
The Diner	2%
Post Office	2%
Parking Lots	4%
Town Hall	6%
Library	6.50%
Shops	6.50%
Veteran's Home	8%
Schools	8%
Domaine Chandon	8.50%
"Country Lane" Feel	12%
Views along Cross Road	15%
Hotels	15%
Parks	16%
Rivers and Creeks	17%
Community Hall	18%
Vintage 1870	23%
Restaurants	25%
Neighborhoods	26%
Narrow Treelined Streets	27%
Pistache Trees in Fall	29%
Big Trees in Town	33%
Places to Meet Friends	35%
Human Scale Buildings	46%
Pleasant Places to Walk	57%
Views to Vinards	84%

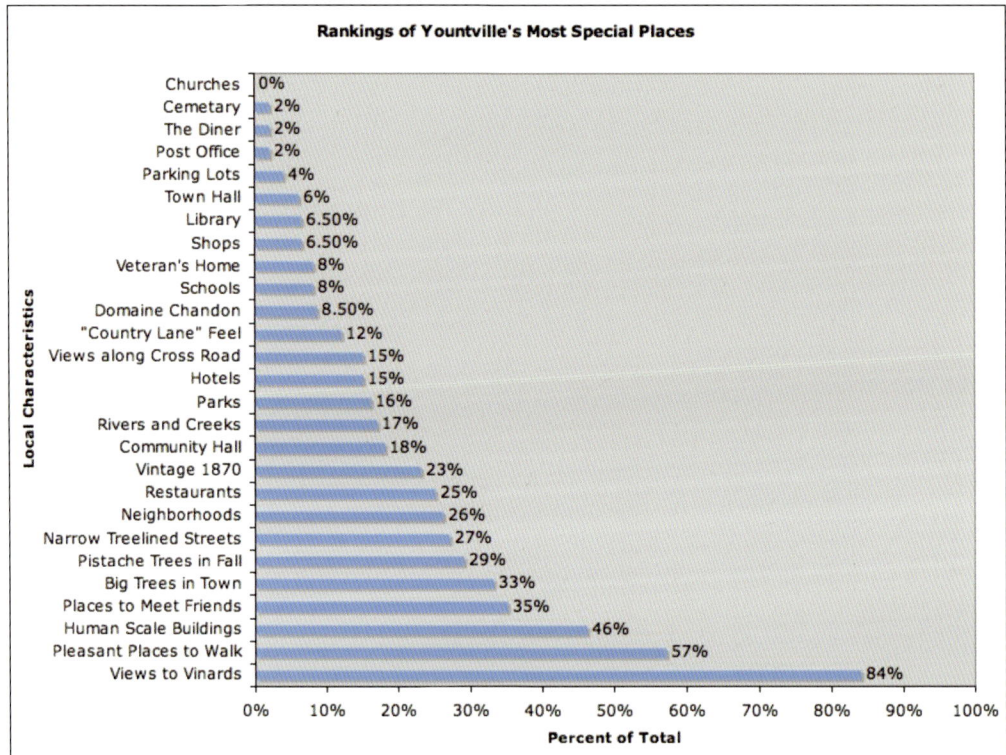

Fig. 56. Residents ranked views to vineyards as the single most special aspect about Yountville. Enhancing those views became a priority in the Urban Design Plan.

The center of the town is the place where most people meet friends (thirty-five percent) with restaurants (twenty-five percent), vintage 1870 shops (twenty-three percent), and Community Hall (eighteen percent) being the most frequently mentioned centers of social life. After all the responses had been tallied, the results were presented to City Council and became a legal public record. During the next year, the council acted to reserve remnants of vineyards in town and initiated an aggressive street-tree planting program. The clear set of data was strong evidence in legitimizing these special places in Yountville.

At each stop on the tour, issues previously identified through surveys and public meetings were discussed. Stop Six (Yount Street) was especially important, because it addressed the particularness of the scale of buildings. On this stop, residents clarified their previously stated concerns that Yountville was becoming overbuilt and losing the feeling of its human scale. People were arguing for lower building mass and height than was presently in the most sensually delightful areas of town, so the tour stopped at a location where the building with the greatest floor-area-ratio in town could be observed. A full story higher than most buildings and filling almost all of its lot, the Maison Fleurie Hotel was one of the city's truly charming buildings. Natural stone and wood, careful craftsmanship,

Stop Six: Yount Street

People in town have told us that it is important to maintain the small-town scale and specifically to not "overbuild."
Which of these are the worst aspects of overbuilding in Yountville? Check the five (5) that you consider the worst. If you do not consider overbuilding to be a problem, check that at the bottom of the page.

_____ loss of views to vineyards and hills from town
_____ not enough open land and green space left
_____ parking lots too big and unsightly
_____ too much development
_____ too many hotels and inns
_____ too many tourist shops
_____ too much new residential development
_____ not enough local-serving retail development
_____ buildings too close together
_____ buildings too big for their lots
_____ buildings taller than one story
_____ buildings taller than two stories
_____ new buildings are too suburban and don't fit the rural village character
_____ too many cars in town
_____ streets being widened
_____ cars going too fast
_____ other (please list): _____
_____ other (please list): _____
_____ overbuilding is not a problem

Fig. 57. This page from the Feedback Form at Stop Six asked participants about what they meant by "overbuilding," which was a hot topic of debate in Yountville at that time.

and a tiny but well attended garden and landscape compensated for mass and height (Fig. 57). This was the perfect place to get residents to consider exactly what they meant by "human scale" and "overbuilding."

Because overbuilding was such a contentious issue, the script required provocative yet nonjudgmental wording in order to get people to respond with their senses. Here, the evidencing served to separate experiential reality of the charming three-story building from public statements opposing any building over two stories. The following is the script for Stop Six. The design team member leading each tour memorized this script and used it to introduce the issues of scale and over building. You might find it useful in orchestrating a similar tour in your community.

Stop Six: Yount Street

Some people in town have told our design team from Community Development by Design that there is a danger that "overbuilding" will detract from life in Yountville. "Overbuilding" can refer to how the development is done, such as the size of buildings,

THEIR DENSITY, THE NUMBER OF BUILDINGS OR THEIR STYLE. ONE OF THE PRELIMINARY OBJECTIVES OF AN URBAN DESIGN PLAN IS TO PROTECT THE SCALE OF THE VILLAGE AND MASS OF BUILDINGS IN THE COMMERCIAL AND OLD RESIDENTIAL NEIGHBORHOOD. WE'D LIKE TO GET MORE FEEDBACK FROM YOUNTVILLE RESIDENTS ABOUT WHAT IS MEANT BY "OVERBUILDING" IN YOUNTVILLE.

IT IS IMPORTANT TO BE SPECIFIC ABOUT WHAT PEOPLE WANT TO PROTECT ABOUT THE SMALL-TOWN SCALE. HERE, WE CAN SEE SEVERAL POTENTIAL PROBLEMS OF OVERBUILDING. FOR OUR DESIGN TEAM, THIS BUILDING AND THE SITE'S DEVELOPMENT SEEM TO BE SENSITIVELY DONE, AND THEY ADD TO THE CHARACTER OF THE TOWN. THE MAISON FLEURIE IS A THREE-STORY BUILDING. PERHAPS SOME PEOPLE THINK THIS BUILDING IS TOO TALL. DOES THE QUALITY OF THE COURTYARD AND ROOF PITCH MAKE THE BUILDING ATTRACTIVE? WHAT ABOUT THE WAY PARKING IS ARRANGED?

LOOKING EAST, THE OWNER OF THE VINEYARD IS CONSIDERING PLANS FOR FUTURE DEVELOP-MENT. WILL THAT MAKE THE TOWN SEEM "OVERBUILT"? ARE THERE WAYS THIS DEVELOPMENT CAN BE DESIGNED SO THAT THE VIEW AND PART OF THE VINEYARD ARE SAVED?

CERTAIN ASPECTS OF FUTURE DEVELOPMENT MAY CONTRIBUTE TO "OVERBUILDING" THAT HARM THE TOWN'S SMALL, RURAL CHARACTER. ON THE OTHER HAND, YOU MAY NOT WORRY ABOUT OVERBUILDING.

Notice that the script explains that the designers are unsure exactly what "over-building" means, so the Community Development by Design team needs precise feedback. The leader points out the features of the Maison Fleurie that might be problems but acknowledges that it seems to be well designed. After posing questions and listing common overbuilt features of buildings, the tour leader points out that "overbuilding" might not be a problem at all, again trying to provide unbiased balance to the discussion.

Experiencing the Maison Fleurie Hotel in person helped people to acknowledge that a two-story height limit was not necessarily the answer to maintain human scale. They needed to make decisions based on concrete experience rather than abstract urban design doctrine. After discussing this site, people were asked to check the five worst aspects of overbuilding from a list. The feedback from this stop was particularly informative. As citizens experienced the potential problems sensually, they were much more precise about "overbuilding" than earlier discussions in workshops to develop the Urban Design Plan, in which there seemed to be a uniform hostility to any new development.

People were able to separate aspects of new construction that were acceptable, even desirable, from negative impacts. This made for a more informed discussion about guidelines for future urban design and planning.

Some professionals worry that the choice of stops on a tour like this is manipulative, pointing out only selective issues to residents while not discussing others or by choosing the extreme example of a stated opinion. Admittedly, these tours can be persuasive, though these stops were chosen only after listening to previous community concerns. To this end, the late Lawrence Halprin, a foremost

---

Highest Priorities

1. Of all the objectives of the Urban Design Plan, which should be the highest priority? Check no more than five (5). Then rank those five from one to five, one (1) being your highest priority, two (2) being your second highest priority, and so on.

_____ Preserve and enhance the character of Yountville as a small, rural, informal community, such that the image of the town as a unique place supports business viability and investment.

_____ Enhance the already-memorable image of town by maintaining views of vineyards and hills from town, planting street trees, and protecting the small-town scale of Yountville.

_____ Make Washington and Yount Streets more walkable.

_____ Connect the separate parts of Yountville and the surrounding landscape.

_____ Encourage shoppers to walk to a variety of stores and destinations.

_____ Create a center that serves local purposes and conveys the identity of Yountville to visitors.

_____ Design details like light fixtures, benches, sidewalks, and curbs to reflect the character of the town.

_____ other (please list): _____

2. Having been on this tour, is there anything else you'd like to tell us that is important to the Urban Design Plan?

Fig. 58. At the end of the tour, people were asked what actions should be the highest priorities in the Urban Design Plan.

landscape architect and innovative participatory designer, felt that raising sensory awareness of careless decisions or abstract logic is precisely the purpose of the public design process.[15]

At the conclusion of the tour, participants were asked to rank objectives of the urban design plan. This question served as a cross-check, and it reconfirmed the sacredness of the overall ambience of Yountville and, specifically, the importance of vineyards and trees (Fig. 58).

In effect, the site-tour strategy intensifies collective awareness and reinforces the power of place. The resulting maps and lists legitimize deeply held values about the landscape that daily touch peoples' lives. The shared experience informs public debate and provides points of reference that are rooted in an actual place rather than a conceptual space (Fig. 59).

For anyone considering doing a walking tour, Marcia has written tips to make it successful. These are based on her thirty-plus years of experience designing tours to get people to experience places first-hand in order to create places more informed by sensual pleasures.

Walking Tour Tips

- PREPARATION IS EVERYTHING. KNOW THE PLACE AND THE MOST CRITICAL ISSUES BEFORE SCRIPTING A TOUR. THIS INVOLVES LISTENING TO PEOPLE IN THE COMMUNITY, SETTING PRELIMINARY GOALS, AND SENSING THE PLACE ON YOUR OWN.

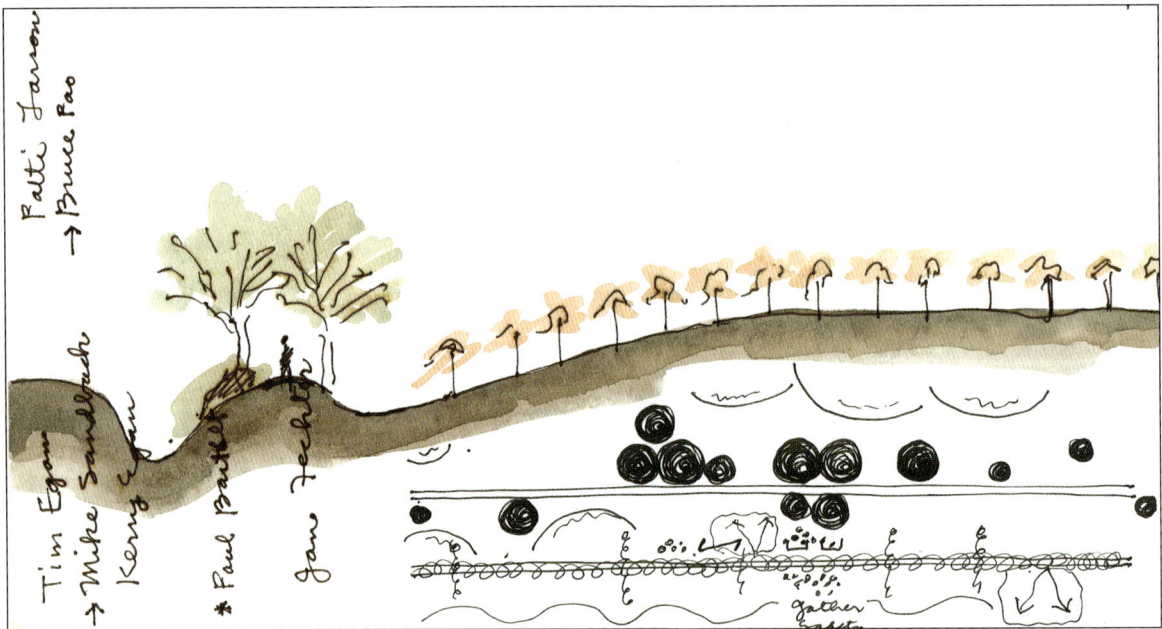

Fig. 59 (left and right). Based on overwhelming evidence of public support, the City of Yountville preserved existing views and created additional views to vineyards along the major promenade where double rows of pistache trees provide shade and spectacular fall color.

- People usually will not walk more than two miles.

- Plan the tour to take half a day or less, with time for breaks.

- Decide what the priorities are and what phenomenological experiences and issues are to be emphasized in a minimal amount of stops.

- Use the tour as a way of cross-referencing previous results from surveys or questionnaires such as most sacred places and concerns over safety and development. You should have collected some such results by the time you have gotten to the stage of a walking tour. In the case of Yountville, we had done goal surveys and mapped sacred places, and there was data from many community workshops. These workshops dated to a Take Part event conducted Larry Halprin twenty years before, in which he discovered how much local people valued walking in Yountville.

- Script what will be verbalized during the walk for each stop to make the visit concentrated and efficient. Call out unclear findings from previous results and ask members to clarify.

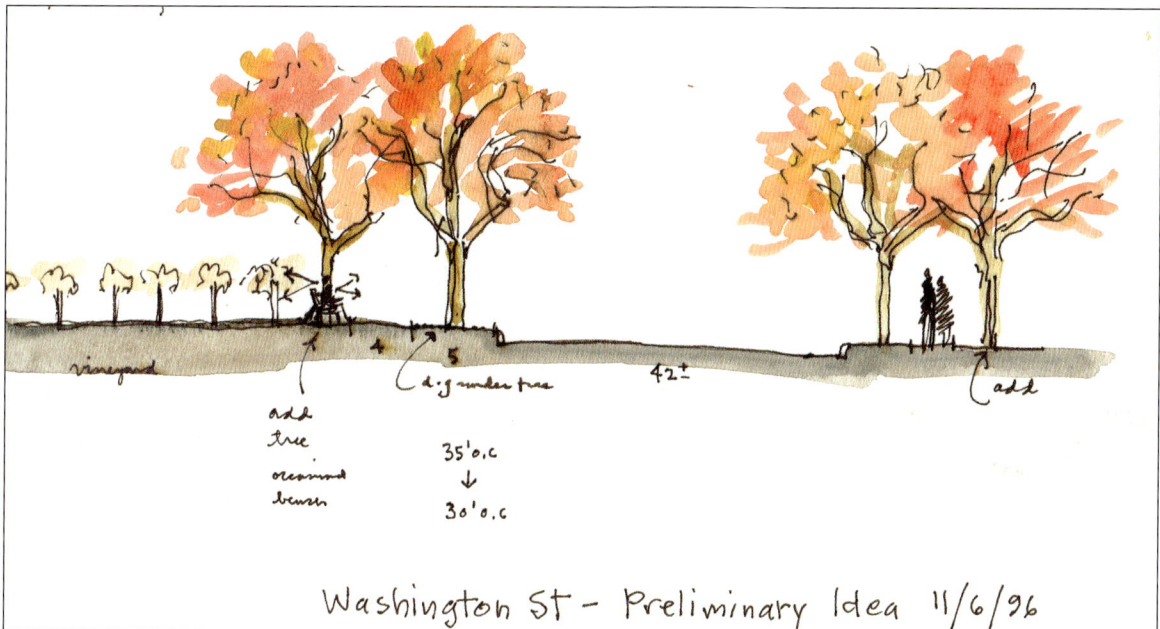

Washington St - Preliminary Idea 11/6/96

• GIVE PARTICIPANTS A FIRM SURFACE TO WRITE ON. FOR EXAMPLE, CUT CARDBOARD TO STANDARD PAPER SIZE AND STAPLE THE PRINTED PAGES ONTO IT. THE CARDBOARD CAN BE REUSED NUMEROUS TIMES IN THE FUTURE.

Other Techniques

A few other techniques are worth note for evidencing. Asking hypothetical questions is an effective way to probe phenomenological responses stimulated by the sensual experience of the place by asking: What uses are appropriate in a place? Some favorite "thinking outside the box" questions are: What would this place like to be?; If this place could speak, what would it say to you?; What lessons does this place offer?; and How would you feel if you were this place? These questions should inform the designer, community participants, and officials about fundamental values and objectives that should be brought into the design and planning debate.

Another helpful technique is asking questions about nature. Although access to nature is sacred to most people, its meaning may be unclear and result in heated public disagreements. The following question focused on a riverfront area in Mount Vernon, Washington, though in other ecologies the questions would need to reflect different issues of "nature":

TO DEFINE NATURE IN A WAY THAT IS USEFUL FOR PLANNING, PLEASE WRITE OUT WHAT YOU WOULD PROPOSE AS APPROPRIATE GUIDELINES FOR NATURE IN YOUR COMMUNITY. YOU MIGHT CONSIDER BUT NOT BE LIMITED TO THE FOLLOWING:

1. NATIVE TREES, SELECTED TO ATTRACT BIRDS, SHOULD BE PLANTED ALONG THE BROKEN CONCRETE RIP-RAP EDGES.

2. MAINTAIN THIS AREA AS IT IS, IN ITS NATURAL STATE.

3. THE CITY SHOULD ACQUIRE THIS AREA TO PROTECT ITS NATURAL CHARACTER.

4. PLANT MORE NATIVE TREES IN THIS AREA.

5. CUT DOWN OLD TREES THAT POSE A SAFETY THREAT.

6. CUT THE UNDERGROWTH OUT EACH YEAR TO MAKE WALKING TRAILS BUT MAINTAIN MOST OF THE LOWER STORY VEGETATION FOR WILDLIFE.

7. PROVIDE A SIX-FOOT PAVED WALKING AND BIKING TRIAL THROUGH THIS AREA.

8. MAINTAIN THE WARM-WATER SLOUGHS FOR SWIMMING.

9. MAINTAIN A WILDLIFE HABITAT ZONE, WITH A MINIMUM WIDTH OF 100 FEET IN ITS NATURAL STATE ALONG THE RIVER'S EDGE.

10. KEEP THIS AREA IN ITS NATURAL STATE, EXCEPT:

      A. PROVIDE WALKING AND BIKING TRAILS

      B. INSTALL SIGNS

      C. PROVIDE RUSTIC PLACES TO SIT AND PICNIC

      D. MAKE AN EARTH MOUND

      E. BUILD A PLAYGROUND

      F. MAKE A SHELTERED PICNIC AREA

      G. BUILD AN AMPHITHEATER

      H. PROVIDE A PARKING LOT

      I. OTHER:_____

11. THIS AREA SHOULD BE DEVELOPED, EVEN IF IT MEANS CUTTING DOWN NATIVE TREES AND REMOVING HABITAT.

12. AT LEAST ____ PERCENT OF THE TREES IN THIS AREA SHOULD BE MAINTAINED FOR A NATURAL PARK, AS WILDLIFE HABITAT, AND FOR ITS NATURAL VIEW.

Fig. 60. Walking tours, combined with field research, engage residents in gathering scientific and sensual evidence about special places. Here, a group measures the effects of erosion from poor siting of a road on their Hollywood, California, neighborhood. Citizen involvement reversed their previous support to dam this natural canyon and engineer a debris basin to control flooding. Their own science convinced them to disperse floodwater into sub-watersheds, slowing erosion with small check dams and vegetation.

13. At least ____ percent of the trees in this area should be removed and replaced with a grass lawn, even though grass is not native to this location.

14. Plant trees or flowers, even if they are not native to this location.

15. Please think of other examples and write them on your forms.

The designers in our firm, Community Development by Design, have also combined walking tours with field analysis such as teaching residents how to map vegetation, wildlife habitat, or pedestrian hazards or how to measure water or air quality (Fig. 60). This kind of fieldwork not only provides invaluable firsthand data that otherwise could never be collected, but also engages residents

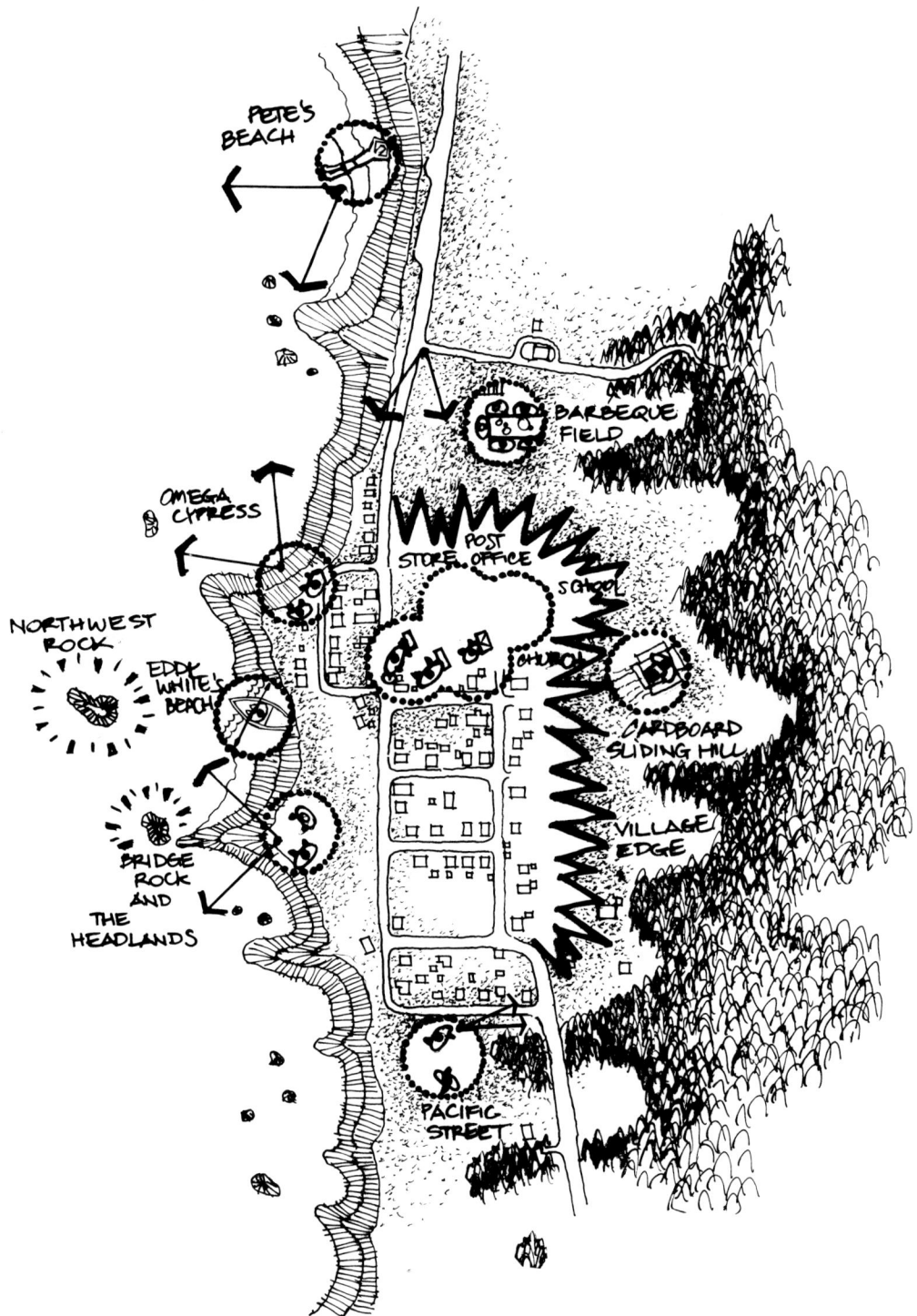

Fig. 61. The Sacred Places Map for Westport, California, provided concrete evidence of values embedded subconsciously in the untamed landscape, the solar orientation of everyday life, and the distinct juxta-position of village and ocean that the residents held most deeply.

with the sense and science of the locality. As it turns out, citizens with only modest training can map complex ecosystems adequately to meet professional standards for the purposes of community decision-making.[16]

The common element in all these techniques is the end product. Without a clear and concise list, spreadsheet, or map to organize the collected evidence, citizens and officials will have no documents to use as a tool or weapon in inhabiting the sacred. In community design and planning, nothing provides legitimizing evidence like a map (Fig. 61).[17] A map of local sacred places has additional power far beyond legitimizing, for it raises a community's awareness and gives ordinary people tools to fight powers that threaten what is most valued in their community. Such a map compiles dozens and often hundreds of individual opinions into a unified voice of a community's sentiments for place. More than a list of valued settings, a map provides proof of the existence of something deeply felt but previously invisible.[18] It creates an observable pattern of what was previously unimaginable. It makes obvious what was experienced or sensed but not grasped or comprehended consciously. A map of the locally valued places turns partly known, separated fragments of experience into an integrated whole that is far more than the sum of the individual parts. The map represents newly constructed knowledge based on collective wisdom.[19]

On the day we were writing the first draft of this section, Amber's family and Fito came by our office for lunch. Fito became transfixed with a map on the wall titled "The World from Down Under," in which the Northern Hemisphere-centric map had been reversed so that Chile, his native country, occupied a prominent location. The North American continent was warped, misshapen, and unrecognizable. He studied the map a long time, deliberately tracing the Chilean coast with a loving finger. He seemed to feel a special pride and amusement of seeing, for the first time, his country given importance equal to the Global North.

For a community to live more intentionally and in tune with deep values toward place requires evidence of what those values are and what their benefits will be. Mapping sacred places provides compelling evidence, creates a collective awareness of sentiment for a place, establishes a shared common ground among competing interests, and reframes nagging challenges and problems. Techniques that gather evidence in participatory ways are especially powerful. Evidencing legitimizes attachment to a place, readies a community for commitment in the public realm, and empowers inspired leaders to guide community groups through the next tough steps of inhabiting the sacred—transforming values of place and organizing a plan of action.

VALUES OF PLACE THROUGH SACRIFICE

Making Choices

IN THIS CHAPTER, we focus on making choices about which values of place are most important to an individual, a family or a community. This process of setting priorities transforms some seemingly mundane places into the sacred. This involves sorting thick from thin values, satisfying the most basic needs, separating deeply held wishes from their monsters, comparing conscious and subconscious values, and creating a means to evaluate the competing choices. We show how to maintain choice when options are restricted. We offer techniques for making sustainable decisions.

Short-term and Long-term, Thin and Thick Values of Place

After sentiments of place are evidenced and converted into maps comes the difficult task of negotiating which values are worthy of a family's pursuit and which are worthy of implanting into the public landscape. Why so difficult? Often personal and collective values are at odds; superficial desires can overwhelm serious intents; and families or constituents often want freedoms without responsibilities. This means that short-term goals and long-term benefits frequently clash. Therefore, it may take soul-searching to forego some personal profits, comforts, and special interests for deeper, more fulfilling family values and the community's long-term good. Once a group is dedicated to abiding values, however, it has the power to visualize a direction and a cohesive plan for the future that may not only stand unwaveringly in the opposing face of internal change or external power, but also manifest a sense of the sacred that satisfies personal and community interests.

Community values fall along a continuum from thick to thin. Simply put, thick ones are enduring, deeply held, and really important. Thin ones are like a passing fancy, not so important when seriously considered. Thick or deep values have most centrality and interconnectedness to biological needs, identity, and a worldview. These thick values, within which sacredness is most deeply held, require time to form and are difficult to change and, if lost, are particularly unsettling, resulting in disorientation and rootlessness. Thin or superficial values are less connected to basic needs and are superficially held preferences of individual taste and style. They are given up less painfully, because they are always changing based on shifts in popular culture.[1]

The Four Wishes and the Four Monsters

Thick values regarding place develop from the most fundamental human needs; places become sacred when they satisfy basic needs and are necessary for human fulfillment. Sociologists refer to these as enduring wishes sought throughout life until achieved satisfactorily. There seem to be four needs-serving settings of sacredness for individuals and communities: places of certainty, places of new experience, places of reciprocal response, and places of belonging.[2] Places that connect people directly to multiple needs in a harmonic balance or exemplify a single wish become hallowed and beloved, while those that connect people only weakly to their needs tend to be profane and unloved.

Places of Certainty

Places that provide sustenance, stability, and safety amidst uncertainty become sacred to individuals and societies. We need settings we can depend upon for support, aid, vital nourishment, and protection from harm. Cognitive assurance of certainty must be constructed to carry out basic human functions, from cooking healthfully and dressing appropriately for a meeting to finding a new destination in the city and coping with climate change. As a result, places that provide ecological, biological, physical, and social safety are as vital as food and water.

Designers and planners can create places that reinforce survival, order, a clear worldview, important rituals, and explanations for the inexplicable. Places with these characteristics help quiet the fear of a chaotic home or the mistrust that some people feel when sharing the public realm with others. Planners provide certainty in everyday life with the assurance of lead-free drinking water and zoning that allows access to healthy food within walking distance. Designers provide certainty with such simple measures as safe sidewalks and shade trees. Apart from these daily activities, religious architecture often tries to explain the inexplicable. A clear example of a traditionally sacred place that fulfills the need of certainty is the Cathedral of Our Lady of Chartres in France. Here, the Christian worldview is confirmed with the display of the tunic worn by Mary when Jesus was born. And three depictions of Christ—his life on Earth, his ascension or second coming, and the end of time—are designed as a system that explains the otherwise unexplainable. On the other hand, places that undermine a sense of security, whether at home or in public, lurk as monsters that can devour vulnerable people and communities.

Places of New Experience

A second source of sacredness are places of growth. Changes within an individual are like the emergence of a moth from its cocoon, outgrowing the nourishing haven of its bounded pupil stage to a more extensive environment. Like metamorphosis, the human world, expands reality from a situation of safety to a less secure state of new experience. Although certainty and new experience might appear as mutually exclusive oppositions, they actually form a process in which one stage of new experience depends upon the previous security. Venturing forth requires a base of certainty and a place beyond to explore, grow, and stretch the boundaries. The combination of places of certainty and growth form identity.

Places that offer opportunity for free expression of identity, creativity, dreaming, and adventure shape a healthy identity. For example, an architect might help a family transform an unused garage into a room for making arts and crafts, satisfying a basic need inexpensively and helping the family avoid buying a new home much larger than necessary. Or a planner might incorporate places for adventures such as rock climbing in the regional plan that are more challenging and fulfilling than any pseudo-adventures such as fake rocks of gunite offered commercially. These planning and design actions are enjoyable and sustainable. Moreover, these actions are affordable for most people who might be unable to travel to a distant corner of the world for the experience of the exotic. Black Rock City, where the annual art festival Burning Man occurs, is one such example that offers its participants adventure and the opportunity to define, test, and challenge limits in Nevada. Burning Man experiments with new forms of art and temporary community. When Amber attended, she was struck with the range of explorations and innovations so close to home. The Department of Mutant Vehicles, for example, turned a truck into a super-sized Praying Mantis, opening her imagination about transportation in the future. Nearby and accessible adventure can calm the monsters of superficial thrills and unsustainable status-seeking that threaten meaningful new experience.

Places of Reciprocal Response

A third source of sacredness are places of reciprocal response, where humanity fulfills the requirement to elicit reaction from another person or place by one's mere being. When the setting provides the necessary sensory stimulus, this reaction is an involuntary, spontaneous impulse that produces a feeling of closeness and understanding that the world around us is interconnected and much larger than a single individual. Such response overcomes the culturally created divisions that separate us from each other, our community, and nature. Reciprocal response encourages intimate and deep experience with a place. The stimulus and response is not a one-way cause and effect but a two-way interaction, a commingling of person and place that gives us pleasure and makes us accountable to each other and the environment we inhabit.[3]

This mutual give-and-take is most visible between two people, say friends or lovers, but it can happen between any two subjects: person and pet, person and plant, person and landscape. Response is emphasized in places that offer multi-sensory experiences, accessibility, morality, or metaphysical transcendence such as meditation. In this way, designers and planners help people reconnect with their surroundings. As Randy recently sketched an ancient gingko tree in Kyoto, an old woman walked up to the tree and gave it a hardy hug. He was taken aback, as the tree seemed to embrace the woman as well. He put down his watercolors and contemplated this reciprocity. It reminded him that he needs to spend more time exchanging oxygen and carbon dioxide with plants and less time on his computer. Providing parks and other natural settings close to home serves this function in daily life. Within the home, potted plants and flowers can offer the opportunity for reciprocity.

Places of Belonging

The fourth source of sacredness are places of social belonging and recognition. We seek to be part of social units that make up our society, and we want to be acknowledged by others within the culture. In order to be fulfilled, we need to join, be accepted, and confirm our contribution. Belonging to a group requires a territory, a home base, a place for group rituals and settings that are visible to other groups in the society. These places distinguish insiders from outsiders, proclaim who is in control, and reflect deep democracy in which people not only vote and complain about government, but also engage in improvements to a community voluntarily and govern locally. The monsters that lurk over belonging are social isolation, exclusion, and mindless competition for control. To counter the monsters, designers and planners can create opportunities for citizen volunteerism, recognition of accomplishments and places that foster group identity. In this way, people may participate in the making of the place rather than simply consume it. Ultimately, being involved helps them reach a healthy level of self-recognition. A kitchen, clubhouse, farmers' market, non-governmental organization, stadium, theater, or anywhere a group of people gather around a common purpose can be a place of belonging. In these places, people share in the wins, losses, and drama of the moment.

Sacred public places do not always fit neatly into one of the four categories above, and, ideally, they should intersect and fulfill several or all of the needs. For example, a community garden can fulfill the need of certainty if people grow food there and the need for new experience if gardening is new to them. It can offer reciprocal response, because they are giving to the earth, and the earth is giving back to them, and it can provide a sense of belonging to the community of gardeners sharing the land.

Yet the four wishes are in conflict much of the time, and our values embedded in place reflect those conflicts. For example, a certain amount of tension between insiders and outsiders and hearth and cosmos is necessary and healthy. But when individuals and societies are insecure, threatened, and/or unsettled, coupled with the fact that many are unconsciously aware of the values of place, these conflicts can become simultaneously desperate and irrational. At such moments, the healthy tension between certainty and personal transformation is replaced with either senseless fear of the other or pseudo-adventuring. Similarly, when public places lack uniqueness and access to nearby nature, reciprocal responsiveness is supplanted by rootless relativity, and recognition gives way to untethered seeking of status. These are not only barriers to inhabiting the sacred, but also are among the most serious problems of contemporary society. These problematic landscapes create four monsters: fear, superficial thrills, loss of nearness, and obsession with status.

In this chapter, we discuss ways to transform values embedded in place and environments dominated by the monsters to healthier values of place by making critical choices and then dwelling in a place with resolve to accomplish the manifesto or other particular values about the place. This is intentional living. Later, in Step 5: Manifesting, we return to these four wishes and their associated monsters to consider the design implications of living intentionally with sacred places.

Transforming Values of Place through Sacrifice

Beyond satisfying the four wishes, inhabiting the sacred inevitably requires sacrifice, the giving up of something of value to attain a more fulfilling state. This sacrifice is a renouncement that eventually may enable transformation in a family or community's values, a shift in city form, or conversion to a new way of thinking, living, and dwelling. Meaningful transformation that enables intentional living requires changes, first, within the individual, then in the community, and finally in the public environment.[4] It is the sacrifice of the four monsters in favor of the four wishes. Although an individual often gives up one quality or belief in the pursuit of another private one, sacrifice in the public realm is distinct. Public sacrifice is more typically associated with relationships with family, the greater society, and, for some, God. The very act of creating a household, family, community, or civil society, for example, requires relinquishing something personally valued for a higher shared good. In committing to a community goal larger than the individual, we relinquish some personally held values in favor of achieving collectively shared values.

Although this may be reduced to self-interest rightly understood for the individual, the act of sacrifice has purposes for the group beyond what is given up or offered in tribute. Sacrifice creates, maintains, or renews a kinship that unites those who participate. This elevates the collective awareness derived from evidencing discussed in Step 2 to an intense and visionary commitment. The vision transforms a collective map of sacred places into a clear declaration of the place-based values worth struggling to attain or even fighting for.

The intensity of commitment to the vision is greatest at the moments when members of the community are assembled together, engaged in thoughtful discussion about communal sentiments, and stirred to action as a result. In pragmatic terms of community planning, this moment is when the community makes choices about the kind of future they seek to create. This bonds people to each other, to their collective values about what really matters in civic life, and to a vision for the future and to their place. In turn, the people, their values, and their place provide support and sustenance to the participants.

Although publicly declaring most basic human needs and a community's values might feel awkward to some people, planners have a long-standing tradition of fighting for exactly this cause. They often defend and promote place-based values with a religious or even evangelistic attitude. Often these big-picture planners fight against pragmatic social scientists who narrowly distill the act of urban planning into arguments of politics, economics, and negotiation.[5] A community that is collectively aware may also need to face a similar challenge, making the step of transformation absolutely crucial if that community is to voice a coherent and powerful counter-argument to some dominating economic, social, or other force that ignores or threatens place-based values.

It is important to bring human nature into the picture. When a community assembly breaks up for any long period of time and its members disperse back to their private lives and the events of daily life, the original energy of the shared commitment progressively diminishes. The group must sustain the momentum through regular assembly or reminders of the shared commitment. Even so, the intense energy of what is sacred to a community is more stable and longer lasting than individual values, because collective representations and avowals are less easily modified or ignored.[6] Although we verify this avowal by believing in it individually, we also submit to its control collectively, and, thus, the community assumes the authority to enforce the sacred. In shaping community through participatory events, citizens consecrate the collective authority through both the process of assembling to make choices about the future and the transformation of a vision imbued with high civic value: the public good.

Assembling for Transformation

To make salient critical choices on a community level that can be committed to, believed in, and acted upon, it is necessary to identify the options for growth and change. Let us assume that a group is meeting, because people are worried about some aspect of their community. Perhaps a well-loved space is threatened because crime is high in their neighborhood or the community is dissatisfied because there is no space in a central location that brings people together. It is improbable that members of the group will agree outright to a singular vision of the future. Therefore, in order to make place-value decisions, the group must systematically consider the best and worst outcomes of the following alternative futures of their community:

1. The current situation: how history has influenced the present and how the future is likely to unfold if no action is taken.
2. The ideal vision of the future if funds are unlimited and no boundaries are placed on change.
3. Visions that are being formulated based on unique community resources and the limits and values discovered through Steps 1 and 2 as well as through an assessment of the current situation and ideals.

4. The existing propositions for change being offered up within the group, in government agencies, or the private sector.

Once these alternative futures are understood by the group, they can weigh the options in terms of how well each satisfies the four wishes. The assembly should be inclusive of a diverse demographic. Everyone should have access to information about each alternative vision, and each vision should be articulated so it can be honestly and fairly compared to others. The aim is to spell out the components of each alternative future and allow people to evaluate them in terms of tradeoffs. For example, to what degree does the current situation offer a place of certainty that a developer's vision may neglect? Can the ideal vision be practically implemented, or are there some restrictions the group must take into consideration before dedicating itself to it? Through this act of weighing place-based values and sacrificing some individual values for collective values, the group will likely formulate a new vision that is neither the ideal nor the worst-case scenario. It should be formulated based on distinct community resources and limits, the intentions underlying the ideal, and the proposals that powerful forces want to implement. It should articulate the community's noblest and achievable intentions so that Step 4: Organizing can be done with a spirit of cooperation and productive discourse, even if there is an element of conflict.

Widespread public participation can greatly affect how a place is built and may open the door to sacred habitation that truly echoes the values of the community. Still, the state of engagement today is often splintered, negative, and narrowly self-interested. In some American cities, public involvement has been described as shortsighted, exclusionary, and motivated by fear. Not In My Back Yard (NIMBY) actions are indications of a frightened public that is knowledgeable of city process and law but whose actions primarily define quality of life in terms of safety, exclusion of the unknown, and real-estate value. This arises from insecurity and the general sense that nothing is certain anymore. We worry that solid ground may, at any moment, melt into air. Such fear debilitates us personally and civically and profanes public space.[7] At present, our participatory rights out-distance our participatory responsibility. Sacredness calls up shared values, personal accountability for civic purposes, and a willingness to sacrifice something for the public good. Only then can we overcome insecure irresponsibility and be inspired to pursue noble values rather than mean-spirited ones in the public domain.

When values are clear, then a plan of action can be discussed. This plan is largely a promise that will require work and occasional acts of faith to envision and commit to the transformation. The intensity of commitment to this image of the future increases if it is bold and worthy yet practical and achievable. It must compute with rational minds but also touch people's hearts. It helps if the plan seems to grow out of the specific history of the place and experiences of the people. Championing uniqueness of a place may invite helpful insurgent action and other acts of contrary intentional living.

Commitment is stronger if self-interests are reasonably considered, even if some dear ones are sacrificed. This tradeoff is easier for most people to make if they understand their role in something bigger than themselves and if they can envision their progeny benefiting from these efforts.

Comparing Conscious and Subconscious Values

A participatory design process to make improvements to the Harvard Law School Child Care Center in Cambridge, Massachusetts, illustrates most of the keys to a successful transformation through assembling, discussing, and making choices. The parents and administrators had decided that, in the process of rectifying deferred maintenance, they might also upgrade the comfortable but funky two-story home that had long ago been converted into a day-care facility near Harvard Square.

A survey of parents revealed an overwhelming preference for a building dramatically different from the converted home. Their responses indicated a desire for a sparkling new building on a site large enough to have on-site parking and the most fashionable play equipment. This ideal site would have to be three times as large as the present one to accommodate all the desires.

The staff was suspicious of these survey results, partly because the center was known for its loving atmosphere and homey appearance. The cramped building and grounds were also a source of self-deprecating pride for families with children there. It *was* Harvard, after all; it could be funky. In the past, any income surplus was spent on the staff, maintaining an enviable ratio of one teacher for every three children. This budgeting explained the poor maintenance that stimulated the design process, but it did not explain the survey's results.

The staff hosted a second parent assembly, in which they re-administered the questionnaire by asking the same questions but in small groups using a guided-meditative technique that is similar to the self-hypnosis described in Step 1: Awakening. They sought responses from the parents' subconscious about the places that were most important from their own childhoods. Parents answered the same questions again, except this time the technique outlined in Awakening was employed. The results of the two surveys varied so much that they seemed to have been answered by entirely different people.[8]

The second survey described settings consistent with the existing day-care center. The building they described was slightly dilapidated and filled with love. It provided a rich variety of experiences for the children. The building was neither fancy nor suburban.

The small group settings allowed each parent to share his or her responses and for the staff to quickly tally and compare the answers under the guided meditation to those of the earlier survey. The assembly enabled a frank discussion not only about the extreme variance in the kinds of futures suggested by the surveys, but also about the current condition of the building, budget for renovations, and trends in the design of day-care centers. The analysis revealed two different philosophical tendencies reflecting the responses in the two surveys: one toward technology-centered stimulation and another toward staff-based nurturing. These represented clear options that could be evaluated in terms of costs and benefits and against the ideal center that existed in the imaginations of the parents. Parents were able to talk through their dissatisfactions. The hypnotic guided meditation changed major frustrations into minor nuisances. For example, a major concern for the parents was drop-off and pick-up, but instead of fighting for more spacious parking, there followed a long discussion about walking from home and campus as opposed to driving. After more deliberation, the parents concluded that they strongly supported the present philosophy of the center.

One parent acknowledged that his answers to the first survey were bogus. He secretly wished for a day-care center like one in a wealthy community nearby. Other parents followed with the same confession. One said she envied the families that she considered a social class above her. Many parents were ashamed of their center when compared to the appearance of the one where their classmates and friends enrolled their children. A spirited discussion followed. Parents returned to deeply held values. They wanted a caring place, but they still wanted some improvements.

Their desires pitted two powerful wishes against each other—the desire for a day-care center providing family-like security versus the desire to have a more fashionable facility like that possessed by the affluent social class nearby After the distinction was made clear, parents could separate prestige from necessary improvements. They wished to enhance the diversity of childhood experiences through modest changes. The highest priority, a memory parents held dear, was to have a tree in the schoolyard large enough for children to climb. They wanted their children to experience nature. The center's site was too small for nature larger than the tree, but an inventory of nearby nature spots revealed impressive resources. There was a creek where children could catch frogs and build dams. There were gardens and overgrown vacant lands within walking distance of the center. Excursions to places with leftover nature near Harvard Square were incorporated into the daily ritual of the center (Fig. 62). Parents also wanted prospect refuges, lookouts, and places to hide, ideas which also reflected their childhood memories. At the most practical level, enlarging the children's' cubbies solved a daily problem in a cold climate where multiple layers of clothes are required and where extra clothes constantly overflow on the floor and then are lost. The larger cubbies were possibly more prestigious and certainly more functional.

In this case, most of the improvements were implemented by the parents and staff via volunteer workdays. After the discussions, more parents made the effort to walk with their children to and from school, and some reported using the inventory of open spaces to identify places for weekend family excursions. Each served as a consecration of firmly held values and solidified the transformation through assembly, ritual, and construction. The parents' actions actually renewed values that had been diminished over time. This created a much stronger commitment to the existing and future intentions of the center (Fig. 63).

Fig. 62. The designer identified a creek and leftover natural areas near the Harvard Law Child Care Center that became part of daily play.

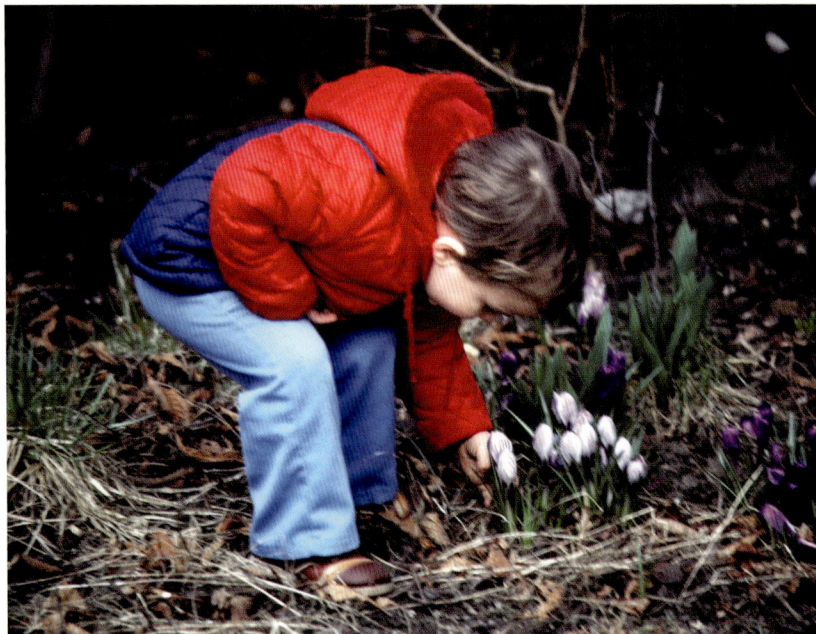

Fig. 63. As their deep values about childhood became clear, parental stewardship increased, resulting in many small volunteer projects.

Fig. 64. After Mount Vernon's citizens developed alternative plans for their waterfront, community leaders placed them in storefront windows, inviting hundreds of other residents to study and vote for the ones they preferred.

Visualizing Criteria for Evaluation

In contrast to the Harvard Law Child Care Center, most communities require a graphic comparison of alternatives in order to make a choice. There must be drawings and text that allow examination of similarities and differences, costs and benefits, and superlative qualities of one option versus others. The process of deliberate choice is facilitated by simple plans and a list of evaluative criteria.

In making a riverfront plan for Mount Vernon, Washington, members of the community developed specific objectives for the Skagit River and then mapped three alternative plans during a weekend workshop. They placed the plans in storefront windows in the center of the city where other residents could compare them, using a feedback form with criteria for evaluation based on the objectives (Fig. 64). The design team had shared the method used in Manteo with community leaders who studied and adapted that technique for their own use. This process of developing a range of alternative plans is much better than presenting only one alternative. A single plan discourages critical evaluation and consideration of the trade-offs between priorities. Often when a community debates the various choices, they create a different and superior plan, one that satisfies the truly highest priority.

TOURIST TOWN MERCANTILE CENTER

DISPERSED CULTURAL AND PERFORMING ARTS TOWN

MANTEO ON SKIDS

Dispersed Cultural and Performing Arts Town
RELATIVE COST-BENEFIT OF MANTED PRELIMINARY PLANS

Cost		Benefit
	Lifestyle preservation	7
	Sacred structure preservation	6
	Village character enhancement	
	Separated parking provision	
	Tax base increase	
	Property tax increase	
	Tourist expenditure	
	Tourist experience	
	Integration of public-private facilities	
	Local store protection	9
	Accessibility of facilities	8
	Diversity of stores	
	Prices suitable for local people	
	Environmental protection	
	Reliance on volunteerism	10
	Provision of jobs	1
	Street paving and sidewalks	2
	Playgrounds for children	5
	Recreation for teenagers	4
	Low income housing increased	3

Key:
Low relative benefit to community
Moderate relative benefit to community
High relative benefit to community
Low relative cost to community
Moderate relative cost to community
High relative cost to community

Manteo on Stride
RELATIVE COST-BENEFIT OF MANTED PRELIMINARY PLANS

Cost		Benefit
	Lifestyle preservation	7
	Sacred structure preservation	6
	Village character enhancement	
	Separated parking provision	
	Tax base increase	
	Property tax increase	
	Tourist expenditure	
	Tourist experience	
	Integration of public-private facilities	
	Local store protection	9
	Accessibility of facilities	8
	Diversity of stores	
	Prices suitable for local people	
	Environmental protection	10
	Reliance on volunteerism	
	Provision of jobs	1
	Street paving and sidewalks	2
	Playgrounds for children	5
	Recreation for teenagers	4
	Low income housing increased	3

Key:
Low relative benefit to community
Moderate relative benefit to community
High relative benefit to community
Low relative cost to community
Moderate relative cost to community
High relative cost to community

Tourist Town Mercantile Center
RELATIVE COST-BENEFIT OF MANTED PRELIMINARY PLANS

Cost		Benefit
	Lifestyle preservation	7
	Sacred structure preservation	6
	Village character enhancement	
	Separated parking provision	
	Tax base increase	
	Property tax increase	
	Tourist expenditure	
	Tourist experience	
	Integration of public-private facilities	
	Local store protection	9
	Accessibility of facilities	8
	Diversity of stores	
	Prices suitable for local people	
	Environmental protection	
	Reliance on volunteerism	10
	Provision of jobs	
	Street paving and sidewalks	2
	Playgrounds for children	5
	Recreation for teenagers	4
	Low income housing increased	3

Key:
Low relative benefit to community
Moderate relative benefit to community
High relative benefit to community
Low relative cost to community
Moderate relative cost to community
High relative cost to community

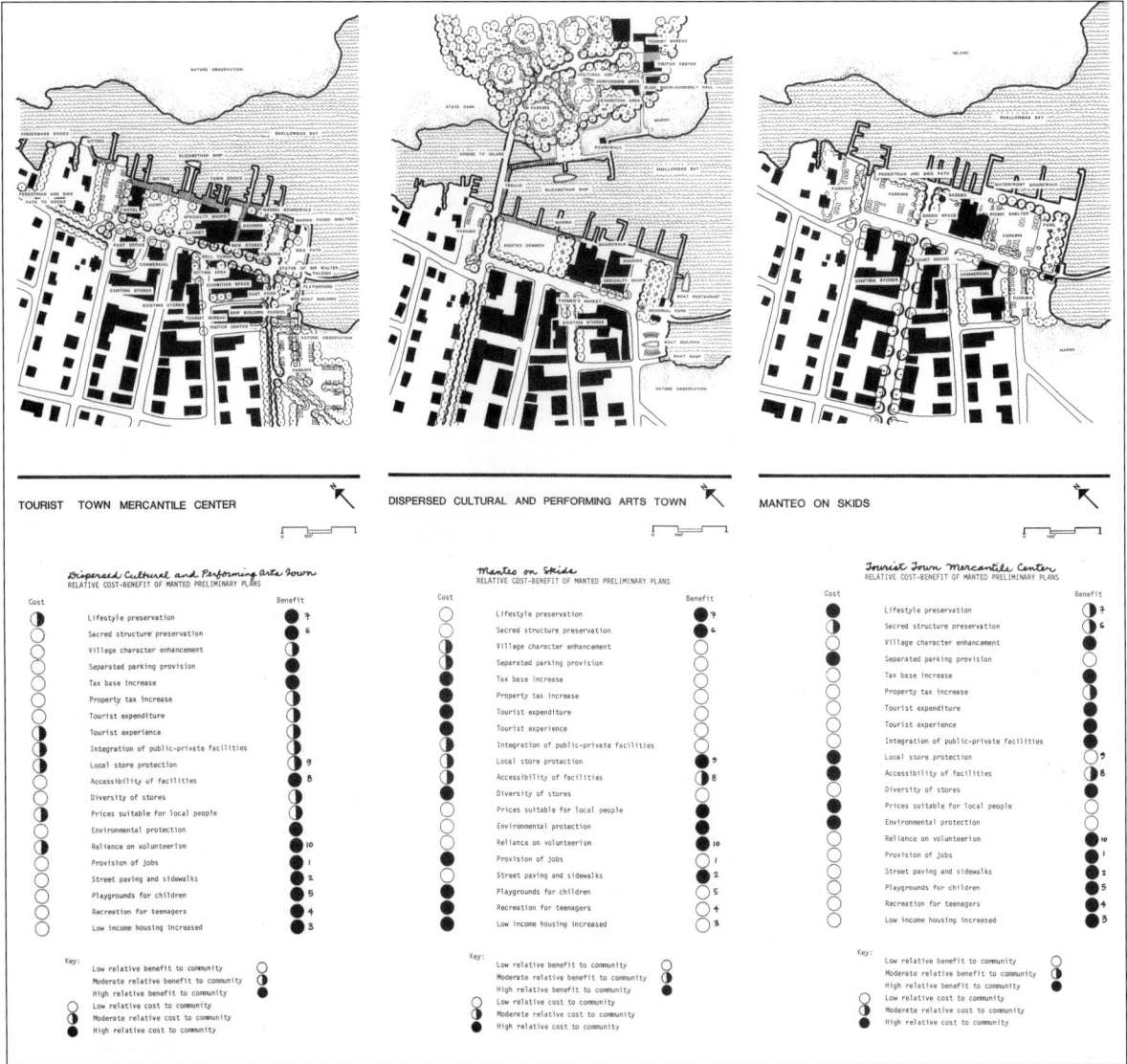

Fig. 65. Citizens must have clear, concrete choices in order to transform values into priorities for a plan of action. The Manteo method of showing a range of choices with evaluation criteria helped Mount Vernon's residents to choose a plan with widespread and dedicated support.

Although the residents in Mount Vernon wanted to make the river more accessible for recreation, they also wanted to reduce the danger of flooding with higher floodwalls. Some wanted to keep the river natural, although it was unclear exactly what that meant. The three plans provided clear choices. In the end, additional floodwalls were sacrificed in order keep the river natural. Floodwaters were diverted to fallow fields and wooded lowlands. Ecological functions were consecrated as their highest goal over all other objectives (Fig. 65).

Providing Choice, Even When Big Powers Object

The process of choosing a future is seldom as local a matter as either the Harvard Law Child Care Center or the Mount Vernon Riverfront Plan suggest. In many cases today, powerful external forces dominate, making it nearly impossible to get the accurate evidence that is necessary for a community's deliberation. Usually, when short-term economic gain is the primary motivation, the stakes are enormous, and the dream of big profits engenders an attitude whereby harm to local businesses and habitat for species is an acceptable tradeoff for investors. In these cases, there may not be any alternative plan to the one proposed by the external power, so the only initial choice is to fight against it. This has certainly been seen recently with efforts at Standing Rock, the Shenandoah Valley, and elsewhere to relocate pipelines to more sensible locations that would mitigate their impact. But there are many examples.

For twenty years, Spoonbill Action Voluntary Echo (SAVE, International), a small nonprofit based in Berkeley, Tokyo, and Taipei, has worked to prevent the extinction of the rarest of all spoonbill birds in the world, the Black-faced Spoonbill (*Platalea minor*). During the early 1990s, the Binnan Industrial Complex, one of the world's largest petrochemical refineries, steel plants, and associated factories, was proposed to be built in Chigu Lagoon, Taiwan. The lagoon itself supported 16,000 jobs in fisheries and related industries, and the edges of the lagoon were prime winter foraging habitat for three-quarters of the entire world population of spoonbills, only about 600 birds at the time.

Families who fished in Chigu Lagoon had begun protesting the industrial plan to fill the lagoon (Fig. 66). They appealed to Randy and National Taiwan University for help, and SAVE was formed as a joint effort between National Taiwan University and the University of California, Berkeley, to conduct research and coordinate advocacy efforts for the fishermen and spoonbills. One of the first studies completed by SAVE revealed that the 320,000 metric tons of water required by the industry each day would necessitate inter-basin transfers and new dams on distant rivers that would not only cause the extinctions of the spoonbill and other species, but also flood nearby aboriginal villages.[9] The industry would produce nearly 28,000,000 tons of carbon dioxide each year, almost a third of Taiwan's total emissions at the time. Fishermen feared that fishing jobs would be lost if the lagoon was industrialized.

In spite of these obvious negative impacts of the Binnan development, the local communities were violently divided over the industrial complex, since only one choice for the future was being

Fig. 66. A local fisherman, Uncle Gao Ong, led protests against filling
Chigu Lagoon where he fished. He helped designers develop an alternative plan that created wetland-friendly industries.

offered, and the proponents of industry promised employment for everyone and their families, more
than 30,000 new jobs in total. With local fishermen and community groups, SAVE drew up an alternative plan that focused on expanding fishing, value-added fish-related industries, cultural and ecological
tourism, and emergent high-technology parks. In the plan that SAVE presented, the Binnan complex
could only be located in an industrial zone inland from the fragile lagoon.

The alternative plan provided choice and allowed comparison of the costs and benefits of each
plan. SAVE, National Taiwan University, and the University of California, Berkeley, assembled various
scientists to evaluate systematically the two plans. The co-chair of the International Union for Conservation of Nature and Natural Resources (IUCN) Specialist Group on Storks, Ibis, and Spoonbills
advised a team that compared how much habitat critical for the spoonbill's survival would be lost in
both plans. Less than two percent of the wetland habitat would be destroyed with the SAVE plan,
compared to nearly forty percent with the industrial complex. The team made two maps showing the
comparative loss of habitat (Fig. 67).

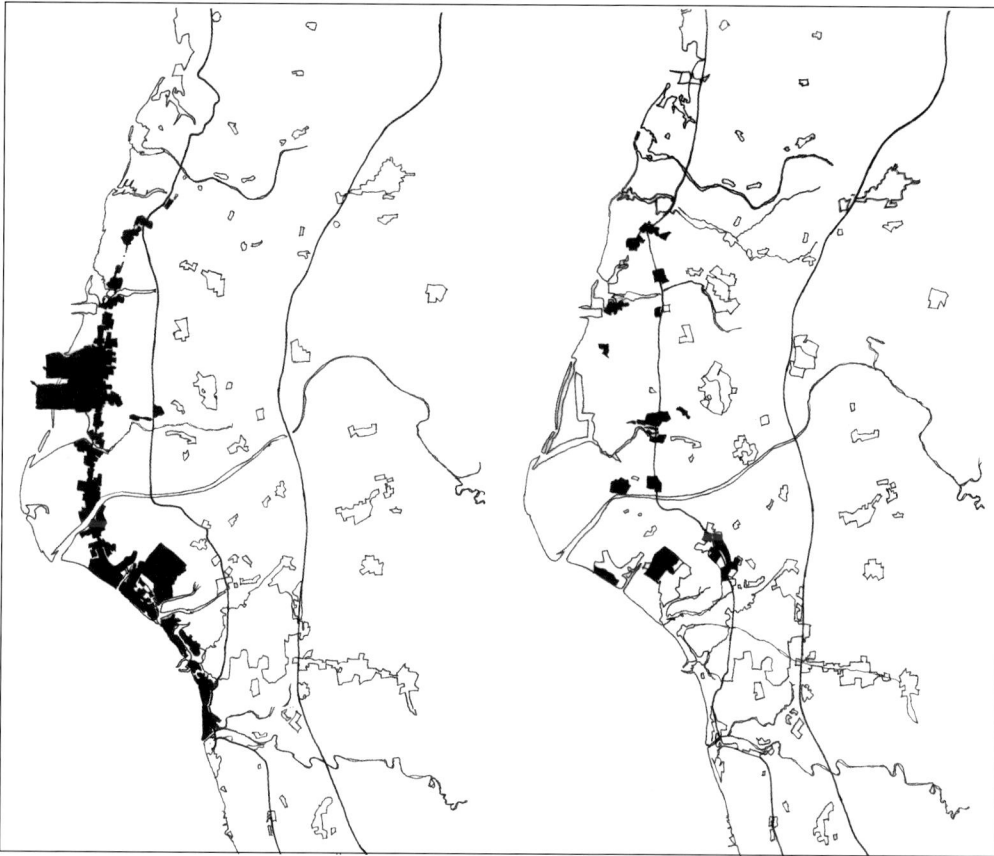

Fig. 67. The Binnan Industrial Complex to produce petrochemical, plastics, and steel would have resulted in a loss of forty percent of critical wetlands (areas shown in black in left image). The SAVE/ Fishermen Plan lost only two percent (areas shown in black in right image).

Another evaluation showed that, although the industrial complex would generate thousands of temporary construction jobs, few of the jobs would be sustained fifteen years later, and most of the current 16,000 fishing jobs would likely be lost. In contrast, the SAVE alternative would create fewer jobs early on, but most would be locally controlled, and, in the long term, nearly 30,000 jobs would be sustained (Fig. 68). Locally, the SAVE alternative is called the SAVE/Fishermen Plan.

These two comparisons depicted specific tradeoffs—the likely extinction of a species and fishing culture due to the loss of habitat versus a terrific influx of construction jobs and associated short-term windfall profits. These graphic depictions were dramatic and undeniable. They mobilized the international community, especially human rights, environmental, and bird groups. The comparisons also raised red flags in the highest levels of Taiwan's national government. Locally, the communities began

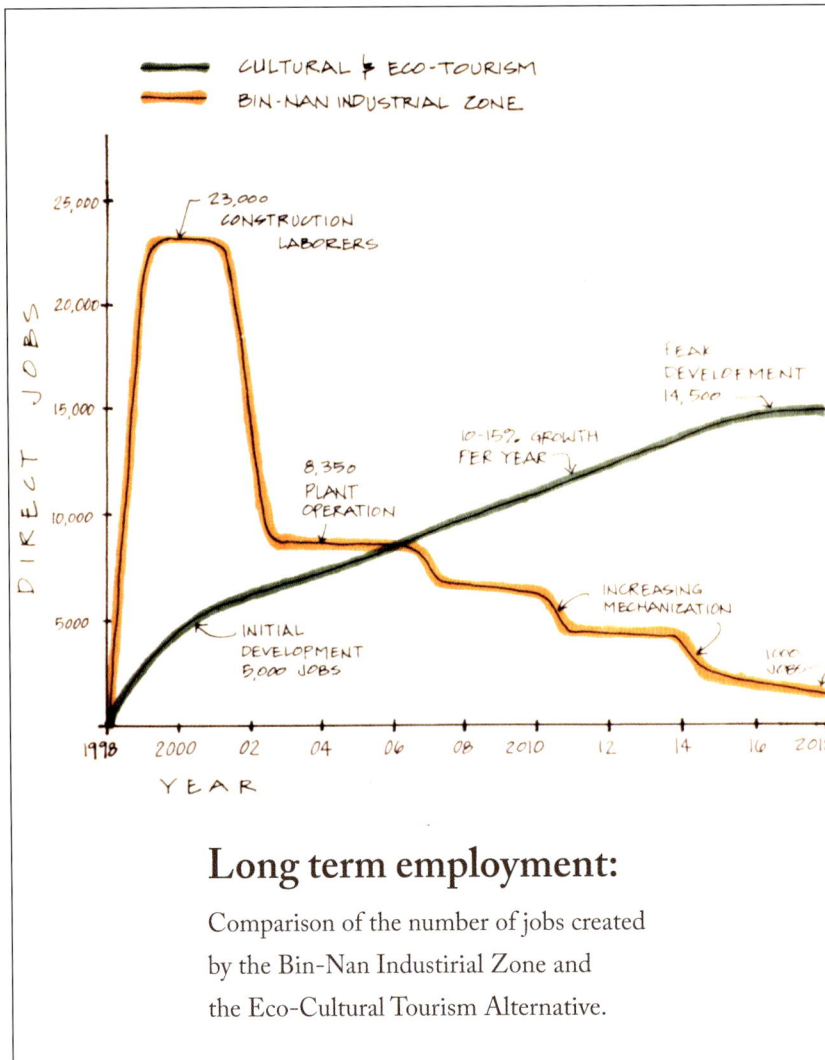

Long term employment:

Comparison of the number of jobs created
by the Bin-Nan Industirial Zone and
the Eco-Cultural Tourism Alternative.

Fig. 68. Comparing permanent and temporary job creation revealed
that the Binnan Industrial Zone Project would produce only several
thousand long-term jobs; the Save/Fishermen Plan has spawned more
than 14,000.

an emotional but more informed process of making a deliberate choice. For them, the two maps compared more than wildlife and jobs. The preservation of the spoonbill's habitat also conserved places the people loved: their villages, wetlands, and waterways. The map had an affectively charged double meaning: habitat for spoonbills and loved places of everyday life. Nonetheless, Binnan's promise of thousands of immediate jobs was far more attractive than SAVE's long-term employment, because families were in peril due to a lack of local revenue, and children were leaving home for distant cities in search of

Fig. 69. People who had never participated in civic life became involved in community discussions, coming together to study the alternative futures. These assemblies became important community rituals.

work. Many people felt they could not wait for the establishment of high technology, cultural tourism, ecotourism, and expanded fishing employment. The choices centered on these factors, and the debate was facilitated by clear, simple graphics communicating the tradeoffs.

The discussions of transformation continued for more than a year. At least one value of great importance would be sacrificed, yet the ongoing participatory assemblies created bonds even between families with opposing views. The deliberate ritual of assembly reconfirmed community in ways that continue to nurture people today (Fig. 69).

After dozens of community assemblies where residents discussed the costs and benefits of the alternatives, public opinion swung firmly towards the SAVE plan and simultaneously guaranteed the election of Congressman Su Huan Chi to the position of county mayor because of his courageous and risky support of the SAVE plan and opposition to Binnan's. As Congressman Su campaigned to become mayor, he sponsored excursions to the lagoon, where he provided expert-led field trips to

Fig. 70. Congressman Su integrated ancient festivals with progressive environmental education to convince residents that the SAVE/Fishermen Plan was better than a polluting industry.

explain to the public the importance of the lagoon to the fishing economy. Each field trip included hands-on experiences like wading in the water and catching fish or crabs (Fig. 70). In the decisive moment to elect Su as mayor, the community collectively sacrificed short-term jobs in favor of a vision of an economy that would grow out of the place, rather than be imposed upon it (Fig. 71). The support of cultural and eco-tourist values has spawned thousands of small local enterprises, attracting 3,800,000 visitors per year and bringing young people back home to new family-owned businesses (Fig. 72). Transforming values imbedded in a place can make even gut-wrenching sacrifice worth the effort (Fig. 73).[10]

Fig. 71. Ecological and cultural tourism have brought new life to abandoned villages, creating multi-generational family businesses like this bed-and-breakfast with gardens made from recycled beach detritus.

Fig. 72. The transformation of deeply held values in Longshan Village resulted in an addition to the temple that featured species like the spoonbill and milk fish, replacing traditional Taoist symbols with locally sacred ones.

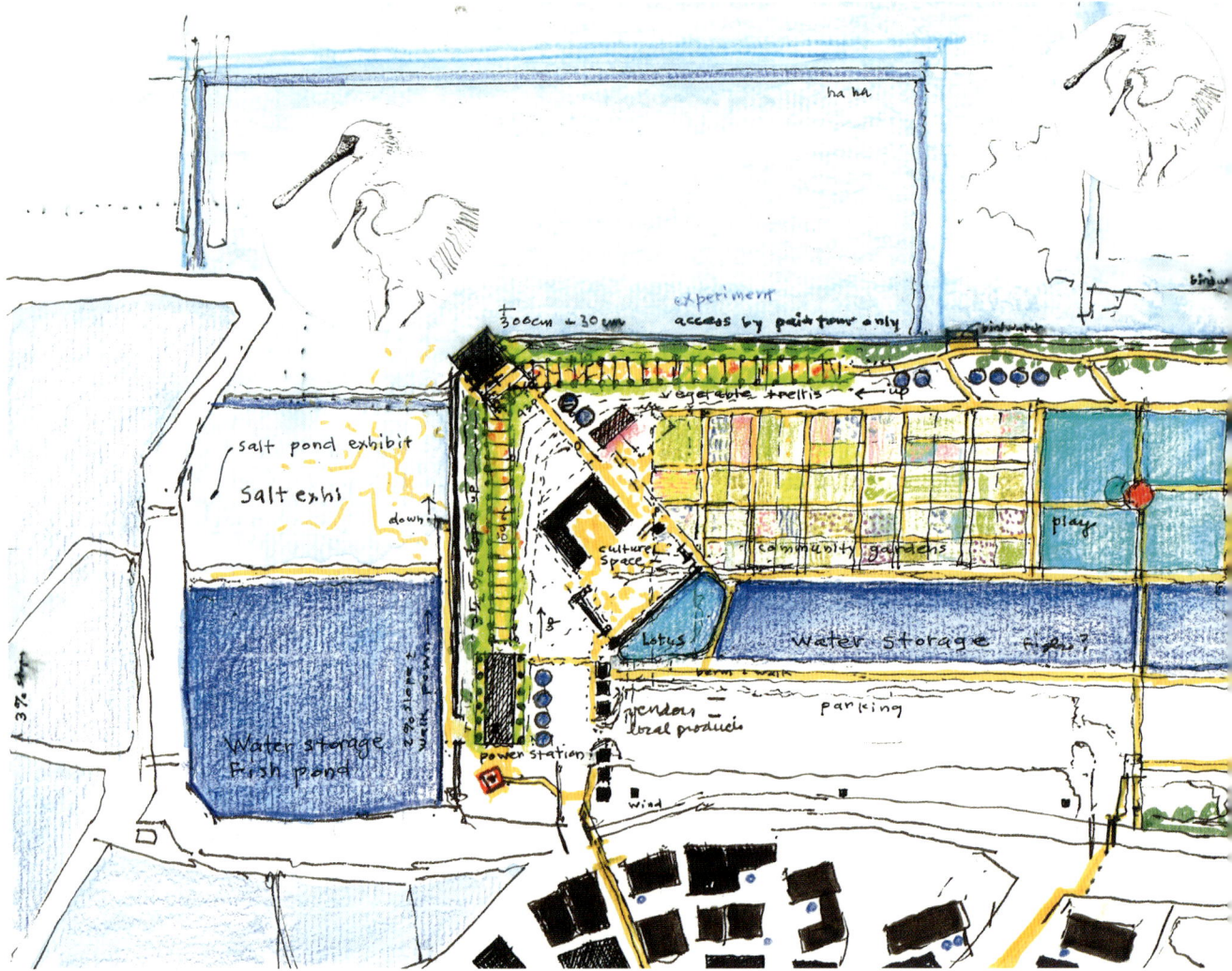

salt pond exhibit

Salt exhi

down

Water storage
Fish pond

3% sl.

experiment
300cm ← 30cm   access by paid tour only

vegetable trellis   up

cultural
space

community gardens

play

Lotus

Water storage fish?

berm walk

parking

vendors
local products

power station

wind

ha ha

ecoslope walk down

biower

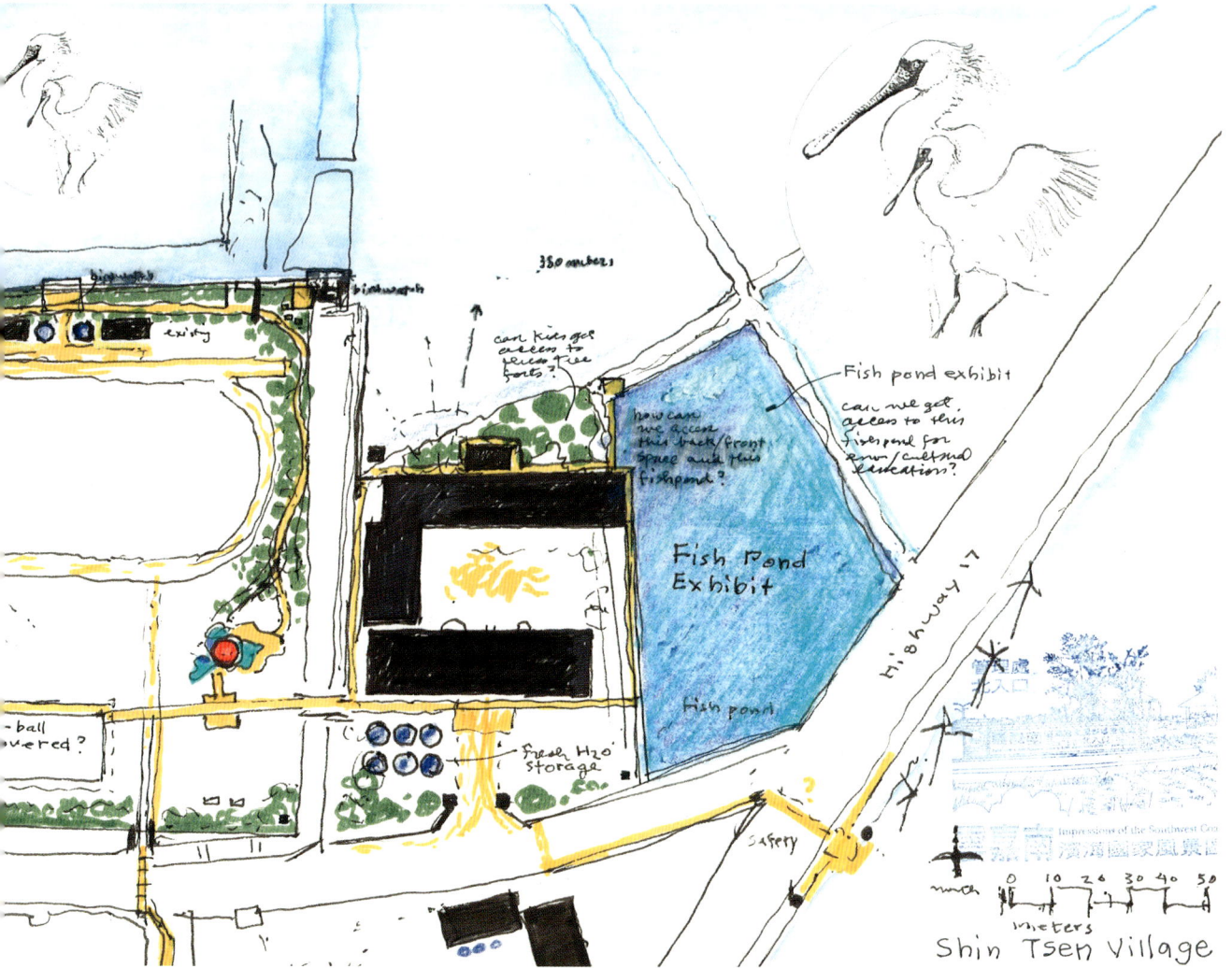

Fig. 73. Value-added fish industries have revitalized local economies, enabling community-improvement plans like this one for Shin-Tsen Town that features recreation, spoonbill-based science, and math for elementary school children.

Techniques for Transforming Unsustainable Values

Today, many of us live unsustainable lives; that is, we aspire to live beyond our means and pursue over-consumption. This also means we can become divorced from the sensual joys of nearby places, distort sacredness, and develop unhealthy values rooted in the four monsters. City makers, who are usually charged with creating healthy public spaces, are addressing these problems with only limited success. Development around public transit, higher-density housing, smaller homes, boundaries on growth, restoration of rivers and waterways, creation and integration of greenways and larger urban wilderness greenbelts, and public programs in environmental stewardship are among the most effective. Underlying these actions are a number of conceptual approaches to involving the public with civic decisions.

Access to Information

Public education, a tradition revered in both the United States and China, is an extremely effective approach. Thomas Jefferson's reliance on an informed public to make wise decisions underlines America's Declaration of Independence and Constitution. Jefferson posited that, given proper information, responsible choices will be made. Environmental education pursues this strategy and is most effective when it combines awareness with sensual experience. This hands-on educational approach was key to the success of the SAVE plan and Mayor Su's election. He combined information for the intellect and senses. This was necessary to overcome the previous lack of access to information, when the government and proponents of industry conspired to keep the public uninformed. Public campaigns to reduce energy consumption also provide access to information and combine it with legal or financial incentives. These efforts assume that the government provides the public access to plans and facts. In the United States, this is minimally guaranteed through the Freedom of Information Act, but often governments withhold material essential to informed debate. In those cases, the only resource to secure information may be via the courts.

Making a community aware of its most cherished values and associated sacred places can also change harmful actions. For example, in Manteo, the collective awareness of its Sacred Structure Map had a dramatic impact in the community's decision to stop sprawl and the filling in of its wetlands. The effect can be even stronger if an inconsistency of values is exposed. Sometimes, a community has deeply held but unjust or destructive values; in such cases, a more aggressive campaign may be required to induce the public to reverse those values. Anti-smoking or anti-drug abuse campaigns use aggressive imagery like your brain being fried like an egg. In other situations, the campaign method distributes information from a highly respected source to create psychological conflict within the public regarding unsustainable actions. If, for example, a revered mayor strongly advocates walking and transit instead of driving, an unstable triad of two positive values and one negative value is created. One may reason that "I value the mayor (+), but I don't value transit (-), and he does (+)." To balance the values, I can either change my opinion of the mayor or of transit.

In the San Francisco Bay Area, Spare the Air Days and the annual Bike to Work Day are highly publicized, providing information on the effects of the automobile on regional air quality. This is combined with requests to walk and take transit periodically in the case of Spare the Air Days when air pollution is unhealthily high or annually on a scheduled date in the case of Bike to Work Day. The publicity emphasizes both civic duty and pleasure. The carefully crafted campaign provokes guilt and provides an immediate substitute behavior to alleviate the guilt. For some, the action, once tried, is pleasurable. This enjoyment allows for repeated positive adjustments in behavior that will eventually be restructured permanently for the betterment of self, society, and the environment.

Experiments and Proof

Most people want to know that something works before they will try it. In response, designers often build experimental environments to test and demonstrate the effectiveness of an innovation. These experiential demonstrations expose the public to new place-based values through precedence and prototypes. They often satisfy those who are skeptical of new technologies or unwilling to alter their routine until given an easy or guaranteed way to adopt change. In recent decades, some architects have championed the pleasures of living in small houses by building beautiful and satisfying domestic places in tiny square footages.[11] Numerous books and popular magazines have spread the message, but none is as powerful as testing out the prototypes and discovering how smallness can be satisfying. In St. Louis, Missouri, EarthWays Center is a retrofitted prototype house made of a brownstone that allows the public to tour and test-out new sustainable technologies.[12] Similarly, architects rely on local precedents to use as proof for doubters. They are more powerful than experiments alone, because they have the advantage of being rooted in the tradition of a place. Even when trying to bring about radical change, there are major advantages to implementing strategies that do not go beyond the actual experiences of the people.[13]

Zoning and local building codes may reflect a community's values, a government's concerns about the public's health, safety, and welfare, professional lobbying efforts, or shifting local or national priorities. All have the appearance of proof but may neither be backed-up with evidence nor appropriate for a locality. For example, Leadership in Energy and Environmental Design (LEED) standards certify sustainable projects, but, in reality, they improve some aspects while ignoring others. A LEED-certified building can save energy while located on a site that destroys habitat of critically endangered species. To address this problem, Sustainable Sites Initiative (SITES) developed criteria that focus on environmental factors associated with each place. No matter how sincere the motivation and effective LEED and SITES may be, designers, planners, and citizens must carefully consider preapproved specifications such as those to be sure that the community's deep values are reflected right up to the last detail of a project.

Attachment to Thick Values

Another approach to transforming unsustainable behavior is linking desired behavior to deeply held "thick" values. Because meaningful attachment to a place is stronger the more directly the sacred spaces are tied to fundamental needs, places that are grounded in personal experience and shared with others in one's important social groups reinforce a community's thick values. In Aurora, North Carolina, all leaders had adamantly opposed land-use regulation of any kind. The former mayor even told designers who were developing the town's Coastal Management Plan that he took every copy of the previous plan and dumped them in nearby South Creek. When townspeople realized that their hunting and fishing grounds would be threatened by a mining company, they adopted an innovative plan to restrict Aurora's growth, preventing mining, from thousands of acres of habitat that were environmentally sensitive. Environmental protection now rode piggyback on their hunting and fishing territory surrounding the town.

The city maker tries to connect sustainable actions to thick values in order to reinforce lasting change in everyday habits and steer citizens towards intentional living. Most Americans value both low-density residential neighborhoods and nearby natural areas to support wildlife, but these land-use patterns are often mutually exclusive. Low-density housing destroys wilderness and habitat. Therefore, Americans are caught between choosing a thin value of desire for large private space or a thick value of providing habitat for wildlife. Fortunately, wildlife protection is such a sacred value that it has the widespread potential power both to reverse many of the worst land-use patterns and to improve overall urban form. One recent urban strategy pairs slightly higher-density housing with the protection of wildlife habitat. More than eighty percent of the Americans who are most opposed to living in higher-density areas support greenbelts that provide habitat for wildlife. This research further suggests that more than twenty-five percent of Americans might accept higher-density living if opportunities to watch birds and see other wildlife are provided in a nearby preserve.[14] Americans are particularly attached to birds and megafauna, but wildlife preferences differ by country. The Japanese public, for example, most values earthworms, dragonflies, bush warblers, fireflies, and tiny native fish.[15]

Thick values are often tied to local myth and spiritual rites. As a result, a community is likely to choose sustainable actions that are associated with important local religious ritual. In India, the majority of forests that have been preserved are associated with sacred temple trees.[16] Likewise, in Japan, only hallowed shrine forests were spared logging during World War II. In the U.S., Arbor Day promotes urban reforestation and is often supported by inner-city religious groups. Similarly, the civil rights movement was empowered by association with religious doctrine. More recently, faith-based community gardens combine theology and ecology to redirect teenagers with criminal records, to encourage intergenerational cooperation and combat obesity.[17] These sustainable actions are transformative, because they recall core values that may have been sitting idle in the subconscious while thin values dominated the conscious realm.

Transforming place-based values through sacrifice requires making choices and even sacrifice, often between competing objectives. To do this, a community must have legitimate choices and access to the information necessary to compare and evaluate the options. Once made, the choice is consecrated with full knowledge of what is being given up. To implement a chosen plan takes organization, the next step in the process.

AN ACTION PLAN TOWARDS
INTENTIONAL LIVING

At some point awakening, evidencing, and transforming values of place make action unavoidable. To act requires organizing a strategy for a community to live more intentionally, to live in a manner fully conscious of deeply held values about the place and the community's goals. Although the process of organizing can be used by an individual or a family for improving one's own private life, the focus in this chapter is on community organizing to improve the public environment. And it is written as if you, the reader, is a primary organizer, the instigator of action. In this step, we address the key points in successful organizing. To do so, we need to define organizing clearly, acknowledge its inherent strength and problems, and distinguish between the contexts in which the organizing takes place. We explain the differences between the efforts to preserve a place, reclaim one that has been lost, or create anew a vision for the future. We detail the steps in organizing a place-based campaign and provide simple guidelines for successful action. We conclude the chapter with a timeless case story about how a passionate landscape architect, Richard Haag, introduced a new vision for civic space in Seattle.

Organizing as an End and Means

Organizing is the act of (1) arranging pieces and/or players into a structured whole, (2) preparing to exercise change for the public good through unified action, and (3) inducing others to contribute to the whole and take part in the decision-making process and subsequent action. Simply put, this requires a vision and an image of what is being sought and a strategy for mobilizing people to achieve it. Although this may seem like two different activities, they actually occur simultaneously and are mutually reinforcing in a healthy democracy. The vision/image (the end) and the assembly (the means) actualize each other. As you may have realized, in this process organizing likely started with awakening (Step 1) and certainly blossomed with evidencing (Step 2) and transforming (Step 3). In fact, the choice of a vision for the future that resulted from Step 3 usually forms the foundation for the vision and image that is sought, and the participatory assembly is the first action towards formulating a strategy for collective action. Through organizing, the vision becomes more inclusive and more precise. It is changed from an idealistic concept to an achievable work plan. This happens as more community members participate in shaping it and as available resources inform it (Figs. 74 and 75).

Figs. 74 and 75. Organizing at any scale requires a clear, detailed vision, yet it must be broad enough to invite participation from many constituents with their interests: from protests against the Gulf War (top) to protests against the location of the Dakota Access Pipeline (DAPL) on sacred lands of the Standing Rock Indian Reservation (below).

Fig. 76. Organizing around issues of daily concern such as speeding traffic in a neighborhood can lead to life-altering action. After considering solutions, many residents of Berkeley stopped driving and started campaigning for "Slow Streets."

Organizing fulfills many of our deepest primal needs of security, growth, face-to-face intimacy, belonging, purpose, and recognition. It is also fundamental to a healthy democracy as evidenced by its inclusion in the First Amendment to the Constitution in 1791. As observed as early as 1835, it is a tradition in the United States to form local associations to solve problems and improve the local environment.[1] The nation is strongest when democracy is an active part of everyday life, as the nation's founders envisioned. Democracy is not a spectator sport; a living democracy cannot be maintained simply by voting and consuming American products. The greatest threat to democracy, says Francis Moore Lappé, is the belief that democracy has already been achieved, making citizens complacent as a result. Organizing prohibits complacency. It rebuilds a sense of community, social capital, self-esteem, and a sense of empowerment to change private and public situations.[2] Organizing teaches skills, empathy, and the value of listening and exposes the shortsightedness of exclusion and fear of the other. It bonds our affections to a place, overcoming environmental anomie. Organizing helps us live civically, intentionally, sustainably, and meaningfully.[3] The organizing assembly provides a support group and enforcement for positive life-change. More directly, organizing prepares a community for and leads to action (Fig. 76).

Effective Execution of Organizing

Organizing can only provide the above benefits if it is executed correctly. We present four overarching frameworks for success:

First, it is a skill that is acquired through a lot of practice. Specifically, a good organizer must be well prepared and knowledgeable, able to talk to strangers, account for different interests, and risk being threatened or humiliated by the powerful.

Second, organizing implies that a change is necessary, and so there may be tension between the old and the new, between collective memory and hope.[4] Major changes can threaten the status quo and its powerful forces that may benefit from things remaining as they are within a passive (inactive) democracy. Organizing not only commits a community to a new vision, but also redistributes power to greater or lesser extent, often exposing forces that can subjugate, placate, or manipulate.[5] Therefore, conflicting interests must be addressed in organizing.

Herein lies the ultimate capacity of seeking to inhabit the sacred in everyday life: Personal disagreements and even conflicting economic and other interests are slain by letting democracy loose, by collectively identifying and prioritizing what is truly meaningful in a community. Organizing is the democratic testing ground for finding this unity, and it must be nurtured and transacted carefully. Success relies on changing the focus from issues to values.[6] When Randy organized to fight the expansion of freeways in Raleigh, North Carolina, residents defined the issue as too much traffic in their neighborhoods that could be solved by building thoroughfares in some other neighborhood. This led to debilitating infighting until Randy realized that all the neighborhoods across the city shared similar values. They longed for safe places for children to walk, and they wanted to protect historic communities from the massive destruction freeways would cause. By shifting focus from narrowly defined problems to values about place, the thoroughfare plan was scrapped in favor of public transit. Although this is a painful and ongoing transition (the freeways were never built, and public transit is still debated), the deep values about children's safety and historic preservation were satisfied.

In organizing for political action, a full range of strategies is essential for success in working with (and sometimes against) players who may wield extraordinary influence and power. When things turn bleak, options must include civil disobedience, boycott, confrontation, and even disruption as well as invention, cooperation, negotiation, and compromise. Conflicts over strategy typically harden along class (economic) and generational lines, but versatility is key in using multiple strategies. Employing a diverse range of tactics is the hallmark of most great organizers, from activist legends like Mahatma Gandhi, Rosa Parks, Martin Luther King, Jr., Cesar Chavez, Malcolm X, and Saul Alinsky to lesser acknowledged organizers like Jane Addams, Jane Jacobs, Jane Goodall, Dennis Hayes, Larry Susskind, Karl Linn, Barack Obama, and Paulo Freire (Fig. 77).[7]

Third, conflicts need to be resolved, but they also need to be nurtured from time to time and never swept under the rug without honest, open, and respectful discussion. Because an assembly and association impose a spirit of cooperation, organizing creates pressure to harmonize, ignore substantive disagreement, and compromise often "before" its time. This can stunt the inherent creative tension in differing views. Avoiding or ignoring internal conflict can short-circuit the extraordinary potential for

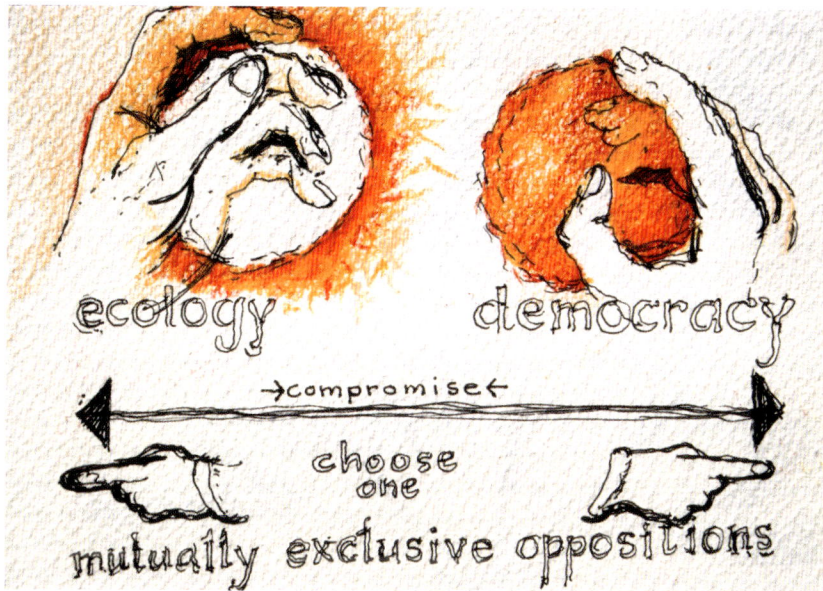

Fig. 77. Simultaneously applying strategies that seem to be mutually exclusive, including negotiation and boycott, is a fundamental source of power in organizing.

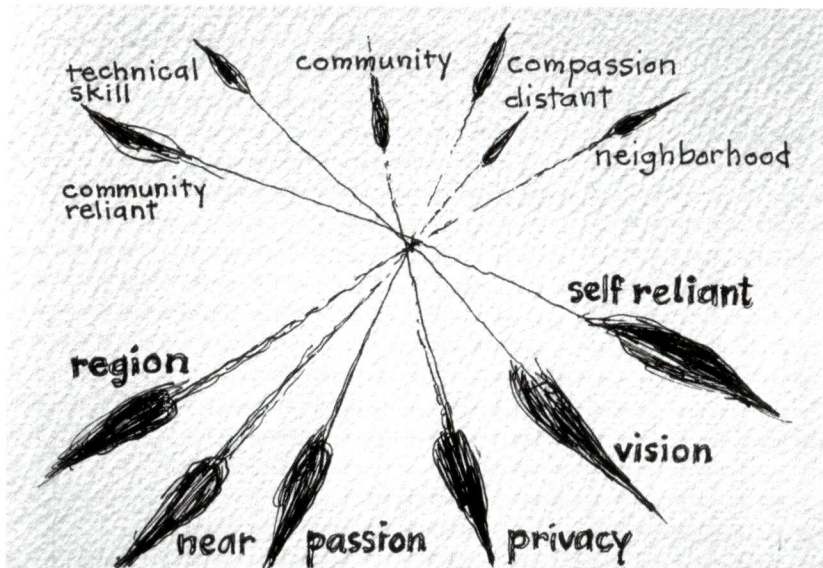

Fig. 78. Conflict between interests such as regional and neighborhood advocates provides the community process a creative tension that designers must embrace in order to reap the greatest benefits of intentional inventions.

grassroots innovation upon which society depends. The pressure to agree too soon also restricts the exercise of power, severely crippling action outside the group. Good organizers make time and space for healthy conflict to be aired and put to good use within the group (Fig. 78).[8]

Fourth, organizing is in perpetual motion, constantly evolving offensively and defensively in reaction to various ideas and attentive actions. Each community goes through stages from childlike and adolescent participation to adult, middle-aged, and end-of-life participation. For example, youthful participation often arises from oppression, paternalism, and protest. It can be rambunctious and disorderly. It embraces civil disobedience. As participation in a community matures, it relies on joint fact-finding and negotiation. These require more refined tactics. The organizer must understand the applicable stage and plan accordingly. Similarly, new participants join the effort at dramatically different stages, and some are involved in "deep democracy" for the first time while others are seasoned activists. The organizer must grasp the level of experience of each new recruit and integrate him or her appropriately.[9]

Preserve, Reclaim, or Create

Although the process of organizing begins with awakening to a problem or opportunity, how the strategy proceeds depends upon whether the awakening is prompted by an opportunity or (more often) a dissatisfaction or even a threat. The context determines which of the three situations—preserving some place that is valued, reclaiming some sacred place that has been lost, or creating a place that will come to be cherished—dominates at any one given time in any given place. A threat to a sacred place typically leads to a desire for preservation.[10] Such protective action is a reaction against some already articulated vision that is being pushed forward by a local or outside authority. Typically well funded and politically connected, that authority is usually perceived by a minority as destructive or exploitative of an existing place. Resistance is often the only strategy available to the less powerful. The resisting parties often enter the process late and are thereby severely disadvantaged. Their goal is not to make improvements but merely to stop the intrusion.[11] Luckily, governmental legislation for environmental protection, freedom of information, clean air and water, and citizen participation is well institutionalized in the United States. Such protection makes the preservation strategy easier than both reclamation and creation for communities with little power to enforce change.

Reclaiming a once-sacred cultural practice, territory, and/or ecosystem that had been colonized, conquered, seized, or destroyed is far more difficult than preserving a place, the rightful use of which has not been taken away. To regain what has been lost has all the difficulties of resistance like coming in late against powerful forces that have money and influence that have created a "done deal" situation. Then there is the additional handicap of the disputed territory having been dispossessed and being used by others for profitable purposes. The legislation that empowers preservation is less helpful after the fact. Therefore, the effort to reclaim or gain access to a place that has been taken away must utilize an organizing strategy distinct from the preservationist view. Reclamation usually requires convincing others in the community and those with authority that a higher purpose will be served by the return to an earlier status or ownership or that some grievous injustice was done in taking the territory. These efforts are not easy, but the return of illegally desecrated, destroyed, or taken landscapes is gaining public support around the world. The process almost always involves a legal court battle that may take years to resolve.

The creation of sacred places can be found all over the U.S. and throughout the world in many communities. These projects originate as one person or group dreams to improve his or her community in significant ways. Success requires a distinct form of organizing that may at first be considered eccentric and implausible by other residents. Through sustained effort, public education and involvement, and sacrifice, most projects gain support from the greater community and civic offices. Such projects can make heroes and heroines out of ordinary people, create local myth, and concretize the best-shared values of cities. They also can turn unused public spaces into well-used civic treasures, as our concluding case story illustrates. Constantly creating, reshaping, and making places sacred in everyday life is the hopeful future for communities everywhere.

No matter the strategy, community groups often struggle to offer a powerful alternate vision; this is the more difficult half of the fight for preservation, reclamation, or creation of the sacred. The visionary dream was likely born from a subconscious dissatisfaction brought to the surface, leading to a powerful awakening that "the world would be better if we pursued this vision" others had not yet considered. At first, the guardian of the alternate vision must fight to gain support and momentum through charismatic persuasion. The organizing strategy to make change begins from the ground, with little public or legal support. An alternative vision is most readily adopted when it addresses a widespread public discontentment, captures the spirit of a community, involves lots of others early on, and is backed with funding.

The Organizing Process

Although the three organizing strategies of preserving, reclaiming, and creation differ from each other and with each case's circumstances, the following pointers may foster effective organization.[12] We describe some things to do to prepare for an organizing effort, what to do first, ways to choose an appropriate strategy, and how to maintain the organized tactic until the goal is achieved. One reward of success is the empowerment to take on other projects; we note how to seize those opportunities when they arise.

In Preparation

1: Identify a problem or an opportunity underlain by a thick, deeply held, and interconnected value. Isolate a situation in your own community that prevents people from inhabiting the sacred, that personally affects a number of citizens, that requires action. Look for causes, not symptoms, and specify

Fig. 79. Find opportunities for better inhabiting the sacred and the specific barriers to realizing them. Then clarify how your personal vision of the future relates to those opportunities and barriers.

them. Relate them to core values. Develop and understand your own vision for desired change in explicit spatial terms and be prepared to test it (Fig. 79).

2: Get the support of a few active people from the community. Discuss the situation with people active in the community. Even people with whom you disagree on national issues are likely to agree with you on local issues such as working together to develop a new park, make more streets pedestrian friendly, or prevent gentrification from disrupting the neighborhood. If their ideas or concerns converge with yours, continue to seek their advice and help. Assess the likelihood of meaningful change; our experience suggests to expect the worst. No matter how minor a proposal for change may be, someone will likely be threatened by action and may become hostile towards you. Keep in mind that, all too often, something worth doing at a community-wide level is going to be unpopular with someone.

At the Outset

3: Check the facts with experts. Nothing can dampen one's argument more quickly than errors in facts, no matter how minor. Ask each of the active people in your group to check some facts with an expert they know. Do not go to experts with the wrong questions or seek expertise from those with whom you disagree on substantive points. As an example, the city traffic engineer is the last person to ask, "Is the new highway really needed in my neighborhood?" He (or she) will always say, "Yes." But he (or she) is the person to ask for basic facts: "Is this project on the Thoroughfare Plan? When is it scheduled for construction? Has there been an environmental impact statement about run-off and other issues? Can you get maps of the project? Which traffic volumes and population projections are used in the project?" (Fig. 80)

Find an expert who appreciates and respects your position. If there is no one in your community, go to colleges and universities. Faculty members are sometimes willing to help, but you must find someone who is knowledgeable and whose research funding is independent of the agency you may be challenging. After you have found an expert, ask this person the direct questions you did not ask the traffic engineer: "Is the highway needed? Can transit, bike lanes, and walking satisfy the same need?" Find out why or why not. Write down his or her ideas. If the expert uses terms you don't understand, ask for clarification. Ask if he or she is willing to express sympathetic views publicly. If so, fine; if not, determine what role the person might play. Ask the expert if there is anything you can read on the subject and if there are other people with whom you should talk. Maybe he or she will introduce you to them. The same opportunities for expertise also lie in nonprofit organizations such as The Trust for Public Land, Trout Unlimited, Southern Poverty Law Center, and Food and Water Watch.

Fig. 80. Know the facts before taking public action. Although civic action is values-driven, good information is essential to success.

4: Get the facts to the community. Each of the active people should be given the task to contact other key people and organizations in the community. Write down the basic facts and duplicate them so that everyone will be on the same page and be able to tell people the same thing. Engage in the dialogue those who are normally left out: the poor, new immigrants, teens, and the shy and soft-spoken. Seek them out by going to the places they inhabit. Hold events consistent with their cultural traditions. For example, our colleague, Jeff Hou, created a game called Design Buffet in order to engage elderly Chinese Americans in a project. They all knew a buffet, which brought them together to design their own parks. Call on ones if they do not speak up. Do not expect them to attend formal public meetings. If feasible, go door to door and talk to people. Go only at appropriate times (these vary from neighborhood to neighborhood). Dress appropriately and be yourself. You may feel nervous about doing this, but it can be great fun, as you meet neighbors you have always intended to meet. Most people will be friendly and will support your cause, because it affects them, too. Usually, they will be grateful, because they were unaware of the situation. If someone is hostile, be especially respectful and even charming. This takes practice. If possible, use a neighborhood phone tree, the Internet, social media, or newsletter to advertise the facts and the aspirations. Organize distribution routes if you use a newsletter or flyer. Recruit people to distribute the flyers. Be sure that households do not get missed.

After listening to folks and synthesizing what specific opportunities exist, determine what should not be changed and what tradeoffs are necessary to achieve change. When your position is well formed and, hopefully, timed to your best advantage, contact the local newspaper, radio, and TV stations along with other interested groups such as nonprofits with your story. Everyone loves a good story and a worthwhile cause.

Strategy

5: Get the community to consider, improve, or get behind the position that you and your group prefer. This can best be done at an open community meeting. Find a suitable and centrally located place to meet. Often this is in a church, school, library, or community center. Your meeting place should be located in the community where your supporters live and, ideally, have a big room (that seats fifty or more people) and a small room (that seats about twenty people). Start in the small room and move to the larger room only if you have many attendees, because holding a meeting of a handful of people in a large auditorium can be the death-knell for a project. Make arrangements well in advance of the meeting date and be sure the building will be open. Restrict the meeting to an hour and thirty minutes. Expect the first meeting to be non-directional. A lot of people will come to present (often gripe about) unrelated matters; they should be allowed to express their ideas and vent their concerns. Equalize power in the process so that no one is imposing, imperializing, or co-opting via a power imbalance.

Remember that something concrete must be achieved for people to be willing to continue to participate. Try accomplishing some or all of the following at this first community meeting to ensure continued participation:

- Select informal interim leaders.
- Establish a primary objective that has widespread support. This can be done by asking for a show of hands after everyone has had a chance to weigh in.
- Determine a preliminary plan and benchmark to achieve an objective. Even if this is achieved at a later date, people need to know that the leaders have a plan of action. Be open to ideas about how to proceed, but be ready to spell out a plan if no ideas are forthcoming.
- Appoint task groups to accomplish the plan of action. For example, one might research the problem in more detail; another might develop a means of local communication; another might get representation from areas or people not in attendance; and another might look at long-range problems in the community.
- Aim to formulate and vote on a motion after appropriate discussion. Even a simple resolution gives people a sense of accomplishment and clarity of purpose.
- Survey the people in attendance about the goals they have for improving the community, creating an innovative place or simply living more intentionally within their neighborhood. This can be easily done with a simple questionnaire filled out during the meeting. A few questions asking people to list their highest priorities for improvements or ranking a list your group has prepared will suffice. Be sure to leave blanks in a predetermined list so people can add ones you did not know about. If you want to ask about problems, do so only after you query regarding visions for improvements. The leaders can then use the results to determine what long- and short-range projects should be undertaken.
- Set the next meeting time and place and describe the tasks to be done by that time.
- Get a list of the people attending, their addresses, phone numbers, and emails. Keep a list of all the people you talked to. Write down their primary interests and skills.

6: Assure the work gets accomplished. If the primary objective of the association is a reaction to a crisis (such as contamination or a natural hazard), that problem must be thoroughly and quickly researched; otherwise, it may be too late for your group to intervene in public action. Be sure the appropriate data are collected and carefully analyzed. Check with your experts if you and your group have questions. Time is usually of the essence in a crisis, but the advantage to situations of crisis is that more people seem willing to work for the community when the problem that threatens them is imminent. Be sure all other task groups are getting their work done. During a crisis it is easy to forget tasks like communicating with other people in the neighborhood, expanding the base of support, keeping in touch with the media, and planning for long-term goals, but these tasks are necessary if the organization is to be effective over a period of time. Try to involve a sizable number of people in these tasks to share the load. Too often, too few do too much of the heavy lifting.

Fig. 81. Develop a strategy for action that maximizes the power that the group has and counters the opposition's strengths. Consider strategies that like Occupy Wall Street, Critical Mass bike rides, and Parking Day that embrace fun.

7: Plan a strategy for action with a core group. Develop a core group from existing organizations or from the leadership of the task groups. Keep in mind that a strategy and plan for action is an exercise of power, and the organization must determine how best to implement its mission. Is power associated with money, knowledge, or numbers of participants? Usually, community organizations do not have the money to advertise their vision, so they must be fully informed, even more than the opposition, and have large numbers of people to support their cause when appropriate (such as at public hearings). Realistically appraise your sources of power. Do you know how the system works in regards to your problem? For example, there are complicated procedures and laws for building affordable housing, pipelines, bikeways, and pedestrian routes. You need to know the standard procedures that are supposed to be followed. Reach out to other groups that are likely to support your position and engage sympathetic power brokers who can effect change without betraying the internal intent. Appraise the sources of power against you to determine who would be hurt or lose power by your success. Encourage bold and innovative ideas. Think of strategies that will be fun or exciting to gain public awareness. You may never do some of the things you come up with, but fresh and creative thinking is essential (Fig. 81).

Usually, a group needs a short-term success—a clear, decisive accomplishment—to build morale, retain and increase numbers, and legitimize the group and its vision. The short-term strategy need only be peripherally related though not counter-productive to the long-term goal, but the long-term strategy must be firmly in mind from the beginning. Choose a strategy that allows a lot of community people to participate. Employ techniques that evoke shared experiences and knowledge to make people self-aware of the implications of their values for their community. The techniques should connect people to people and people to place by direct experience, kindle noble civic identity, and impel change.

Choose a strategy that will "cost" the least but still get the job done. For example, if a phone call to the city manager will get him (or her) to consider funding a bikeway, do not have a big demonstration at City Hall demanding the funds. A strategy that is inappropriately harsh will not only require more time and energy to organize, but also cost you public favor.

A slow escalation of tactics will keep your public support steady and may be more effective. If you are unsure about the appropriate level of strategy, use an established course first such as meeting with members of a city council. If that is unsuccessful, then escalate. Settle on a best strategy to present to the community but have alternatives at hand that have been brainstormed within the core group if your best strategy is challenged. Don't be intimidated by corporate or government experts. You, your core group, and other residents know better than they what you want for your community.

Fig. 82. After getting support from the community and determining what agency to target, take action and maintain a simple message about the change you expect.

8: Make the final strategy decision in an open meeting. Sometimes, in really high stakes conflicts, strategies must be worked out in secret, but not often. In many cases today, public-private partnerships develop strategies cooperatively and intentionally make the strategy as transparent as possible.

The Reward

9: Take action. Be sure your group knows exactly what it wants to do and do it. Be direct and do not get sidetracked. Show force. This is where public support is vital. Knock at the right door. This is where knowledge of the system comes in. Be sure you are not demanding the wrong thing from the wrong agency. Even when you get the right agency, it is not guaranteed that its personnel will know how to deal with public demands. Bureaucracies often do not know what to do about citizen participation, so have your facts boiled down to the essentials and make public statements clearly, succinctly, and respectfully. Do not talk about side issues. Do not talk over the head of the average citizen. Have a few sound bites that express the essence of your goal in a memorable way. Be sure your effort is well coordinated and presents a unified front. Pay attention to details such as where, when, and how a certain council or commission meeting is to be conducted. Continue to meet with the core group to make changes in strategy. Keep your supporting public informed (Fig. 82).

10: Persevere until successful. Be persistent. If a bureaucrat tells you he (or she) will do something, check to see that it is done. Even after a change has been made, keep a watchful eye to be sure the change is not undone. "Eternal vigilance is the price of liberty," to quote one founding father.[13]

11: Advertise success. Use the Internet and all kinds of media to spread the word of your accomplishments. Communicate with supporters and look for new ones; now is the time to broaden your base of support. Emphasize the noble value gained, not the politics exercised. Be gracious and do not gloat. Credit everyone before yourself.

When Opportunities Arise

12: Undertake other projects. Remember to evaluate the previous project so mistakes are not repeated. If the previous project represents a major step forward, freeze it by taking steps to prevent the action from being undone. If you are interested in other ways to inhabit the sacred, now is the time to start while you have the community's attention. Expect some of the hardest workers to retreat

Fig. 83. Celebrate each successful outcome with other, even bolder ideas for other actions that allow you to live more responsibly and meaningfully at home, regionally, or globally.

for a period of time. Try to produce a periodic newsletter or other alert to describe the activities of the task groups to keep the community informed and legitimize the group. Be prepared to use a small window of opportunity to induce change that may appear through serendipity. You may want to begin working on the longer-term projects. After success at the neighborhood level, you may be ready to take on issues at the city, regional, or national scale (Fig. 83).

Techniques for Organizing to Protect Sacred Places

Many techniques can be used to organize successfully to identify, protect, reclaim, and create sacred places. The following story about Camp 4 in Yosemite National Park illustrates some of the techniques that work well to empower a community towards protection. Drawing from community resources, expanding the group, legal complaints, showing precedence, and having face-to-face conversations about conflicts were all employed to strengthen the organization and present a compelling case for preservation.

Drawing from Community Resources

Since 1941, Camp 4 has been the base for rock climbers of Yosemite. In 1997, Camp 4 was threatened with destruction by a new road and expansion of Yosemite Lodge, dormitories, and other buildings on the valley floor. Typical of preservation fights, the plan for growth had gathered strong

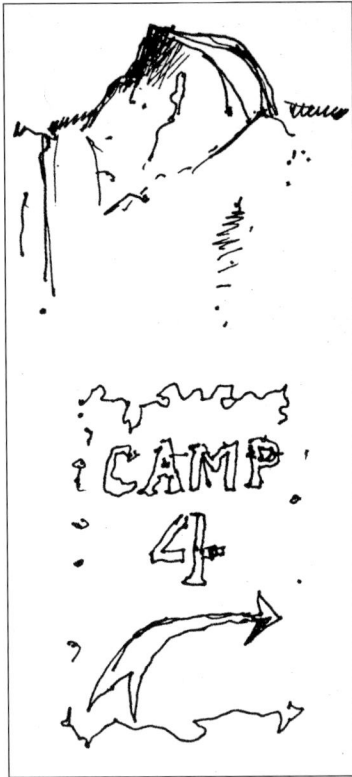

Fig. 84. Camp 4 is the sacred center of rock climbers throughout the world, but it was dismissed by National Park Service officials as looking like all other NPS campsites in details as small as the rustic sign.

support within the National Park Service's (NPS) hierarchy long before the public was informed and opposition became organized. Yet Camp 4 has great significance as the base for the world's greatest rock climbers who have tackled the boulders around the camp and the vertical faces that enclose the valley.[14] The climbers insisted that Camp 4 exceeded the criteria for protection under the National Register of Historic Places, but they lacked the "hard proof" to justify it to an audience that only understood quantitative evidence. The camp had already been dismissed by a NPS historian who noted that the trees, rocks, and campsites looked like those at hundreds of other parks (Fig. 84).

The climbers decided to fight for the camp's preservation, so their lawyer, Dick Duane, a climber himself, came to Randy for advice. After hearing the stories of incomparable physical and mental toughness, Randy suggested that the climbers map their most valued places around the campground. Within a few days, the most active contester against the development delivered a handmade map of Camp 4 drawn from memory (Fig. 85). He had located every campsite and hundreds of individual rocks strewn across acres of the gently sloping surrounds. He knew which climbers occupied each camp and when they had made great ascents from that staging area. He drew every opening in the pines to scale and described the experience of the sky from each. Dozens of rocks were sketched with shapes so precise they could be identified in the field. Each was named, often for the person who had first figured out how to free climb it or for the movement required to scale it. Rocks were labeled Yvon Chouinard Overhand, Royal Robbins Offwidth, Chuck Pratt Mantle, Ron Kauk Face, Jerry Moffatt Stick It, and Jim Bridwell Boulder, among many others. The scattered granite was like a climber's Hall of Fame. Then there were rocks named Elegant Gypsy, Blue Suede Shoes, The Sloth, Swan Slab, Thriller, Dominator, Twinkle Toes, Shiver Me Timbers, King Cobra and Tendons Give Traverse (Fig. 86). There were even three "midnight" rocks—Midnight Cowboy, Midnight Lightning, and After Midnight—famous for free climbing in the dark. Midnight Lightning is among the most infamous boulder problems in the world; only about two-dozen climbers have ever made this ascent, and many have been seriously injured trying. The climber had placed a large red heart beside the rocks most important to him. The most astonishing discovery was that he insisted that every avid climber could make his own map of sacred structures.[15] They could draw with such precision, because they had to sense the rocks spatially

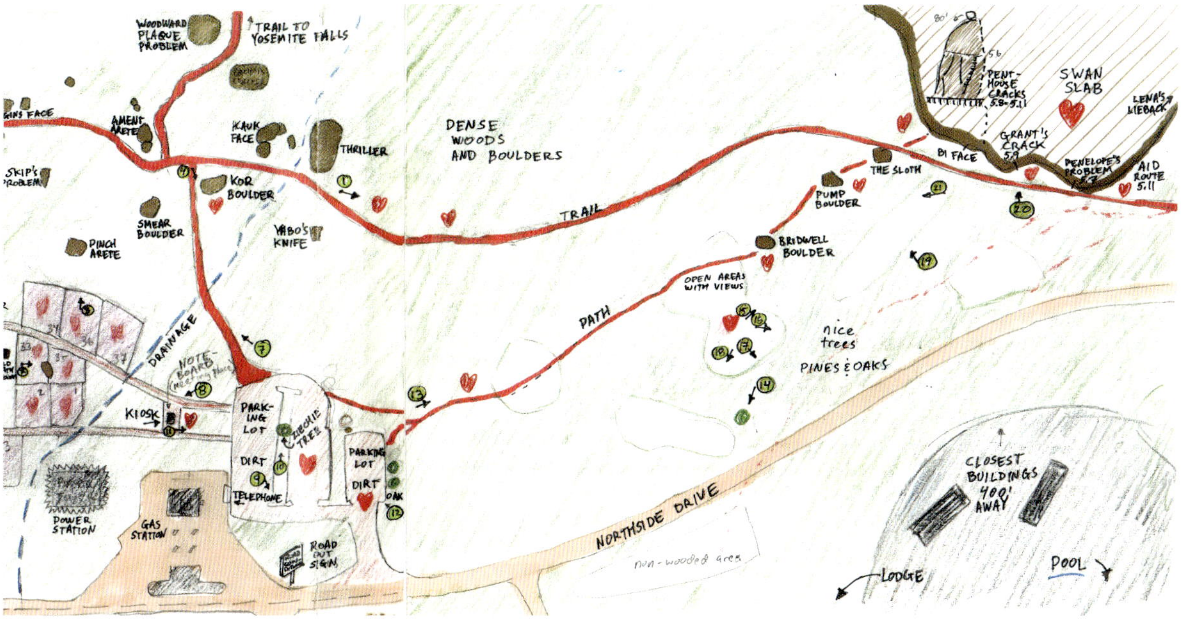

Fig. 85. One of the climbers drew a map from memory that was accurate enough to substitute for an "as built" document. Climbing required that he knew every inch of the rock faces.

in order to climb them. Their ability to draw was a previously untapped resource, like fish heads and tails discarded after the fillets have been removed. Finding strategies that utilize unique skills of the group is a key to successful organizing. Their drawings were powerful as art and data. They now had some evidence for legitimization!

Expanding the Group

The lawyer devised a questionnaire that was sent to major rock climbers all over the world, asking them to draw or list the most sacred spots around Camp 4. He compiled their responses into a map and list of the rocks and other most sacred aspects associated with Camp 4 (Fig. 87). Respondents from dozens of countries called Camp 4 "the home place of climbing," "Mecca," "our spiritual home," "the embodiment of a pure ethic," "a valley floor of inspiration," and "a pilgrim site." Dozens of the world's most important climbing feats had been staged here, about which hundreds of books and articles had been written. In short, the history of climbing in Yosemite was told in the mapped rocks at Camp 4. What had looked like ordinary granite debris to the NPS suddenly took on new meaning. By questioning climbers from vast areas of the world and mapping their responses, the climbing community could offer a physical counter-argument of equal political weight to the proposed plan for development. As the group expanded, so did their clout. The climbers' stories dominated the planning from that point forward. The strategy to organize climbers worldwide had succeeded.

Fig. 86. Each rock had a name, memorializing a person, event, or the specific skill necessary to master it.

Legal Complaint with Stories

Dick Duane filed suit in a federal district court. He demanded injunctive relief to prevent any construction at Camp 4 and the whole Swan Slab rock area. The complaint noted typical procedural violations but then took twenty pages to paint an affective picture of the plaintiffs and their individual stories at Camp 4. He felt that the legal missteps of the NPS were less important than the narratives of struggle, sacrifice, and heroic achievement on the mountain. He wanted to make stories about the place rather than legal issues the focus of the court decision, a risky but powerful strategy among the judiciary.

Conversations amongst Conflict

Duane also initiated meetings between climbers and NPS personnel, longtime foes in Yosemite National Park. Duane's approach was to communicate the compelling story of Camp 4 and to engage key people in heart-to-heart exchanges. To that end, one of the plaintiffs told the NPS in a court proceeding, "I am suing you, because I love you; we were kids in Yosemite together; you (Park Service officials) are not the bad guys." The lawsuit proceeded. Duane orchestrated the sharing of stories between climbers and NPS officials through informal meetings outside court. As they listened to each other, Yosemite's officials grasped the meaning of Camp 4 to the climbers. These meetings created a bond between the park's staff and climbers, some of whom had tried years before to enforce NPS rules on the then-youthful climbers who were viewed by the NPS as outlaw troublemakers. Most were now elderly, and their memories from opposing viewpoints in their youth tied them together as a community in old age (Fig. 88).[16]

Show of Precedence

As part of his legal preparation, Duane had read the entire process of revitalization that occurred in Manteo. He cited in court many times the stories of the use of the gravel parking lot for "hanging out at the waterfront" and "newsing" at the post office, two key everyday sacred events in Manteo. His aim was to explain how seemingly ordinary places can be of central importance to people. To him, the climbers' sacred places map became Camp 4's Fourteenth Amendment.

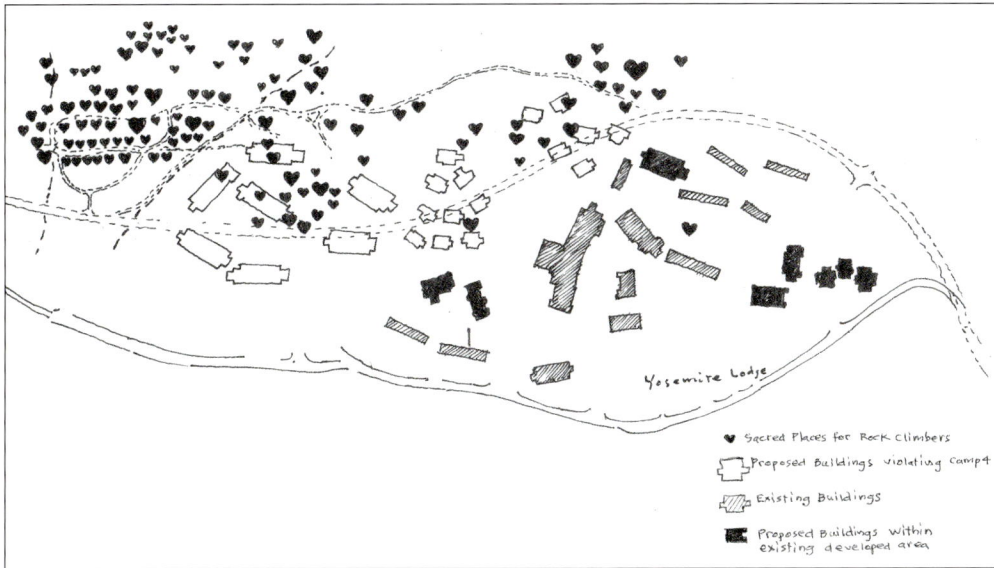

Fig. 87. The lawyer for the rock climbers compiled the responses of climbers all over the world into a single map showing hearts for the most sacred spots and where sacredness conflicted with NPS's plans for expansion. This map was submitted to the court as primary evidence.

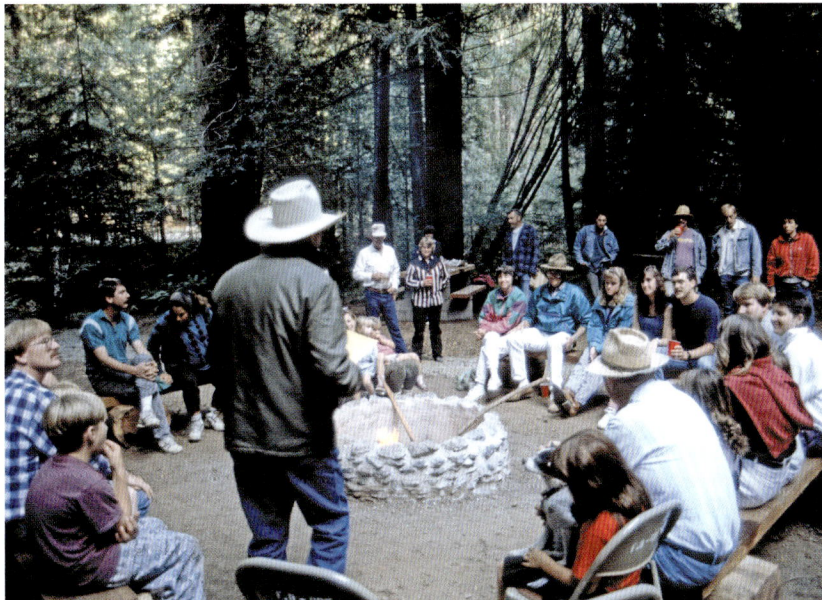

Fig. 88. The court proceedings were secondary to informal meetings between climbers and National Park Service officials, where sharing stories about renegade young climbers and youthful NPS law enforcers allowed all to view themselves as part of a historic adventure.

In time, even the highest-ranking NPS officials acknowledged that Camp 4's mere "sites, trees, and rocks" were hallowed. The judge in the case drove to Yosemite, walked among the boulders on the climbers' maps; and grasped the import in one afternoon. Without further resistance, Camp 4 was soon placed on the National Register of Historic Places.[17]

The actions of the climbers were finally successful, and their influence was manifested in many changes in the development of Yosemite. The plans for large-scale development nearby were curtailed, some proposed facilities were relocated out of Yosemite Valley altogether, the road near Camp 4 was removed, and the total footprint of buildings was reduced in the park. The main lesson here is to take the risk, even in community situations, to pursue the sacred. It can become an equal force to economic desires, if it is legitimized with sound techniques and a clear method, especially important in public situations with high stakes and legal ramifications. The result is worth the potential embarrassment.

Techniques for Organizing to Reclaim Sacred Places

Some of the techniques used in Saving Camp 4 are applicable to reclaiming places that have been stolen. In the next story, however, native Hawaiians had to employ different and drastically more difficult strategies to reclaim lost sacredness. We focus on mapping facts about the landscape and culture from opposing viewpoints, calling for inclusive management and slow organizing.

Mauna Kea is a snow-covered dormant volcano rising around 13,800 feet from the warm seas surrounding the Big Island of Hawaii. It is the single most sacred site for native Hawaiians and represents both the symbolic and literal body of the gods and goddesses of creation; it remained part of the Royal Kingdom, even after the Hawaiian government was illegally overthrown, in part, by the United States in 1893.[18] This area is so hallowed to Hawaiians that structures of any kind are forbidden to exist upon it. Even burials of the royalty were distanced to the shoulders of the stony alpine peaks (Fig. 89). The height and extremes of this landscape formed a unique ecosystem of rare and endemic species that exist nowhere else on Earth. The land, its plants and animals, and the spirit of the mountain were protected by the sacredness Hawaiians bestowed upon Mauna Kea. The mountain continues to be sacred long after the state claimed control of the land.

A few years after statehood in 1959, the University of Hawaii began construction of what has become a leading international center of astronomical research. In 1968, only one telescope had been located at the summit, but the impact and destruction of the land drew protest from native Hawaiians. One recalled her grandfather's passionate speech at a hearing, "Sacred Mountain no Place for Telescope." In spite of the fact that the State Bureau of Land Management lease allowed only one telescope on the mountain, by 2006 there were thirteen. The lease, which runs until 2033, is continually contested by the "first people" who claim that the land was illegally seized and leased without jurisdiction (Fig. 90). For ten years, the University of Hawaii expanded the scientific facilities with no plan to guide development.

Fig. 89. Mauna Kea, literally meaning the Gods and Goddesses of creation, is the most sacred place for native Hawaiians. It is so sacred that no one, not even the highest royalty, can be buried on the summit.

Fig. 90. Although only one telescope was allowed on Mauna Kea by law, more than a dozen have been built, with their foundations piercing the bodies of the Gods. More telescopes are planned.

Fig. 91. In order to counter misinformation from government agencies and advocates of telescopes, native Hawaiians did field studies to construct their own maps of the sacred places. With professionals from fields as diverse as cultural anthropology and landscape architecture, they mapped sites never before acknowledged by state authorities.

Retroactively, it produced a series of plans that were adopted to legitimize the illegal activity. The plans largely ignored standard U.S. cultural and environmental legislation, and even the state auditor found the state's agencies negligent.[19]

A local *hui*, which is a small group—in this case a group comprised of native Hawaiians, cultural practitioners, environmentalists, grassroots activists, and the Royal Order of Kamehameha, a society of native Hawaiians committed to defending the sovereignty of the Kingdom of Hawaii—became the leader in challenging the destruction of Mauna Kea. Its members employed many of the same techniques that the climbers did in saving Camp 4. They took legal action and mapped the sacred sites (Fig. 91). They sought outside support to show precedence and to gain international attention for their cause. They personally engaged the power brokers to the extent possible. Additionally, they proposed alternative futures for the mountain on the basis that the present lease requires the astronomical industrial complex be removed in its entirety in 2033 and the mountain be restored to its former state. Later, the group proposed an inclusive management system between all parties for the mountain. Eventually, their collective voices were heard and legitimized, though the *hui* still fights to secure rights to Mauna Kea.

Mapping Facts from Opposing Viewpoints

Although many voices speak for Mauna Kea, two explain the extraordinary difference in world-views that surround the mountain and complicate the process of reclaiming the sacred. The first voice is Kealoha Pisciotta, a native Hawaiian: "The mountain is the first born of Wakea and Papa, parents of the Hawaiian race. Mauna Kea is the umbilical cord of Island Child that connects land to heavens."[20] The second voice is Henry Joy McCracken, an astronomer: "It is a sad state of affairs when [the endangered weikiu] bug, or even the outdated traditions of ancient worship, can take precedence over getting to grips with the universe."[21] Representatives of this second voice dominated the published information and plans for the mountain for forty years. Each plan used incomplete, fabricated, or inaccurate data to show that the astrological industrial complex would have no significant impact on sacred sites or ecosystems.

In 2006, the *hui* hired experts to map the mountain's geology, hydrology, flora, fauna, ecotones, and cultural practices. Their maps exposed scientific flaws in the previous data on which the university's plans were based, to such an extent that those plans were rendered invalid. The maps exposed that the state-supported astronomy industry had misrepresented the areas occupied by endemic species and sacred ritual routes of native Hawaiians and gerrymandered the data to allow construction of telescopes in the most sensitive areas.[22] The courts ruled similar findings in a Contested Case Hearing. The *hui* had gotten the facts straight, exposed the state's misinformation, and informed the public. One map showed the distorted science offered by industry and helped the *hui* enlarge its constituency (Fig. 92). This technique of comparing the facts proved an especially powerful strategy for organizing when the dominant powers either used faulty information or purposefully falsified the information. Look carefully at the subtle differences in information mapped. Look carefully at the subtle differences in how the information is mapped (Figs. 92 and 93).

Call for Inclusive Management

Another organizing strategy was a call for a single jurisdiction for management of the whole mountain that would plan and regulate all uses on the mountain—for astronomy, recreation, habitat, and culture—as equal partners. This made sense to people who were frustrated by the fragmentation of authority and the imbalance of power that ignored other uses besides astronomy. The *hui* argued for a moratorium on expansion. Even though most members of the *hui* favored removal of all telescopes incrementally by 2033, they called for the new management authority to create a comprehensive plan with widespread input from the community. Rather than advocating its own vision, the *hui* argued for the opportunity for others to participate in a meaningful way. This, too, appealed to a broad public, increasing the *hui*'s support. The *hui* wished to "run the *aina* (that is, hold gatherings over the entire land, from one end of the island to another)," explaining the proposal to each village, clan, and settlement, but the State of Hawaii has not responded favorably to this proposal.[23]

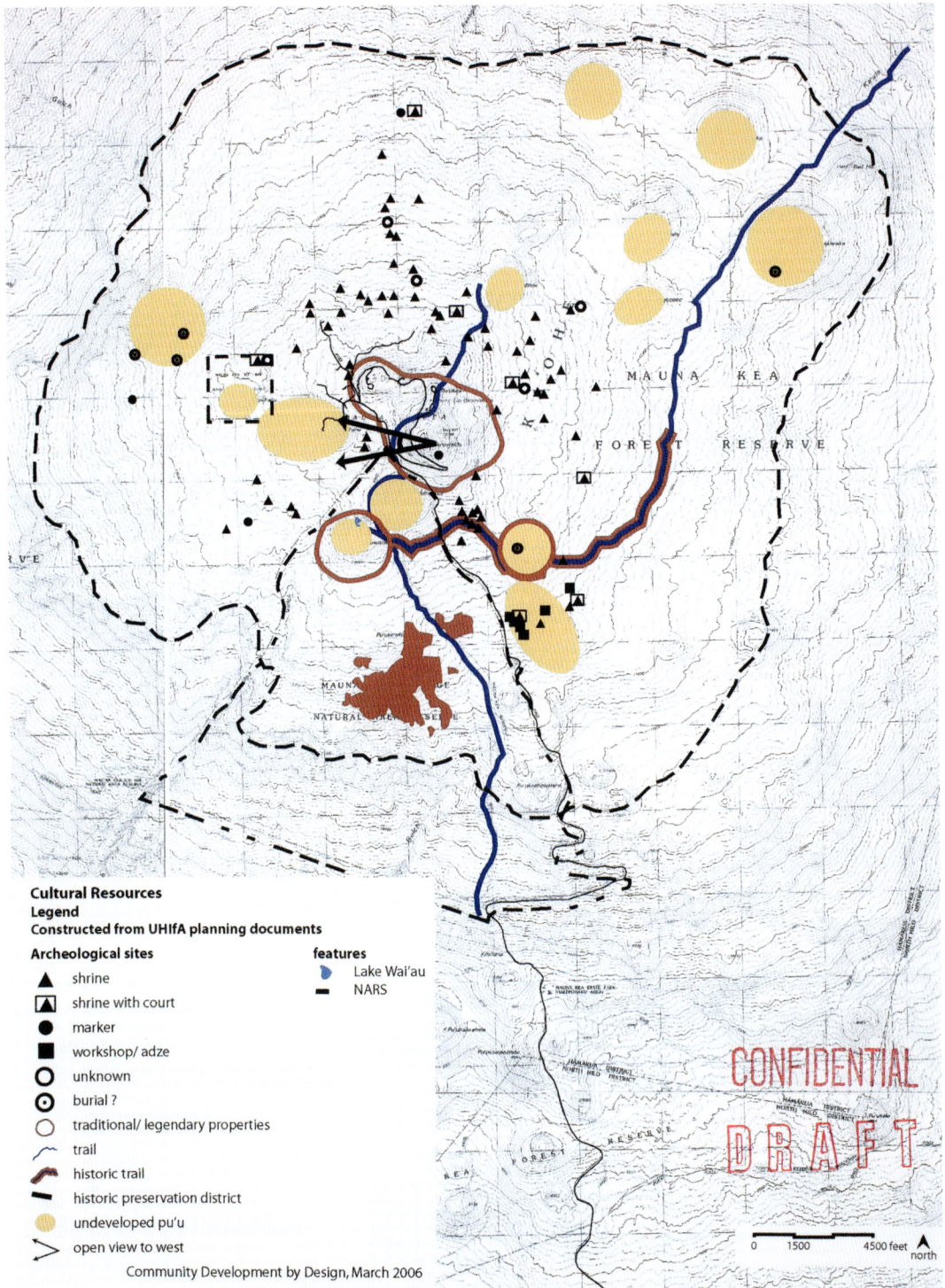

Cultural Resources
Legend
Constructed from UHIfA planning documents

Archeological sites

▲ shrine
▣ shrine with court
● marker
■ workshop/ adze
○ unknown
◉ burial ?
◯ traditional/ legendary properties
⟋ trail
historic trail
historic preservation district
undeveloped pu'u
⟩ open view to west

features
Lake Wai'au
NARS

Community Development by Design, March 2006

CONFIDENTIAL

DRAFT

0   1500   4500 feet
north

Fig. 92. The official map of cultural resources map had long neglected to record the sacred aspects of Mauna Kea, allowing construction of telescopes in the most sensitive areas for religious practices and endangered species.

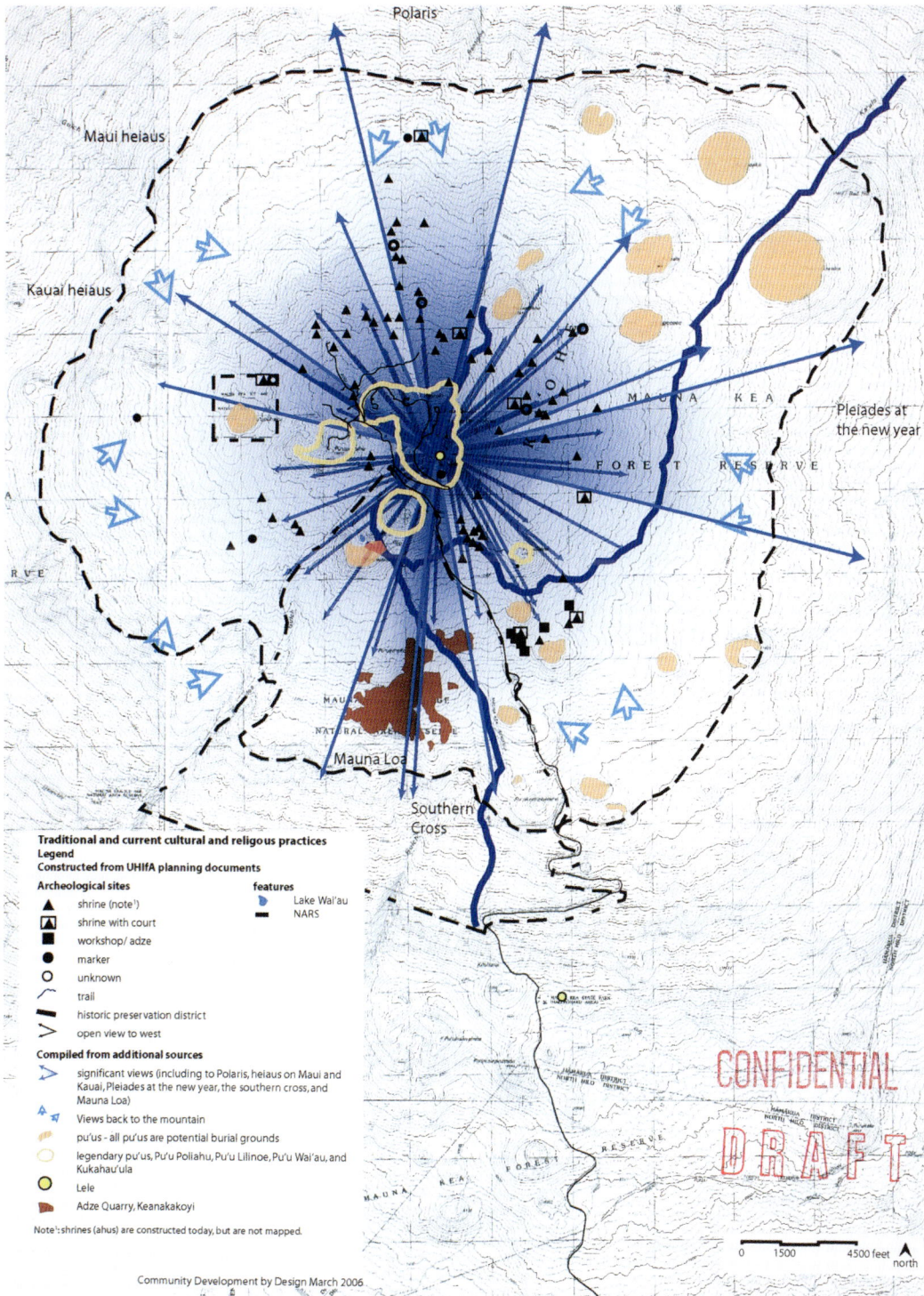

Fig. 93. The map prepared with the native Hawaiian hui replaced incomplete data with accurate information about the values embedded in Mauna Kea, changing public opinion and winning legal challenges.

Fig. 94. The hui and other groups led by Kealoha Pisciotta continue
to coffer gifts to the Gods and counter proposals to those who want
to expand the industrial complexes of telescopes occupying the
sacred mountain.

Slow Organizing

The first meetings voicing concern about the theft and abuse of Mauna Kea occurred before a
single telescope was built during the 1960s. The *hui* has been an advocate for the mountain for more
than a decade and has gained significant ground, though the struggle continues. Why is the *hui*'s
progress in organizing an effective constituency so painfully slow? First, the astronomical-industrial
complex and its international partners have a near monopoly of power, resources, information, and use
of the mountain. By comparison, the *hui*'s resources and power offer little more than a minor nuisance.
Second, the dominant powers have successfully labeled those native people who seek to reclaim the
mountain as radical separatists who seek an extremist secession. The *hui* is too small and underfunded
to counter this reputation. Third, the native community is divided. Some have been bought by state
agencies; others are confused; and many are passive (Fig. 94).

This case serves as a cautionary tale. Organizing is never easy, is often time consuming, and
frequently is stifled by the dominant culture, especially when the economic stakes are high. It also
demonstrates several vital reasons for hope. First, never underestimate the power of a few committed

individuals with good science and reasonable proposals, even if they are labeled radical. The *hui* with a few dozen activists has won court rulings and compiled more accurate scientific data than a global industry of people calling themselves scientists.[24] The tiny *hui* has exposed how powerful interests can distort science to fit their purposes. Second, is the matter of time. We may view the *hui* as moving too slow, but slowness is an island reality. The *hui* knows it can only push so far so fast, but it also knows their time will come.

Techniques for Organizing to Create Sacred Place

There are times when someone has a dream for their community long before anyone is prepared for it. Such visionaries are true inhabitants of a place, deeply rooted and committed to living in the everyday sacred. They know their places from long-term reciprocal experience and critical analysis. These wise citizens are perfectly positioned to see opportunities that no one else comprehends. In these cases, they often impose personal acts of creativity and devotion on the public landscape. Such actions may stir debate about the deeper meaning of a place and how to live in a more active democracy. They may meet mundane needs but often seem like divine inspirations, radical measures to correct critical problems that a community may unknowingly suffer from. These projects usually begin with a new idea or prophesy, an unexpressed but deeply held value, and a need to create.

In Seattle, Washington, landscape architect Richard Haag spent nearly twenty years building Gas Works Park, first determining what was most valuable on the site, then battling public opposition in order to save the derelict remnants of the industrial gas works. He practically lived there, nurturing the project, designing the place, and, in time, overseeing the site's transformation from an object of controversy into one of Seattle's most beloved civic places (Figs. 95 and 96).

When the City of Seattle purchased the ugly, defunct site decades ago and proposed to demolish the industrial ruins for a park, Haag and everyone else in the city was pleased, because the industry was an eyesore on the waterfront. Six years later as Haag studied the place, he discovered sculptural beauty in the despised black pipes and towers. Haag recalled that the guardian spirit of the place told him to leave the ruins and build a park around them. By this time, Haag had fallen in love with the place and its haunted sculpture. He spent thousands of dollars of his own money to renovate an old blacksmith shop and moved his landscape architecture office there. A mentor suggested that the value of its preservation would be appropriate "way down the road," but no civic leaders agreed. Haag was convinced that only he knew what the gasworks plant should be.

People in Seattle found Haag's idea outrageous and said so. Since innovation involves changing the way things are done, they were skeptical and hostile and certainly not forthcoming with the resources necessary for its implementation. "Newspaper columns, his peers and enraged citizens attacked him," reported one publisher; only someone as "stubborn and committed as Haag could have survived the

Fig. 95. Although his vision for Gas Works Part was bold and expansive, Haag knew he had to get feedback and support from each community group, one at a time. He referred to this as "organizing the capillaries" rather than "going for the jugular."

Fig. 96. Haag's idea to make the old gas works into a central feature of the park was a radical idea to Seattle's citizens, but it became a magical, unconventional playground for youthful minds.

community's ridicule."[25] Many of his best friends and associates privately voiced their doubts to Haag as well. Some supported a formal rose garden on the site instead of his outlandish dream of converting an industrial site into a new kind of public park.

Organizing the Capillaries

It was essential for Haag to get official recognition, because few people were willing to participate in an unauthorized project that ultimately required civil disobedience and trespass. Quasi-illegality was attractive to "radical innovators and a few comrades" who occupied the site and set up an office without proper authorization. Their camaraderie increased when they were evicted from the blacksmith shop-office by Seattle's authorities during a driving rainstorm. Still, official approval was prerequisite to widespread acceptance and involvement.

For long-term success, Haag had to develop a strategy to attract the support of elected community leaders and officials. Haag knew his group of radical supporters would run out of energy, so he tried to persuade community and civic groups to endorse his idea. He saw this organizing strategy as "going for the capillaries, not the jugular." He hoped that they, in turn, would persuade the unwilling mayor and other city leaders to consider and adopt his plan.

Public Education

In order to persuade the public to end the opposition to his idea for saving the gas works, Haag developed a slide show that he used in a three-year educational campaign.[26] The slides portrayed the gas works as multipurpose and timely art. He gave parties on the site and sponsored bus trips so local officials could look at and understand firsthand the possibilities as he proposed them. The slide shows neutralized abstract opposition. The tours on site elicited sensual responses and excitement. After nearly three dozen public showings, Haag had opened many eyes and minds and a few hearts to the potential beauty of the site. In short order, people began to respond with more tolerance and occasionally enthusiastic support. The organizing laid the groundwork for action.[27]

Inspiring Spirited Civic Life

Three years lapsed between the time Haag obtained the contract to design Gas Works Park and the time construction began. In the meantime, he knew he had to show improvement. Only months after he had the contract, he converted the blacksmith shop into his office. This act showed he was dedicated, and it persuaded some people that the filthy gas ruins could be used. For the first phase of construction, he chose visible and popular facilities: a picnic and play area, a grassy mound with trees and shrubs, and an observation station to oversee the whole site. His vision was to regrade most of the

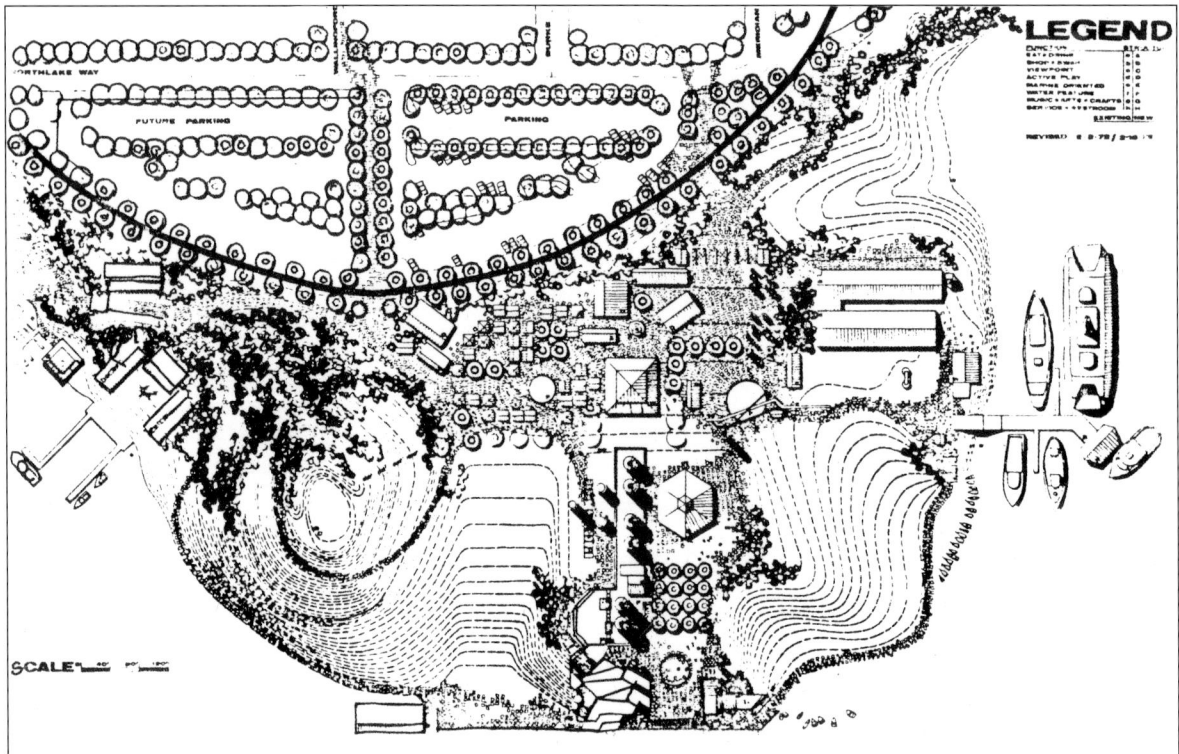

Fig. 97. In designing the precedent-setting Gas Works Park decades ago,
Rich Haag experimented with many ways of community organizing,
from trespassing to public education. These are still "go to" techniques.

site to create a sweeping and majestic hill overlooking the beautiful inner waterfront that defines
Seattle to residents and visitors alike. From this overlook, remnants of the gas plant appear as art
growing out of the earth, subservient to the big earth mound, the climb up the hill and the view Haag
created. Only after initial landscape construction had finished did he receive consent to begin work on
recycling the industrial relics. The park was open to the public in 1975, twenty years after the industry
left the area (Fig. 97).

Haag finally gained official recognition for his accomplishments in Gas Works Park when he
was awarded the Presidents Award of Design Excellence from the American Society of Landscape
Architects. Then, in 2013, the park was added to the National Register of Historic Places for housing
remnants of the sole-remaining coal gasification plant in the nation. Still, it maintains its legacy as a
place of controversy. The park was supposed to be named Myrtle Edwards Park after the city council-
woman who rallied support to obtain the land for public use but died shortly before its opening in a
car accident. In her vision for the park, all evidence of the gas works would be removed and redesigned
as a gardenesque park, so when the city decided that the gas works would remain, her family requested

that her name be removed. A Seattle entertainment guide said, "Gas Works Park is easily the strangest park in Seattle, and may rank among the strangest in the world."[28] Yet even with its quirks, it expresses the essence of Seattle as a community with rich history, unusual civic commitment, and willingness to live differently. It supports a wide variety of activities that are not expected in the center of the city, and people say it is the best place for Fourth of July fireworks, kite flying, and views of the city. Gas Works Park has become a precedent for other grassroots uprisings in support of deep democracy in Seattle. Projects like it have become an important part of the city's public landscape, making a living tradition of a creative, public serving disobedience and distinctive ways to dwell.

Organizing shapes a unified image from disparate or conflicting pieces, prepares a group to take political action, and engages the broader public in the process. Preserving something sacred, reclaiming it, or creating new sacredness require distinct strategies. These strategies can be learned. It is imperative to remember that organizing is never static, evolves through stages, and requires some confrontation. As powerful as organizing is, it can only do so much. Inhabiting the sacred requires changing the world in which we live and making the sacred manifest, the next step in the process.

FOUR WISHES THROUGH PLANNING AND DESIGN

WHEN KING ARTHUR convened the knights, he ordered that a giant round table be made for the meetings. When planners introduced community participation as an essential part of redesigning Tokyo's neighborhoods, they started the "Round Table Movement." When Cornell Walker wrote his manifesto, described in Step 1, his second promise was to help his wife find a round table for their kitchen. In each case a deeply held, though abstract value was manifested through the design of an explicit setting. The practical purposes varied. Arthur wanted to avoid conflict between his warriors. The Japanese planners wanted citizens and professionals to work together collaboratively. Mr. Walker's wife wanted a place where the whole family would sit and eat together and discuss the events of the day. She specifically outlawed texting at her table. She may have also wanted to be able to keep an eye on each child's behavior. But each round table made the abstract value of creating a less hierarchical setting tangible for everyone involved. No one occupied the "head of the table." This act of transforming values into physical form is the essence of manifesting.

It is impossible to act on values without concrete images of those values. We require physical expressions of our worldview, identity, morality, and accomplishments. We may hold images of these in our heads and hearts, but we also need real places that make those values tangible. The physical world we make gives form to our sense of security, adventure, and relationships with other people and the ecological world of which we are a part.

Design manifests values by revealing them plainly in the built environment. This is easy to say and difficult to achieve, making manifesting a troublesome step. It requires a transparent process so citizens, designers, and planners can discuss the precise form their values should take. Most of us are not accustomed to making deep values legible. We know the shape of a baseball field or community center but seldom do we think about, much less draw, things like survival, identity, reciprocity, status, or a sense of belonging. So we have to adapt to the purpose of communicating values. This may sound like "design speak," but the choice of appropriate tools to exchange symbolic information is essential. No single tool is likely to deliver a manifestation of the everyday sacred. Together with professional designers, the community can, however, intentionally oscillate between intuitive and precise tools to keep their skill set fresh and combine this with imagination, creativity, theoretical and practical knowledge, and previous experience to invent a stunning proposal. Drawing tools matter, but this is just the beginning of the difficulty of manifesting, because this step requires tracing core values back to their roots, deciphering the research about attachment to a place, connecting the research findings to the everyday experience of the family or community, and applying these to the situation at hand. This must not be done by a professional designer alone but in collaboration with the client group. This relies on a new language to communicate ideas inherent in revealing the sacred.

In this chapter, we describe a framework and language to facilitate the manifestation of what is truly cherished. It is more technical than previous steps. It introduces concepts and words central to sacredness not used in daily conversation. Some may seem unnecessarily abstract at first, but we have found that this framework and language is the most effective and efficient means to designing the sacred of all the methods we have tested. The framework is based on the most basic needs that the sociologist W. I. Thomas (1863–1947) described as four wishes. We organize this step of manifesting around these four wishes, describing each wish as a series of types of settings that satisfy that wish. For example, the wish for certainty is evident in settings related to survival, order, and a worldview, explaining the inexplicable and ritual. Then there is a brief review of research that informs communication about how to conceive and create places of certainty, followed by suggested design actions to manifest certainty. We then describe how each wish may turn into a monster if taken to an extreme. Using the wish for certainty again, excessive measures for making places for safety and security actually generates more fear and creates risk-adverse environments, which, in turn, negatively affects other wishes such as new experience. One example are playgrounds that are safe but so boring that child-development goals are stifled, so children do not enjoy playing there and the playground instead becomes a meeting place for drug deals. In this chapter, we offer ways to satisfy the basic need for certainty without the disastrous side effects caused by the monster of fear.

Although it is awkward, we must begin by acknowledging the framework that W. I. Thomas provided. Recall the four wishes from Step 3: certainty, new experience, reciprocal response, and belonging and their counterparts of excess, the four monsters. These four wishes, reminiscent of basic needs described by Thomas a century ago, encapsulate the domains of sacred place. [1] Thomas is best known for his seminal work on Polish immigrants to the United States, though he directly addresses the topic of the most basic human needs in a 1923 research report. In that, he describes four "forces which impel [people] to action." He coins them the wishes: the desires for security, new experience, response, and recognition. Read them within their historic context. Pay attention to the essence of each wish and not the literal words of his time. Think about how the places you love satisfy each wish. He details them as follows:

Security. "The desire for security . . . is based on fear, which tends to avoid death, expresses itself in timidity, avoidance, and flight. The individual dominated by it is cautious, conservative, and apprehensive, tending also to regular habits, systematic work, and the accumulation of property."

New experience. "The desire for new experience is . . . emotionally related to anger, which tends to invite death, and expresses itself in courage, advance, attack, pursuit. The desire for new experience implies, therefore, emotion, change, danger, instability, social irresponsibility. The individual dominated by it shows a tendency to disregard prevailing standards and group interests. He may be a social failure on account of his instability, or a social success if he converts his experiences into social values, puts them into the form of a poem, makes of them a contribution to science."

Response. "The desire for response . . . is primarily related to the instinct of love, and shows itself in the tendency to seek and to give signs of appreciation in connection with other individuals . . . In general the desire for response is the most social of the wishes. It contains both a sexual and a gregarious element. It makes selfish claims, but on the other hand it is the main source of altruism. The devotion to child and family and devotion to causes, principles, and ideals may be the same attitude in different fields of application."

Recognition. "This wish [of recognition] is expressed in the general struggle of men for position in their social group, in devices for securing a recognized, enviable, and advantageous social status . . . The showy motives connected with the appeal for recognition we define as "vanity"; the creative activities we call 'ambition.' . . . Society alone is able to confer status on the individual and in seeking to obtain it he makes himself responsible to society and is forced to regulate the expression of his wishes. His dependence on public opinion is perhaps the strongest factor impelling him to conform to the highest demands which society makes upon him." [2]

Yes, you have to get beyond the gender discrimination, old-fashioned judgments, and 100 year-old conventions to see the utility of Thomas's framework. This framework encapsulates classic and recent research about deep attachment to place, and it is concise enough to be used in relating the research directly to design. It creates a simple language for sorting values about place into categories that can be demonstrated in physical design. In this chapter, we expand upon the principles of the four wishes, interpret them to be more culturally relevant today, and suggest planning and design actions that can be used to achieve the wishes and tame the monsters in one's physical place at home and in the community.

Once manifesting happens and a sacred landscape exists, it plays multiple roles: Place is a causal agent, a partner in the process of formulating values and also the symbol of those values.[3] Because values about place may be acknowledged consciously within the individual and community or subconsciously held as a memory and in dreams, a sacred place provides multiple ways of experiencing and knowing these values, not distinguishing between reason and emotion.[4] A homogeneous society tends to share an integrated set of abiding attachments to a place, while a diverse society's attachment is more complex, with fewer shared values related to a place. Though meaning embodied in a place varies from person to person and society to society, no one is divorced altogether from a deep attachment to place, which Yi-Fu Tuan long ago labeled *topophilia.*[5]

As we saw in Step 1: Awakening, childhood plays a particular role in attachment to a place and the formation of values. Landscapes that manifest security, identity, and reciprocity are sought-out early in life and form the basis of personal understanding. Landscapes of adventure and social recognition continually contribute to and expand a person's values about place. Places empowered with values maintain the ability to trigger thoughts, emotions, and morality throughout life. They become more sacred as we maintain and tend them through firsthand involvement and sustained commitment; they cannot nourish us without being nourished in return. [6]

Because the process of making deeply held values evident through design is complicated by its difficulty, a few words about how to use this chapter are in order. We suggest reading the entirety to understand the types of settings that reveal the four wishes and some possible planning and design strategies to achieve each objective. As you read, think about the environmental issue or design project you are presently trying to address, or consider this chapter in context of your manifesto or actions stimulated by earlier steps in this book. If one wish strikes you as singularly central to your life or present work, concentrate on that wish. Try to apply the theory, research, and strategies to your project. Yet do not be limited by the strategies we offer. Create your own when ours do not fully help you. Your imagination might be more effective than solutions we offer. Untangle the wish from the monster. Draw possible ways to manifest the sacred. Try new tools to communicate with your family or community using the language of that wish. Apply the results in a participatory design process. Do not be afraid of screwing up something as you apply this method. Remember, it is difficult to master right away. Practice on some easy projects. We begin this adventure by manifesting the wish for certainty.

Wish 1: Places of Certainty

Securing rootedness in a place is essential for our sense of certainty. Places of certainty provide safety, survival, and order amidst the chaos we perceive around us and give us the opportunity to develop a worldview and fulfilling rituals. Without such places, there is no protection for survival, no foundation from which to venture, and no origin point to compare oneself in relation to others. Security-pursuing behavior is markedly conservative and stasis seeking, resulting in places that maintain or recreate comforting previously experienced settings. Certainty typically originates as personal space, beginning as a small territory surrounding the body. This territory provides a protected center with safe enclosure and clear boundaries. [7] For most, the home place is the primary setting that stimulates security and grounds us in the safety of self, family, neighbors, and the larger society. Later, home usually becomes a memory and a symbol of protection. So important is a secure setting that, if there is a prevailing sense of rootlessness in a person's life, self and community development are likely irreparably stunted. [8]

We identify five types of settings of certainty that provide distinct benefits and implications for the design and planning of habitation: settings of survival, order, worldview, explanations of the inexplicable, and ritual. Before you read further, think about the places where you feel the safest, the most secure. Then consider the places where you feel unsafe. Make a list of your safe and unsafe settings. Describe what makes them so. Think about how you can make unsafe places safer.

Survival

For most of human history we have depended directly on the environment to help us live long enough to reproduce without being eaten, catching a fatal disease, or dying catastrophically. We have recognized safe places that allow us to survive through intimate local wisdom of, attachment to, and consecration of the inhabited landscape. This dependence on the landscape partially explains the profoundly respectful relationship that indigenous people have with their environments. Some first people, farmers, and fishermen still retain these bonds with the landscape they inhabit, because if they did not, they would perish.

It is often assumed that people living comfortably in developed countries lack such intimate dependence on their landscapes for survival. Recent discoveries, however, suggest that acknowledging sacred places is a survival tactic for all societies, even the most developed. The simple conclusion is that we have inherited a love of living things and landscapes from ancestors with genetic traits extraordinarily in tune with their local landscape. [9] They were the few who survived to reproduce successfully to become the population we are today. Therefore, we, the survivors, are genetically synchronized to our environment. According to this thesis, we have chromosomes that sanctify the territory that provides us with shelter safe from danger and suitable for reproducing.

Genetic topophilia has programmed us to covet places from which we can see and not be seen, to sense danger without being discovered. The observer is in a superior and hidden position, raised above the surrounding with an expansive view. [10] These settings of surveillance are often sacred personally and collectively, though often unconsciously. In one research project, Randy and Marcia included "to look out and not be seen" in a long checklist of reasons why certain places in a community are valued. Over and over, when the list was read to interviewees, there would be a pause followed by a smile of discovery and then a verbal response like, "Why, yes! I never thought of it before, but yes."

Such areas of surveillance are provided by prospect-refuges, archetypically a wooded mountain-top surrounded by open land that offers unobstructed views from a place of hidden safety. Observe a deer approach a clearing from a forest: It invariably pauses, unmoving in the camouflaged vegetation and shadow, nostrils open and quivering, posture alert, eyes, and ears sensing safety or danger in the exposed openness beyond. This setting of unobscured surveillance unquestionably affords the deer's survival. Of course, people today do not fear being eaten by a predator in daily life as does a deer, but we do feel a level of security in settings where we are hidden and have a view of or over the landscape. An aedicula on a hilltop, an attic window, or a treetop perch overlooking one's neighborhood can provide such valued settings. [11] Likewise, a savannah landscape or scattered trees in a grassy park may trigger survival genes, telling us we are safe.

Safety in daily life has a powerful social overlay beyond genetics. Urban survival requires street smarts and knowledge of how to read the cultural dangers of places. We learn to cherish areas of "low crime" and condemn "crime-infested" territories. The dangerous unknown, overgrown, dark, or public places are to be avoided. The presumed safety provided by gated communities and locked and alarmed houses are sought out by those with means. Conversely, some seek neighborhoods dense enough so that residents keep their eyes on the street to prevent criminal activity. [12] These settings may spawn sacredness just as powerfully as an aedicula or savannah landscape.

Besides physical and social safety to survive, we must also have the security of shelter, food, water, and disposal or reuse of waste. The places and territory that provided these essential resources were sanctified originally by genetic triggers and later by cultural convention. Home included not only shelter, but also a community or region from which we derived food, water, and additional resources for clothing, good health, and prosperity. Personal space and expanded territory were and are imperative needs. [13] More sophisticated societies typically lose sight of their direct connections to these resources until they are threatened. In recent generations, the anxiety of a mobile culture has been somewhat curtailed by strategies to secure resources necessary for survival such as the back-to-the-land movement, the Clean Water Act of 1972, our impulsive gardening, the farm-to-fork movement, and the legislation to preserve agricultural land. In each case, old territories and places are resanctified when the society awakens to the reality of a threat to their landscape (Fig. 98).

The most vulnerable populations, however, are constantly reminded of the value of precious resources. They are denied shelter, food, and water by war, natural disasters, corruption, and neglect. These populations are not all residents of foreign countries; the working poor survive in the U.S. as well by a tenuous dependence upon their marginal territories. For example, a homeless friend of Randy's, Joe Speed, slept in the stairwell of a parking garage until he was evicted by the police. For a time, he earned the eight dollars a day to buy food and warmth at the homeless shelter. He did this by washing office windows and the cars of lawyers downtown. But he considered the shelter more dangerous than sleeping in an abandoned car, so he moved. He nearly froze to death one January when a long rain interrupted his work. He knows how his life relies on his environment and says he is constantly learning new ways of the streets. Prison life was much easier for him because survival was guaranteed through the provision of life-giving services—food, water, bed, toilet, shower, table, and chair. Joe works hard, never begs, and continues to build his business through inventive ways of washing cars at the street curb, but the basic needs of life are never certain for him. He hopes to have a place all his own.

For most of us threats to survival are increasingly indirect. Dangers like climate change, air pollution, genetically engineered foods, lack of exercise, and the increase of new consumer entreaties threaten us in abstracted ways that lack a direct connection with personal safety. We have been bombarded with nascent threats since 1962, when Rachel Carson, in *Silent Spring*, sounded the alarm about chemicals that were poisoning us in the name of progress. [14] These dangers defy genetic preparation, urban savvy, and the traditional places of safe retreat. They require complex reasoning and intelligent problem solving across disciplines, scales, and social barriers. They require places where we can take

Fig. 98. Advanced societies paid little attention to food security until recent health scares. Now, an increasing number of cities, both in the U.S. and abroad, are preserving agricultural land to provide local, organic produce directly to urban households.

action to combat these arising threats. The settings that will be sanctified in these efforts already are expanding the survival heritage to include the Kyoto Protocol, Paris Agreement, Ramsar, and river-restoration and food-justice movements.

How should we reconfigure our habitation to address these issues? Because these problems are so overwhelming, it may seem pollyannaish to offer suggestions, but we must start somewhere. These actions range across every urban scale, from regional form to details of site and building design. At the largest scale, these actions are appropriate:

- *Secure the essentials locally.* Reshape our towns and cities to produce basic resources of clean air, soil, and water, healthy food and housing, energy, and recycling within the region and design the places of their production so they are experienced as part of everyday life. Consider modest examples. Schoolyard gardens allow students to harvest their own food and learn firsthand its nutritional value and safety from pesticides. Garage apartments increase diversity and provide affordable housing by integrating renters into single-family, owner-occupied neighborhoods.
- *Supply life-giving provisions.* Each urban area should provide for the basic needs of underserved populations. At a minimum, this includes places to sleep, wash, eat, and relieve oneself. Public

restrooms with showers, soup kitchens, and homeless shelters may provide these temporarily as long as they are integrated within the community. Lasting solutions include inexpensive owner-built housing and places to work according to ability and to grow one's own food.

- *Address indirect threats.* Identify opportunities for citizens to participate directly in healing diminished local ecosystems and taking personal action to address threats to personal and environmental health. As examples, reforestation projects increase wildlife habitat and sequester carbon; reintroduction of top predators balances ecosystems; repair of coastal wetlands improves water quality and reduces storm damage inland; restoration of rivers saves endangered species, supplies fish markets, and reduces flooding; safe sidewalks, walking trails, greenways, healing gardens, and urban wilderness areas encourage people to improve their own physical and mental health.

At the smaller scale, these actions are important:

- *Survey for safety.* Enhance the sense of security in public places by increasing the number of "legitimate users," those who adhere to norms of conformity within a society, using appropriate dress, language, and behavior. Non-conforming or marginal people like new immigrants, the poor, homeless, and even teenagers are often considered illegitimate users who scare others away, but when more "legitimate" people use a place, the "scary" people become less scary. Conforming people attract many types of people to a place, making the place seem safe by diluting the dominance of any one group and inviting diverse users. Likewise, design adjacent land uses to guarantee eyes on the street and provide sight lines to see danger at a distance, making a place feel safer. A park with open space in the center edged by a canopy of trees affords such surveillance.
- *Look out without being seen.* Create prospect-refuges within the public landscape. This may manifest as an aedicula on a hilltop or roof, an observatory on top of a promontory, a hilltop in a park, a tree in a grassy expanse, a public room on the top floor of a tall building, or a bridge overlook. Now, think about a few additional actions you might take that would enhance your sense of safety and survival. Are there actions you would add to your manifesto? You might consider growing more of your own food organically, working to save an endangered species from extinction, building housing for homeless people, or any number of manifestations of basic certainty.

Order

A second security-seeking need is for order. When the environment we inhabit becomes excessively disordered, some even go into a rage for order. Rage highlights its import as a source of security. At its most basic, ordering provides a sense of orientation (Fig. 99). To our primal selves this begins

Fig. 99. The lighthouse (left) and lighthouse keeper's home (right) at Corolla, North Carolina, order the world around them, providing orientation for ships for centuries and serving as an enduring center for generations of the keeper's family.

with reading the landscape so we do not get hopelessly lost, whether in a fearful forest, alien neighborhood, or large parking lot at the mall. Am I deeply inside the woods or close to a clearing leading out of the woods? Does this street appear major enough to lead me to the center of the neighborhood, or am I going in the wrong direction to the boundary with another neighborhood? Am I parked in the middle of Section B or just outside it? Orientation requires primarily a clear sense of center and boundary, which together establish inside and out. Also helpful are design mechanisms that distinguish clearly between near and far, up and down, front and back, beside and on top of, above and below, within sight or beyond the horizon. Each is grounded in the relationship of our bodies to the earth and surrounding landscape. We must know not only where we are, but where we are headed, how to get there, and how to recognize when we have arrived. Urban designers facilitate a sense of orientation in the city by making the public environment as legible as possible with clear nodes, edges, landmarks, paths, and districts. [15] Amber is away from St. Louis for long enough periods of time that she often gets turned around exploring a new part of downtown. When she does, she pauses and scans the skyline until she finds the Gateway Arch to the east. By studying its shape from her vantage point she can determine whether she is northwest or southwest of a desired destination.

For most people, home is the primary means of ordering. Home provides the concretization of inside and out, up and down, and near and far. [16] It is our physical and emotional center. This is as true for the family home in a Los Angeles suburb as it is for the pole staked in the ground wherever nomadic tribes spend the night or for thousands of African Americans returning to North Carolina and other places in the South where, in spite of lingering racism, they feel their emotional roots calling them home. [17] Home is full of majestic dullness: "Home is a place where the nondescript is sanctified by its necessary place in a system, where sublimity and predictability coincide, and moral grandeur results from the combination of alertness with incapacity for boredom in boring surroundings." [18] Our need for order makes the home sacred, because home defines a clear center and boundary.

Beyond a sense of space and direction, in our rage for order we seek ways to arranges things so they make sense to us as individuals, usually by creating generalized categories of similar items, establishing hierarchies and social position, and planning steps to be followed. With categorization accomplished, we can maintain a state of peace and serenity, because "everything is in its place." This expression rightfully indicates that order is dependent upon and practically impossible without being grounded in a place. Having everything in its place helps us understand life's inconsistencies and paradoxes. Hip as it may sound to live amongst constant change in our surroundings, we usually are more content with an orderly and understandable environment from which to contextualize irregularities. [19] Simplified oppositional classes—such as city and nature, big and little, light and dark, and black and white, clean and dirty, winter and summer color—are especially useful in constructing categories of security.

We also order the world in terms of desirable scale still based largely on Leonardo de Vinci's drawing, the Vitruvian Man (ca. 1490 CE). This standard is grounded in the relative proportion of parts of our bodies, our body to architecture, and architecture to cosmos. These comparative relations supposedly give a harmonious relationship, proving a sense of balance and stability from the nearby environment to what we perceive as the distant, including the universe beyond what we know. We further project and intermix self and landscape in descriptions such as "headwaters," "mouth of the river," "foothills," "shoulder" of the mountain, "finger" lakes, or the "brow" of a cliff. Landscape personifications serve to humanize the surroundings and establish a subconscious security in places of human scale, measurable in hand size, arm's length, and eye level. These connect us to places of proportions we find proper in the regional landscape.

Ordering suggests the following actions for shaping our habitation:

- *Clarify orientation.* Provide a sense of center and boundary, in and out, up and down, and cardinal direction in a project and in civic design. Reinforce natural and person-made landmarks, edges, nodes, travel routes, and districts to make the environment legible. Simplify unnecessary complexity in the public landscape to express what is fundamental, not incidental. Avoid ambiguity in spatial layout. [20]

- *Order with simple categories.* Create a hierarchy of inhabited space with centers of home life, neighborhood, city, and region and of natural boundaries for each neighborhood and city. Use simple oppositional classes in designing the public environment. Uncomplicated and familiar contrasts like light and dark, open and closed spaces provide comforting order for most people.

- *Scale the city to the body.* Reform cities in a human scale with buildings made of materials from hand sized to average height and arm span. Monumental buildings should be reserved for expression of noble public values. Avoid overly large corporate and governmental architecture that suggests the insignificance of individuals and community. Embrace figurative art. Connect the body to the region by emphasizing recognizable local landscape features like headwaters and finger lakes in the design of the city.

Worldview

A worldview also provides certainty. More complex than ordering, a worldview establishes relationships between people, the local community and environment, and the rest of the world. Beginning with a primal order of a local center where we structure an explanation of what the immediate and faraway universe is, a worldview goes beyond to explore how our place works and how we think it should work.[21] The places associated with a worldview give form to individual and group attitudes, beliefs, and values. At the most protected core, we usually place ourselves and home. The center is defended by a boundary beyond which we form associations with others and the landscape.[22] For security we instinctively try to keep this worldview fixed and invariable.[23] Nonetheless, we modify, reshape, reconstruct, and reorganize our worldviews into fabrics of personal meaning as we grow with experience. A worldview is an intertwined bundle of fundamental social values and environmental mores, forged largely by the environments we experience around us and our reactions to new pressures from the outside. Its framework may be flat or round, urban or rural, wooded or barren, new or old-fashioned, optimistic or hopeless, inclusive or exclusive, egalitarian or elitist, vigorous or passive. A healthy worldview is confident about the certainty of fundamental principles yet flexible enough to evolve as experience informs it.

Worldviews are not just constructs in our heads; we find or make some literal place that reflects our worldview back to us. That place is the symbol by which we refer to our worldview, and it allows us to come to grips with the world as it is or might be.[24] A worldview remains hopelessly abstruse and prevents function in daily activities until made solid in place.[25] Placing a worldview requires both a concretized schema of a best possible, idealized world and an image of that world expressed in the form of our habitation and the built environment. This manifestation of the world is powerful, because it locates us in time, space, relationships, and beliefs and directs our behavior.[26] Every era, generation, nation-state, city, community, and person has a prevailing worldview manifested in how they plan and build. A most important spatial quality for a confident yet flexible worldview is holism and consistency of architecture and city design, based on the local landscape and economy (Fig. 100).

Fig. 100. A worldview that is well-articulated in the built environment manifests a vision and values for all who pass by. This park communicates Taoist and Buddhist teachings through ritual practices.

The form of home often reflects our personal worldview in microscopic scale.[27] It can be a machine for living in which a technical order replaces or complements a moral order. It can be a commodity or a real-estate investment rather than a homestead. It can be a complex mechanism surrounded by a garden or an ancestral hearth of unambiguous simplicity.[28] We may make it with our own hands or have it mass-produced. Our worldview can be dominated by the fear of the outside, internal power relationships, or visions of the future. For example, the arrangement of some African villages expresses a protection from the outer world relative to the most cherished aspects of the tribe. A boundary of thick thorn brush fortifies defense against the threatening outside. The primary assets of society—the chief, men, cattle, and other animals—are placed at the most protected center, indicating they are most valuable in this worldview. Women occupy the least secure outer realm. On many Depression-era farmsteads, the rural American house remained unsecured while the smokehouse was locked, where an essential though meager supply of meat was kept. This worldview suggests that the security of the food supply was more vulnerable and valuable than anything else. Although we do not surround our homes with thorn bushes or lock our stores in the smokehouse, we are similarly preoccupied with securing our computers and entertainment centers with passwords and virus protection.

From these conceptions of home, a worldview radiates outward to the civic landscape. There, it may collide with other worldviews, creating conflicts between a community and individual, sympathy for and destruction of nature, or quantitative and qualitative progress. The view may be traditional or hypertraditional, a spectacle or authentic experience.[29] The larger landscape may be constraining or limitless, domestic or wild in the American mind.[30] The enclosed schema of the cloister garden and the open plan of the plaza express contrasting worldviews from the Middle Ages and Renaissance. Similarly, the grand axes in the expansive gardens of Versailles versus the modest pathways at Shugakuin reflect contradicting worldviews. Interstate highways and autobahns reflect our exuberant embrace of freedom and mobility in the modern era just as the fantasy landscapes of Dubai now echo post-post-modern views of fragmentation.

Change is slower for individuals and societies in isolated, traditional communities and much accelerated in global cities. Tension arises when the natural formation of a worldview, which is inherently both static and changing, is interrupted. Tension converts to outright resistance when the interruption threatens the worldview with sudden and brutal change due to accelerated growth, conquest, colonialization, conversion, globalization, disaster, exploitation, or advances in technology.[31] The ongoing controversy about removing Confederate memorials illustrates the point. Although simmering after decades of Jim Crow, the worldview of Black Lives Matter brought racism into public debate in a way that a collision of deeply held views was inevitable: The dominant memory of white Southerners of heroic rebel ancestors and the Lost Cause squared off against a worldview in which statues celebrating racist oppression must be forever removed as daily reminders that black lives did not and do not matter. Public officials and the public in thousands of towns face critical choices. Will removal reduce racism or simply promote "out of sight, out of mind" forgetfulness? Are there alternative solutions inspired by the fearless girl standing up to the Wall Street bull, the conversation across the water between the Martin Luther King, Jr. and Thomas Jefferson memorials, a monument to victims of lynching, the Civil Rights fire hose and police dog sculptures in Kelly Ingram Park in Birmingham, or Joe Minter's nearby found-object interpretations of overcoming racism? Thoughtful depictions of this moment when American worldviews turned prevailing views upside down might create new meaning to places that embrace resistance.

Design helps form and nurtures healthy worldviews but only if designers understand and evaluate the prevailing worldview(s) where they work. Unfortunately, most designers simply give form either to their personal or the dominant worldview, even if it is unhealthy or unjust. To inhabit the sacred requires designers to offer counter-views to the placelessness that results from repeating a single dominant worldview.[32] Some of the implications for inhabiting the sacred by manifesting healthy worldviews include the following:

- *Nurture confidence and flexibility.* Neither parochial nor ungrounded worldviews serve us well today; worldviews that are both centered and richly expansive are essential. We must provide environments that inculcate thinking across scales and disciplines, that microscope and telescope from minute details of locality to regional and international flyways.[33] Because the home is most central to the formation of a worldview, parents and architects must carefully assess the impact of house form on child development. We advocate avoiding home as a machine, threat, or commodity. We urge stability, simplicity, and compassion to create a secure core that, with time, expands to embrace complexity, mastery, and empowerment. A kitchen table around which the family gathers daily might exemplify security. Places to build forts, meet other cultures, and explore nature might later encourage flexibility.

- *Ground the worldview.* Unify neighborhoods and civic areas by using primarily the building types most distinctive of that place. Repeat patterns that are suitable to the climate such as adobe and deep-shaded arcades in the American Southwest. Root every design in the ecology of the region. Use topography, hydrological patterns, plants, and climate to express the inherent regionality. Native materials do this best and should dominate the landscape. Allow the natural systems to provide the necessary diversity to encourage healthy choices. Avoid unnecessary fragmentation of the town or city, which often occurs when an architect imports an inappropriate style. Although designers in our era champion the new and different, healthy worldviews are nurtured through a sense of holism. Nurture local economies based on the distinct resources of each region that allow and encourage people to stay in one place long enough to form worldviews grounded in place rather than continuously migrating elsewhere in search of work.[34]

- *Manifest various worldviews.* Make invisible power tangible in the design of public landscapes so people understand the external vested interests shaping their worldviews. In the process of city making, designers should help communities identify distinct and conflicting worldviews. The tension may uncover values that must be resisted or consciously changed to better inhabit the sacred. In some cases, the conflict may spark innovative solutions for longstanding problems. Eco-revelatory design does this by exposing multiple layers of a site's history, industrial wastes, and toxic land uses and contrasting those with garden-city landscapes.

Explaining the Inexplicable

Mysterious human occurrences have always terrified and fascinated us.[35] The best-informed science cannot account for everything; therefore, we are compelled to explain God, illness, death, luck, and natural catastrophes. To do so myth, religion, and history are constructed.

Humankind tends to tame the utterly mysterious by making it sacred. As a small example, the four-year-old daughter of a colleague was extending bedtime in the shadows of her father's late-night discussion about this topic. Seemingly oblivious to the serious talk, she suddenly inserted, "Letterman turned mystery into history." She had grasped the essence of this human need and described it in terms of the conflict between Letterman and Spellbinder, cartoon characters on public television who taught children to spell through the battle between evil Spellbinder who created chaos by stealing letters from words and replacing them with confounding ones. Spellbinder might insert "R" for "C" in "Cat," instantly making "Rat," creating chaos in the preschool world. Letterman, like all good action heroes, would save the day and create security by returning the stolen letters. In this case, Letterman created certainty by turning metaphorical "mystery" into "history." History is sacred to many cultures, because it becomes an authority of the past so that we no longer debate it and can use it as a reference to the present and future.

Creation and our relationship to God are particularly confounding. Our need to comprehend origins and connections to higher powers shapes myth and then religion and, in turn, some of the most powerful places of sacredness.[36] We designate notable settings where things are born or originate, where the sun and water are sacred. In most cultures, there are places where God first created this world or humankind. Mountain tops, rocks, springs, forests and individual trees, or unusual geologic formations stir our memories of godly intervention. For example, on Mount Kurama in Japan, God came to Earth several million years ago and inhabited an outcrop of rocks. Shintoists not only worship there because the landscape represents godly forces, but also to communicate directly with the *kami* (godly spirit) who inhabits the rocks. This place explains the inexplicable and subsequently symbolizes these explanations; a rock can be God and represent God simultaneously. Once we have constructed a thesis for these matters about which we are uncertain, we become inflexible in our defense of that reality, as can be observed in present debates about creation, global warming, abortion, genetic engineering, gay marriage, and many civic design and land-use decisions.

In addition to making elements in the landscape sacred, religious faith structures the way we build our habitation and places of worship. Myth confers orientation by a set of fixed points some of which are conceptual and others topographical. Geometry from its beginning was rationalized as a gift from God that led to a system of spatial arrangements in which the mystery of life's difficulties could be solved by positioning things properly (Fig. 101). The proper form of the building—religious, civic and domestic—was descended from a heavenly prototype, representing either the form we imagine a more heavenly place to be or the way we think the gods want it arranged.[37] Gothic cathedrals prescribe to a strict code of proportions that allow the vaulted ceiling to tower high above the heads of the congregation, symbolizing the power of God over man. In the American context, early Anglican churches were single-story rectangles, with the main door facing west and the altar in the chancel at the east end. Dissenting religions felt the church referred only to the congregation, the living body of Christ; they refused to sanctify the building structure itself. Quakers, among others, call the place of worship a meetinghouse unembellished by crosses and towers, appointed only by benches around a central pulpit. Each represents distinct interpretations of proper geometry to satisfy godliness.

The heavenly prototype informs not just religious institutions, but also public buildings and home. *Feng shui* has directed the layout of imperial cities and the site plans of individual dwellings for centuries, down to the minute detail of locating a shokesan, a small ceramic warrior, on the street-facing roof to ward off demons and other mischief. Similarly, from the sixth dynasty in Egypt a winged disc

Fig. 101. Religious architecture like Kiyomizudera in Kyoto conveys clarity about the proper relationship between self and other, grants wishes, matches lovers, and transforms mystery into history.

representing the sun was placed on the side of building to banish evil. Such ornamentation served as a body-like tattoo to protect important structures.[38]

To satisfy our need to honor the deceased and cope with impermanence, we make death and other losses comprehensible in built form as memorials. Memorials take many shapes but typically focus on a single spot that marks the body or tragedy in a precise location. This place then centers grief, celebration, and direct communication with the mortal. Commonly, death is sanctified in pyramids, cemeteries, earth-mound burials, and, in some cases, natural features in the larger landscape. Tragic loss of life creates the most emotionally charged of all public places, like Gettysburg and the Holocaust, Vietnam, and 9/11 memorials. At a smaller scale, personal losses motivate individuals and family to create shrines and gardens. Fito's Place celebrates a life, reminds the community that no suspect has been identified, and provides Amber a spot to continue cultivating their love. Randy's home place at Hester's Store, North Carolina, has a family cemetery and a circle of love, a protective ring of native cedar trees, which his cousins and children planted to honor the affection received from aunts and uncles. The fourteen cedars interlocked in loving embrace now create a contemplative enclosure to show gratitude for family security, to praise ancestors for their moral instruction, and to remind us of our commitment to extended family (Fig. 102).

People also have a need to comprehend and cope with misfortunes such as unlucky household events and natural disasters. To account for such vagaries we enshrine methods of fortune in buildings and landscape. As examples, in Cambodia the form of the dwelling was shaped by the belief that the shade of a tree or tree roots under someone's home brings bad luck.[39] The house had to adapt to its site to avoid calamity or trees had to be removed. The Tongva Indians of Southern California sanctified fault lines by avoiding them altogether and performing rituals at a safe distance in an effort to keep the sleeping giant from destroying the earth with his violent shaking when he was angered.[40] Today, we may simply be unaware of, deny, or ignore the risk. Generally, we reduce the risk artificially rather than sanctify dangerous territory through avoidance. We may think our technology is invincible, which then allows us to buy earthquake-disaster insurance and build in spite of the taboo terrain, fault zones, and alluvial soils. Nonetheless, myths about luck infiltrate our lives, because our understanding remains limited. Natural hazards like floodplains, steep slopes, barrier islands, and coastal damage from a rising sea are just recently being reconsidered in light of uncertainty, emerging ecological science, and lingering conflict between native wisdom and profitable progress.[41] Contentious debates about these lands are common, and the outcomes of the conflicts will determine whether the land is sacred or profane and to whom. Many of the things that are inexplicable in our present world relate to ecological catastrophe and the collapse of an ecosystem. Our myth-making can help us reverse the trends or allow us to retreat into denial. Nonetheless, we need spaces where we can gauge our efforts to the betterment of humankind in a fragile environment.

As a whole, our efforts to comprehend the incomprehensible shape habitation in powerful ways, giving us ritualistically sacred architecture in the form of a heavenly prototype and landscapes where

Fig. 102. From cedar circles to open fields, the landscape around the
Hester's homeplace in North Carolina provides opportunities for the
present generation to communicate with ancestors about good fortune
and terrible loss.

God, faith, death, and their symbols reside. Inexplicable luck or misfortune is also the terrain of many
of our most contested urban and wild lands. Landscapes that embody both uncertainty and threats to
survival, like ecosystems about to collapse, are particularly unsettling to our sense of security. Uncertainty has inspired some of the world's most sacred architecture, and myths surrounding our deepest
unknowns can do the same by following these design directions:

- *Acknowledge doubts about origins and God.* Choose a few places in each community to collect
  and express the facts and uncertainty of science, experience, and belief. These places might
  be traditionally sacred sites like places of worship, burial, or nature. Or they might take new
  forms as Libraries of Uncertainty or Museums of Present-day Myths. Use them to make
  places for collective and individual expressions of bewilderment, grief, faith, enlightenments,
  and the confusion of science. Combine these with the science that is known to clarify evolution,
  social trends, poverty, and ecological principles.
- *Manifest transience and loss.* Create markers where impermanence and tragedy are noted, not
  avoided. Spontaneous memorials are one of the most genuine expressions of feelings about
  uncertainty; they should be encouraged in the public landscape.

- *Express faith.* Respect places of primal belief as well as organized religion and science. Preserve and restore natural places to communicate with the gods. This includes landscapes as grand as Mauna Kea in Hawaii (discussed in Step 4) or as inconspicuous as a hidden artesian spring that Jimmy Jay Winslow took Randy to in Bushy Fork, North Carolina. To him it was a worthy sacred place.

- *Avoid unnatural misfortune.* Acknowledge phenomenological experience and faith-based knowledge as well as hard science in the participatory process of city making. Sift carefully through these to find inspiration for urban form that avoids the misfortune of what we often label as natural disasters. They are not natural; rather they are manmade and predictable and can be annulled. Avoid these unnatural catastrophes by sanctifying territories of ecological instability like floodplains, storm surges, rising sea levels, liquefaction zones, and steep slopes. Then focus on the incomprehensible nature of ecological collapse and the complexity of poisonous living; develop a framework that combines myth with science to address causes not symptoms.

Ritual

Repetition of the same activity over and over in the same place gives a sense of certainty, makes places of habitual behavior sacred, and creates local tradition.[42] There are hundreds of patterned behaviors in our everyday lives, and all offer a certain amount of security. Some behaviors reinforce negative values, and others promote healthy values and improve ties with friends and family or physical fitness. Some are mundane and feel like chores, while others are special, even when performed daily. What behavior is sacred to whom depends on basic needs, individual values, and the quality of the place where the ritual occurs. For example, to teens and those in the fashion business, dressing may be special, but it is primarily a means to an end. For some, meals with family are sacred. Dressing is a necessary but thin value dependent upon quickly changing styles, but meals nourish the body, reinforce family values, and occur within special areas of the home. The clothing closet is usually utilitarian in its meaning, whereas the kitchen is often a sacred setting of everyday life, with inviolable patterns of spatial allocation, seating, speaking, and chores intermixed with love, mutual support, and communication with God. Randy's niece just objected to these generalizations. Nonetheless, only ritual activities with fundamental needs and strongly held values become habits of the heart. These may be everyday, routine actions or regularly recurring seasonal, annual, or episodic events. The flow characterized by regular recurrence is reassuring. In each of these habits there are rules, etiquette, and sequences to be followed, much like a Japanese tea ceremony. This habitual behavior becomes ritual, a ceaseless quest for conception and orientation. How and when things are done is often more important than what is done.[43] The rhythm of habit makes everyday and seemingly mundane places sacred. This reinforces the importance of locality, the utilitarian landscape, home, and neighborhood. Repeated interactions over an extended period create the strongest mark on our concept of valued place.[44]

Fig. 103. The ritual of luau in Haleiwa, Hawaii, is not only a festive gathering for food and music for native people, but also a means by which a sense of community and culture is maintained and conveyed to children.

Ritual behavior through special celebrations have long reinforced a sense of community and attachment to local landscape (Fig. 103). Events like parades, county fairs, and seasonal festivals celebrate national and local values. In Hillsborough, North Carolina, the Festival of the Eno calls attention to the Eno River's ecosystem. Classes help people make costumes and floats that represent native plants and animals. A parade of the creatures emerges from the river and proceeds up the main street, teaching viewers about critical environmental issues. The parade is centrally located, and the costumes are coordinated to produce a repeating unity. Events like the blessing of fishing fleets, rain dances, and consecration of crops expressly ask God to overcome unfavorable conditions such as rough seas, drought or famine that threaten safety and survival. Pilgrimages seeking God's grace or cures for illness are similarly governed by set procedures. The grace or cure is usually embedded in a particular place, making that spot the most holy, the culmination of a consecrated route. In most of these instances, elements of architecture and landscape intensify the ritual. Repeated columns, lancet arches, hundreds of *torii*, or blooming cherry trees heighten the drama of the event. Such syncopation of architecture provides a rhythm that evokes a sense of security.

Design, from the smallest detail of a dining table to the regional scale of a landscape, can support security-serving habit. Some simple directives can add significantly to a sense of certainty:

- *Ritualize healthy activity*. Create settings for healthy behavior that reinforce individual certainty and support family, neighboring, and civic engagement and connection to the local landscape. Identify places where shared rituals already occur, and make them more special through enhanced design. For many Americans, this needs to start with such basic things as designing a local park so it encourages neighbors to share in the community's events and daily rituals.
- *Celebrate community nearby*. Ritual events should be held in areas denoted as a parade ground or public open space so the event can occur in the same location each time. Locate these civic spaces centrally to make them available for everyday community life as well as special occasions. Design with repeated elements and typologies to heighten the drama of the special event and provide security in everyday use. When a successful public event outgrows its space, resist moving to a remote location; this relocation almost always diminishes the event's original specialness.

Monster 1: Fear

As we seek certainty we create our deepest and most abiding attachments to a place. These places ground us and provide a sense of place. They allow us to survive and thrive, to order everyday experience, to develop a worldview, to explain the incomprehensible, and to form ritual with others and the landscape. Until places that provide these needs are secured, we cannot function healthfully. We remain preoccupied with finding places that offer us certainty.

When uncertainty overwhelms certainty, fear dominates our lives. Uncertainty destabilizes us and renders our world as unreliable. It occupies us with doubt, confusion, skepticism, a lack of conviction, and, in extreme cases, utter nihilism. Uncertainty then fills us with anxiety, apprehension, or indifference about daily life and the years ahead. These incubate fear, which then gives rise to ruthless behavior and, in turn, destroys communities, defiles the landscape, and undermines democracy. Fear makes inhabiting the sacred impossible, because certainty is the basis from which the other wishes— new experience, reciprocity, and belonging—can be satisfied. Ever-present are sayings such as "Fear dominates all other stimuli"; "the driving force in human minds is fear"; "we hunger after certainty"; "we hold fetishly to a stable structure as a resort or haven against chaos"; "when we feel the world changing too fast, we evoke an idealized and stable past"; and "it is not power that corrupts, but fear." Excessive fear is a monster that robs us of life.[45] As our friend, Emily, stated succinctly after she did the awakening exercises, "The past hurts me; the future scares me."

There are fear-producing uncertainties everywhere today. Crime, economic instability, and housing foreclosures threaten our basic sense of daily safety. Large populations from other places, the homeless, gangs, and others we do not understand make us distrustful of the abstracted "other" and cautious about sharing public space with them. (The "other" is anyone different from us.) Rather than building friendships with new people, we install security systems and obsessively lock our homes and cars. Social and environmental dangers, both real and imagined, make us apprehensive about letting our children walk to school or play in nearby woods and creeks. Compounded with family crises, poor health, and job insecurity, fear can cripple us. It is further debilitating amongst rapid restructuring in our workplaces, advancements in communications and technology, and changes in the social makeup of our neighborhoods. War and terrorism keep us on edge. Oil spills, global warming, tweeted threats of nuclear war, and other ecological catastrophes flood the news and add to our anxiety. Many people grieve, despair, and feel powerless in the face of these environmental crises. This gives rise to ecoparalysis that debilitates the public and allows profiteers further unconstrained destruction of critical resources. A vicious cycle of greed, calamity, and disempowerment accelerates. Apprehension, alarm, and chaos dominate far too many worldviews. The world seems "senseless to many people because for the first time in modern history, it is relatively placeless."[46]

Excessive fear causes Americans to seek security in the wrong places. Temporary, false security is frequently achieved at great cost through an oversimplified, incorrect, or harmful order. As we sense the outside world becoming more chaotic and uncontrolled, we withdraw into the private domain of illusional safety and sometimes outright denial. People stay home or in safely controlled places that exclude the undesirable. Financially successful people lock up their homes and protect their assets, as if every passerby were a thief. Their assets include entertainment centers, pools, and sports equipment that were once part of community life. NIMBY attitudes maintain the fear-fuelled status quo.

The public domain is abandoned, as each household satisfies its needs privately. Few of us are out on the town, walking, celebrating with our friends, and talking to strangers, creating by our presence the safe civic environment we need in order to inhabit the sacred. Without more of us, the civic landscape becomes ever more frightening. We participate less in local public affairs. Community suffers and cannot nurture us. Democracy itself is weakened.

False security results in an unjust system inflexible to change or a self-defeating order grounded in a dysfunctional center.[47] This explains in part why some former slaves never left their plantation home places, reporting in old age that life was better before emancipation and why abused spouses might suffer repeatedly without escaping the abusive environment.[48] For some women and children, home becomes a ghetto or prison, a place where the only certainty is violence or the struggle of survival.[49]

False security also lulls those of us who are well-off and best equipped to address fear. For example, many who live quite intentionally are disempowered by the counterfeit certainty that thinking globally and acting locally offers. True, this helps, but it cannot defeat the local fears that are derived from distant forces of virtual capital and corporate privileges that are largely immune to any local action except resistance.

Taming Fear: Design for Intrepid Assurance

Fear appears to be a hopeless extinction vortex from which we cannot escape, but it is not. Fear can certainly cause panic, encourage mindless action, or turn to dread and completely immobilize us, but it does not have to. Rather, fear should alarm us into willful action and reformation.

The strategies for taming fear are actually straightforward. The alarm of fear has to be personally and publicly acknowledged. Then it needs to be sorted into categories of what can be directly addressed and what cannot. The goals must be both aspirational and practical. A foundation of reasonable assurance that encourages personal and public bravery must be created. At the same time, it is necessary to acknowledge that achieving absolute certainty is neither possible nor healthy because no change would ever occur. Ideally, strategies are shaped to allow tension between certainty and uncertainty, taking risks that lead to innovations that may make us more secure in the long run. Since fear originates both within and beyond ourselves, we must address both realms. This requires personal awakenings described in Step 1 and democratic actions similar to those in Steps 2, 3, and 4. Essentially, to convert fear into security, our communities must be familiar and friendly so that people recognize their neighbors and neighborhood, feel comfortable getting out of their cars and homes, and spending leisure and civic time in public places. Fortunately, a sense of security in the community is achievable with a few democratic actions to design our neighborhoods and cities, utilizing fear's energy to shape a hopeful future.

- *Make nostalgia progressive.* Preserve traditional buildings and walkable neighborhoods. Reuse of them for changing purposes accommodates both historical and contemporary needs. This design strategy might be thought of as progressive nostalgia, because it provides a secure framework for radically reshaping a future that is grounded in the glorious past and everyday present. It is also more sustainable than demolition and rebuilding.
- *Secure the center and boundary.* Likewise, a town or city can be made more secure by forming it with clear centers and natural boundaries. This provides access to nature and legibility in the landscape. Clarity is further enhanced through repetition of familiar and indigenous landscape and building patterns rooted in the region. Simplify overly complex urban areas to reduce an overload of excessive information. Do not add meaningless clutter. Build at a human scale. Resist making the city so safe and clean that it sanitizes life. The city must be clean enough to be safe and dirty enough to be happy.
- *Produce essentials locally.* Reinforce certainty by producing the most essential resources for daily life within the immediate region. This provides food security and energy, the assurance of clean water, soils, and air, and reuse with minimum waste. These processes should be integrated into the landscape that is experienced daily to reassure their healthy presence. This may influence land-use patterns to be multi-use and economies to be distinctively of the place.

- *Make risk transparent.* The most threatening natural processes need to be acknowledged appropriately: floodplains, liquefaction zones, slopes that are prone to landslides, and land below sea level should be sanctified, set aside, and protected for the purposes that natural processes require. Remove development from these areas or make the edge more naturally resilient. Use these areas to provide the essential ecological processes of food, fiber, water, and energy. These actions are a first step in combating ecoparalysis.
- *Acknowledge fear.* Cities should publicly acknowledge uncertainty with a special space to process fear and with rituals that transform fear into collective action. Americans are skilled at solving problems once brought to the public's attention, so fear should be similarly managed. An annual ritual of burning last year's fears might be appropriate as a community's New Year's event to help raise public awareness of those debilitating apprehensions. The Good Enough Festival described later in the section, "Wish 4: Places of Belonging" (pages 231–47), might inspire solutions to fears. Similarly, local stages need to be set from which false securities are exposed. Borrow from Fred Shuttlesworth, who planned local Civil Rights confrontations, hoping to provoke an over-reaction to stir national outrage to counter Bull Conner's brutal enforcement of segregation in Birmingham, Alabama. Virtual capital and corporate privileges should be so challenged from local places. Combine flash mobs, fire hoses, police dogs, and batons to galvanize national action against placeless investment and corporate advantage.
- *Celebrate many and create one.* To overcome fear of others, city policy must encourage rituals to celebrate *e pluribus unium*, oneness and diversity, our differences and our shared destiny. City design must create spaces where difference can be acknowledged face-to-face while conflict is negotiated. Parks with a large, central, and shared common space surrounded by raised small niches for distinct subcultural events provide one model for this. The alien "other" is not nearly so frightening, once known.
- *Secure housing for all.* Providing for the basic needs of those considered marginal is a similar matter. We do not talk much these days about the need for affordable housing and a safe homelife for all citizens. The poor and homeless scare us more when we feel our own finances and homelife threatened, and we become less concerned for others. This is a problem for all of us. The failure to secure housing for all of us threatens the safety and security of all of us. Secure housing must be made a national priority.
- *Revive participatory democracy.* Finally, active participation in everyday democracy banishes fear while securing and empowering us. Making our own places allows us to inhabit the sacred everyday. Participation in local politics and the local economy as part of daily life provides us with an unmatched sense of civic security. Participation in repairing degraded ecosystems like restoration of a stream heals broken landscapes and us simultaneously. Working to produce affordable housing builds healthy, diverse cities and a sense of shared destiny.

Participation in groups that address large-scale concerns provides us the means to assess our ecological and cultural footprints, take actions to reduce our negative impacts, and contribute to community building elsewhere. In concert, these strategies secure us, enable us with certainty enough to proceed, harness fear, and put it to good use. Before you leave the wish, think of the single most important spatial manifestation of certainty in your life. Then think of one new manifestation you would like to create in your home or community. Keep these in mind as you explore the next wish for new experiences.

Wish 2: Places of New Experiences

Places of new experiences stimulate risk, exploration, and discovery. These places are associated with the irresistible spice of danger, vulnerability, potential harm, and adventure.[50] They become sacred to the person or community both for their active role in the human or community growth they foster and their symbolism of that accomplishment. Growth is about the process of becoming something, reaching full potential, realizing one's complete capacity. It requires change. Growth is often associated with a child or city simply getting bigger, but this shortchanges the essence. Plenty of children and cities get bigger, taller, and fatter without becoming what they are capable of becoming. City designers now distinguish between urban expansion and a community's development. The first is about getting bigger, the second about reaching the city's collective potential. Reaching full potential is a fundamental tenet of inhabiting the sacred. It is a truly scary but fulfilling process that includes the exploration of new experiences and the making of places to develop identity, creativity, dreams and adventure.

New experiences do not arise independently; they generally require a secure platform to build upon. Formation of identity depends upon a certainty about a place that offers the confidence to test new roles, to take chances, to explore deeply. Similarly, growth requires certainty about a place to provide orientation for intentional change. Dreaming and creative activity contribute to the production of one's worldview and vice-versa. Daring adventure stimulates excitement largely in contrast to safety. Security and radical transformation depend upon each other.

In spite of their interdependence, places of transformation are valued for reasons starkly contrasting to places of certainty. New experiences require detachment from a safe haven, intense connection to a new environment, and reconciliation of the old and new. New experiences embed powerful meaning in places of passage, growth, invention, and peak experiences. These settings possess an air of openness, exoticism, distance, and the unfamiliar "other."

Places of new experiences are unpredictable and may appear dangerous, disorganized, or empty. We typically think of new experience as occurring in far-away places, but this need not be the case. In fact, places near home and one's neighborhood are most frequently the settings for adventure, dreaming, and testing one's identity. What is seen by one person as wildly adventurous may seem utterly conservative to another. What is riotously creative to one may be old hat to another. Still, there are distinctive spatial patterns and settings associated with new experiences. We now discuss four types of settings that nurture various aspects of venturing activity: places of identity, creativity, dreams, and adventure.

Identity

Pause for a moment and think about the place that most reflects your identity today. Then recall what place most reflected your identity five or ten years ago or when you were eighteen and ten years old. Write them down chronologically. It is likely that the places changed drastically with each phase of life. Keep this list in mind as you read this section to see if your places match our observations. Identity is a combination of certainty, new experiences, and confirmation that makes each of us unique and each town and city distinct. Healthy individuals are grounded in places that satisfy basic needs for survival, order, worldview, and ritual, but they require springboards outward from that secure base, because certainty alone is not enough to form identity. There must be interaction with society and landscapes to test and reconfirm the self. Our identity is a dialectical movement between shelter and venture, attachment and freedom.[51] Identity is formed where certainty and uncertainty intersect and collide. These collisions are internal, with family, friends, mentors, strangers, the fearful "other," and with places as well. Roles must be tried on for size and choices made about how they fit. We have to find purpose. Desirable role models must be found, followed, mastered, and overtaken, all the while avoiding the pitfall of marginalization.

Like Icarus, we may have to fly too close to the sun and adjust to, conform to, rebel against, and resolve crises to form an identity. We may need adults to introduce us to these places that test us and shape our identity, but we must be allowed to explore them on our own. In a Korean creation story, an abused and abandoned brother and sister are chosen by God to be the sun and moon respectively. The sister is unsure if she would be a good moon; she is somewhat afraid of the dark, so she explains to God that she would prefer to be the sun. After listening intently to her explanation, God agrees and makes her the sun. But she is shy about everyone watching her throughout the day, so she shines brighter and brighter so no one can stare at her as she warms the world. We, too, must honestly assess what we are and what we are capable of becoming. We must develop purpose consistent with ability. Do we have the characteristics needed to carry out a desired identity? If so and if there is accurate recognition of our intended identity by those people and places with whom we interact, that identity takes hold. This provides selfhood with authenticity, integrity, and depth (Fig. 104).

Gender and place interact to shape identity. Just as certain behaviors are stereotyped by sex, so, too, are places. Clichés like "the woman's place is in the home" or garden or library or elementary school classroom form identity.[52] This environmental sexism begins early in life, when girls imagine their

Fig. 104. Enduring identity is formed when we test ourselves by venturing outside our sense of security in acts as simple as climbing higher than we thought possible or as difficult as challenging gender stereotypes.

identity as a quiet, reflective pool of water and boys envision themselves as a stormy sea.[53] Girls and boys need equal access to a full range of environments to develop robust selves.

Identity may seem to be solely a cultural creation, but it is also dependent upon place and can be fostered by design. Identity is formed from the social and environmental materials at hand. Cal Ripken, Jr. needed his father's genes and inspiration to play baseball, but he also needed bats, balls, and fields. John J. Audubon needed native habitats to paint birds. Rosa Parks needed a bus to challenge segregation. We all need access to environments that we interpret, edit, and process relative to ourselves in order to develop identity. Access to diverse places enhances the opportunity for distinctive identity.

Place is central to identity through processes of forming, testing, reflecting, confirming, and marking. As identity takes shape, we reflect it back to ourselves and others through symbols of our uniqueness. Clare Cooper Marcus first called our attention to this in her research on the house as the symbol of self. She and others since have noted that we all need to make ourselves visible in the places we inhabit, in the home, and, to a lesser extent, at work and elsewhere. Places are images we hold of ourselves. The interior of the home specifically represents how we wish to present the self to the self; the front yard and facade of a house represent how we consciously or unconsciously wish others to see ourselves. The effort put either inside or at the street front may indicate whether one is inner or other directed.[54] These concrete expressions of self not only mirror, but also reconfirm our identity. Since identity is necessarily evolving, it is neither comprehensive nor stable, even to ourselves unless we anchor it to a place. The place reminds us. Such simple things as a room of your own, natural lighting, architectural details, construction materials, garden, music, tools, books, video games, or television may figure in the formation of self. Access to nearby nature and the characteristics of that nature also shape the self. In teaching architects and landscape architects, we have observed a recurring pattern of formative childhood experience with the built or natural environment that leads students to the professions they choose. Most architects built rooms, forts, fantasy cities, or other constructions as children. Most landscape architects developed deep and abiding relationships with the natural world. The larger landscape similarly shapes our identity. Those who grow up in temperate forests are distinct from those in coastal plains, the Great Plains, or desert Southwest. You can take the child out of the country (or city, or temperate forest, or coastal plain), but you can't take the country out of the child.

As our life unfolds and challenges are faced and mastered, changes in identity and key points of transformation are marked in settings.[55] Places that we personally participate in making produce a strong and positive self-image. Places that challenge our physical ability and endurance likewise build self-esteem and confidence. These settings are mere moments in the landscapes of our lives, but the places, or the memory of them, serve as bookmarks of our personal narrative. These places recall the highlights of our personal stories. We note our growth—physically, emotionally, spiritually, and socially—in a place. Many people have a doorjamb marking childhood heights with inches and time. These are the tree rings of our lives. Place makes time visible. First kisses, broken hearts, marriage, moments of bliss, and triumphs over our demons are likewise celebrated and remembered through their sites. The places, conceptual and actual, become more practical as we mature into adulthood.[56] For example, people report that, after living in a big city, they grow more independent and self-reliant.[57] Just as children, adults stretch identities through the challenges they master.

Growth is accompanied by uncertainty, fear, and strenuous effort. Therefore, we celebrate not only the outcome, but also the struggle itself. Both are sanctified as personal passages and pilgrimages, respectively. When Martin Luther King, Jr. proclaimed, on the evening before his murder, that he had been to the mountain top, he celebrated both the achievements of the civil rights movement and the sacrifices of the journey to freedom.[58] The journey from the mountain of despair to the stone of hope marks his memorial in Washington, D.C. We make our personal developmental journeys sacred for good reason.

Architectural passageways, like thresholds, gates, bridges, and arches, both provoke and evoke passages in our growth. The threshold is sacred, because it defines territory and divides domains. Moving from inside to out or from darkness to light through a portal is an architectural element that divides space but is also a subliminally powerful metaphor for intense interaction that may permanently transform us. A passage may guard the forbidden, remind us of our birth, or connect us to the departed. Landscape axes, alleés, mazes, and meandering paths, even changing seasons, remind us of difficult periods of growth. These periods may be portrayed as paradoxical spaces that admit and exclude, that provide sanctuary and confusion. A rose garden within a labyrinth or a secret garden with no entry convey initiations into a goodly place through struggle.[59] These design elements symbolize departure from a safe haven, going beyond a previous boundary and embracing the dangers and opportunities embedded within transformation. These are the counterpoints to the design qualities of repeated rhythms that offer us security. They cast home in a different light: Home is a starting point, and to remain at home is to be imprisoned, stunted.[60]

Places mark our achievements and failures, our high and low points. There is the heart-wrenching story, told by Sandra Cisneros, about the young schoolgirl, Esperanza, whose identity is punctuated when the Sister Superior exclaims in disbelief, "you live *there*?," as if no worthy being could possibly live in that neighborhood. The house on Loomis Street symbolized poverty and depravity, and the sister's comment forced the same qualities onto Esperanza. We inherit the qualities of the places we inhabit, for better and worse.[61]

The markers of identity are among the most emotionally loaded places. These settings that symbolize selfhood often become sacred. Although core identity is formed in childhood between five and twelve years old, identity evolves throughout one's life, and key points are commemorated in a place. We speak here about the individual, but this applies to communities and regional populations as well.[62]

Today, identity is becoming less grounded in place. This may be socially acceptable, but the psychological costs are considerable, and the secondary impacts on ecosystems are cause for alarm. Therefore, the implications of identity are critical in reforming the city. Since identity combines security and new experiences, the settings necessary for certainty must be satisfied as a starting point. Then we must attend to the following:

- *Make places for selfhood.* Provide a diversity of built and natural settings that are accessible to youth—boys and girls alike—to interact with positive role models and mentors. Design the places with multiple raw materials to try out many selves. Allow children to process and edit the places on their own, even if some messiness and danger are involved. Redesign play areas for children that allow them to choose for themselves. Likewise, the entire city and not just parks should be considered for "child's play" to increase choices of selfhood.
- *Express identity in everyday places.* Make available places, however modest, for every person to express his or her identity and reflect it back to the self and others. This can be accommodated by a room of one's own, a family bulletin board, a front yard or garden, a climbing tree, or a street corner or local park over which one has legal or symbolic ownership.
- *Determine authentic community.* Help communities ascertain their deep, distinguishing public identity and build on that for the future. Document and manifest healthy patterns particular to the city, so they become consciously known, not just subconsciously felt. The Windy City (Chicago), the City of Towers (Dungeons and Dragons), and the City of Trees (Washington, D.C.) express environmental patterns. The City of Brotherly Love (Philadelphia), the Bull City

(Durham), and the Country Music Capital (Nashville) express dominant and abiding social values, not superficial marketing schemes, which are to be avoided. Uncovering positive attributes of marginal communities is especially important in both personal and neighborhood development.

- *Ground identity locally.* Build on precedents close at hand. This may be as simple as constructing with brick or creating blocks with playful alleyways to reflect historic economies or as complex as expressing suppressed histories that might foster youthful minority aspirations. For example, in Durham, North Carolina, each block of Parrish Street was recently adorned with sculpture describing the events that made it the Black Wall Street of America during the early twentieth century. Parrish Street was home base where African-American entrepreneurs created large and powerful insurance and banking corporations. The sculpture not only recounts the past, but also offers positive benchmarks for identity formation today. Encourage such official expressions in major public places and provide for spontaneous ones in less conspicuous spots. These may come to capture meaningful local identity and encourage deeper attachment to place.

- *Designate and dare growth.* Make public settings to mark a community's struggles, growth, triumphs, and aspirations for development. Conceive of these places like graduation that celebrates the accomplishment but challenges the community to proceed to a higher level. Design with thresholds, *paseos*, and *aleés* that provide movement from dark to light, from closed to open space, and from one time to another. Such qualities serve to designate the previous and dare to attempt the following. Do not eliminate fearful places that are essential for growth; rather mark the passage to them clearly. The Martin Luther King, Jr. Memorial in Washington, D.C., uses many of these devices to connect civil rights struggles to present-day racial prejudices; they exhort us to attempt visionary equality through a metaphorical conversation across the tidal basic with the Thomas Jefferson Memorial.

- *Make struggle physical.* Provide natural places that require strenuous physical effort to experience fully: hills to climb, waters to swim, wetlands and deserts to navigate. Each serves the purpose of challenging us to evolve individually and collectively.

Creativity

Before you read further, think about the settings where you are the most creative. Write a list of these places, and make notes about how each encourages your creativity. It may help to draw some of the places in order to uncover what stimulates your inventiveness. Then, as you read, consider your places relative to the theory and applications we present.

We have an essential need for creative expression. It provides joyful satisfaction and control over our lives. It can keep us sane or advertise our insanity. It can serve as a weapon against automation, the denigration of daily chores, or the disintegration of our lives. Most importantly, creativity affords us a focused effort and a moment of delightful rejoice. All activities of making are art, not necessarily in the specialized sense of high art but in the original sense of creating. Creativity is the ability to make things anew, a singularly distinguishing characteristic of human beings from most of the rest of nature, crows excepted. We must make art to be human, and everyone has the capacity to create artistic works.[63] The artist simply makes an intelligible equivalent commensurate to his or her particular experiences. The creation becomes the person's body and soul. The creative act is both profoundly security-seeking and transformative. This is especially true of home and garden, where a large percentage of people invest creative energy.

The places we make are undoubtedly sacred to us. As noted previously, they produce a strong and positive self-image. They typically combine the creation of secure habitation with the concretization of a worldview and identity. To make a world is intricately related to a sense of identity. This is as true of building our own home, decorating a room, and cultivating a garden as it is of drawing, sculpting, painting murals, or designing a city.[64] Simply changing, adding to, or adorning an environment makes it more desirable to us as individuals and as communities.

Similarly, settings of creative action like making crops, crafts, and meals, giving birth, sewing, performing, or working, or planning a new city hall make places as diverse as kitchens, agricultural land, workshops, hospitals, stages, office desks, and city centers sacred. Each of these may be marked as hallowed ground for inventiveness in personal or public life.

Of particular interest is the nature of environments that stimulate the imagination, complex thinking, and creativity. In childhood, malleable and appropriately scaled materials like small objects, sand, water, rocks, wood, and mud are important.[65] Proper tools and knowledge of various materials are usually required for adults along with a work area that accommodates risk taking and making a mess with a set of variables or loose parts (Fig. 105). The loose parts include tools and raw materials that come from many sources, ones that don't normally go together, some for which the purpose is unknown and ones that can readily be moved about and reconfigured. Forest-made forts, shallow creeks, all-purpose workshops, attics, junk piles, and dump heaps are often cited as nurturing creativity.[66] In the public environment, small spontaneous expressions of creativity often invite others. These occur in places of ambiguous ownership and neglect. Public action can legitimize these and encourage more participants. In contrast to these messy places are settings for meditative intellectual creativity characterized by simplicity and quietness such as a spare, enclosed room or a seat surrounded by restful nature. The Japanese philosopher Kenko described this essential quality declaring that, "Emptiness accommodates everything."[67]

Creative needs suggest a number of actions in city design:

- *Inspire inventiveness.* Stimulate the development of the imagination and inventiveness by making loose parts, sand, water, junk piles, meditative gardens, and wild nature a part of the everyday landscape. When Amber's daughter, Ramona, was one year old, she discovered sand at the beach near her home in Paraty, Brazil. This opened a whole new world of play. She

Fig. 105. Creativity can be cultivated or stymied by the environments available to children. In spite of parental preference for tidy equipment, the loose parts of this school yard encourage adventure and invention.

could not yet walk, but she wriggled her body through this new texture, burying her belly as deep as she could. She sat up, grabbed hands full of this magic stuff, sifting the sand through her little fingers. Again and again she sifted, faster and faster, pausing now and then to share her joy with her mother. In an urban context, a creek or a pile of construction sand or wood chips can often make a more delightful place to play than play equipment. For grownups, provide a spot, however small, for spontaneous creation in every workspace. Save some space for emptiness.

• *Make creativity public.* Provide places to encourage creativity in the public environment. These should include centers for instruction in the arts and other inventions, community gardens, performances, cooking, experiments, and music. Put these activities in the center of the city, because they exude energy and give vitality to community. The American Visionary Art Museum is the singular model for this. Located in the Inner Harbor of Baltimore, it is like no other art museum. Instead of passively viewing art and being intimidated by its mastery, the museum founder, Rebecca Hoffberger, envisioned art to celebrate and stimulate creativity. The place rocks with energy. It is noisy. Kids and old people scream with delight, "I could do something like that!" The art is dazzling, but a generous portion of space is an open studio where visitors make their own art. The energy spills out onto the street and across the harbor.

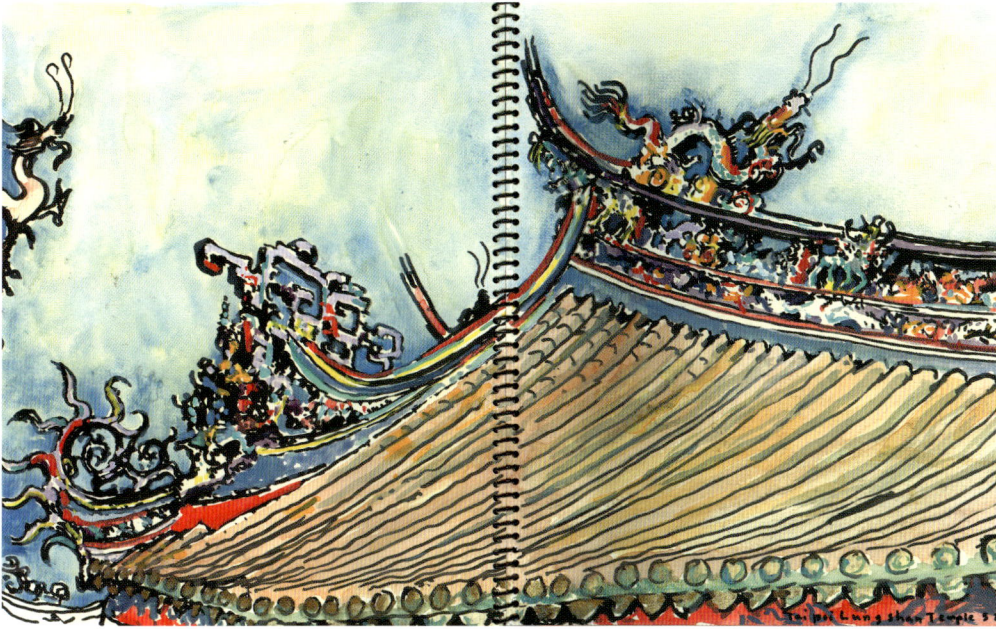

Fig. 106. The design of some landscapes and architecture stimulates the imagination, revealing dream worlds from which new ways of conceiving and living arise.

One leaves with a conviction to inhabit the sacredness of creating something oneself and to lobby for more places that encourage informal or spontaneous outlaw art as well as formal commissions. In Paris, some of the most provocative art occurs in squats, vacant buildings taken over by artists. The Albany Bulb in California is a public setting where informal art challenges the dominant culture. Some of it is terrifying. There should be many opportunities for people to contribute by fixing up old buildings, constructing an urban farm, or making art we cannot imagine.

Dreams

Whether asleep or awake, dreams expose us to unimaginable new experiences. Dreaming supplies us with hyperbolic fantasies and illusions of life. Dreaming can also make the strange familiar and the familiar strange, combine irreconcilable oppositions, and take us to imaginary places where strict boundaries of scale, time, and mores are violated. These may reveal the exotic, provide interpretive fodder, or show us new ways of conceiving and thinking (Fig. 106).

Philosopher Gaston Bachelard considered the home as the primary setting to encourage insightful new experiences. He used houses as a way to study the human soul and realm of dreaming. His poetic house was multi-story, with an attic and basement. Its height gave it sacredness, as the vertical axis reached towards the heavens and inspired dreams. Most houses today, like the horizontal ranch style, he noted, lack the verticality necessary to be whole. Among his many insights that became foundations for the study of topophilia, he realized that the vertical house is comprised of a single fabric of imagination, dreams, thoughts, demons, and memories. Dreamy imagination inhabits shells, nests, and other found objects, while corners provide the dream places of rest and solitude. The house protects the dreamer; it is a deep-dream shelter.[68]

The attic, being the highest room usually serving as storage, stirs imagined history. Unopened boxes and chests of drawers inspire speculative discovery of the tangible sacred. Openings like doors and thresholds encourage dreaming or daydreaming about what is beyond. In Japan, there is a tradition of including a moon-viewing room or platform as part of the homes of cultured philosophers. The landscape designer and public servant Ishikawa Jozan constructed a slightly awkward appendage to his small hermitage retreat at Shisendo for the specified intention of moon viewing. Its very sight stirs the imagination, partly because today, closed to the public, it can only be inhabited through mental fancy. This suggests two types of dream spaces: One like the unopened box, which Gaston Bachelard championed, explores the hidden inside, and the other, like the space Ishikawa Jozan created, is where the unknown outer cosmos is poetically searched.

The house as a repository of dreams can stimulate the imagination and be an object of desire. The dream house is an aspiration, usually big and fancy, maybe on a hill in a remote or exclusive location. The dream house attends to the self, not the public, and is often sought out as an escape from poverty or the world itself.[69] It is a particular challenge of our time to dream of small, energy-saving and transit-friendly houses.

The landscape can also serve the purposes of dreaming. Caves, hollows, secret gardens, lazy water, pools, and open grassy fields, with cumulus clouds or stars or a new or full moon overhead prompt reverie in various scales. Landscapes that are not sharply defined, misty, soft, soothing, and vague give rise to dreams. Panoramic and deflected vistas, places we can see but cannot reach, stir illusions and anticipatory speculations. In the landscape, the dreamer expands and withdraws.[70] Connections between the hearth and cosmos are played out. We microscope and telescope simultaneously.

In dreams, we take on multiple forms and identities; everything grows as it pleases.[71] This kind of dreaming is particularly important in changing unhealthy cities into sustainable ones. Since dreaming gives free rein to the imagination, some dreamy brainstorms may be impractical but others brilliantly implementable. The task of the designer is to help communities find their existential foothold by concretizing such dreams. The redesign of the city should give form to people's heroic insights and visions.[72] Manifestations of dream settings might begin with the following, but be sure you expand this list of actions based on your own imagination.

- *Protect the dreamer.* Make places in the home to stimulate the imagination and dreams, thoughts, and memories. Employ verticality, nautiluses, and corners literally and poetically.

- *Set the stage to dream.* Create settings in the public landscape that provoke dreaming about the city. Panoramic overlooks of the community, grassy fields open to the sky, gardens, and soothing water seem especially good for this.

- *Imagine visionary futures.* Create public forums where citizens feel safe and free to envision the future in non-traditional ways that explore deeply held values through dreams and other media. Tolerate the impractical; search for the visionary. Children are especially gifted at this. In a workshop in Adachi, Japan, elementary school children suggested that bus stops should have book shelves for short-term reading or longer-term borrowing. They also suggested that there should be strawberry fields along the walk to each school. These ideas challenged adults to think deeply about life's daily priorities.

Adventure

Danger enriches space with irresistible forces. Depending upon our life-cycle stage and personality, we enjoy and contrive situations where life and limb are at risk. We live dangerously and look for trouble in those moments.[73] Adventure momentarily shatters the confines of centeredness and familiar boundaries. To live fully, we must venture forth. Usually, but not always, we return afterward with renewed respect for the safe and secure. Space accommodates adventure; place represents safety.[74]

We think of adventurers today as those who travel to and explore exotic places, life-threatening mountains, rivers, deserts, and rain forests. The danger arises precisely because the explorer is alien and unfamiliar with the locality of the specific landscape, ecology, and culture. The adventurer is confronted with ambiguity, incongruity, surprise, uncertainty, or illegible complexity. He or she must quickly absorb intimate details or perish, unless one is guided by an insider who knows the lay of the land from experience. In either case, senses are aroused from the experience.[75] The adventurer gets a high or peak experience. Few people have truly extreme adventures, but most have challenging ones. We mark those events in our memories for the peril we experienced. If we survive and perform well in meeting the challenge, we consecrate the place of that accomplishment. This is why we usually recall camping trips and travel that involved near disasters.

Eleanor Roosevelt said that we should do a least one thing every day that removes us from our comfort zone and scares us.[76] Interestingly, settings of adventure—the other, outer, unfamiliar, and faraway—need not be located far from home. Traveling to a different neighborhood or city may be exotic enough to be challenging. There may be risk or merely a welcome change of scenery. The adventure may be tamed by a packaged tour or completely unplanned for free and independent travelers. In the mildest form, a move to a new landscape, a walk in the woods, or a hike through a nearby neighborhood

Fig. 107. Untamed nature where risk, danger, and fear are encountered provides essential adventure for healthy child development.

may provide the necessary elements of adventure: uncertainty, mystery, fear, and discovery.[77] Finding adventurous settings within walking distance simply requires imagination, engagement, and a fresh perspective on discovery.[78] Unfortunately for the very young, elderly, disabled, and poor, the abundance of adventurous experiences close to home are limited due to cost, inaccessibility, or local mores.

For a young child, adventurous exploits can be found in the backyard, a park, or some forbidden spot where risk is taken, danger is encountered, fear is overcome, excitement is stirred, the unknown is explored, and mastery is gained. These experiences are essential to develop field independence, confidence, and selfhood separate from parental control. Natural landscapes are critical in this regard. Almost everyone who has done the awakening exercises in Step 1 has listed childhood adventures in wild nature among their most sacred places. Children need to climb to high places, move fast, handle dangerous tools, experience water, fire, and other natural dangers, wrestle and play rough, and wander alone from adult supervision (Fig. 107). All of these involve risks essential for child development. For example, children who fall from a climb and are injured before the age of nine become less fearful of heights than other teenagers. For youth, adventurous settings serve to temporarily violate secure center and boundary, so they generally prefer exotic, dangerous, and rugged environments more than older people.[79] Youthful new experiences are most fulfilling if they involve breaking adult rules related to distance, danger, and/or social class. Abandoned buildings, wild nature, an unknown part of the city, or industrial infrastructure will provide a teenager with adventure, because each can only be successfully navigated by quickly learning details of the terrain, where to venture, and what is forbidden.

By adolescence and later, adventure often entails romance and requires a normalized setting: a secret place appointed by lovers, a "trysting place." It might be a park at dusk or pear tree in bloom.[80] It assumes an old-fashioned and routinized home with boundaries for the breaking. The act of breaking this home boundary exerts freedom. These settings become markers of independence and contribute to the formation of identity. The design implications of adventuring, exploring, and discovering reflect central issues of our time. Professional designers continue to believe that cities need their creative signatures of adventurous perceptual opulence when, in reality, cities provide more than enough of that already. What people need from city designers is cognitive clarity.[81] At the same time, parental fears and unfounded legal actions have led to sterile, adventureless design for children's environments. We should try the following design actions:

- *Access diverse adventures.* Although cities are perceptually complex enough to satisfy the adventurous, many people do not have access to new and healthy experiences in their neighborhoods and cities. Providing access by foot or public transit should be made a priority in reshaping urbanity.
- *Supply natural adventures.* In homogeneous-looking neighborhoods, create greater choice for adventure. Provide more wild nature for authentic adventures, exploration, and discovery close to home. Allow it to be natural with rocks, hills, and trees to climb. These may seem dangerous to parents, but children test nature at their own paces and skill levels. Urban wilderness, camping areas, adventure playgrounds, and natural parks are good examples to emulate. Make children's play areas more adventurous, with opportunities for speed, using tools to build things, manipulating water, and building fires. Avoid technological simulations of nature. For example, to climb real rock faces is generally better than sprayed concrete surfaces; body surfing in the ocean is preferred over wave machines.

Monster 2: Superficial Thrills

A process of attachment, disconnection, intensification, and reconciliation to place is essential to cultivating new experiences. Permanent detachment or indifference to a place can negate new experiences. Identity that develops without strong sentiment for place, either positive or repulsive, is incomplete, disengaged, and vulnerable. If experiences with a place are shallow, the resulting identity is shallow. These are some of the ingredients for the second monster: superficial thrill seeking.

There are other insidious factors weakening new experiences and similar impediments to certainty, but fear is foremost. It makes us seek risk-free places, safe but superficial thrills, and pseudo adventures. It makes us overprotect our children from almost every danger, without providing them access to dangers necessary to actualize. We do not let them climb to the top of a tree or monkey bars, play alone in wild nature, cross the street, or venture into a diverse neighborhood. Instead, we lavish them with manufactured adventures on television, at the mall, or on the computer, at Disneyland, and ultimately in the car or at organized events. These new experiences are fabricated by others, and the adventure is second-hand, trivialized. When no genuine adventure is present to offset these safety concerns, children lose the power to imagine internally, discover adventure individually, and gain substantive confidence.

The automobile provides freedom, mobility, and danger simultaneously, or so it seems. For youth, driving is indeed far more dangerous than wild nature or bad neighborhoods, but ironically this is one risk parents embrace. Different from authentic adventure, the freedom is accompanied by little responsibility either to the place left or the one visited. The knowledge required of the new place is minimal; only Global Positioning System (GPS) is needed. American mobility has become a form of voyeurism and tourism. It contributes to rootless, shiftless, and unaccountable actions, superficial knowledge of and indifference to place, and a lack of intimate social contact. It undermines security and centeredness while still being dependent upon them. Yet precisely for the unfettered freedom and mobility it offers, the car is sacred to many. Many of the young people we know today seem wise to this and are not learning to drive at all.

Mobility has allowed adults to become migrants to escape the oppressive security of one place and to search for better opportunities in another. This migration has the characteristics of adventure. There is risk. Uncertainty rises. Environmental and cultural knowledge of the new place must be quickly learned to reap benefits from the opportunity. Yet the knowledge required in moving about the United States today is less about the ecological process and more about the social institutions of the new setting. This diminishes ecoliteracy, attachment to place, and a sense of community.

Another aspect of this monster is the professionalization of creativity. As it becomes the exclusive domain of artists, the rest of us are discouraged from developing that most precious outlet for thinking, problem solving, and self-expression. Along the way we commodify dreaming. Dreaming provides insight, vision, and stimulates creativity, though today's "dream house" is primarily a materialistic excess that provides more status than contemplation and inspiration. Youth seem to be socialized early on to discard places of imagination and substitute them with materialistic "dream house" aspirations. A recent analysis of the ideal homes drawn by fourth graders revealed few places of fantasy and an abundance of unusually large houses or McMansions. Out of 147 drawings, only three spoke of childlike reverie—a boathouse with a kind ghost for a captain, a cupcake house with a cherry on top and an ice cream tree leading to a banana mountain, and a peaceful place to read a book. The others were many thousands of square feet, at least four bedrooms with many extras. One was indistinguishable from a real-estate ad that accompanied the exhibit. It promoted a huge 27-by-15-foot family room highlighted by a gas log fireplace on a *cul-de-sac*. In such cases, dreaming is more a matter of financial dependence than reverie, demonstrating that children have learned to equate wealth with happiness.[82]

Together, all these factors create a multifaceted monster. Identity that embraces risk-free risk, pseudo adventure, professionalized creativity, and commodified dreams contributes a snake from the head of Medusa. Like the Gorgons, it is difficult to slay these complex forces threatening new experiences without becoming cold and lifeless.

Converting Cheap Thrills into New Experience

None of us is Perseus, but collectively we can overcome the monsters that demoralize new experience. This requires intentionally and aggressively reshaping our lives and our cities.

- *Put place in identity.* We need to help our families and communities discover and employ authentic identities grounded in our history, architectural traditions, native landscape patterns, ecological functions, and regional culture. Use place-based identity to inspire the remaking of the city to be more resilient, enabling, and impelling.

- *Reconsider mobility.* We need to assess carefully the costs of escapist mobility. Voyeuristic travel or relocating from one region or home to another frequently has benefits as well as costs. Destabilized identity, diminished knowledge of a place, and loss of a community are significant consequences. City design should encourage staying in one place by providing abundant experiences locally and making it a matter of pride to experience the locality in great depth.

- *Access existing experiences.* We need to keep in mind that there are plenty of genuine opportunities for new experiences in most communities already. We can tap into them by making them accessible, especially for young people through walking, biking, and public transit.[83] The opportunities must be equally available to boys and girls, rich and poor, young and old.

- *Free creativity.* We need to curb second-hand experiences that rely on a safety net or technology to entertain us. These pseudo adventures, from the car to computer games, diminish our humanity. Instead, we must make natural and formal settings available in the neighborhood for adventure, creative endeavors, and dreams. We need to mentor children to recognize new experiences, then free them from the mentor so they internalize discovery on their own. Children need to be able to take risks, face reasonable dangers, and develop a less hysterical fear than what dominates our present lives. Provide wild nature, gardens, creeks, grassy fields, junk piles, and lots of loose parts in public landscapes. Also make structured settings for the instruction in the arts, ecological thinking, civics, stewardship, cooking, performance, and experimentation. Be aware that creativity exists in the most unusual places. Amber lived for a few years in a favela on one of the hillsides in downtown Río de Janeiro, Brazil. These are the least desirable areas of the city, with houses made of scrap materials, many lacking basic services. This is home for the city's most impoverished people, mostly Afro-Brazilian, stigmatized as uneducated and violent. Yet the favelas are places of extraordinary creativity, from samba to carnival, as witnessed in the opening ceremony of the 2016 Summer Olympics. Carnival would not exist without the year-long preparation of music, costumes and parade events staged in the favelas. Explore your own community for such centers of creativity.

- *Dream better cities.* Encourage widespread participation in re-making the city. Bring people of different backgrounds, generations, and cultural experiences together to share goals and dreams. Pay special attention to creating public forums where citizens feel free to envision the future in imaginative, non-traditional ways, discover deeply held values, and create new ways to inhabit the sacred. Now that you have contemplated multiple manifestations of identity, creativity, dreams, and adventure, consider which is most needed in your own home. Make a list of a few things you might do to achieve them. Then think about a few actions to provide new experiences that would most enrich your family and community.

Wish 3: Places of Reciprocal Response

Your new-born niece cries, you gently pick her up, and, holding her in both arms, cuddle her to your warm body. As you rock her softly, singing "Swing low, sweet chariot," she wriggles, and you feel her snuggling to you. She stops crying. You return her to her cradle, rockers echoing your song. You exhale, sensing an unexplained warmth throughout your body. This simple act in this setting captures the basic principles of reciprocal response. The setting—bedroom, bodies, cradle—are essential places, expressing and concretizing the experience of devotion to a family.

Places of reciprocal response manifest the physical connections between self and others and between self, community, and landscape that are necessary for a healthy life. At the deepest level, these connections are expressed as the desire to love and be loved. This requires giving and getting, gifting and receiving. I acknowledge you in an intimate way, and you respond to me in kind. Or I acknowledge a place, and it acknowledges me in return. The giving and getting may be reasoned, but the response is an involuntary impulse, stimulated by the mere physical presence and sensory qualities of another person, group, or environment.

Reciprocal response is complex. It accounts for familial devotion, deep friendship, empathy, altruism, topophilia, and biophilia. It accounts for sensory joys of visual, olfactory and tactile beauty, and sexual arousal as well as selfishness, self-indulgence, and commitment to ideals and causes. The contradictions inherent in reciprocal responses are mediated through gaining a sense of relatedness, a mature awareness of self as a part of and apart from others.[84] Gaining an understanding of relatedness requires both thoughtful reflection and a sensory intimacy with another person or place. This intimacy is attained through nearness, being close enough that one can see, smell, touch, and feel the other, whether the other is a person, community, animal, or landscape. Nearness depends upon being in the same place at the same time and alert to who and what are sharing that place with you. This sensory intimacy provokes a way of thinking and feeling that combines intellectual rigor with our animal kinship with the people and land around us, providing us with a carnal empathy with other people and the environment This creates a oneness between the two, similar to the reciprocal pronoun "each other."

We next introduce four forms of sacredness manifested in places of reciprocal response: sensing, reciprocity, morality, and transcendence. We begin with sensing, because it is the foundation upon which other places of response are conceived and expressed. It is also the basis for genuine sensory pleasure. Places of reciprocity inculcate relatedness, expressing a sense of self and other as one, as well as give and take. Sacredness in these places derives from a feeling of unity and mutuality: that you nurture the people and place, and the people and place, in turn, nurture you. Intimate reciprocity with the natural world also underlies the capacity to commingle with and be reminded by the landscape of our most cherished values. Relatedness also serves as the catalyst in forming morality and as the stage for transcendence. Each reciprocal relationship requires particular settings and interaction with those settings.

Sensing

Before reading further, think about the senses upon which you most depend as you go about your daily activities. Then think of a place where all of your senses are activated in such a way that causes you to pause and feel great joy.

Early *Homo sapiens* depended upon keenly developed senses that allowed them to see and not be seen, smell and not be smelled, and hear and not be heard by meat eaters larger and faster than them. Nearness, an alert presence in time and space, guided action. Our senses combined with intuition and movement told us when to flee, hide, procreate, or find water and food. As we evolved, our dependence on the sensate environment animated human endeavors beyond our needs for food, shelter, and clothing. Aesthetics, for example, derives from the classic stimulus included in the showy display that aroused the senses in order to attract a mate.[85] Senses rather than abstracted reasoning informed and still inform our primal actions.

Today, nearness is being transformed and, in some conditions, supplanted. Mobility and technology compress time and space and allow seeing and hearing remotely. These senses now divide their attention between an experiential place and a distanced space, diminishing nearness and complexifying our perception of vision and sound. Senses of taste, touch, smell, and kinesthetics, which are still bound to nearness, are sublimated. Repressed nearness can be revived through prolonged sensual engagement with a place. To know a place is to sense it deeply and intimately, so knowledge of a place cannot be separated from our senses. Knowledge, abstract reasoning, and problem solving evolved entirely from our senses, though we tend to think of them as products of reason alone. We touch, move, feel, and taste, and only then do we know.[86]

Nonetheless, our experienced knowledge may conflict with our conceptual knowledge. Abstractly we know that the world is round; we also know that it can be flat, rolling, and hummocky. From science we learn that Earth revolves around the sun; in its rotation Earth rises and sets, creating day and night. In opposition to this we experientially know that the sun rises and sets, not Earth. We know this with enough certainty that we call these events sunrise and sunset.[87] Which then is correct, the scientific or the experiential fact? Both! Not only thinking, but sacredness itself is embedded in the seamless integration of scientific and experiential knowledge. We sense and think; therefore, we are. Mental worlds are shaped from sensory and kinesthetic experience.[88] Topophilia, in turn, is formed by sensitivity and sensibility as one. Continued human evolution is dependent upon reclaiming the sensual intimacy of nearness and the development of knowledge from a combination of conceptual reasoning and physical experience. This, in turn, depends upon spatial qualities that stimulate all senses simultaneously. To fulfill our potential as humans, we need multi-sensory places that impel us to be attentive to space nearby and learn holistically through all our senses.

The meaning of place also lies in the sensual pleasures it gives. Sensualists argue that the joy of the senses is the greatest good. The need for sensory satisfaction is a constant among people and other animals. Vision has become the preeminent sense in defining cultured gratification; so prized is the pleasure of visual stimulation that the branch of philosophy called aesthetics, the study of beauty, is dominated by the visual arts. In the landscape, focal views along pathways, long and panoramic views, and open views to the sky all give us these sensual pleasures.[89] These pleasures mirror the aesthetic experience of art, which is typically described thusly: The viewer is separated from the picture object, and his or her attention is firmly fixed on the object, usually with only one sense, in this case, sight. There is a beginning and an end to the experience contained within the frame. Furthermore, the painting exists within created virtual space, which is entirely self-contained and independent. Depending entirely upon the qualities of the object itself, the experience is more or less intense. There remains a discontinuity between the art and the space in which we normally live. This may adequately detail the visual appreciation of two-dimensional art, architectural facades, and distant views but not three-dimensional place in time.

Experiential space of our everyday lives is known by more than sight alone; pleasures of daily life come from multiple senses, including touch, relative humidity, motion, smell, and voice.[90] The arousal of all the senses heightens the joy of making love in a manner looking at art cannot. Bird song, the smell of freshly baked bread, the taste of salty air, or rolling down a grassy slope give us as much pleasure as a panoramic view or framed painting. These experiences are fundamentally different than the aesthetic experience of art and framed views (Fig. 108). In these daily experiences of place, we are surrounded and enclosed by a place, yet our attention is seldom fixed on it. We focus on what is important for the activity at hand at the moment, and there is far too much information to grasp every stimulus in the room. Therefore, most of the sensation of space upon which sensual pleasure depends is unconsciously received with subliminal intensity.[91] There is no defined beginning and end of the sensation of space; the experience is sequential and ongoing and involves all the sensing organs, not just the eyes.

This is not to suggest that the sense of place provides no sensual pleasure; quite the contrary is true. The aesthetic gratification, delight of the senses, and multi-sensory satisfaction provided by place is unmatched by other arts, because the nature of experiencing a place is direct. The delight is integrated into everyday life. Because we engage space with our whole body, our body becomes the measure of

Fig. 108. Sacredness manifests in places that arouse all the senses at once through textures, sounds, and smells that provide pleasure and sensual knowledge.

the experience of place. A place achieves reality when our experience of it is total, when all the senses are engaged. The sense of space can be understood as a metaphorical walled enclosure, completely dark, that intensifies sensual attention, centers interest, and makes our body shrink. Sight becomes fuzzy and out of focus, so we rely on touch, taste, smell, and sound alone.[92] The rest of the world is erased for a moment while these senses are concentrating on one activity. This nuanced stimulus arouses in us a feeling of intimacy like private conversation, holding a baby chick, or making love. In contrast to intimate space, open space removes physical or metaphysical barriers. The body expands in response and encourages uplift, open arms, and deep breaths. One may scream, skip, or fly involuntarily in the presence of a landscape's expanse provided by a treeless hillock, an open meadow, a canyon overlook, a rock outcrop, a rainbow, fields of row crops, a full sky, or a minimalist roof garden. In both contracted and expansive space, the body responds primarily to others and the environment through the sensation of space; this multi-sensory experience evokes unselfconscious delight.

The design implications of sensing are simple and direct. Actions must be taken in the city to enhance the appreciation of nearness as it improves our knowledge and capacities to solve problems. Additionally, we must provide the full range of pleasures offered by the sensation of space:

- *Reawaken nearness.* Heighten the sensual qualities distinctive of the region in the design of the city. Honolulu does this exquisitely by accentuating the naturally soothing embrace of the climate and slack key guitar with seductive fragrances of stands of lei and aromatic planting throughout the city. The perfume invites the use of public places and, in turn, is invited indoors via traditional building styles. True, not every city is blessed with Honolulu's sensual joys, but even harsh qualities can inspire. In Taipei where summer is brutally hot and humid, building arcades lower walking temperatures by day then transform into night markets that make the balmy evenings a social extravaganza that excites every sense. Such city designs evoke sensual pleasure and inculcate sensual knowledge of the place. Do not tolerate architects concerned primarily with how their buildings look; insist on a description of the full sensual experience, from movement to sound, within every new building and civic landscape.

• *Fulfill pleasures.* Take advantage of existing vistas and panoramic views of the city or create new ones that mimic classic art appreciation. Then satisfy other sensual pleasures with intimacy and expanse. Make places for intimate sensing in public landscapes. Shape them with delights like gardenia, honey locusts, tuberose, or native stone. In Child's Park in Northampton, Massachusetts, there is a large rock that snuggles you like a small child in its voluptuous grace. Formed from glacial and erosive processes particular to the region, it provides a niche for privacy or affection, a place to lounge or recline at the edge of a large public space. It converges the senses of touch and smell. In contrast, make places that expand the body; find treeless hillocks and rock outcrops; make extensive open meadows and fields of row crops, sunflowers, or salvia. Juxtapose enclosed and expansive spaces to heighten the experience of both.

Reciprocity

Reciprocity is a relationship of mutual exchange of resources between two or more beings. This give-and-take becomes a symbiotic obligation, a necessary interdependence for the health of all parties. Reciprocity derives from relatedness, the simultaneous awareness of both an intimate kinship with other people and natural ecosystems and a personal identity apart from them. It is a fundamental need for lifelong human wellbeing. The realization of being a part of and apart from serves primary purposes in childhood and throughout adult life.[93] It is the means by which we empathize with other living things and the rest of our surroundings. Relatedness has four major effects. First, it fosters an appreciation for and acceptance of other people and the more general "other." This transforms the "other" into "each other." Second, relatedness eases painful and anxiety-laden states of feeling. Third, it fosters self-realization, develops trust, and clarifies identity. Fourth, relatedness deepens the perception of reality. When children between five and twelve experience separateness for the first time, it is important that they form relationships with the environment and nature as process. Pets, trees, and other natural parts of place and built elements in the immediate neighborhood can serve this purpose. Interaction with the nonhuman environment provides practice in how to relate to other people, creatures, and places. Relatedness is enduring, close-up, hands-on and personal. Complex knowledge of other people, cultures, individual species, functions of the entire ecosystem, and the personality of the region grows from it.[94] This knowl-

Fig. 109. Places where a person experiences an intense sense of oneness with something or someone else manifest biophilia, as when this Red-Spotted Purple Butterfly (*Limenitis arthemis*) shared the sweat on Randy's finger for half an hour.

edge is grounded in sensual experience, but it only develops with the elevated cognizance of unity and separateness. This creates a place-specific empathic intelligence shared by all who truly inhabit the place, those who are permanent residents of that region. This intelligence is the foundation for native wisdom.

Although relatedness originates from an insight into the silent rhythms we share with all living creatures in the world around us, empathy is socialized with age. We soon empathize primarily with people of similar backgrounds. It is more difficult to bring the lessons of relatedness with people different than ourselves and the non-human world into adult life.[95]

The sense of oneness has a biological and evolutionary basis, a claim addressed recently in the literatures on biophilia and phenomenology as well as in the narratives of native people. Biophilia extends the idea of sensual response beyond stimulus-reaction or relatedness to reciprocity. This suggests that we love other living beings and the land not only because we are interconnected with them via abiding friendship, marriage, food webs, and other exchanges, but also because these connections make us one being, much as soulmates become one (Fig. 109).

The Gaia hypothesis, formulated by the scientist James Lovelock, broadens relatedness and reciprocity to Earth as an ecosystem in its entirety, not as a personified goddess but as a living oneness.[96] Native Canadian Thom Alcoze clarifies this distinction when he says, "I love the earth not because she is like my mother, but because she is my mother." Earth is no mere symbol; she is our mother. For most of human existence, this was likely the prevailing conception of our being.[97] Only beginning in the era of Socrates did we separate and subordinate the rest of the world to humankind's reason. Prior to that time, our thinking, our breath, and the wind were one and the same. Rational awareness did not separate us from the rest of nature but invisibly joined us. We commingled with the world around us. We didn't separate ourselves from the world around. We were part of it. We also literally commingled with plants by exchanging carbon dioxide for oxygen. We continue to commingle. The everyday environments we inhabit, far from inert, actively participate in our daily lives. We become intermixed with, united, and joined with the places in which we truly dwell. This is the essence of mutual interaction to the advantage of both: "The world and I reciprocate one another."[98] The landscape we directly experience is not an object but rather a realm that responds to our emotions and calls forth feelings from us in turn. We have a dialogue with the surrounding landscape; we exchange ideas and share our very life-breath. We move back and forth alternatively with our surroundings. Through a sympathetic relationship with the environment, our bodies and our entire selves possess and are possessed by the place we perceive through dwelling.

A Cherokee myth illustrates reciprocity between people and place at the societal level. The Appalachian Mountains were a landscape of enduring health for the Cherokee, promoting their physical well-being and originally preventing inhabitants from becoming sick. For some reason, the Cherokee disrespected the wild animals who, in turn, created diseases as a retribution. The disease spirits then inhabited particular features of the landscape like rivers, thunder, fire, and certain animals or their ghosts, but the plants of the region felt the diseases were too harsh a punishment. Without being asked, they provided a cure for all the diseases animals had caused. The plants themselves exerted the commingling with humans that is still exhibited in the life of the Eastern Band and their landscape.[99]

We sometimes observe a child hugging a tree and, at a certain age of scientific inquiry, exchanging carbon dioxide for oxygen. Rarely do adults reciprocate so directly, but a traditional tai chi-like exercise similarly unites the elderly Chinese body with low branches of mature trees. In a performance much like Tao Dance Theater, the human body and limbs intertwine with and slowly grow into the shapes of the tree branches themselves. In many cases, these interactions are repeated daily for decades, improving the health of both tree and person.

Reciprocity forges bonds between people and place. It is a process advancing from dissatisfaction between two beings, through asking and searching to arrive at an encounter, then trying to accept and eventually accepting the other. This creates synthesis, literally the growing together, which prompts understanding, caring, and mutual stewardship. Reciprocity is more than connection; it is a relationship in which the two beings have a real stake in each other, creating a togetherness. Commingling can only happen through nearness. Proximity and intimacy are requisites. Place is simultaneously the indispensable setting, the active participant, and the symbol, but it is the commingling that gives place deep meaning. By corresponding with the world, sacredness is acquired.[100]

Reciprocity suggests the following as design strategies in the city:

- *Prompt relatedness.* Provide access to non-human environments and nature for every child in the everyday landscape. Create settings that invite interaction, not just viewing from a distance. Make situations for relating like shallow water where aquatic life can be touched and considered or trees small enough to embrace fully a child's hug.

- *Design empathy.* Create public settings that enable interaction across age, class, ethnicity, gender, species, and other divisions to encourage empathy for others different than oneself. Parks with a centered open space surrounded by settings for different activities offer a wide range of interaction for users. If the open center slopes gently inward, it invites multiple uses like kite flying, soccer, Frisbee, *tai chi*, and red rover. Community gardens and water fountains similarly attract different ages and ethnicities and encourage intimate relatedness.

- *Steward damaged communities and landscapes.* Create opportunities for reciprocal stewardship with programs and places in cross-cultural and social-class exchanges, restoration of urban streams, community gardens and farms, urban wilderness, and expansion of wildlife habitat. Such places allow people to nurture and restore damaged parts of the community and to be nurtured in return.[101]

- *Commingling with small nature.* Make places that encourage commingling with the natural world and combine sensual commingling with an understanding of underlying ecological processes. This can be accomplished in tiny spaces like Tokyo's ecotone parks, often no larger than an eighth of an acre, that create the full life-cycle requirements for insects like beetles, fireflies, and dragonflies. In turn, the fireflies, for example, produce light shows that thrill people of all ages, invite them to learn metamorphic requirements, and teach the reciprocal dependency on clean water. In Berkeley, Andy Liu's butterfly habitats fit into traffic circles less than thirty feet in diameter. Butterflies astonish residents by living in such cramped quarters and by engaging people with colorful clothing. They inform and relate. Such habitats for small species should be incorporated into tiny open spaces in even the densest cities.

- *Accommodate adults.* Make places for commingling for adults as well as children, understanding that the design must overcome adults' self-consciousness about this. Adults should be encouraged to do summersaults down a grassy hill, taste wild plants, dig earthworms, embrace a tree or vegetable to exchange carbon dioxide for oxygen with a tree, walk barefoot in the mud, or become part of a tree sculpture or dance with trees. If we understand our dependence upon place and how dependable it is, we can anchor ourselves as trees do.[102]

Morality

As you read this section, consider what moral values are currently most obviously expressed in your home and community. Think about ones that are missing that you would like to see manifested. Figure design strategies to express those values.

At the most fundamental level, morals describe proper relationships between the self and other. Good and bad judgments determine how we act and respond to others.[103] A stimulus provokes an action that is sensually motivated and consciously or unconsciously tempered by reciprocity. The Golden Rule—"Do unto others as you would have them do unto you"—defines one proper relationship in terms of reciprocity. This give-and-take exchange engages both emotional and thoughtful response as well as responsibility. In certain situations, we have an obligation to conduct ourselves in a particular way, a duty to the other. The other can then depend upon that duty being performed. When these principles of reciprocity are codified, they become rules of conduct or morals that guide behavior for individuals, groups, and society. Every moral action is a deliberate choice to do right over wrong, even when that choice may be clouded by conflicting values, rapid upheaval, changing customs, or loss of traditions of relatedness. This likely requires modifying the rules that govern our actions. We also need to understand the role of place in forming, making, teaching, and enforcing morals. We need to know what responsibilities of reciprocity are important to creating better habitation for all today.

We typically imagine moral lessons to be delivered verbally by elders—a parent, teacher, or religious leader. This verbal transfer of morality is essential, yet the message endures only when the elders' daily actions reflect their words. Peers similarly influence our judgments of right and wrong, as do secondary sources like stories, fables, morality plays, and the landscape we inhabit.

The cities we make reflect moral principles just as they do the worldviews of their builders. Environmental equality or injustice result from conscious or subconscious choices of right and wrong. Generous open space or lack thereof in neighborhoods symbolize moral judgments about who deserves what, conveying the decisions about the proper relationships of people and resources. The fact that poorer neighborhoods typically have fewer parks and open space than affluent neighborhoods might seem to be simply a political decision, but it also reflects an ethical failing. Most of us do not think about places reflecting right and wrong, but these subliminal messages about collective morality are especially powerful manifestations. They need to be evidenced and judged and then critical decisions made about appropriate responsibilities.

The landscape around us plays multiple roles in shaping and instructing morality. It marks good and bad choices of elders and can sometimes enforce morals. For the family, similar decisions are reflected in our homes. Critical moments of choice of right over wrong are marked as sacred and remembered in our domestic and public space. Wiley Bradsher, a particularly powerful black preacher who filled the landscape with moral lessons, lived in the community where Randy grew up. He created a store, never attended by employees, where you took what you needed and left payment in a box on the

quercus alba in snow 1 10 2004 ... noon

Fig. 110. Although it has been nearly eighty years since Wiley Bradsher hanged a car from the oak tree at his church, the tree reconfirms the moral lesson for passersby today about the automobile being the ruination of the black man and possibly all of us.

honor system. It reminded all of the youth the value of honesty. His farm reminded us of his frequently preached sermon that tenant farmers should buy land. As a result, the county had one of the highest percentages of black ownership in the region. Rev. Bradsher also felt that the automobile would ruin the black man by uprooting him from his land, so he hanged a car from an oak tree near his church to make the point. The car dangling from the tree reminded people of a dark past, and today the oak itself reminds us to be critical of technological progress (Fig. 110). All of these markers of the preacher's values instructed us and reinforce his moral teachings.[104]

In a Western Apache ethic, elders indirectly reprimand misbehavior by telling short moral histories about a place where some event happened. The place itself becomes the enforcer, reminding the offender never to behave as such. These tales that "shoot the offender with an arrow" begin and end with landscape features such as "coarse, textured rocks lie above in a compact cluster," which prevents incest, and "big cottonwood trees stand spreading here and there," which warns of the consequences of meddling in the affairs of one's children, both of which resulted in death for the offenders in the historical narratives.[105]

One story is told by a woman whose granddaughter had worn her hair in pink plastic curlers to a coming of age ceremony. Apaches know that the event is only effective for the initiates when everyone has free-flowing hair. The granddaughter violated ritual by acting like her white friends at college. At a different gathering a few weeks later, the grandmother shot her with an arrow by telling the story of "men stand above here and there," which is a point on a low ridge with a commanding view of the valley to the south. Years before an Apache had been demonized for following the laws of the white men. He became stupid and forgetful, an absurd and laughable figure. The story ends with, "It happened at men stand above here and there." The granddaughter knew she had been shot and left the party without saying a word, humiliated. She threw the curlers away and remembers the lesson each time she passes "men stand above here and there." She had formed a lasting bond with the ridge; it made her "want to live right." The grandmother who told the story may die, but the ridge will endure to enforce the moral to both the girl and others who know the story. In this way, the ridge becomes a narrative landscape recounting the lesson like a moral play, except the landform has a permanent presence in daily life. The landscape narrative may be embedded in some natural feature like the ridge and preacher's oak tree or in a constructed landscape like the preacher's store.

Instructing morality through the built landscape is widespread.[106] In the case of Buddhist rock gardens, one type teaches about the life of Buddha, his seven steps at birth, enlightenment among craggy mountains, and the four noble truths. Rocks lying prone remind us that suffering is caused by insatiable greed; an upright rock offers the contrasting message that life is fulfilling and meaningful. The teachings expressed in stone continue to instruct centuries later.

The preceding lessons about greed, cultural mores, honesty, and technology underlie proper inter-personal and community relationships. Today, much of the ethical instruction is helping us to learn to reciprocate with our environment and increase understanding of land ethics. Statements such as "Reduce, Reuse, Recycle," "Do not spoil the waters from which one drinks," and "Live lightly on the land" serve practical purposes, and each informs a land ethic. Frequently, the land, or features in the landscape, remind the inhabitants of the moral bonds with and bounds of ecological limits. The Dust Bowl, strip mining, and extensive clear-cuts convey messages of excess with little give and take. Crop rotation, strip cropping, and forested swales more positively and gently reflect an ethic of reciprocal restraint. One of the most influential environmental ethics is the narrative in Aldo Leopold's classic book, *A Sand County Almanac and Sketches Here and There* (1949). To Leopold, land is a holistic organism of which we are only a part. He wrote, "A land ethic changes the role of *Homo sapiens* from conqueror of the land community to plain member and citizen of it." Each member must respect all other members and the community as an entirety. The land community has value far beyond the "hopelessly lopsided" short-term economic self-interest. This noncommercial value provides the threshold of sacredness in public life. Some landscapes are too valuable to be profaned; their ecological integrity and sheer joy must be protected. Leopold was a scientist and practitioner of rational best practices of land management, but his knowledge was based on a firsthand relationship with the earth. His land ethic is simultaneously sensible and sensitive. It avoids both scientific determinism and spiritual idealism, both of which preclude reciprocal encounters, because they emphasize "I" versus "other" instead of "oneness."[107]

Such writings help reconnect us to the land, especially those of us who previously only had abstract relationships with the environmental crisis. Many who wish to live sustainably are confronted by machines in the garden and confused about how to live healthfully.[108] Some had lost native wisdom and moral principles regarding locality. They suffer hopelessness and emptiness. Many estranged from their natural selves had declined into mere consumers. In hopeful contrast, some are "reinhabiting" or becoming native to a place, apprenticing self to landscape through projects to increase local knowledge and restore damaged ecosystems. These actions combine rigorous ecological thinking and our animal kinship into an ethic that integrates rational abstraction and sensual responsiveness. This leads to the restoration of native habitat, and the development of urban agriculture, urban wilderness parks, and backyard certification as wildlife habitats.[109] All these concretize an emerging land ethic that sanctifies the landscape.

The city design actions derived from morality include the following:

- *Manifest honorable morality.* Design the public landscape to express and remind us of our most noble community values. Do this unashamedly and in spite of the religious right and spiritual left. In many cities, the creation of Peace Parks and Martin Luther King, Jr. Boulevards urge less militaristic and more nonviolent ethics respectively. Similarly, Michelangelo's slaves struggling to escape from stone and Rodin's Burghers of Calais call out the moral imperatives of freedom and responsibilities to the community by every citizen. Recent works celebrating lesser known heroines like Biddy Mason and Pauli Murray echo these moral themes. Mason was born a slave, was freed in California, and succeeded as a midwife and land developer. She founded a church and school for black citizens. Today, she is honored in the Biddy Mason Park in Los Angeles. Pauli Murray battled discrimination against women, blacks, gays, and lesbians. In her hometown, she is now remembered with murals throughout the city of Durham. Her home, which people tell us that Murray described as having her grandfather's stubborn character, has been recognized by the Trust for Historic Preservation and will become a museum to advance the causes for which she fought.[110]

- *Employ the moral landscape.* Use the dominant landscape features of the region to impart morality. Values should be reflected by prominent location, accessibility, height, size, and contrast. Mountains obviously do this well for the Western Apache as well as the City of Los Angeles. Here, the HOLLYWOOD land sign has represented central values for decades, starting as a real-estate advertisement, morphing into a symbol of the movie industry, and today proclaiming the importance of the hillsides as green lungs for the city. Even where dramatic features are absent, the landscape can portray morality, as Wiley Bradsher's oak tree does.

- *Express emerging ethics.* Encourage the manifestation of place-based ethics that explore interconnectedness of people and people, land and people, and democracy and ecology. Do this through public education, adult education, civics, and action. Among appropriate actions are design for alternative habitation and production like cohousing, mixed-income apartments, organic farming, and self-governing neighborhoods that give expression to emerging ethics.

Transcendence

The human urge to go beyond the limits of material experience, to be separate momentarily from the confines of human knowledge or even the physical universe, leads us on quests for transcendence. This may be done through spiritual, intuitive, or extrasensory awakening or through the pursuit of metaphysical deduction. For most, this is a temporary separation from the physical world and often provides deep insight. We transcend commonplace consciousness when we exercise to exhaustion, communicate with the deceased, take drugs, make love, play music, meditate, or pray.

Despite the fact that it requires fleeting existence apart from the material universe, transcendence is dependent on time and place. In the same way a novel requires a real setting to make fiction convincing, transcendence needs an exceptional setting, both to stimulate the separation and for contrast to the realm beyond the physical. Psychic experience is portrayed to our consciousness as natural form and in recognizable places.[111] Transcendence depends upon nearness. It must activate the senses to capacity and open us to an extrasensory experience (Fig. 111). Usually, this experience is achieved by altering both the landscape and our consciousness, either in an imagined journey through a designated spot or a literal journey through a sequence of spaces.

Japan offers cases: the meditation garden and the *sando*. They are consciously designed to concentrate and elevate sensual perception in order to separate us from it. Natural and built forms are used in both to intimate underlying myth and provide altered awareness. The meditation garden is typically a simple composition of a few landscape elements consisting of little more than rocks and plants, with few flowers and little color. It represents a larger domain, perhaps the cosmos. The observer or, more accurately, the sensor sits on a plain wooden step and contemplates the composition of objects and voids, imaginary pathways and elements concealed from casual observation. In the early morning, only the sounds of nearby birds and gentle bells break the silence. A faint smell from flowering trees beyond the garden walls blends with the smell of the aged-wood step. The wood is smooth to the touch, more human than plant. The senses are focused on the simplest forms of purity in nature. The journey awakens internal beauty by following patterns of physicality that lead to transcendence. At Ryoan-ji in Kyoto, the focus is enforced by a south-facing seat that creates warmth but also glaring sun that obscures all the world except the contemplation rocks and raked sand, resulting in an experiential reality that is more real than physical reality. To the native insider, there are complex meanings that speak from the senses to the spirit. Rocks surrounded by sand, for example, may be a tigress and her cubs swimming. The rocks are the hardest material of physical reality but also a symbol of lasting virtue; the sand is the earth and water as well. It is the concentration of multiple senses within the confinement of a relatively

Fig. 111. Places like Gio-ji Temple in Kyoto, Japan, stimulate transcendence when they lead us on a journey from physical reality to an extrasensory experience, in this case along a meandering runnel of water.

devoid but orchestrated physicality that magnifies nearness so that invisible forces and energies can be observed. These elements freeze time and evoke transcendence. Gardens are portals to space beyond.[112]

The experience of a *sando* is a physical climb to transcendence. A *sando* is a path that leads pilgrims from secular to sacred space, typically from the city to a mountain top inhabited by the *kami* (gods). The steep, exaggerated climb exhausts the climber and makes him or her receptive to transcendence. There is a sequence of dominant landscape elements that lead a pilgrim through domains of increasing sacredness, using contrasting repetition of open and enclosed, light and dark, near and far, slow and fast, expectation and sensation.[113]

At Muroji Temple in Uda, the unifying landscape elements are cedar trees on a near vertical slope of a thousand feet. At Mount Kurama in Kyoto, native stone walkways are arranged varyingly as formal stairs, irregular stepping stones or markers of treacherous dirt surfaces tie together the mixed forest. At Fushimi Inari-taisha in Kyoto, it is the hundreds of repeating *torii* leading up the mountain that unifies. Enclosure and openness are achieved by the arrangement and density of trees at or above eye-level. The atmosphere changes, formed by a single *torii* (gateway) that signals movement from one domain of sacredness to the next. Contrasting textures, turning axes, landmarks with lanterns, water features, or shrines signal transition. Such concentration is required for walking alone, and elements along the *sando* seem to appear suddenly out of nowhere. At Mount Kurama, the pilgrim walks beneath several undersized *torii*, which force him or her to stoop with lowered head. After emerging from the last *torii*, the pilgrim is confronted with the eye of the dragon from an uncomfortable nearness. As the pilgrim nears the *okunoin* (the inner-most sanctum), the pace of transition quickens. Openings and enclosure repeat more frequently, the path narrows, and the climb steepens. Combined exhaustion, excitement, and anticipation prepare the pilgrim for transcendence. Finally, the destination is reached: an extensive rock outcrop with unusual shapes where God first came to Earth. The pilgrim's inner and outer environments are synthesized. In experiential reality, he or she is without physical bounds. A pilgrim often feels the body lifted off the ground and senses a distinct existence beyond the known world.

These sequenced routes to transcendence can be found all over the world in the form of dream tracks, high-altitude mountain treks, Hopi Indian ritual runs associated with Basket Dances and Snake-Antelope ceremonies, Henry David Thoreau's extended walks in the Massachusetts landscape, or the daily lives of the Tarahumara footrunners of Mexico. Transcendence requires a place from which to go beyond. The landscape that enables the experience must itself possess extraordinary sensual power. With care, such places can be found or created in more modest form in the city as well. The implications of transcendence for city design include the following:

- *Make places for meditation.* Create quiet places for transcendence in the likeness of meditation gardens. These need not literally imitate Zen gardens, but attention to their underlying principles will help the designer. Healing gardens often achieve much of the meditative effect by concentrating on natural simplicity.
- *Encourage transcendence.* Find or make places for transcendence in the larger landscape, based on the unique features of each region. Make them accessible to people in their daily lives. These might be pinnacles to climb, strenuous trails to run, deserts to cross, or ephemeral landscapes like a trillium bloom in the Connecticut River Valley.

Tips for Designing and Planning with the Sense of the Landscape

Because the landscape has such power to evoke the sacred, cities that express their native contexts are the most beloved. Wise city makers apply both natural symbolism and sensual responsiveness in urban design. This is done by following these principles:

- Make the natural landscape more of what it is. If it is hilly, emphasize hilliness. That's why San Francisco is cherished. If it is riverine, make the most of the meanders and riparian vegetation, even when flood protection is considered, as in Albuquerque where the Rio Grande Bosque reconnects to ancient spirits. If the landscape is formed by mountains juxtaposed with ocean, as in Honolulu, form the city within that framework. Never diminish the landscape.

- When expressing the essence of a landscape, do not junk it up with other stuff. A rock is a rock. It should not be mollified, and it need not be apologetically elaborated. It and its surroundings should be simplified if necessary by removing distractions to its "rockness." This is also the power of a mountain, a plateau, an orchard, or a river's headwaters.

- The built environment and our habitation should reflect the essence of the landscape. The power of place attracts us to build dangerously close to hazards. The landscape and its hazards should inspire the architecture so the hazard is not excluded but integrated as part of everyday life. In that regard, a braided floodplain is better than a flood wall. Buildings are more sacred when they respond to local landscape factors of climate and topography and are built of regional materials. Sienna, Italy, does all these. It is literally built of the natural yellowish or burnt reddish-brown manganese oxides of the area. More recently, the architecture of Glenn Murcutt captures the soul of the Australian outback. He addresses the harsh climate and limited resources with buildings of modernist clarity and ecological function. They conserve energy and fit into the landscape. Beyond the building, the constructed landscape should also reflect its specific location. This may be grandly done with native-plant communities, distinctive land-forms, or hydrology. At the smallest detail, the ground plane itself should exude the sensuality of the place as do the black-and-white pavement mosaics of local stone in Lisboa, Portugal.

- Be careful not to be too literal with human necessities. If natural materials can serve the function without additional built elements, let them. As an example, a place to sit need not be a manufactured bench in a rocky outcrop or in woods with downed trees.

- Design for the ephemeral moment (sunlight through cumulus clouds, fog, fall color, or the sound of birds claiming territory), even if it cannot be controlled or always be present. Chances for sensory transcendence can be increased through design with nature. The unpredictable sighting of wildlife, for example, can be made more likely by careful provision of appropriate habitat. The fleeting moment of landscape is surprising and joyful, even if managed.

- Make the layering of history obvious by designing with the artifacts of previous events. These leftovers tell valuable stories of how culture resolves tensions with the natural landscape and between competing societies. Seldom should a place be wiped clean, even if the past is unpleasant. Sensing it in fragments is more useful than merely reading about it.

- Design the place for relevance over time by maintaining its inherent structure and its basic sensual qualities to provide organic flexibility and reciprocity. Most landscapes with one dominant and several subordinate spatial orders—for example, the regular pattern of a few small meadows and successional saplings in predominantly mixed hardwood forest lands—provide settings for multiple activities and constantly regenerating sites for relatedness. When the sensual structure is tapped in the natural or created landscape, it provides visceral pleasure and cognitive awakening.

These seven principles applied to design in concert can give distinctive character or what is sometimes called particularness that is important for the formation of a unique personal, community, or landscape identity. Theses design principles can also heighten primal multi-sensory response. Combined, they reenchant the natural world and create inspiring habitation.

Monster 3: Lost Nearness

Sensing the nearby environment allowed our ancestors to develop language, complex knowledge, and pleasure. This instinctual nearness underlies our sense of place and community, native wisdom, ecological literacy, and stewardship. It enhances identity and a worldview while mitigating material poverty. Yet we are severing our connection with nearness. We began losing this useful connection when sensing was separated from reason beginning with Cicero. For hundreds of years, our sensory view has been increasingly devalued in favor of rational thought. Reason (*ratione*) afforded us enlightenment and allowed us to progress beyond our primitive superstitions and pantheistic tendencies. The body came to be considered sinful, sensual arousal ungodly, and nudity immoral. Reason flourished as taboos controlled touching and smelling. What the senses sought was repressed in favor of what we were taught to admire from a distance. Two centuries ago, Thomas Carlyle noted that people were becoming mechanical in head and heart, estranged from the natural self and living and dying in artificial ways.[114] Carl Jung observed that modern man, freed from superstition, lost moral and spiritual values to a dangerous degree. Likewise, European aesthetics pointedly emphasized the eyes and ears. In such a world, other senses were disregarded as unpleasurable or barbaric.[115] Visual arts disconnected from identity, a worldview, and other thick values are erroneous interpretations of the experience of place, yet we are well acclimated to their dominance as the primary sensual experience. Modern Cartesian space abstracts the body so it is machine-like, minimalizing interaction with others and the environment.[116] The body floats freely in placeless space.

Mobility and technology compressed time and neutered space. The Internet now allows people to be several places simultaneously. As beneficial as these advances often are, the disastrous drawback is that places lose meaning when we see and hear remotely. Sensing is divided between places near and far. Vision and sound are complexified while taste, touch, smell, and kinesthetics are simplified, weakened, or dislocated altogether. Our experience of nearness is supplanted by abstract knowledge of farness. Nearness doesn't disappear; it simply loses its import, because anywhere is everywhere.

This does not mean the virtual interpretation of reality is useless. It provides us enormous advantages when used in concert with nearness, but virtual sensing can never substitute for sensing that which is near. We need to be aware of the limits of virtuality, its bogus claim to be truly sensing and its potential negative impacts on nearness. How much have you ever enjoyed kissing someone over the Internet? We need to understand the difference between a thought embodied within a technology and a thought embodied within a biological body. The virtual is never dependent on place, although it may require some ubiquitous physical space in order for us to interact with it. The virtual can be a threat to nearness and sensual place if it dominates, if it diminishes our capacity for sensual knowledge, if it grossly oversimplifies reality, if it becomes a substitute for truth or pleasure, if it enables us to withdraw from face-to-face civic life, if it alienates us from nature and place-based stewardship of the ecosystem, or if it reduces our capacity to inhabit the sacred. The sensual body, our most telling measure of the world, needs to be consulted on these matters, just as we take our temperature when we are sick or weigh it when we overeat.

As nearness is disembodied, we suffer worldwide disorientation.[117] Remote sensing and virtual realities shape only part of the monster. Synthetic communication in many other forms reduce face-to-face sensually and democratically charged encounters. Mechanical devices for controlling personal micro-climate and satisfying daily comforts further dull the keenness of our near senses. In some cases, this threatens our lives. For example, some pilots who rely almost exclusively on computerized flight controls have lost the skills to fly manually; they do not know how to recover from problems when the automation fails, leading to hundreds of deaths.[118] Our personal loss of sensual control is usually not so immediately life threatening, but this has cumulatively weakened us, made us sluggish mentally, and diminished us in ways we do not yet comprehend. There have been negative impacts from things we take for granted to be improvements in our lives. Appliances made our senses inconvenient. Technological inventions provided artificial movement and rendered body kinesthetics unfashionable. Our eyes and ears are overstimulated. Our eyes seek refuge from over-saturation by only intaking the most aggressive images, forgetting how to see and appreciate the quieter ones. The automobile reduces New York City and New Jersey to one virtual space, despite being separated by the Hudson River. Locality consists of the steering wheel, pedals, and dashboard instruments while the outside space is merely a perceived abstraction, a projection of reality made manifest by the car. Such mobility frees us from direct contact with a place, diminishes native wisdom, and allows us to act irresponsibly and ignorantly towards the people and landscape around us. These forces reduce a place to an artificial, virtual, and synthetic space. In none of these does the entirety of our senses inform us. When nearby senses are unused, the virtual and real are indistinguishable. Unfortunately for our community, biological functions, plants, animals, and, ultimately, our own species, virtual space does not nourish us as a healthy ecosystem does.

As we lose nearness, we become senseless. It is our senselessness that is the real monster. When we are senseless, we act without knowledge of anything outside our sparsely constructed reality. Our decisions have permanent disastrous effects on ourselves, other people, and the environment. Ultimately, everyone loses.

In recent years, people have begun to concern themselves with the detrimental outcomes of faulty reality. Our senseless acts that contribute to the collapse of a local economy, ecosystem, and diversity affect individual health as well as the entire democratic system. When people see these problems as insurmountable, they are disempowered to become active participants in effective change. This allows further environmental destruction and facilitates a vicious downward spiral of widespread paralysis in a community. We can despair or construct solutions, become psychologically overwhelmed or be spurred to conscientious problem-solving by employing sensual knowledge of nearness as well as abstract, theoretical science.[119]

Manifesting Nearness with Reciprocal Design

We have several choices of action. One is simply to go along with the crowd, adapt to the loss of nearness, sharpen virtual skills of seeing and hearing, and abandon other senses until catastrophe forces us to relearn lost survival skills. A second course is to escape, to withdraw into a private world of our own. This is appealing, because it restores nearness, pleasure, and transcendence, but it negates civic relatedness, reduces reciprocity, and undermines democracy, furthering the gap between the haves and have-nots. A third choice is to resist the forces that are destroying nearness. This response allows us to recultivate nearness and protect places we value, but it does not contribute to a living democracy. A fourth choice is not only to resist, but to, identify core values and live intentionally. This alternative revives both nearness and democracy, allowing inhabitation of the sacred through concerted community action. We would profess the right to inhabit our landscape with sensual nearness, to establish our community's identity, and accept the responsibility to care for the nearby landscape and community.

Fortunately, visionaries have begun to see answers and suggest courses of action. Medical research has recently verified the importance of nature in the prevention of and recovery from illness. This has been accompanied by a rapid increase in the creation of healing gardens, urban wilderness, and nature parks.[120] The need for regular exercise has likewise increased the value of pedestrian routes, bicycle lanes, and walkable neighborhoods.[121] The deadly air pollution caused by trucks and automobiles is another matter, because our health conflicts with other core values of freedom and mobility. As a result, less aggressive action has been taken. Hopeful prescriptions for calming traffic and making neighborhoods more livable have nonetheless been offered at the scale of city design by Allan Jacobs and Elizabeth Macdonald.[122] In their work, they attend to the context of regional movement while reemphasizing qualities of the nearby environment.

Still, there is much to be done before we are no longer vulnerable. These actions may reestablish our relationship with nearness:

- *Reawaken the sense(s).* Foster city form that cultivates nearness by creating places that arouse all of our senses simultaneously and cultivate carnal knowledge, using powerful stimuli and symbols derived from the region. Think about Honolulu as a precedent. The landscape there fills one with gentle breezes, smells of plumeria, tastes from multiple cultures and the tropics themselves, and sounds of endemic birds. Within walking distance there is preserved and created wild nature. In the everyday landscape, everyone has places to commingle, experience transcendence, and practice reciprocity with the natural world. There are plenty of places for adults to exchange carbon dioxide for oxygen with mango trees. Palms are a taller challenge.

- *Multiply sensual delight.* Use the body as a measure of the city. Get the body moving with great places to gather, walk, dance, perform, and celebrate. Provide panoramic views but pay more attention to the design of places that concentrate and expand the body. Make places that encourage intimacy and relatedness like walking barefoot, catching doodle bugs on a blade of dried grass, and tasting wild fruits and grains.

- *Resist the foes of nearness.* We must fend off the forces that undermine sensual nearness. Restrain powers that rely on and/or promote primarily one mode of sensing. Consciously reduce the impact of the car by intentionally walking or biking instead of driving. Design to inconvenience the car as some European cities are doing by closely spacing red lights to torment drivers, reducing speed limits to twelve miles per hour, or removing parking spaces.[123] Control placeless technologies by using senses and not just machines to solve problems. Adopt only necessary tools of remote virtuality. Stand firm against those who ruin sensual pleasures of place, community, ecosystems, cultural and biological diversity, and democracy. Expose greed. Raise factual awareness about the destruction of nearness so the community can carefully evaluate the impacts of technology, communications, and mobility on sensual knowledge. Champion forms of habitation that provide new alternatives to prevailing developments of homogeneity and placelessness.

- *Democratize nearness.* Encourage deep democratic engagement in making nearness possible. Develop local land ethics derived from the ecology of the region. Teach civics and embrace a living democracy and environmental activism. Reeducate those who have lost sensual knowledge and native wisdom. Use the landscape and built environment to express cherished community values and remind the citizenry of its moral principles. Provide hands-on participation in stewardship of community and the regional ecosystem. Use Frances Moore Lappe's *Liberation Ecology* to break the vicious cycle of powerlessness and create a living democracy.[124]

Before we move on, reflect a moment on the possibility of enhancing places of reciprocal response in your own private life, your home, and city. If you could make a single change to manifest the value of sensing, reciprocity, morality, or transcendence, what would that be? What form would that action take?

Wish 4: Places of Belonging

Just as we seek security, new experiences, and sensual responses to be fulfilled, we must be part of social units that make up our society and be acknowledged by them. We need both to belong, be recognized, and be needed. We need roles that fit our ability.

Physical space becomes the medium of exchange for belonging and for relationships between individuals in a group and between one group and the next. Every group needs a territory of its own, a home base for rituals and a setting to make itself visible to people within and outside its membership.[125] The size, location, and quality of space allotted various groups reflects their standing in the community. How space is allocated within the group for their members determines the hierarchical or egalitarian nature of the group. Therefore, places of belonging are the most socially complex of any of the four wishes. They are personal and public, physical and virtual, natural and synthetic, traditional and modern, threatening and threatened. As a result, they are often conflict-ridden, and with each conflict the places are made ever-more hallowed in the public domain. When one has to fight for a place, it becomes more sacred. These negotiations for place define who has access, who gets what place, and who is welcome; in short, who belongs. It is here that we most clearly see deep democracy at work as not only a process of community participation, personal fulfillment, and identity politics, but also a contest for place, a competition for symbols of the group's prestige, and what the groups consider a fair distribution of space and public resources.

For the past five years, Randy and Marcia have been part of a group of neighbors trying to manifest a tiny open space in downtown Durham, North Carolina, with a sense of belonging that includes every segment of the community. The process brings up most of the issues of belonging. This case underscores the difficulty of determining who belongs and how as well as to whom public space belongs.

Created when old buildings were removed, the quarter-acre open spot was acquired by the city, which had long considered it a future building site. Over the years, it evolved into the most democratic public place in all of downtown, lovingly maintained by Kevin Lilley but funky enough to be welcoming to the most established residents, the most marginal, and everyone in between. Along the way it acquired the name Chicken-bone Park. As downtown was reinhabited from a handful of residents twenty years ago to nearly 5,000 today, Chicken-bone Park became an increasingly essential open space.

But a new restaurant wanted to expand its outdoor dining into the space, in the exact location where a church group feeds the homeless. Neighbors and advocates for the homeless fought the restaurant's takeover, because they knew this would privatize the open space, pushing the marginal people out. Still, city staff and officials supported the privatization. The mayor was quoted (I still hope incorrectly) as saying, in reference to some of the homeless, that he did not want those people in his downtown. The neighbors and advocates pushed back, arguing for an even more democratic design. Marcia organized a series of community meetings to do so. The participants ranked an inclusive design as the highest priority, protecting existing uses plus inviting the elderly by providing pathway lighting and benches with backs, encouraging parents with small children and teens to a free play area and everyone to a big round table, with porch swings and walls for seating—all the while acknowledging Durham's struggles, failures, and successes with racial equality.

Then, African-American participants raised a thorny issue: the name. Chicken-bone was seen as an offensive, possibly even a racial slur. After months of revealing discussions about race and class, Chicken-bone Park was renamed Black Wall Street Garden. Mickey Michaux, a black leader, had said that one of the good things about Durham was that, at least we could sit down and talk about race. More places to sit and talk face-to-face were added to the design. The redesign was nearly complete, when Brian Smith pointed out that Black Wall Street Garden lacked a center. The design was adjusted to create a zocalo-like center in hopes of making the open space even more inclusive.

Consider this story as you read about ways to manifest belonging in your homeplace. We will next discuss five aspects that generate meaningful places. These include active belonging, acknowledged accomplishments, influential roles, group identity, and status. We share a typology of settings related to group identity that are particularly important in designing public places. Then we turn to the monster of unhealthy status obsession and how to reverse its negative influences on individuals, families and communities through creative policy and design.

Active Belonging

All people need to belong. This means to be a part of some larger social unit, a member of one group or hundreds. Membership is satisfied differently by various individuals and cultures and occurs on many levels—within the family, social group, neighborhood, city, region, and beyond. Often, being a part of a family or a nation dominates and satisfies us. Part of American identity is that we are joiners and participators in local community affairs. The French diplomat Alexis de Tocqueville, during his visit to the United States in 1831, observed the behavior of colonists at the inception of the United States and concluded that Americans are largely unable to act alone but have an exceptional capacity to form local associations to tackle the problems we then faced.[126] This active democracy that impressed him is now part of our collective consciousness. From barn raisings to community gardens we verify his view. This participatory approach through which we assertively engage in group activities and community improvements distinguishes American democracy and our pursuit of belonging.

In order to belong, we participate. Through participation we make places meaningful. Belonging literally means to have a proper or suitable place, both within a group and within a place. We belong to the place, and the place belongs to us. Participation in place-making by the people who live and work there not only makes meaningful territory, but also fulfills fundamental needs and contributes to deep democracy. Commitment to those places develops over time.[127] Most people participate initially close to home on small projects. Places are made from the inside out, evolving from the direct efforts of people who care most, and then grow from small projects to larger, from neighborhood to region and from selfish concerns to more inclusive ones (Fig. 112).

In some aspects of civic life, there is diminishing collective action.[128] This may signal a retreat from public engagement fundamental to democratic societies, a shift from some endeavors to other voluntary activities, or it may be a phase in which an aging democracy has to be revitalized.[129] People need to be able to affect the making of the city directly to develop affection for it.[130] In a poignant literary example, the protagonist in Sandra Cisneros's novel, *The House on Mango Street* (1984), declares that she is leaving her rundown neighborhood and will never return. Her friend insists that she will come back, but Esperanza shouts, "Not until somebody makes it better." The friend retorts with sarcasm that

Fig. 112. When people actively participate, they gain a sense of belonging. Emerging from martial law, youth in Taiwan assertively engage in designing improvements to their elementary school.

springs off the page, "Who's going to do it? The mayor?"[131] This is a familiar participatory theme. If we want to make our homes and civic environments better, we must do so ourselves and with neighbors, without relying entirely on government-inspired miracles. We either participate and therefore belong or we give up belonging and, consequently, profane ourselves and our space. Volunteerism is essential for the society to work and is critical for each individual, because it satisfies deep personal needs and improves our communities. Although participation in various civic affairs waxes and wanes, environmental activism in neighborhood planning has increased since the civil rights movement, partly because it allows us to improve our local world.[132] Local volunteerism changes our worldviews, gives us higher purpose, makes us more empathic, sharpens our capacity to make critical choices, and prepares us to inhabit places more respectfully.

The following design imperatives will help to entice belonging, initiate local participation, and remake the city from the inside out:

- *Provide places to belong.* Every neighborhood should be supplied with places where grassroots participation can be initiated and sustained. Neighborhood parks and open space are excellent training grounds for democratic action. They are close to home and small enough to invite participation. Most can be shaped and programmed to distinct local needs using volunteer action. Some people want to help build the facilities, others want to envision places to meet changing needs. Create opportunities for citizens to participate in planning, design, construction, and maintenance of their public landscape. Promote small neighborhood places for people of all abilities and inclinations to participate directly, face-to-face, hands-on.

- *Assist Volunteerism.* Actively encourage community self-help and volunteerism with assistance and incentives from the local government. Even meager public funds can have a major impact on the sense of belonging. In Setagaya, Japan, a small community fund offers seed grants on a competitive basis for neighborhood's open-space improvements. The modest funding has created distinctive parks throughout the community, including firefighting wells and habitats for dragonflies. The improved sense of community has created a local culture of caring. Local governments should also sponsor continuing education in civics, grassroots democracy, affordable housing, regionalism, and intentional living to encourage widespread and informed public involvement.

- *Nurture big belonging.* Locate public places centrally where groups can meet to work together and with other groups to cross-fertilize the broad public good. Be sure that the settings are designed to accommodate a variety of social interactions, from private, intimate, and small-group discussions to large public events.

Acknowledged Accomplishments

Beyond the need to belong, we want to be recognized for our contributions and accomplishments.[133] This may be in the family, neighborhood, volunteer sector, at work, or in any group of which we are a part. To be recognized is to have an externally verified identity. Because hollow approval is unfulfilling, acknowledgment satisfies our need only when it is authentic. Recognition must be for a worthy task that the group considers important and consistent with the individual's sense of self.[134] Satisfaction increases when we have performed a valued task with skill that few others could have achieved and others acknowledge the accomplishment as a job well done. But for the sense of accomplishment to feel genuine, the gratitude that the group affords must match our own view of the achievement (Fig. 113).

When individuals are acknowledged by their group and when groups are validated by an exterior entity, the settings of our accomplishments are often sanctified. A young man in Fort Bragg, California, who was coping with a serious mental disability was interviewed about the most valued places in his community. One was his mother's garden, in which he had done most of the labor and for which he had been recognized by the family. The other was the Georgia Pacific lumber mill where he had a rather dangerous job working with oversized industrial conveyor systems and moving heavy timbers. There, too, he received genuine praise from both fellow workers and the supervisors for consistently doing a difficult task well. Recognition is particularly important in the family as well as public and voluntary sectors. The most successful mayor Randy ever worked with had a sign on his desk proclaiming, "There is no limit to what you can accomplish if you are not concerned with who gets the credit." He lived

Fig. 113. Settings where jobs well done and other accomplishments are recognized by others are often remembered as special years after the event.

these words by spreading the praise far and wide for every accomplishment. The mayor posted the praise in an informal City Hall of Fame. Other groups do this with certificates for Volunteer of the Month hung in a prominent place like a public lobby. The places of accomplishment manifest the success and call attention to contributions to the civic welfare.

To acknowledge jobs well done, the following design action might serve as a precedent:

- *Acknowledge volunteer accomplishments.* Make places in civic buildings and the public landscape where big and small accomplishments may be immortalized. Volunteers who provide exceptional service to the community's welfare should be recognized in public environments at the neighborhood and regional levels. At the entry of Berkeley's Shoreline Park, a sign tells the story of three women who prevented the San Francisco Bay from being filled. They started a movement, now an organization called Save the Bay, that reversed years of dumping, pollution, and filling tidal flats and wetlands for new development that would have eventually destroyed San Francisco, reducing it to a concrete channel to the Golden Gate Bridge. A picture of the leader Sylvia McLaughlin occupies the most prominent location, signaling to passersby the accomplishment of saving the bay and also the importance of fearless activism. The bay belongs to them, and they to it. All residents today belong to the bay as a result of their work. Thanks to the women's action, today the bay is the most sacred landscape to hundreds of thousands of Bay Area residents.

Influential Roles

Another source of belonging is achieved through the exercise of power within and outside the group. To influence decisions through leadership, seniority, specialized knowledge, friendship, debts, networking, or charisma satisfies the need to have an influential role. Such roles may be those typically associated with exercise of power by virtue of some official position in the public or private sector, but they may also be subtler. Political actions may occur in the spotlight or in the background. Typical settings include the glamorous stages of public debate, backroom arm-twisting, the campaign trail, the halls of Congress, lobbyist-paid junkets, the streets of protest, or behind closed corporate doors. All of these places mark the influences of the politically overt. For many, power is exercised more quietly by arranging the furniture for a community workshop, walking door to door to register voters, facilitating a round-table discussion, gathering field data to present as evidence from an expert witness, or distributing an image of racial brutality over the Internet. These more modest settings also punctuate the exercise of power. Any of these may well be sanctified by an individual or group as a signature of influence, the post where notice was served (Fig. 114).

Likewise, influential roles may be inscribed into places with a plaque or sign that demarcates an acquired parkland, preserved historic district, or a freeway that is stopped. These markers claim territory and may acknowledge the expansion of influence beyond the original turf of the group. At the most intimate scale of the organization, influence may be expressed by a chair reserved for a natively wise elder or a garden for secret negotiations on the top floor of a corporate headquarters.

Exercising influence can empower people, but it can also work in reverse when influence is exercised upon people to cause a sense of debilitation. Therefore, power reflected in the built environment can be liberating or oppressive, depending on whose power is expressed onto whom. Today, the most powerful groups are typically corporations, think tanks funded by billionaires, and the government.[135] Corporate control is most visible in financial districts of major cities, but, when partnered with government, corporate values extend into every detail of the public environment.[136] This is appropriate unless your community's values are in opposition to those of the corporate and political authority, which is often the case for those seeking to inhabit the sacred. When they do conflict, resisting is often the first action that prompts other responses from deep democracy at the local level. Here, power is less about elections, lobbying, and consuming and more about integrating domestic work and civic lives.[137] Authority of resistance stems from relationships in daily life, distributing power instead of concentrat-

Fig. 114. Working under the protective eye of architect Yasuhiro Endoh, children in Japan assumed central roles in calling attention to the joys of street life when automobile traffic was blocked. A pedestrian-friendly design for their neighborhood resulted.

ing it, and celebrating each small victory of community values with symbols of resistance and reclaimed democracy.[138] Many of the most dramatic urban reformations such as community gardens or removal of a freeway have grown from the seeds of local change that provided a more appealing vision of the city and democracy. The impact on the built and inhabited environment is striking and no longer small scale. [139] How influential roles should be expressed in the public landscape is often a controversial issue. Elected officials and corporate sponsors often want their power inscribed by size and naming rights. Grassroots influence lacks resources for such expressions. City form can recognize the authority, positive and negative, of dominant powers more directly and simultaneously express the rising influence of grassroots democracy with the following actions:

- *Make power transparent.* Expose unhealthy influences that undermine a living democracy and inform the public of the dangers of concentrated or one-sided authority. This can most readily be done by making power transparent. As an example, at the base of Taipei 101, at one time the tallest building in the world, there is a marker celebrating the corporation that financed the structure and one honoring the laborers who died during the building's construction. Such reminders give fair warning.
- *Manifest grassroots influence.* Create public spaces that celebrate urban reformations that grow from the grassroots and implement visionary civic life like People's Park and the colorful traffic

barriers in Berkeley. Mark bottom-up influences that encourages more intentional living. Posting notices of modest neighborhood improvements like a cooperative bakery, affordable housing, and a pedestrian-friendly street will command power in the future.

Group Identity

Pause for a moment and make a list of about a half-dozen or more groups with whom you most identify. Then mark the ones that are most important to you and list the places you associate with those groups. Consider the location, size, and qualities of those places. As you read this section, compare the places you listed to the types we describe. Do your places fit these categories, or do you have different ones? How do your kindred-spirit groups most effectively express their identities?

Like individuals, a group must secure its distinct personality with a shared worldview and ritual behavior. The group must clarify its purpose, test and confirm its intended identity, weather crises that challenge its sense of self, and determine if it has the characteristics and power it fancies. To sustain a sense of belonging, a group must develop an identity that appeals to its members and reflects its authority and commitment to outsiders. The public environment is an important setting for forming, testing, reflecting, confirming, and marking a group's identity to the rest of the community.

When Amber first moved to a small colonial town in southern Río de Janeiro, she noticed strange looking, over-sized doors attached oddly to buildings in the historic center of town. The doors matched each other but seemed out-of-place architecturally. She could not imagine what they concealed. The mystery lingered until Holy Tuesday, when she arrived at the main plaza to discover one of the doors open, revealing not a room but an altar, complete with a picture of a crucified Jesus, flowers, and a prayer bench in front. The other odd doors were also open. Amber discovered these to be Stations of the Cross, each a stop along the way for the annual procession of *semana santa*. For believers, these secret doors were no secret at all. They were reminded of their religious identity passing by them every day.

Almost every group, whether a church group, an amateur sports league, or a nation state, places itself initially at the center, creating an ethnocentric topophilia (Fig. 115).[140] This is usually the home base. At the neighborhood level, the surrounding landscape reflects the group's identity in house form, yards, and gardens. There is a unified expression of culture or social class within each group, whether in the dooryard gardens of Puerto Rico, xerophytic yards in Tucson, or agricultural plots in North and South Ethiopia.[141] Landscape style is also a symbol of group identity in wealthy communities where alpha landscapes are slightly seedy, overgrown, and rural, reflecting the security of old money and dominant identities needing no embellishment. Beta landscapes communicate that these owners are less confident of their new class. They know they are secondary to those more established and try to compensate by creating ostentatiously manicured yards with showy houses in view from the road. The larger landscape reflects similar distinctions of class. Higher classes separate themselves with woods and overgrown underbrush from others who prefer more orderly landscapes.[142] Today, the places of

August 8, 2012

A Maravilhosa Maracanã na Construção

Fig. 115. Maracaña Stadium has been a center of Brazilian identity for more than sixty years, at one time seating more than 200,000 soccer fans in a soccer-crazed country but often appearing unfinished and in need of repair.

group identity are often far more complex than these neighborhood expressions of social distinctions. Social class and insider/outsider group identities continue to dominate, but group definitions based on culture, alternative lifestyles, sexual preference, environmental values, and old timers/newcomers reflect increasingly fragmented social and political identities. For the homeless, those struggling against foreclosure, new immigrants, transnationals, refugees, and women, the group may have places of confused, double, or hollow identity or may be robbed of identity altogether. Likely, they lack a centering home base.[143] Marjorie Agosin, a Chilean-American author of Jewish parents, speaks poetically for many people today when she acknowledged that she has no country and no citadels, only a dream, stones, and rivers. She acknowledged her lack of group identity grounded in place as she contemplated that she always feels as if she is from some place else.[144] This becomes an ever-increasing problem when refugees flee to places where they are unwanted.

One of the first priorities in establishing group identity is to lay claim to a place that provides certainty. This home base can be within the private domain, but most often the group requires the appropriation of public space and some imposition on the public and private lives of others. This can cause conflict among old and emerging groups over both the space and the mores governing its use. The dispute both threatens and solidifies identity. The public space becomes symbolic of the struggle for group identity through a spiral of increasing intensity that creates ever more hallowed place.[145] Other than resource exploitation, group identity fuels the most fiercely conflicted battles over place of any factor.

Ongoing conflicts of identity over territory take multiple forms, but all focus on highly symbolic land. This may be as local as turf wars between street gangs, racial struggles to claim parts of a city's history or community gardeners claiming vacant lots.[146] Conflicts may also be as international as the contest over the West Bank, India and Pakistan's disputed border, or China's claim to the island of Taiwan. These land disputes are more than political quandaries. In the case of the Taiwanese dilemma regarding Chinese versus Taiwanese identity, it is changing the way the landscape of Taiwan is viewed and remade by its inhabitants. Until recently, the 100,000 nationalists who retreated there in 1949 after the Chinese communists drove them from mainland China considered Taiwan a temporary address until they recaptured China. They formed little attachment to the island and oppressed the groups who had deep roots there, partly to control them and establish a nationalist identity and partly to exploit the land for short-term profit, since the nationalists never intended to stay. Only in the past few decades have the cultures of the native people and the early Han Chinese been recognized as the foundation of a unique Taiwanese culture. A strong Taiwanese identity is emerging, expressed not only in passionate democratization and diversity, but also in growing attachment to the new homeland. The island is finally becoming sacred to hundreds of thousands of people who had little regard for it even two decades ago.[147]

The symbolic value of place rises dramatically when identity is being formed, tested, lost, or violated.[148] The case of Taiwan is a dramatic instance of the reestablishment of affective identity, but similar turmoil in the meaning of place is associated with every migration, conquest, colonization, protectorate, or act of imperialism.[149] Psychological turmoil regarding place, although seldom as physically violent, delineates crises of identity and initiates assimilation of youth, new immigrants, minorities, and marginalized people. Some cultural identity is genetically and socially inherited, but increasingly it is constructed, and this, too, creates confusion. Our colleague, Anna Holand, insists that people in Norway are simultaneously pressured to be both the best and like everyone else, creating unbearable conflict. Today we have multiple choices of group identities, largely due to an increase of mobility and reliance on the Internet. This flexibility unsettles people and their places, because they create unpredictable patterns of habitation but still exhibit predictable needs of the group. Acknowledging this challenge can help us understand the underlying values of the group, highlight their conflicts, and consider possible solutions.

In our professional practice, we often are confronted with serious conflicts regarding how the identities of various groups can be manifested in places we are designing. We have continually witnessed what can be described as typologies of place identity. These typologies help us sort out the issues and resolve disputes through redesigning the places. These patterns of conflicted habitation in public settings include continually contested places, enclaves, places to preserve culture, tourist places, hybrid places, shared places of unity, marginalized places, and places without identity. Although some of these habitations occur in private or virtual space, all involve at least a public face essential for group identity. Consider the characteristics of each setting:

Continually contested places. Some places are continually contested, usually because it is in the best interest of one or more of the competing groups to maintain instability, because neither group has sufficient authority to resolve the territorial dispute, or because the values represented by the space are inviolable and cannot be negotiated.[150] By virtue of the ongoing struggle, the contested place becomes more sacred. This makes resolution less likely. Jurisdiction over Jerusalem is one example. Oil and gas exploration in national wildlife refuges is another. Similarly, at the most local level, battles for the same space between cars and pedestrians, shoppers and the homeless, store owners and panhandlers are seldom resolved. The same is true for the territory that evenly matched gangs fight over; each may control a home base, but the overlapping edges are constant flash points. In some cases, in deadly gang warfare, demilitarized zones are created, which become places without identity or meaning for either side, because a new identity emerges to create a safe haven or peace park. At the larger scale, as in the case of Korea, the Demilitarized Zone represents an unending war, painfully separated families, 50-plus years of propaganda, immature tweets from leaders about destroying each other, the elusive possibility of reunification, virgin land to be exploited, and one of the most biologically diverse and complete ecosystems in all of Asia.

Enclaves. Usually, stability-seeking behavior resolves conflict over territory in the creation of segregated enclaves with a singular identity internally shared. They often result from a top-down process of power exerted by a dominant society to create enclaves of race or class disparagingly labeled "ghettos."[151] Nonetheless, enclaves may also be formed from the bottom up by the subcultural group that belongs to it.[152] In Los Angeles, these present-day ethnospaces can be identified in parks and commercial areas where new immigrant groups tend to cluster their businesses, often revitalizing a dying strip for development. The concentration of subcultural capital regenerates the buildings and creates nodes of culturally specific activity. Usually, these are segregated by highly public enclaves. Some become tourist attractions like Chinatowns or a home base for urban adventurers like the Mission District in San Francisco.[153]

The enclaves of recent Puerto Rican immigrants, second-generation Hmong families, gay communities, and organized bodies of dairy farmers foster a sense of security and identity by separating themselves, as do gated communities of the affluent. In these separated enclaves, security breeds spontaneous expressions of culturally distinct public space and enhances a group's identity. Identity politics often grow out of segregated propinquity.[154] In contrast, some neighborhoods define themselves by diversity of ethnicities, classes, or life-cycle stages and gain a reputation for their variety. They are known for respectful heterogeneity rather than homogeneity.

Preservation of culture. Places are sometimes preserved, because they represent society's fundamental identity. For example, America's collective sense of a big and wild self is expressed in national parks, wildlife reserves and wilderness areas. Historic preservation movements protect areas and structures that link national identity to past events and people.[155] Often, a type of place deeply ingrained in a culture's identity will continue to be replicated long after its utility has declined. Mexican-American communities traditionally made *paseos* as part of their central plaza, so that men circulated in one direction and women in the other in courtship. As dating changed, *paseos* were no longer used the same way, though they are still frequently included in Mexican-American parks as a reminder of cultural identity.[156]

Today, there is a push to maintain unique cultural diversity through the preservation of architectural heritage.[157] These efforts often involve the deliberate use of traditional building forms, materials, and processes.[158] In some cases, it entails uncompromised devotion to the historical procedure and form, as at the Ise Shrine in Japan. Most often, the subcultural group employs a combination of vernacular and modern techniques. This is the preferred approach of John Liu in his work with the Taiwanese Dahul house, a housing type that is traditionally made of stone and wood, partly underground with no utilities. He incorporates a toilet and modern kitchen while maintaining the ancient form.[159]

Tourism. When subcultural identity is maintained in buildings and the landscape, those sites often become tourist destinations. The identity is so strong to outsiders that the culture, the built artifacts, or both are marketable.[160] Tourism temporarily enhances identity, but the commodification often diminishes cultural homogeneity in time. It may lead to a manufactured culture, though, if economically successful, tourism seems to bolster group pride.

Hybridity. Anytime an alien force is introduced into a space occupied by tradition, hybridity may result if there is commingling between the new and old cultures. As cultural identity is expressed spontaneously and where identities intermingle, hybrid space of borders and mixes arise. This hybridization may create new forms of public places with enriching juxtapositions where a Chinese New Year dragon joins a Cinco de Mayo parade or where bok choy grows amidst rap music or pedestrians and cars share a woornerf or cul-de-sac. On the other hand, such space may threaten longstanding identity. In Monterey Park, California, the first American city with an Asian, predominantly upper-class Chinese majority, old timers (Anglo Americans, Japanese Americans, and Mexican Americans) felt invaded. One longtime resident told researchers that she felt like she was in a foreign country, "I don't feel at home anymore."[161] Another wished for the time before the Chinese takeover, when Monterey Park was the Mexican Beverly Hills. She resented the forced fusion. Hybrid space upsets old identities and formulates new ones, both of which are sacred to distinct groups.

Shared Unity. Even in communities of segregated enclaves or hybrid identities, there are usually some settings that express cultural unity.[162] These may be tourist areas or places specifically associated with a group's territory that are shared on special occasions. Places of shared unity may be previously contested space that has meaning for several groups simultaneously, because it represents the capacity to reconcile earlier conflicts. These places symbolize truly democratic space or the few values that are broadly agreed upon by groups who otherwise battle over identity politics.

Marginalization. Even marginalized groups have places that confirm their identity positively and negatively. These areas include low-income neighborhoods, squatter settlements, gang territory, homeless encampments, and derelict teen hangouts.[163] Outsiders may stigmatize these areas, but they still serve as a means of group identity and are not disgraceful for the insiders. In his classic study from the 1950s, Herbert Gans found that low-income families held their West End Boston neighborhood in high regard despite scheduled clearance from Urban Renewal. It was viewed by the dominant culture as an unlivable blight that had to be removed. Residents considered it a good place to live.[164] They valued its low rents and readily available services, and they cherished it for the highly identifiable, supportive ethnic village it was. It was eventually bulldozed at great cost to the inhabitants. Gentrification now creates the same impact on previous residents that the bulldozers did during the era of Urban Renewal. They get pushed out without any affordable place to go. A significant difference is that the housing in gentrifying neighborhoods, instead of being viewed as blight, is seen as attractive to the new residents. To resist gentrifying forces, some communities try to retain their marginal visual qualities or seek special protections from government agencies.

Non-identity. Some geographic areas lack identity altogether. After doing his research in which respondents left various areas blank when making cognitive maps of their cities, Kevin Lynch labeled the blanks "gray areas." They were simply unknown parts of the cities. In other cases, residents of an area may lack any shared sense of being an identifiable group. During the 1960s and 1970s, antipoverty community organizers tried to build a sense of identity in areas with disenfranchised citizens to initiate collective power and authority.[165] More recently, it has been acknowledged that this lack of neighborhood identity is more widespread and is more likely in wealthier than in poorer neighborhoods. Accustomed to privatized lifestyles, these residents lack a shared identity of place and motivation to work together.

These patterns attest to the complexity of needs, spatial qualities, design actions, and democratic processes required to support various group identities and to resolve their territorial conflicts. Think about the particular patterns of places of identity in your own community. Add those to the list we have presented. Then think of ways to celebrate positive patterns and improve problematic ones. We offer several planning actions. In city design, we might begin by undertaking the following:

- *Nurture emerging group identities.* Provide places for groups to form, test, reflect, confirm, and
    mark their identities. It is especially important to accommodate new groups in civic places
    as they create centers and establish territories for emerging identities. Acknowledge that
    new groups are essential in a living democracy to address changing problems, even if they
    are threatening and make life uncomfortable for old orders. Typically, public policy makes
    this difficult. Witness the struggles to claim space of gays and lesbians, new immigrants or
    teenagers. Sensible design policy would create "incubator" or "experimental" spaces in com-
    munity centers and public open spaces for fledgling groups.

- *Accommodate difference.* Respect the informal operating rules of enclaves, places where groups seek to preserve their cultures and their hybridized and marginalized places. Their rules may be divergent from the dominant culture, requiring exceptions to normative planning processes, design form, zoning, and codes in order to facilitate everyday life. Policy actions as simple as allowing food carts and trucks, multiple small owners of shopping centers, or extending the hours of business operation to allow nighttime markets can accommodate cultural differences. Design actions such as providing picnic tables big enough for extended family gatherings, pavilions for morning exercises, and quiet spots for *tai chi* allow groups to continue cultural traditions.

- *Process conflict anew.* Develop a fair process to air conflicts over public space arising from identity politics and a means to use such conflicts to inspire new city form. Processes like conflict mediation, Lawrence Halprin's RSVP cycles, Randy's 12-steps, De la Pena's Design as Democracy, or MIG's participatory workshops may be appropriate for different contentious situations.[166] We should expect innovative forms of participatory democracy to emerge from these efforts.

- *Share group identity.* Create central places where distinct identities can be shared and hybrid identities that supersede differences can be celebrated. For example, a *bocce* court can invite multicultural and cross-generation participation beyond the stereotypical users of old Italian men. July Fourth parades celebrate our shared praise of freedom. Places for similar events should remind us of our responsibility to deep democracy. We all need places for refresher courses in civics. Assess the potential for cooperation across the divisions of local group interests in order to develop a united agenda to resist and undo external powers that would prey on local divisiveness to exploit a community.

Status

Status verifies our standing within our familiar groups and to the unfamiliar world beyond. Expressions of status are essential for all individuals and all groups. Status establishes order, makes social hierarchies clear, supports identity, marks accomplishments, and reinforces authority. Architecture, the landscape, and city form always reflect status.[167] It can be as subtle as the distinction between a dramatically uplifted swallowtail roof line and a more modest curve on Chinese houses or as in-your-face as the tallest building in the world. In traditional place-based communities, the expressions are hierarchical yet nuanced. Standing in the community may be determined by honesty, selflessness, wisdom, or wealth. When everyone knows each other's position, minimal displays are necessary. In more mobile and placeless societies, however, seeking status becomes more ostentatious and competitive. Having more space becomes a worldwide symbol of prestige.[168] Bigness, the possession of the rare, an address in a distinguished neighborhood distanced from undesirable land uses, cleanliness,

Fig. 116. When advocates for sustainable development sought precedents
for conspicuous non-consumption, they found them in strange places like
St. Louis neighborhoods with houses less than fifteen feet wide.

and conspicuous consumption are methods to distinguish our position, because we do not otherwise
know one another.

Displays of status can be directed inward but most often are outwardly directed. They reflect
unfulfilled desires to belong yet be distinguished apart from others. Symbols of prestige can express
that a person or community is either healthy or insecure in its identity. They can denote accomplishments, a lack of need to compete with others, or a withdrawal from civic life. When combined with fear
and insecurity, status seeking becomes an obsession. When combined with belonging and intentional
living, status seeking can delight us with newfound prestige. This is the power of groups that support
their members in healthy status play. For example, in Davis, California, the residents of Village Homes
practice conspicuous non-consumption with small houses, solar energy, skinny streets, and limits on
technological display. Such cases provide precedents for others (Fig. 116).[169]

To address issues of status seeking, we might consider the following actions:

- *Fashion contrary status seeking.* Design civic buildings, neighborhoods, and landscapes to
  express healthy symbols of status. Emphasize smallness, the commonplace, proximity,
  heterogeneity, and conspicuous non-consumption. For example, make buildings as small
  as is feasible.

- *Expose status publicly.* Create public forums to discuss the negative impacts of status seeking. Stimulate more intentional living with parodies of obsessive status seeking.

Monster 4: Obsession with Status

Objects of status verify our standing to friends, associates, and those whom we know less well, the anonymous others of the larger society. As a culture becomes less rooted, more mobile, and impersonal, increasingly visible and blatant objects of status are required to express social standing for individuals and the groups and communities to which they ostensibly belong. Consumptive status-seeking undermines a sense of belonging, satisfies the need for recognition in unsatisfying ways, and eventually erodes a positive sense of self and community.

There has been a recorded rise during the last fifty years in "insecure individualism" that makes American society both unruggedly individualistic and anonymously other directed at the same time.[170] Status symbols are "quick fixes" of confidence for underdeveloped, shallow, or unhealthy identities. This does not diminish the importance of symbols of prestige, but obsessive status seeking replaces sacredness grounded in place with sacredness grounded in consumption.

Obsession with status empowers corporations that prey on an anxious, busy, consumer society.[171] Many of us do not find time to vote (often less than ten to twenty percent of eligible voters bother to vote in non-presidential elections), but we indulge ourselves with packaged prestige like lifestyle shopping. Because our individual objects of status reflect upon corporate profits, we are hopelessly reliant upon the very companies that are undoing our democracy, our environment, and our communities. So the monster is both the corporate structure and our obsession with consumption. One within and one without. Eventually, we must dismantle the privileges that corporations enjoy that we do not and that are wasting our democracy. Before we can be effective at that, we must fully understand the specific needs that drive us to obsession with status. Let us begin by defining the various qualities of status seeking that are expressed in the environment:

Size. Bigness is the primary means of making prestige visible. As one measure, the average American house since World War II has become twice as large, even as it sheltered nearly one person less. The pursuit of gigantism inflicts almost every group, community, city, and company.[172] Big usually spreads out and is now the single greatest factor in the extinction of species due to loss of habitat.

Vertical mobility. The pursuit of the social class above our present position explains more about attachment to and detachment from place than any other factor.[173] Not only does the place associated with the previous lower position have to be discarded, but it also must be treated with disdain. The pursued place is made all the holier and the previously sacred turns profane in a reversed double denial of false sacredness. Even highly functional and meaningful aspects of the patterns of inhabiting a place, of previous "relative poverty" are disregarded as deprived.[174]

Horizontal mobility. Being mobile serves as a badge of status in addition to providing freedom and escape. In daily life, commuting divides place into two realms with less time to know either intimately and fewer chances to form a relationship with the space between. Also, the ease with which we can relocate for better opportunities reduces loyalty to any one place. Migration allows us to flee places that do not work out, move and pretend that place does not matter. Among other detriments, this precludes sustained ecoliteracy and native wisdom.

Posing. Insecurity and feelings of inferiority fuel the search to be something a person or city is not and often does not have the capacity to be. Unrealistic pipedreams often prompt communities to imitate more prestigious cities, almost never successfully and at the tremendous waste of scarce resources and funds.

Homogeneity. Exclusive homogeneity conveys prestige.[175] This requires keeping out anyone who is different, whether the distinction is color, social class, age, health, country of origin, religion, sexuality, or lifestyle. Homogeneous subdivisions and exurban addresses remain desired addresses of most Americans. Social and environmental uniformity enhanced by height and natural setting serve security and group identity as well as status.

Rarity. Possessing the rare is symbolically impressive. One-of-a-kind or the very best, whether a home or landscape, has more power to impress than any commonplace habitation. Common but practical vernacular building forms and meaningful regional life patterns become less desirable.

Cleanliness. Clean and antiseptic places free of blemishes rank high. Once a legitimate health concern, our preoccupation with the immaculate now exceeds practicality. The corollary stigmatizes dirt, garden soil, farms, junk yards, swamps, jungles, mud flats, and mud holes.[176]

Gluttony. Conspicuous consumption, squandering limited resources, and ostentatious waste impact ecosystems. Possession of disposable technologies and conveniences confer status.[177]

Newness. Possession and display of the new and novel express high status, making us susceptible to fads, which feed crazed consumerism and gluttony. Even sustainability has become a fashion statement in selling real estate, cars, and other consumer products. Some "green washing" marketing schemes label their product green, even when ingredients or materials are environmentally hazardous.

These patterns of excess are detrimental to nearly every precious aspect of life. In concert, they form a nearly insurmountable barrier to healthy group identity, community belonging, and participation in a deep democracy. Obsession with status renders recognition hollow, fuels wasteful consumption of scarce resources, and exacerbates environmental injustices. We become extravagant and senseless. We chase false idols, making the manifestation of the truly sacred more difficult but also more essential.

Designing and Planning to Belong

Status-seeking, pursuing bigness, extravagance, and being the best distinguish individuals and communities, often at great cost. Youth in Norway suffer under such great pressure to be singularly the "best" that they are stressed to the point of mental illness. Many do not want to live anymore. Our colleague and landscape architect, Anna Holand, worried incessantly about the problem. She knew that one out of five students were struggling with mental issues, and most were medicated without follow-up. She sensed that youth were unusually insecure, because they felt unneeded in their communities and no longer belonged. One day she knew she had to act. Her idea was to create a "Good Enough" Festival, or *God Nok* in Norwegian, to counter the impossible pressure not only to conform, but also to be the very best.

The festival featured "Talks of the Day" by experts, discussing sensitive topics of life-threatening depression. The talks encouraged the community to communicate to each other about unspeakable tragedy. Afterwards, frank and informed discussions resumed around a bonfire and walks along the coast. Music, theatre, and art reinforced the sense of God Nok, calling attention to the positive aspects of the community and the landscape (Fig. 117). For thirty years, the community had produced an outdoor drama that celebrates a legend from the place. It is a Viking story somewhat like Romeo and Juliet that stresses the tender humanity of the community. God Nok reinforced this positive aspect of the community.

Rather than providing stock answers, participants determined for themselves how to implement "good enough" in daily interactions. Parents now share their feelings more honestly with their children. A group offers mental-health counseling. God Nok received national attention, spurring people to attend the festival and begin dialogues in their own communities about the deepest problems afflicting Norwegians.

Why was the festival so successful? It was a topic that touched people's hearts. Almost the entire community volunteered to help. Design played a big role. Ms. Holand and her friends designed the festival space to create a sense of belonging among a temporary community, determining that only a thousand tickets would be sold: big enough to feel festive, small enough to be intimate. No one would feel lost in the crowd. Everyone would belong. For the site, she chose a charming beach that local people cherished in the Municipality of Steigen overlooking the Lofoten Islands. The original plan spread activities out, locating the main stage away from the water to accommodate the crowd, but the group realized the plan didn't create the sense of belonging they desired. With only weeks remaining

Fig. 117. Like the Good Enough Festival in Norway, the Amis of Hengchun Peninsula half a world away celebrate the positive values of their community and the power of their landscape. Priestesses teach young people how the place makes them a distinct and worthy culture in spite of discrimination.

Fig. 118. The Amis' festivals create a sense of joyful belonging in a temporary shelter, made from local materials, just big enough to accommodate traditional dance and song so intense that they harmonize with waves crashing below.

Fig. 119. Successful festivals not only celebrate, but also create settings for thoughtful discussions, often during a meal, about community issues. For the Amis, "talks of the day" focus on ways to accommodate matrilineal ownership in the face of transient global economies.

before the event, they shrunk the entire layout to be more personal and better integrated with the landscape. The main stage was relocated only a few meters from the water (Fig. 118). This juxtaposed performances with the fjord and overcast midnight-sun sky, creating a setting few had ever experienced. Some danced barefoot in the sand. Some snuggled into tall beach grass. Others wandered among the boathouses for food and exhibits, within social distance of each other. All gathered at the beach to hear the "Talks of the Day" (Fig. 119). Holand's festival might serve as a model for other communities to create settings to overcome difficult-to-discuss troubles.

Our cities must be reshaped so they encourage people and communities to be what they are, not pose as something they are not. When thoughtfully designed, cities can encourage people to avoid unhealthy obsessions with status and invite people to belong. If people feel they belong to their city and their city supports their development, they will participate more, dig in, and relocate less. Local associations, a fundamental American tradition, are the basis of long and healthy lives and a robust democracy.[178] They provide the support for belonging. Belonging to groups offers us a proper and suitable place, but those groups must have proper and suitable places.

- *Make places for associations.* To facilitate local associations, cities must be reshaped to make settings for groups to center themselves, claim territory, and make boundaries. This is especially important for new immigrants and transient societies. City design should make it easy to form, test, reflect, confirm, and mark old and emerging group identities.[179] There should be diverse opportunities for people of all abilities and interests to belong, through community planning, construction, programming, and maintenance of the public landscape. Volunteer organizations engaged in collective self-help need to be supported by local government with staff, incentives, and modest funds.

- *Seek sensible status.* Each group and the city itself should pursue sensible status seeking, avoiding harmful impacts to community, ecosystems, and democratic process while fulfilling the needs for influence and recognition. Groups should be what they are and become what they can be by using resources indigenous and endemic to that locality. The use of common local materials instead of rare, imported ones should be rewarded and made a matter of pride. Making group territories and facilities as small as possible should also be recognized as a manifestation of public interest. Home space should be similarly designed. Randy and Marcia's home in Berkeley was only 400 square feet and so freshly sustainable by almost every standard that a prestigious car company wanted to use it in an ad to sell cars. Randy and Marcia didn't even have a car, the garage and driveway of the previous owner having been converted to a studio and garden. They walked everywhere and lectured extensively on the damage the automobile does to a community and the environment. Using their home to market the car was a no brainer. They refused the offer.

- *Make belonging central.* In every community, there should be a place that is centrally located and most lavishly attended where shared values and identity are celebrated. This place must remind inhabitants of their collective responsibility to each other, the locality, and the region that sometimes supersedes smaller identity. Like individuals, groups within a locality are prone to compete with each other. This is partly due to values and interests vested in each group, partly due to who is included and excluded, and partly due to rivalry for resources, recognition, and authority within the community. Conflict may also be fueled from without by government, lobbying, and corporate interests wishing to exploit divisions within the locality. Each community needs to sort out what conflicts between local groups are genuine and which are manufactured. Both unhealthy influences from within and without should be exposed. This is easier to do if there are central places in neutral turf where different groups can come together for cooperative and symbiotic efforts. It also helps to assess the potential for unified action to resist and undo harmful external powers. Special recognition should be given to grassroots efforts that encourage intentional living, express status sensibly, and manifest the blessings of belonging. These efforts should be denoted in central places.

- *Share authority freely.* Democracy is well served when established groups and dominant authorities can openly acknowledge that, although new groups may threaten their power, they can embrace the spread of power. Repressing challengers may prolong authority for a while, but that eventually leads to internecine struggles that drain the energy from all groups. Old groups often solve old problems. New groups address new problems. Only together can old and new groups solve those new problems. Established organizations can provide access to other powers and proven strategies for improving the local community. New groups bring insights into emerging problems, creativity, and energy. Both contribute to the community and a living democracy. The community and the local democracy grow stronger when there exists a fair and transparent process to air conflicts and when they use tension to generate creative resolutions. Communities should minimize places that are continually contested, because such never-ending conflict usurps energy well spent on other endeavors. Dominant local powers should also respect the informal rules of enclaves, places to preserve cultures, hybrid places, and marginalized space. In some cases, exceptions to formal procedures and regulations are necessary to accommodate the healthy diversity these places offer.

Having just considered how to create places of active belonging, accomplishments, influential roles, group identity, and healthy status, think about which of these would most improve the quality of your home and community. Maybe your family or community needs more places that recognize the civic contributions of citizens. Maybe there needs to be a place to discuss seriously and propose strategies for problems like drug suicides, racism, lack of affordable housing, and food security so often swept under the rug. Maybe new immigrants need a place at the table of decision-making. Or something else. Now is a good time to reflect on this and manifest your own solutions.

In Step 5, we have structured a means to organize the deepest desires of individuals and communities into a framework of four wishes—security, new experiences, reciprocal responses, and belonging. We have noted that we cannot inhabit the sacred without expression of these deep values in places that make those values tangible. Manifesting transforms our values from abstractions into the physical world. We have shown how to manifest places of security and safety, places of new experiences, places of reciprocal responses, and places of belonging for our individual, family, community, and civic lives. Some of the prescriptions suggested require painful personal change. We must face the monsters of fear, shallow adventure, loss of nearness, and obsessive status seeking in our personal lives and reestablish a commitment to civic life and deep democracy. To do so, we must reform our towns and cities to create settings that facilitate new lives rooted in fundamental needs. In Step 6, we inhabit those places.

IN THE EVERYDAY LANDSCAPE

WE ARE ABLE TO CREATE the opportunity for inhabiting the sacred through an organized process of awakening consciousness, evidencing sentiments about place, transforming values, organizing action, and manifesting the four wishes through design and planning. But inhabiting means more than our physical presence in a landscape, more than occupying space, more than living somewhere. Inhabiting is to be alive fully in our place. Inhabiting is to live intentionally. Inhabiting satisfies the four wishes—certainty, new experiences, reciprocal responses, and belonging—through a powerful bond between self, place, and community. The place offers the inhabitants these four wishes, and the inhabitants offer the same to the place in return. The landscape is imbued with meaning and power, because it is shaped from fundamental values. The phenomenon is not mystical; rather, it is a matter of awareness, cooperation, and action. Yet when an everyday sacred place is entered, people feel that it is a special, wondrous realm.

Ways of Inhabiting the Sacred

You are likely already inhabiting the sacred to some degree. How one does this varies from person to person, depending on how one engages with a community and the surrounding landscape. It requires all of us to reawaken and live attentively every day. It requires us to be motivated internally and externally empathic. We must be centered and civic. Inhabiting the everyday sacred can be experienced through various actions: constructing, dwelling, stewarding, ritually visiting, and advocating.

Constructing

As discussed in Step 5: Manifesting, we are likely to form a lasting affection for a place that we help to construct. We saw this when Ward redesigned his home to invite more sunlight in. We saw it when Emily painted her rooms. We see it in barn raisings, community gardens, and Habitat for Humanity houses. As does a professional architect and landscape architect, we begin to know meaningful spaces when we build them. A place eventually becomes sacred to us personally, because we embed our needs there. Making this space in the public realm will further enrich the experience, because we benefit not only from our own feedback and the response of the landscape, but also the feedback and response of others. We learn how our ideas of a sacred place coincide or conflict with others. Constructing is a source of new skills, personal pride, and accomplishment to see and share physical proof of our efforts.

When we make our place, the building materials respond to us. We come to know them and they us. We reciprocate with the wood we sand, the brick we mortar, the stucco we cast, the trees we plant. Each is near, tangible, and appreciated with all our senses. For most of us, making a place teaches us how to do new things. This is often an adventure that empowers us, conveys security, and grounds us. Although only a minority of Americans build their own homes from scratch, it is a most powerful ingredient in inhabiting the everyday sacred.[1] Therefore, people should make and remake as much of their own homes as they can. It should be done with their own hands with the help of skilled friends. Even if a home is rented, modest but meaningful changes can be made through modifications to the interior and furnishings. If it has outdoor space, a garden can be made.[2] Making your own place satisfies all four wishes.

This satisfaction from making your home place also applies to your larger home—your community. In Step 4: Organizing, we illustrated how to seek a community's involvement in the design and construction phase of a public place that cements neighbors' love for their landscape or kick-starts the interest of people who have not yet been centrally involved. Civic clubs, teenagers, young adults, and retirees are especially well-suited for volunteer labor. Involving them creates a mutually beneficial partnership, but skilled craftspeople are still needed who can teach others. This also creates a partnership across classes, generations, and genders. Local businesses are usually generous with donating materials, professional labor, and small sums of money to support worthy community-based projects. Again, this is a beneficial relationship for both sides: Community outreach is good publicity for any organization, and, for anyone involved in the construction of a project, the recognition received for their effort satisfies the essential human need of civic belonging. Other benefits to the community include enhanced social capital and a can-do identity. These positive values root us in place, allow the place to nurture us, and encourage us to be engaged residents. Constructing a place makes dwelling in a place more meaningful.

Although we can recount hundreds of public projects we have witnessed become beloved as community members made them, the Exhibit Hall in Castle Rock, Washington, stands out. When Mount St. Helens collapsed and then erupted on May 18, 1980, Castle Rock lost not only lives, but also hope for the future; the city quickly declined. After ten years of despair, citizens began a revitalization effort focused on creating a local museum that would tell about their relationship with the volcano (Fig. 120). They had been assured of a state grant to construct the museum, but that fell through just before groundbreaking. The town again was deflated. Marcia McNally called a meeting of key locals, locked the door, and said no one could leave until they had a new plan for construction. Within two hours, a grassroots plan of donated materials, and volunteer labor was devised (Fig. 121). Hundreds of people pitched in, doing every detail of the construction with their own hands (Fig. 122). At the opening of the Exhibit Hall months later, a celebration the likes of which had never been seen in Cowlitz County rocked the town. People loved the Exhibit Hall for many reasons but primarily because they made it themselves (Fig. 123).

Left: Fig. 120. The economic revitalization of Castle Rock focused on reusing an abandoned building as a small museum.

Right: Fig. 121. After government funding fell through, Marcia McNally organized community volunteers to build the museum themselves.

Dwelling

To dwell is to reside actively for an extended amount of time in one place. It requires us to pay attention to the place with all our senses and knowledge. This keeps us alert, gives us pleasure, and continually enables us to extract new experience from what may seem to others to be the most ordinary environments.[3] This is one of the great lessons of Henry David Thoreau's life at Walden Pond. To dwell requires moments of slower paces than career-driven people typically live. To dwell is to linger, to be here now, to hang out. Even a few moments of lingering allows nearness to accompany us throughout the day. Dwelling invests us in our place, allowing us to belong. Dwelling strengthens bonds that extend beyond family to neighbors. Dwelling depends upon proximity, the physical nearness between inhabitant and place, and the quality of the design and planning.

In the home, the minutest decisions can encourage dwelling. A kitchen table with comfortable chairs, well placed to receive morning sun, can make a moment of purposeful slowness for the whole family before entering a day of hectic events. A view to a bird feeder, butterfly bush, or outdoor

Fig. 122. Involvement in the project at Castle Rock became heroic, eliciting donations of machinery previously used to remove volcanic muds that had destroyed the Cowlitz River. The symbols of death became the source of new life for the town.

Fig. 123. The museum at Castle Rock was christened the Exhibit Hall when people donated cherished family collections that encouraged children to study local history in distinctive and engaging ways.

thermometer can awaken our senses and make us pay attention. Near-space that ignites the five senses, like the smell of cut flowers on the table, the feel of the rug under bare feet, or an open window that lets in the sounds of life outside, is essential to dwelling. Each aspect of a home can be designed to encourage us to dwell. In addition, we must curb the amount of time and attention given to email, social media, and virtual space and refocus that energy on being present.[4] If we are not present and attentive to our immediate proximity in time, sense, and place, then we cannot be nurtured by the flowers, rug, or breeze. After all, when else besides the present is something *actually* happening?[5]

Amber's father recently became a first-time homeowner. Amber remembers the rented house, just vacated, as being a typical suburban brick home with a large garage. The first room was the living room. The main feature of this room was the giant high-definition, flat-screen television. The Lazy Boy and plush couch made it very attractive and relaxing to watch TV. Even Amber, who has not owned a TV since she was seventeen, made a habit of curling up there on her family visits and soaking in whatever mainstream media offered her, but she was aware that time spent with family was rare and not to be taken for granted. She especially treasured the mornings when the light would come in the eastern window, and they would sit around the table and chat about life over coffee.

One holiday trip home to visit family was special, because she was to help them move in to the new home. Her father had told her that the new house was in the same middle-class neighborhood and built at about the same time as the rented home, so naturally she expected this one to be similar. She will never forget the moment she first walked into their new house and saw the most distinctive feature to be a floor-to-ceiling picture window covering the entire back wall. The rest of the house's design contributed purposefully to the window's importance: The ceiling slanted upwards from the front entrance and peaked at about twelve feet, then jumped another two feet up to form a clearstory window before descending again to the back wall of eight-feet-tall windows, which overlooked the forest in their backyard.

The architecture formed in this way drew Amber to that window like a magnet. When it became time to place the television, it was put by default in the corner, where the cable hole was drilled in the floor by the previous owners. Yet when they noticed that the giant flat-screen covered some of the window, they relocated it to the bare side wall. There was no cable connection the first few nights, so they sat together in the fading sunlight, casually talking and watching nature outside on freshly fallen snow. They saw cardinals and rabbits, blue jays and deer. The highlight was when an owl flew to a branch just ten feet away in broad daylight. Even Amber's teenage brother emerged from his video game den to stare with jaw-dropped silence at its magnificence (though he retreated back to the den within two minutes). The mornings at the table were replaced by mornings sitting at the window in simple chairs, feet huddled around the floor vents, cupping coffee and musing about what summer would be like in the new forest they would now lovingly steward (Fig. 124).

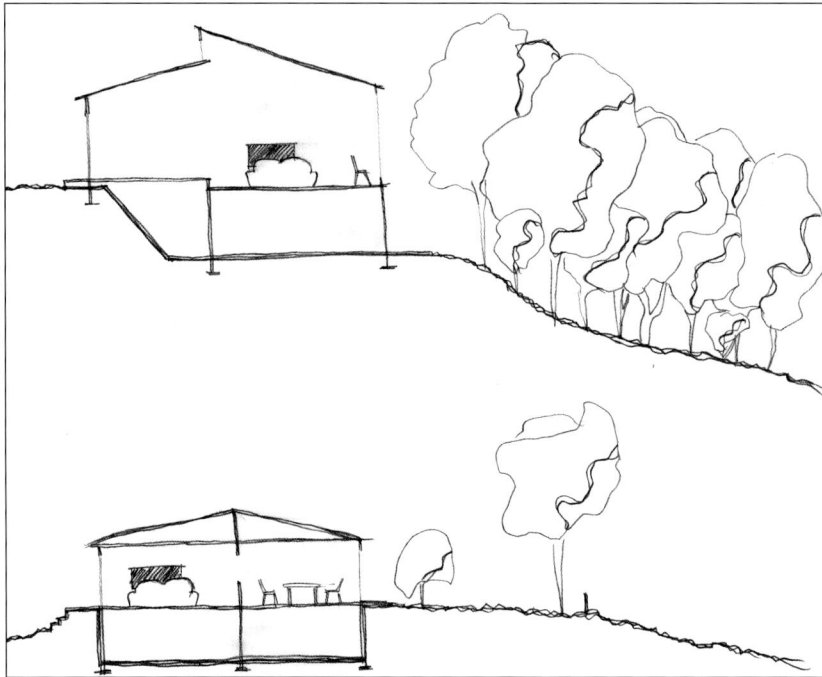

Fig. 124. When the family moved from a house dominated by a giant
flat-screen TV (bottom) to a home with a floor-to-ceiling window
(top), the TV was relegated to a side wall, replaced by watching the
ballet of wild nature outside.

This is simply one example of how dwelling happens in the home, but there are infinite ways design promotes dwelling both in the home and in the larger context of the community. Within the larger community beyond the home, convenience and other practical matters influence whether we truly dwell in neighborhood or public space. Dwelling can be encouraged with simple design elements such as a stoop, front yard, or garden. Bus stops with benches, for example, can encourage neighboring, chatting, lingering, and belonging. We are more likely to frequent places that are nearby and accessible to home or work. If a place serves the activities we need or want, it is likely to become part of our daily lives. We often go to places regularly where other people we enjoy meeting are likely to be, either by chance or prearrangement; and when we wish to avoid others, we seek places where we will be certainly alone. Factors like physical comfort, safety, policy, and cost also influence our consistent use of a place.[6] If the place serves the activities we need or want, it becomes part of a routine; the regularity creates everyday sacredness.

To dwell completely in a place requires more from that place than other places. We expect that place to satisfy multiple conscious and subconscious needs. Regular presence in a place—be it passing through, eating lunch, meditating, playing, or socializing—gives the inhabitant a sense of casual formality with the place. This makes dwelling secure. A place that becomes sacred to the dweller must also offer intimacy and adventure.[7] It must allow us to belong, find our place in it, and shape it to our identity as individuals and as a community. It must excite our senses and invite us to own it. Otherwise, we take it for granted.

Many of these are matters of design were discussed in Step 5: Manifesting. We must upset the monopoly of superficial speed, because dwelling in a place only occurs fully at a deliberate pace. In private and social moments of each day, we must slow down, linger, and even delay.[8] Dwelling makes us an intrinsic part of a place and qualifies us for its rights and privileges; in return, we feel a responsibility to steward it.

Stewarding

The conscious thought that "I am the steward of a sacred place" may never have entered your mind until reading this book, but you already know subconsciously that any place you take care of is special. The most essential and least glamorous aspect of inhabiting the everyday sacred is taking care of a place in both large and small ways.[9] How a place is maintained is perhaps most important to its ability to remain sacred long-term. Keeping a place clean enough to be healthy and in good repair are necessary parts of dwelling, because it is in those moments when we literally hold the place in our own hands. Sacredness is sustained only so long as it has formal and informal custodians—the users themselves—to love and care for it. Another measure of affection for place is to defend the spot when it is threatened with disrepair and change. A guardian would probably be motivated to fight for its preservation because of its importance in daily life.

To steward the community as a sacred place requires knowing its ecology and people, its strengths and weaknesses, and conveying that knowledge to others. Then the place can offer benefits not only to individuals, but also to the community and environment. For example, the repair of broken communities and restoration of degraded ecosystems invite urban stewardship today just as the introduction of contour plowing and strip-cropping slowed erosion and maintained good soil on the Depression-era farm. Removing invasive or non-native plants to restore wildlife habitat, replanting the urban forest, daylighting culverted creeks, and making schoolyard gardens are some of the ways voluntary stewardship is serving the health of both the participants and their ecosystems.[10] Through such stewarding, people become educated about the local ecosystem, eventually caring for it out of both obligation and joy for tending "their" land. Effectively, they become symbolic owners and native to their land; paper titles are simply a formality at this level of stewardship. This mutualistic relationship between a steward and stewarding strengthens a reciprocal response to the point where it is indistinguishable between who is really caring for whom.

Stewardship often starts in our individual households by growing our own food, curbing our cars, walking more, using renewable energy, and avoiding the shallowness of conspicuous consumption. All of these are important acts of family-based stewardship. Once a family is engaged in acts of stewardship at home, it becomes impossible to ignore the neighborhood and larger community that extends beyond the home and bioregion nearby and beyond. As our stewardship expands beyond the home, neighborhood, and community, we become aware of the external forces that can diminish a place and prevent others from inhabiting the sacred. The call of service may be answered by volunteer work in distant communities, across national boundaries like Heifer, International, Doctors without Borders, or SAVE, International. Alternatively, the answer may lie in direct political action to reduce the influence of ideologies and lobbyists who often represent global corporations that damage or destroy local culture and economies. Protests against Wall Street excesses and actions for amendments that eliminate undue corporate privileges can free communities to steward a place by overcoming these invisible powers and insidious powers from without.

Caspar, California, is an extraordinary community in part because people are acutely aware that they must tend to the place and its larger context, the coastal bioregion and the Pacific Ocean. Judy and Jim Tarbell epitomize this sentiment. More than twenty years ago, they led an effort to map the sacred places in Caspar, to protect its vulnerable coastal and river ecosystems, and to redesign the village center with a focus on enhancing civic life (Fig. 125). Casparados, as they call themselves, now engage in seeking a collective consensus in decision making about stewardship more radical than New England's town-hall meetings, and then they do the dirty work of maintenance, such as removing exotic plants from endemic habitats and the removal of trash from local beaches. Judy "mothers" the community gardens, a furniture-making operation, and a fund-raising effort for repairs to the community center and leads the all-volunteer civic association. More than three decades ago, she and Jim started *The Ridge Review*, a bioregional journal that provides forum for critical issues, leading to local study circles to solve problems the mainstream had not even realized were problems. Soon Jim realized that local, even bioregional, stewardship alone was inadequate to address the most critical issues. He now is a major force in Justice Rising, a group whose mission is to challenge corporate corruption that threatens every aspect of life in Caspar from afar (Fig. 126). Judy is setting up a local land trust.

Expanding stewardship will likely take us into uncharted territory to tackle threats that others are unwilling to address. These include unpopular topics like adoption and population control, preservation of threatened ecosystems, endangered species, and cultures, and the redistribution of resources. In this regard, voluntary stewardship is both the antidote to the current monstrous withdrawal from public life and the hope for national reform and worldwide improvements. A community flourishes when citizens tend it like a garden, and democracy requires daily care or it will die on local and global stages.

The aesthetics of stewarding can take many forms. The most successful strategies reinforce hands-on learning and physical labor. The landscapes are usually close to home, small, and needy but not overwhelmingly hopeless. There is no rule that demands stewards to make a place look like it should be on the cover of the newest design magazine or maintain it to the point that it feels sterile.[11] If too styled or spotless, the place may disinvite stewardship. A better strategy is to plan from the beginning to promote stewardship and allow the place to be comfortable as well as invitingly clean with enough rough and loose parts to welcome caring attention. As we steward beyond the home and neighborhood,

Fig. 125. The Casparados steward their community with passion and intelligence that began with mapping sacred places and devising a plan to preserve those places while enhancing civic life.

Fig. 126. Caspar's residents take their responsibility to the earth seriously, from the smallest local action of landscape maintenance to bioregional education and national political action through Justice Rising.

the driving forces are courage, political strategy, and will, and we need to partner with others who make the decisions about the details of how their locality is shaped and how it looks.

Ritual Visiting

By the standard definition of "sacred," ritual action is religious and requires places where hallowed events may take place repeatedly. Churches, mosques, temples, cemeteries, memorial gardens, and other religious structures and areas are sacred to their respective congregations in this way. They are visited daily or weekly, seasonally or once in a lifetime as a holy pilgrimage. One may seek spiritual nourishment, improved health, favors, or an audience with one's God. These visits may include activities ranging from a group celebration of an annual holiday or an individual retreat for thinking or grieving. Though one's religion may not be the subject of the visit, the intensity of the feeling evoked from presence in the place is on scale with worship in a house of God.

We distinguish between daily rituals that are a part of dwelling and those that occur less often as an infrequent though returning visitor. In places that we can visit only periodically, we are both insiders and outsiders, for the rituals and the places are usually not ours to control. We are alien, though we visit them for their sense of place (and even historic design) or exceptional meaning. A pilgrimage to Florence may be to experience firsthand its architecture and civic places, whereas a pilgrimage to Mecca may be primarily for its spiritual meaning. In many cases, the faraway place is sacred both for its form and meaning.

In contrast, local rituals require our attention to the ceremony, location, and design of their settings. Local parades and festivals celebrating historic events need the community's input and a central location to elevate it from a one-off event to a recurring tradition. Ritual visits to ephemeral landscape phenomena such as cherry blossoms, salmon runs, crop harvests, wildlife migrations, and moon cycles increase literacy about the local ecosystems, support local causes, and bring together a community around shared history and central values. The spaces are especially rewarding to visit if appropriately designed to accommodate large numbers and to attract people with different interests. To heighten the experience for the visitors, a mundane space may be temporarily transformed to arouse all the senses and provide an exciting new experience. Likewise, centrally located and well-crafted museums and exhibit halls open our eyes to unimagined futures. Subcultural events such as Chinese New Year celebrations and international festivals invite others to enclaves for yearly events adorned with distinct ethnic design that acknowledges diversity and encourages tolerance of other cultures. Visits to places of ritual fulfill either our need for certainty of ordered repetition or new experiences of growth and adventure and often times both. These are important episodes in inhabiting the sacred because they connect us to memories, help us relate to our community and landscape, and enliven excitement about the town and city we might create tomorrow.

In areas of defined seasons, annual festivals are especially important. The public places where the festivals occur become sacred places. For Amber's parents, the Missouri Botanical Garden is sacred for

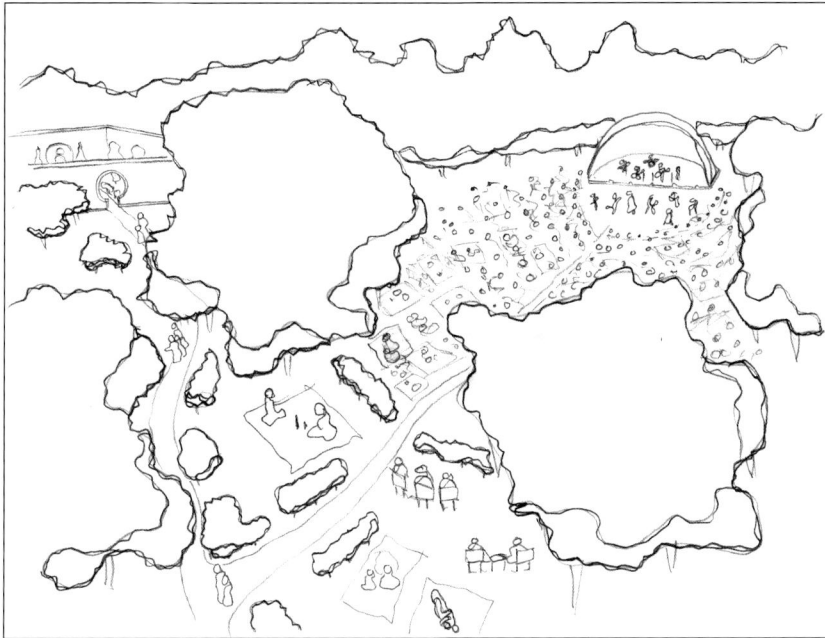

Fig. 127. Repeated visits to the Missouri Botanical Garden in St. Louis satisfy both the need for the certainty of a ritual and the promise of adventure, because the garden accommodates experimental music concerts into the historic collection of plants.

its value as a setting for one of their favorite summer activities. The garden sponsors a series of free musical concerts in the park, hosting local bands weekly throughout the summer months. People are encouraged to picnic together anywhere in the park. Thousands of people attend this event each week, bringing their picnic supplies and setting up amongst the historic flower beds that botanic superstar Henry Shaw established in 1859 as one of the nation's first botanical gardens. There is no exclusionary "Do Not Cross" fencing nor restrictions about what can be brought into the park by guests to help them have a comfortable and enjoyable evening. There are gatherings of all races, ages, and economic levels. Typically, an event so large would never give visitors this level of freedom. Yet "concerts in the park," as her parents call them, are so sacred to so many St. Louisans that the only visible hired employees at the event are the much-needed bathroom attendants. Groups tend to sit within ear-shot of the music, and there is always a spontaneous dance floor at the front. Further off, people walk the garden to discover or rediscover the beauty and rich history which surround them. For even the garden's most frequent visitors, it is a unique opportunity to view the gardens at night. This is a win-win situation for the park, the bands, and the attendees: Each is treated with mutual dignity and respect, and a great sense of commonality is shared. Before these concerts, Amber's parents never visited botanical gardens. Now they are not only frequent visitors during the concerts, but also members of the garden and visit this and other botanical gardens as a pastime (Fig. 127).

Fig. 128. By sharing the joys of intentional dwelling, we become advocates for places we treasure and the values they represent, passing on the places and values to the next generation.

Fig. 129. When residents, designers, or visitors are touched by the power of a place like the Dragon's Eye Waterfall north of Kyoto, they often champion those places as exemplars to neighbors or distant audiences.

Advocating

As we inhabit the everyday sacred, we often become advocates for the settings and values they represent. As we willfully dwell and steward, we serve as role models, encouraging others by our daily actions (Fig. 128). Sacred places and the people who advocate for them serve as demonstrations of the advantages of inhabiting the everyday sacred. We may advocate by making them, lecturing about them, and showing them as exemplars to distant audiences who may employ certain elements in their own places.

Designers advocate the sacred places they know by including such projects in their portfolios, Websites, and presentations to clients. Tourists may blog, photograph, and create scrapbooks about their experiences (Fig. 129). Locals may do as little as share their sacred places with distant friends and family or as much as become serious evangelists for the cause. This book, after all, is a product of adamant advocates evangelizing for sacred places!

People become advocates, because inhabiting the everyday sacred makes lives more fulfilling, more pleasurable, and healthier. We are civically minded advocates, and our work helps communities to improve. We know our places sensually and intimately and feel we belong in them. We observe and are participants in a living democracy. We believe that intentional living sustains us and our planet. As rare as it is, confidence about a place is contagious and may inspire others who have read about or visited a sacred place to try an innovation themselves.

Sometimes, a place advocates for itself with its charismatic power that cannot be denied. The place may lift the spirits, move people to tears, or spur them to action on the place's behalf. One such place is an outcrop of granitic rocks near Hester's Store, North Carolina. As a youth, Randy sensed but forgot its internal might; after visiting Mount Kurama near Kyoto, Japan, decades later, he named the Hester's Store outcrop Kurama.

Recently, Randy took his grandson, Atticus, to the outcrop for the first time. It is nearly a mile's hike through pastures, hilly oak-hickory forest, and treacherous creeks. Soon, Atticus stopped at a fence crossing and said, "Shoulders," indicating he had walked far enough and wanted a ride with a view. He kept up a joyful running commentary the whole trip, especially delighting when he had to shout out, "Don't step in the cow poop." As they entered Kurama, Atticus instantaneously fell silent for the first time that day. Without a word from Randy, Atticus had sensed something special. He quietly and respectfully surveyed the rocks. They are distinctive: not rounded by exfoliation but right-angled and table-sized slabs, not piled but spaced as if designed for a ritual ceremony within.

Atticus cautiously settled from Randy's shoulders to one of the moss-covered table rocks. Randy had never observed him hushed by any situation nor be so attentive. Atticus was not interested in snacks or the treasured toys Randy had brought along in case of emergency. After a long stillness, he reached out and caressed the moss (Fig. 130). Then he noticed a woodpecker's hole in an elderly oak tree shading his mossy rock. He spoke for the first time, "Who lives there?" After a long while, he talked about what he observed, smelled, felt, and heard. He noticed piles of leaves snuggled at the base of rocks. He explained the moss was hard and soft. There was a musical rustle from the lingering beech leaves. Then he turned to Randy, "We need to have a conversation."

He wanted to know exactly why his grandfather does not use a cell phone or watch television. These matters had obviously been troubling his three-year-old mind, and this seemed to be the appropriate place to have them clarified. "How about it?," he asked. Randy's long explanation was broken by the sounds of resident chickadees perched two arms lengths' away. Atticus was ready for a snack, then carefully explored the most immediate rocks and paths, which, at his eye level, seemed maze-like. He asked several times what the name of the place was (Fig. 131). Then he requested "shoulders" so he could visually explore the surrounds again in silence. As they left Kurama and started downhill toward Big Branch, Atticus asked, "Grandy, why do you think God created Kurama?" Randy's reasoning was inadequate, but the mere question reinforced Amber's argument that some places have inherent power to speak to us in ways we may not comprehend, to advocate in a language we cannot speak but sense nonetheless (Fig. 132).

Fig. 130. Sometimes a place is powerful enough to speak for itself, silencing the most talkative youngsters. This rock outcrop silenced Randy's grandson, Atticus, because he sensed it was special.

Fig. 131. On one visit to Kurama, Atticus had insistent questions about why his grandfather didn't use a cell phone or watch TV, concluding his inquisition with, "Why do you think God created Kurama?"

Fig. 132. When Atticus crossed Big Branch and saw his reflection beside the reflection of the moon in the still water, the expression on his face indicated he understood about cell phones and TV.

Labors of Love

One of the greatest powers of sacred places is how they can satisfy all four of the wishes simultaneously for individuals and communities. Returning to Manteo, Jule's Park illustrates how constructing the park earned Jule recognition, how dwelling by neighbors gave them a sense of certainty, how stewarding made citizens reciprocally responsive, how having reason to visit it ritually united the community on a spiritual level, and how advocating for the park solidified the most expressive identity of Manteo.

Let us remember from "Randy's Story of Manteo" that the downtown area was in a state of near abandonment and total disrepair when Jule Burrus began creating his vision for a waterfront park. His fellow townspeople were suspicious, and the City Council was unwilling to supply funds for a park in this derelict district. His colleagues at the Duchess Restaurant disapproved and made fun of his idea to his face and behind his back. People thought it was downright crazy trying to beautify such wasteland. Jule ignored the criticism as best he could, although he told Randy the year he died how much the scorn of his friends had hurt. Fortunately, he had the strength needed to pursue his vision and managed to imbue the park with the value of perseverance, which are still evident.

Fig. 133. After discovering a concrete cross in the rubble of Manteo's old elementary school, Jule Burrus and Guy Midgett began a labor of love that inspired a dramatic revitalization of their town and today symbolizes the community's highest values.

Jule waged a personal campaign to win support and resources. He worked without official endorsement, and some questioned his ownership of the site, which was murky at best. His first breakthrough for support was when he decided to use the rubble from an old school that was being torn down. Generations of older townspeople had attended the demolished school, so the rubble had sentimental value for many residents. Jule aimed to involve them in his project by using the theme "building from ruins" for his proposed park, a phrase that related to the many catastrophes the town had overcome in the past. He persuaded a local contractor to move the ruins of the school to the waterfront at no cost and began shuffling through the debris. People gradually warmed to his idea, and he persuaded the City Council to endorse his efforts as part of an upcoming historical celebration (Fig. 133).

When Jule got this official approval, he was finally able to solicit the help of others. A local handyman collected beach sand that had blown across nearby streets from an Atlantic storm, and Jule deposited it between the rubble to fill gaps with a smooth surface. The local electric power company sold him park lamps at cost, and residents paid for them as memorial dedications to loved ones. Jule

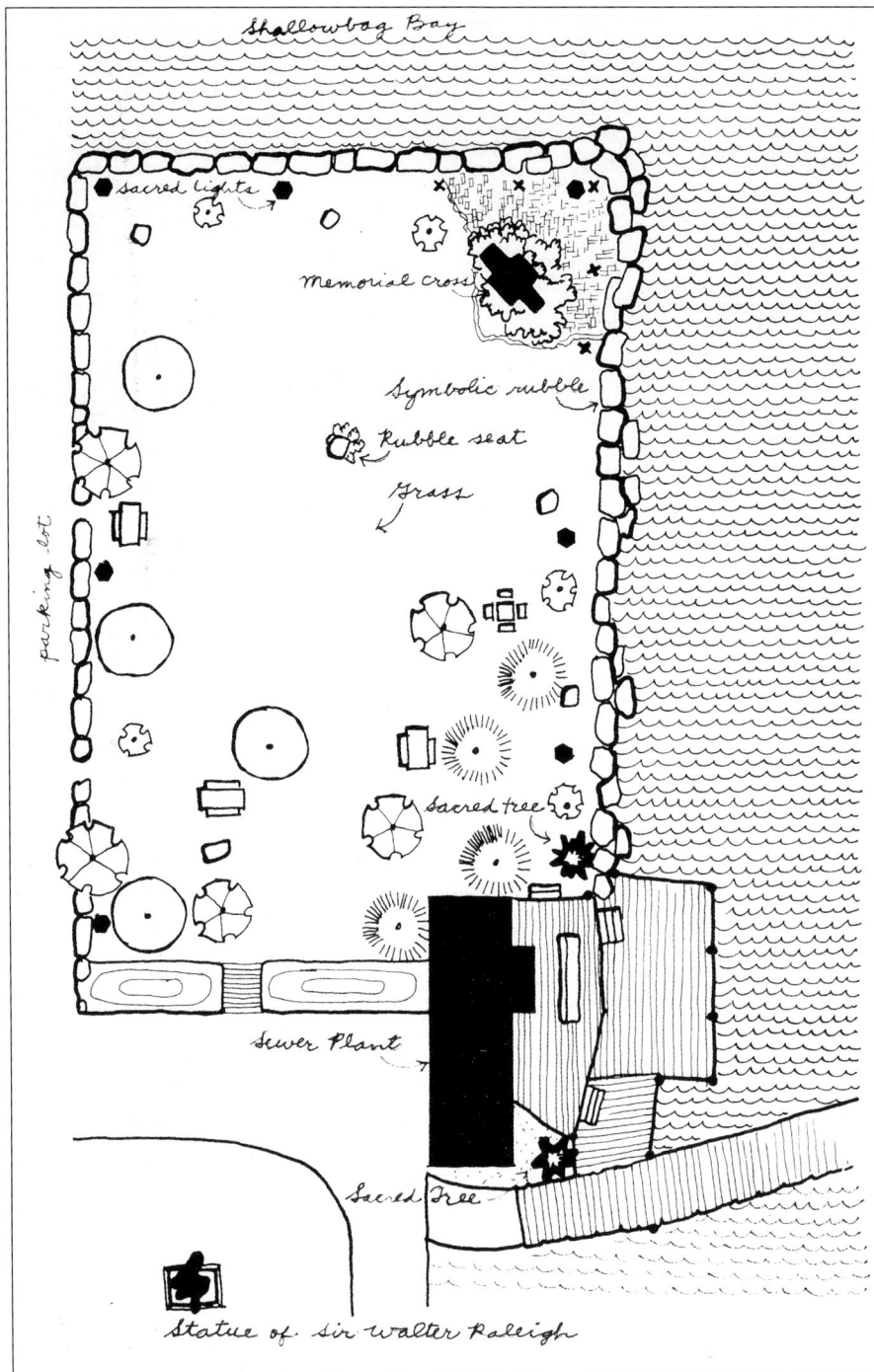

The illustration is a hand-drawn plan labeled with:

Shallowbag Bay

sacred lights

Memorial cross

Symbolic rubble

Rubble seat

Grass

parking lot

sacred tree

Sewer Plant

Sacred Tree

Statue of Sir Walter Raleigh

Fig. 134. Jule Burrus designed a place for specific hallowed events at the spot where Manteo faced the dangerous shoals known as the graveyard of the Atlantic, but he made his plan simple and flexible to welcome the ideas of many other people in his community. This resulted in a park much beloved by the entire town.

asked a local cement company to erect a monument, using a piece of rubble broken into the shape of a cross. This was years before the same symbol became pertinent again during the aftermath of 9/11. Jule was the daily leader, organizer, and solicitor of help, and he completed the majority of the physical work himself with help from one other resident. At one point, he became seriously ill, some later testified from working in the contaminated water. This heightened sense of his sacrifice served as a moral example to others. The combination of powerful imagery, words, and personal sacrifice raised the project to a patriotic plane, connected the effort personally to other residents, and allayed the initial skepticism.

The first phase of Jule's Park was completed in just over one year, and its quick turnaround made it easy for the rest of the community to embrace the project. The initial phase consisted of a grass lawn with an extraordinary view over Shallowbag Bay. This lawn was suitable for hundreds of daily activities plus community festivals, religious rituals, and civic functions. In the next phase, trees were added during a volunteer day of planting. Involvement by the town and private donations continued steadily after the initial effort became visible. The timely manifestation of grass and trees was a convincing result that inspired people into voluntary action and public commitments. Nearby residents maintained Jule's Park for many years. One group of friends went on evening walks and performed voluntary trash pick-up to keep the park clean. Another eighty-year-old woman mowed the lawn for years, as if it were an extension of her own backyard (Fig. 134).

One might expect that such a visionary idea born of disobedience, resistance, and unpopularity would be rigidly designed, formal, and overwrought, but the contrary was true. His labor of love in the public domain had a clear, unifying structure that Jule saw as inviolable. His framework was indeed rigid yet not overworked. His park invited so many other investments of affection that the large, flexible public space gradually got filled with trees, playground equipment, and other claims of symbolic ownership. Jule actually resisted too much "stuff" in order to maintain the versatility of his original plan: a simple, open, and un-programmed space suitable for adaptation and creative use. It was like a mantle, which he imagined would collect new facilities and the gifts of others but periodically be cleared of the additions. This open-endedness attracted others to continue what Jule started and makes the place beloved today. Just recently, a new inscription was mysteriously added to the base of the cross, honoring Jule Burrus and the values he represented.

Jule's Park illustrates how his and neighbor's fundamental needs were met by creation of a public sacred place. Jule chose to make this park, because inhabiting the sacred filled him with purpose. It provided him with certainty and adventurous nonconformity. It allowed him to belong and be recognized for the difference he made in his community. In turn, the community stewarded his park and felt reciprocal response and reason to visit it ritually. The community united on a ideological and spiritual level. The park still thrives and is one of the most expressive tokens of identity in Manteo.

Projects like Jule's Park typically begin as an individual's idea and is moved forward with passion. They are neither participatory nor populist in origin, but they eventually capture a community's values for place if they are to thrive. The dreams of others are accommodated in order to secure their help.

LOOKING FORWARD TO AN EVERYDAY SACRED WORLD

THE SACRED PLACES of everyday life provide us with security, new experiences, sensual responses, and a sense of belonging on a daily basis. Sacredness of place gives us a sense of certainty. It stimulates joyful exploration of the local landscape. The sacred fulfills our need to be recognized by the groups with which we identify. Belonging gives us rights and duties and connects us responsibly with others and the larger community. In return, we gain a profound sense of purpose. This purpose ennobles us and our communities and strengthens our democracy.

Living intentionally requires that we constantly pay attention to the powerful inner forces that can misdirect the way we live and always take preemptive action that reinforces thick values. If we do not, the profane monsters ingrained in our culture and our individual lives may silently overtake us. It will take work to undo the uncertainty that fills too many of us with debilitating fear, renders too many of us as powerless, and makes too many of us retreat from the social and natural landscapes around us. Artificial dangers and superficial thrills that stunt our growth must be replaced with new experiences that test our courage and skill. The distant and remote, though enticing and fulfilling in a limited way, cannot supplant the pleasures and knowledge that the nearby landscape offers us each day. Obsession with status can transform us from caring human beings into mere consumers and wreck our lives, communities, environment, and ability to govern ourselves must cease.

In this book, we have shown how to undo the monsters and assertively create a healthy and beautiful home and community. Hopefully, the six steps have and will continue to help you defuse your town's monsters and shape a better place for all to dwell. Both of us periodically, even ritually, reawaken ourselves, gather new initiative, transform values through sacrifice, organize an ever-evolving action plan towards intentional living, and manifest our wishes to remake the places we inhabit. We urge you to do so as well.

Designers and planners who spend time to engage the public in seeking out the sacred will be counted amongst those who contribute in a real and positive way to our communities, though the task is daunting. There are many practical barriers, and we need to be guided in our place-making with simple focus. To create homes, towns, and cities that touch the heart, we must reconstitute reason and emotion into a singular way of knowing and meet our community's fundamental needs. Without meeting these needs, people are unable to excel in other parts of their lives. In a world of threatening environmental collapse, from the devastating floods of Hurricane Harvey to rampant deforestation in Amazonia, the priority is likely to shift to survival only, but the psychological realm of our humanity is equally, if not more important, because it is so subtle and elusive. A colleague researched the poetry and excerpts from the *Koran* (*Quran*) inscribed on the tiled walls leading to the Court of Lions in the Alhambra and found, in a dark corner just above the ground, a prayer written in basic Arabic that asked Allah to "Let my work be filled with love." We would be far along should all city-makers and place-makers be guided by that simple value. If love is to guide us in our work, then courage and sensibility must inculcate our every action. Our humanity, communities, and democracy depend upon love, courage, and sensibility.

Inhabiting the sacred has seasons. Sometimes, we focus most on constructing or dwelling. At other times, we steward, ritually visit, or advocate. To live intentionally amidst the everyday sacred we must keep each aspect of our place close at heart and mind and always move toward the positive. Inhabiting the sacred requires a commitment to place, community, and values that imbue life with significance. We have to stay in one place long enough to have a long-term, intimate relationship with the landscape. We must know our place rationally and sensually. The constructed and wild landscape must be engaged reciprocally, a continual ebb and flow of mutual respect. When the landscape in which we permanently reside is exalted, glorified, and intensified, it can fill us with unspeakable purpose and pleasure. As we form sacred places, sacred places form us.

Introduction: Why Inhabiting the Sacred Matters

1. Edward C. Relph, *Place and Placelessness* (London, UK: Pion, 1976), 9.

2. Yi-Fu Tuan, *Space and Place: The Perspective of Experience* (Minneapolis: University of Minnesota Press, 1977); Frances Moore Lappé and Jeffrey Perkins, *You Have the Power: Choosing Courage in a Culture of Fear* (New York, NY: Jeremy Tarcher, 2005); James M. Fitch, *Architecture and the Esthetics of Plenty* (New York, NY: Columbia University Press, 1961); David Abram, *The Spell of the Sensuous: Perception and Language in a More-Than-Human World* (New York, NY: Pantheon Books, 1996).

3. Harold F. Searles, *Collected Papers on Schizophrenia and Related Subjects* (New York, NY: International Universities Press, 1965).

4. David W. Orr, *Ecological Literacy: Education and the Transition to a Postmodern World* (Albany: State University of New York Press, 1992).

5. Daniel Solomon, *Global City Blues* (Washington, DC: Island Press, 2003).

6. Andrea F. Taylor, Frances E. Kuo, and William C. Sullivan, "Views of Nature and Self-discipline: Evidence from Inner City Children," *Journal of Environmental Psychology*, Vol. 22, Nos. 1–2 (2002): 49–63; Yi-Fu Tuan, *Cosmos and Hearth: A Cosmopolite's Viewpoint* (Minneapolis: University of Minnesota Press, 1999).

7. Randolph T. Hester, Jr., *Design for Ecological Democracy* (Cambridge, MA: The MIT Press, 2006).

8. Randolph T. Hester, Jr., "Portraits of Haleiwa," *Places*, Vol. 8, No. 2 (1992); Susanne Langer, *Philosophy in a New Key: A Study in the Symbolism of Reason, Rite, and Art* (Cambridge, MA: Harvard University Press, 1957).

9. Gaston Bachelard, *The Poetics of Space* (Boston, MA: Beacon, 1994); John B. Jackson, *A Sense of Place, a Sense of Time* (New Haven, CT: Yale University Press, 1996).

10. John Ayto, *Dictionary of Word Origins* (New York, NY: Arcade, 1991).

11. Caroline Humphrey, *Sacred Architecture* (Boston, MA: Little, Brown, 1997).

12. James A. Swan, *The Power of Place: Sacred Ground in Natural & Human Environments: An Anthology*, Spirit of Place Symposium (Wheaton, IL: Quest Books, 1991).

13. Randolph T. Hester, Jr., "A Womb with a View: How Spatial Nostalgia Affects the Designer," *Landscape Architecture*, Vol. 69, No. 5 (1979): 475–81.

14. Kenneth Grahame, *The Wind in the Willows* (New York, NY: Grosset and Dunlap, 1966), 88–89.

15. Setha Low, *On the Plaza: The Politics of Public Space and Culture* (Austin: University of Texas Press, 2000).

16. Frances Moore Lappé, *Getting A Grip 2: Clarity, Creativity and Courage for the World We Really Want* (Cambridge, MA: Small Planet Media, 2010).

17. Randolph T. Hester, Jr., "Labors of Love in the Public Landscape," *Places*, Vol. 1, No. 1 (1983): 18–27.

Randy's Story of Manteo

1. Information from Aaron Tuell, Public Relations Manager, Outer Banks Visitors Bureau, in an email (April 25, 2017) to the publisher.

2. Randolph Hester, "Do Not Detach: Instructions from and for Community Design," in Lynne Manzo and Patrick Devine-Wright, eds., *Place Attachment* (London, UK: Routledge, 2014), 190–206.

Amber's Story of Fito's Place

1. Amber D Nelson, "Dimensioning the Public Sacred" (College of Environmental Design, University of California, Berkeley, 2012); available online at https://berkeley.box.com/s/4022lrpeeu65jsn7bbts.

Step 1: Awakening New Thoughts and Feelings about the Everyday Landscape

1. Christine Overdevest, Randy Hester, and Marcia McNally, "Operationalizing Place Attachment: Mapping and Planning for Place Values on National Forests," in *Integrating Social Science and Ecosystem Management: A National Challenge General Report SRS-17* (Ashville, NC: USDA Forest Service, Southern Research Station, 1997), 98–102; Marcia McNally, "Participatory Research and Natural Resource Planning," *Journal of Architecture and Planning Research*, Vol. 4, No. 4 (1987) 324–28; Randolph Hester and Marcia McNally, *The Language of Wildlands and Appreciation* (Berkeley: United States Forest Service Pacific Southwest Forest and Range Experiment Service, University of California, 1987); *Community Development by Design* (internal documents with the EPA Chesapeake Bay Program, 1998).

2. Charles Piot, *Nostalgia for the Future: West Africa after the Cold War* (Chicago, IL: University of Chicago Press, 2010).

3. Marcia McNally, "The Affective Landscape: Discovering Forest Values," in Graham Hardie, Robin Moore, and Henry Sanoff, eds., *EDRA 20 Proceedings* (Oklahoma City, OK: EDRA, 1989), 274–78.

4. Victor Flemming, Director, *The Wizard of Oz* (1939).

5. John Fowles, *The Collector* (Boston, MA: Little, Brown and Company, 1963), 37.

6. Marcia McNally, "Valued Places," in Randolph Hester, Shinglin Chang, and Shih Wang, eds., Living Landscape: Reading Cultural Landscape Experiences in Taiwan and America (Taipei, Taiwan: United Force Culture Enterprise Company, Limited, 1999), 126–33.

7. Community Development by Design (Internal document from mapping sacred places at Bushy Fork, NC, 2006).

8. Viv Bernstein, "Going Home Puts Stewart on Right Track," *The New York Times* (August 7, 2005): S1.

9. Marcia McNally, "96 Valued Places," in Mark Francis and Randolph Hester, eds., *The Meaning of Gardens* (Cambridge, MA: The MIT Press, 1990), 172–77.

10. Personal communications between Will Hooker and Randy Hester (May 1987), Raleigh, NC.

11. Dell Upton, *What Can and Can't Be Said: Race, Uplift, and Monument Building in the Contemporary South* (New Haven: Yale University Press, 2015).

12. David Weitzman, *My Backyard History Book* (Boston, MA: Little, Brown and Company, 1975).

Step 2. Evidencing Sentiments for Community Place

1. Melvin M. Webber, "Order in Diversity: Community Without Propinquity," in Gerrylynn K. Roberts, ed., *The American Cities and Technology Reader: Wilderness to Wired City* (New York, NY: Routledge, 1999), 201–10; Clare Cooper Marcus, *House as a Mirror of Self: Exploring the Deeper Meaning of Home* (Berkeley, CA: Conari Press, 1995); Randy T. Hester, Jr., "Subconscious Landscapes of the Heart," *Places*, Vol. 2, No. 3 (1985): 10–22.

2. Yi-Fu Tuan, *Topophilia: A Study of Environmental Perception, Attitudes, and Values* (Englewood Cliffs, NJ: Prentice-Hall, 1972).

3. Randolph T. Hester, Jr., "Sacred Structures and Everyday Life: A Return to Manteo, North Carolina," in David Seamon, ed., *Dwelling, Seeing, and Designing: Toward a Phenomenological Ecology* (Albany: State University of New York Press, 1993), 271–98; Frederic O. Sargent, et al., *Rural Environmental Planning for Sustainable Communities* (Washington, DC: Island Press, 1991); Anne W. Spirn, *The Language of Landscape* (New Haven, CT: Yale University Press, 1998).

4. Mimi Wagner and Peter F. Korsching, "Flood Prone Community Landscapes: The Application of Diffusion Innovations Theory and Community Design Process in Promoting Change" (presented at the Society for Applied Sociology, Denver, CO, 1998); Everett M. Rogers, *Diffusion of Innovations* (New York, NY: Free Press, 1995).

5. Mark Francis, *Village Homes: A Community by Design* (Washington, DC: Island Press, 2003); Mark Francis, "A Case Study Method for Landscape Architecture," *Landscape Journal*, Vol. 20, No. 1 (2001): 15.

6. Setha Low, *Rethinking Urban Parks: Public Space & Cultural Diversity* (Austin: University of Texas Press, 2005); John Zeisel, *Inquiry by Design: Tools for Environment-Behaviour Research* (Cambridge, UK: Cambridge University Press, 1984).

7. Victoria Chanse and Randolph T. Hester, Jr., "Characterizing Volunteer Involvement in Wildlife Habitat Planning" (presented at the CELA 2002: GroundWork, Syracuse, NY: Council of Educators in Landscape Architecture, 2002), 39.

8. Ken Belson, "Doubting Assurances, Japanese Find Radioactivity on Their Own," *The New York Times* (July 31, 2011): A1.

9. Setha Low, *On the Plaza: The Politics of Public Space and Culture* (Austin: University of Texas Press, 2000); Frank Palermo, et al., *First Nations Community Planning Model* (Halifax, NS: Cities & Environment Unit, Faculty of Architecture, Dalhousie University, 2000).

10. Stephen Carr, et al., *Public Space* (London, UK: Cambridge University Press, 1992).

11. Keith H Basso, *Wisdom Sits in Places: Landscape and Language among the Western Apache* (Albuquerque: University of New Mexico Press, 1996).

12. Mark Francis, "The Everyday and the Personal: Six Garden Stories," in Mark Francis and Randolph T. Hester, Jr., eds., *The Meaning of Gardens: Idea, Place, and Action* (Cambridge, MA: The MIT Press, 1990), 206–15.

13. Carl G. Jung, *Man and His Symbols* (London, UK: Aldus Books, 1979).

14. Janisse Ray, *Pinhook: Finding Wholeness in a Fragmented Land* (White River Junction, VT: Chelsea Green Publishing, 2005).

15. Lawrence Halprin, Randolph T. Hester, Jr., and Dee Mullen, "Interview with Lawrence Halprin," *Places*, Vol. 12, No. 2 (1999): 42–51; Lawrence Halprin, *The RSVP Cycles: Creative Processes in the Human Environment* (New York, NY: G. Braziller, 1970).

16. Eleanor Ely, "Macroinvertebrate Data: Volunteers Vs. Professionals," *Wild Earth*, Vol. 11, Nos. 3/4 (2002): 24–27.

17. Denis Wood, *Rethinking the Power of Maps* (New York, NY: Guilford Press, 2010).

18. Edward R. Tufte, *Envisioning Information* (Cheshire, CN: Graphics Press, 2005), 26–27.

19. Randolph T. Hester, Jr., "Native Wisdom Amidst Ignorance of Locality," in John K. C. Liu, ed., *Building Cultural Diversity through Participation* (presented at the Third Annual Pacific Rim Participatory Community Design Conference, Taipei: National Taiwan University, 2001), 416–53; Connie L. Knapp and Orton Family Foundation Community Mapping Program, *Making Community Connections: The Orton Family Foundation Community Mapping Program* (Redlands, CA: ESRI Press, 2003); Freyja L. Knapp, "Making Maps That Make a Difference" (Berkeley, CA: International Rivers, 2007).

Step 3: Transforming Values of Place through Sacrifice

1. Milton Rokeach, *Beliefs, Attitudes, and Values; a Theory of Organization and Change* (San Francisco, CA: Jossey-Bass, 1968).

2. William I. Thomas and Florian Znaniecki, *The Polish Peasant in Europe and America: Monograph of an Immigrant Group* (Boston, MA: R. G. Badger, 1918); William I. Thomas, *The Unadjusted Girl: With Cases and Standpoint for Behavior Analysis*, Criminal Science Monographs 4 (Boston, MA: Little, Brown, 1923), 4.

3. David Abram, *The Spell of the Sensuous: Perception and Language in a More-Than-Human World* (New York, NY: Pantheon Books, 1996).

4. Martin H. Krieger, "Planning and Design as Theological and Religious Activities," *Environment and Planning B: Planning and Design*, Vol. 14, No. 1 (1987): 5–13.

5. Ibid., 8–9.

6. Emile Durkheim, *The Elementary Forms of the Religious Life* (New York, NY: Free Press, 1965), 482.

7. Marshall Berman, *All That Is Solid Melts into Air: The Experience of Modernity* (New York, NY: Viking Penguin, 1988).

8. Randolph T. Hester, Jr., *Design for Ecological Democracy* (Cambridge, MA: The MIT Press, 2006), 101–03.

9. Ibid., 175.

10. Wan-ching Lai, "Ten Years of Effort Glory of Taijiang: A Brief Historical Retrospect on the Establishment of Taijiang National Park," *National Park Quarterly*, Heal the Scar of 8/8 Flood (December 2009): 52–63.

11. Michelle Kodis, *Blueprint Small: Creative Ways to Live with Less* (Salt Lake City, UT: Gibbs Smith, 2003).

12. "The EarthWays Home - Visit Our Urban Green Home"; http://www.earthwayscenter.org/demonstrations.html.

13. Saul D. Alinsky, *Rules for Radicals; a Practical Primer for Realistic Radicals* (New York, NY: Random House, 1971).

14. American LIVES, Inc., "1995 New Urbanism Study: Revitalizing Suburban Communities," paper presented at the Urban Land Institute Seminar on Master Planned Communities 2000 and Beyond (November 2, 1995), 31–33.

15. Vikki Chanse, et al., "Wildlife Across Cultures," in *Wildlife Habitat Exchange Proceedings* (Kyoto, Japan: Kyoto Department of Landscape Architecture, Kyoto University, 2001).

16. M. G. Chandrakanth and Jeff Romm, "Sacred Forests, Secular Forest Policies and People's Actions," *Natural Resources Journal*, Vol. 31, No. 4 (1991): 741–56.

17. Fred Bahnson, "Field of Teens: If You Pay Them, They Will Come," *World Ark* (Summer 2011): 30–35.

Step 4: Manifesting Four Wishes through Planning and Design

1. Alexis de Tocqueville, et al., *Democracy in America* (New York, NY: Alfred A. Knopf, 1945); originally published in 1835.

2. Frances Moore Lappé, *Getting a Grip: Clarity, Creativity, and Courage in a World Gone Mad* (Cambridge, MA: Small Planet Media, 2007), 29–37; Frances Moore Lappé, *Democracy's Edge: Choosing to Save Our Country by Bringing Democracy to Life* (San Francisco, CA: Jossey-Bass, 2006), 309; Randolph T. Hester, Jr., *Community Design Primer* (Mendocino, CA: Ridge Times Press, 1990), 10; Robert D. Putnam, *Bowling Alone: The Collapse and Revival of American Community* (New York, NY: Simon & Schuster, 2000).

3. Robert S. Ogilvie, *Voluntarism, Community Life, and the American Ethic* (Bloomington: Indiana University Press, 2004).

4. Howell S. Baum, "Ethical Behavior Is Extraordinary Behavior; It's the Same as All Other Behavior: A Case Study in Community Planning," *Journal of the American Planning Association*, Vol. 64, No. 4 (1998): 411–23.

5. Sherry R. Arnstein, "A Ladder of Citizen Participation," *Journal of the American Planning Association*, Vol. 35, No. 4 (1969): 216–24.

6. Lappé, *Democracy's Edge*, 156; Benjamin R. Barber, *Strong Democracy: Participatory Politics for a New Age* (Berkeley: University of California Press, 2004).

7. Malcolm X, *By Any Means Necessary* (New York, NY: Pathfinder, 1970); Saul D. Alinsky, *Rules for Radicals; a Practical Primer for Realistic Radicals* (New York, NY: Random House, 1971); Mahatma Gandhi, *All Men Are Brothers: Autobiographical Reflections* (New York, NY: Continuum, 2005); Rosa Parks and James Haskins, *Rosa Parks: My Story* (New York, NY: Scholastic, 1994); Martin Luther King, Jr., and James M. Washington, "Letter from a Birmingham Jail," in *I Have a Dream: Writings and Speeches That Changed the World* (San Francisco, CA: Harper, 1992), 83–100; Cesar Chavez, in Ilan Stavans, ed., *An Organizer's Tale: Speeches* (New York, NY: Penguin Group, 2008); Jane Jacobs, *The Death and Life of Great American Cities* (New York, NY: Random House, 1961); Lawrence Susskind, *Breaking Robert's Rules: The New Way to Run Your Meeting, Build Consensus, and Get Results* (Oxford, UK: Oxford University Press, 2006); Barack Obama, *The Audacity of Hope: Thoughts on Reclaiming the American Dream* (New York, NY: Crown Publishers, 2006); Paulo Freire, *Pedagogy of the Oppressed* (New York, NY: Continuum, 2000).

8. Randolph T. Hester, Jr. and Lara Hamsher, "Geometry and Activist Geometry," in *Democratic Design in the Pacific Rim* (Osaka, Japan: Awajishima Press, 2010).

9. Randolph T. Hester, Jr., "Life-cycle Stages of Participatory Democracy," in Organization of Urban Re's (OURS), ed., *Citizen Participation in Urban Governance: International Community Planning Forum Proceedings* (Taipei, Taiwan: Department of Urban Development, Taipei City Government, 2005), 558–80.

10. Yi-Fu Tuan, *Space and Place: The Perspective of Experience* (Minneapolis: University of Minnesota Press, 1977), 171.

11. Randy Shaw, *The Activist's Handbook: A Primer* (Berkeley: University of California Press, 2001).

12. Hester, *Community Design Primer*, 72–78.

13. Thomas Jefferson, "Eternal Vigilance Is the Price of Liberty.,"; http://www.monticello.org/site/jefferson/eternal-vigilance-price-liberty-quotation.

14. Steve Roper, *Camp 4: Recollections of a Yosemite Rockclimber* (Seattle, WA: Mountaineers, 1994); Daniel Duane, *Lighting Out: A Vision of California and the Mountains* (St. Paul, MN: Graywolf Press, 1994).

15. Kevin Worrall, "Rockin' the Cradle in a New Age in Old Camp Four," *Climbing*, Vol. 24, No. 144 (June 1, 1994): 78–89, 151.

16. Randolph T. Hester, Jr., "Personal Communication with Dick Duane," meeting and telephone notes (March 28, 1998).

17. Peter Fimrite, "Yosemite's New Breed of 'Rock Rats'," *SFGATE* (September 10, 2006): S1.

18. Richard A. Wisniewski, *The Rise and Fall of the Hawaiian Kingdom: A Pictoral History* (Honolulu, HI: Pacific Basin Enterprises, 1979).

19. State of Hawaii and University of Hawaii, "Revised Management Plan for the UH Management Area on Mauna Kea," March 10, 1995; http://hawaii.gov/dlnr/occl/random-files/mauna-kea-files.

20. Kealoha Pisciotta, "The Meaning of Aloha: Personal Communication between Marcia McNally and Kapai Malay" (March 30, 2006).

21. Henry J. McCracken, "In Hawaii: Insects Before Astronomy?," *Spiked Online* (August 30, 2006); http://www.spiked-online.com/index.php/site/article/1573/.

22. Community Development by Design, *Mauna Kea Management Plan* (Berkeley, CA: Community Development By Design, 2006).

23. Lynne C. Manzo and Douglas D. Perkins, "Finding Common Ground: The Importance of Place Attachment to Community Participation and Planning," *Journal of Planning Literature*, Vol. 20, No. 4 (2006): 336–50.

24. Kevin Dayton, "Audit Says State Fails to Protect Summit Resources," *Honolulu Advertiser* (December 29, 2005).

25. Randy Hester, "Labors of Love in the Public Landscape," *Places*, Vol. 1, No. 1 (1983): 18–27.

26. Joshua Cohen, "Deliberation and Democratic Legitimacy," in James Bohman and William Rehg, eds., *Deliberative Democracy: Essays on Reason and Politics* (Cambridge, MA: The MIT Press, 1997), 67–92; Henry Sanoff, *Community Participation Methods in Design and Planning* (New York, NY: John Wiley, 2000).

27. John F. Forester, *The Deliberative Practitioner: Encouraging Participatory Planning Processes* (Cambridge, MA: The MIT Press, 1999).

28. Geoff Carter, "Gas Works Park"; http://events.komonews.com/Gas_Works_Park/v173003022.html.

Step 5: Manifesting Four Wishes through Planning and Design

1. William I. Thomas, *The Unadjusted Girl: With Cases and Standpoint for Behavior Analysis*, Criminal Science Monographs 4 (Boston, MA: Little, Brown, 1923).

2. Ibid., 4, 12, 17, 31, 32, 78.

3. Susanne Langer, *Philosophy in a New Key: A Study in the Symbolism of Reason, Rite, and Art* (Cambridge, MA: Harvard University Press, 1957). See, also, Erich Fromm, whose five needs of relatedness, transcendence, rootedness, sense of identity, and intellectual orientation provide an alternative way of organizing interaction with community and place.

4. Gregory Bateson, *Steps to an Ecology of Mind; Collected Essays in Anthropology, Psychiatry, Evolution, and Epistemology* (San Francisco, CA: Chandler Publishing, 1972).

5. Yi-Fu Tuan, *Topophilia: A Study of Environmental Perception, Attitudes, and Values* (Englewood Cliffs, NJ: Prentice-Hall, 1972).

6. Edward C. Relph, *Place and Placelessness* (London, UK: Pion, 1976).

7. Paul Shepard, *Man in the Landscape; a Historic View of the Esthetics of Nature* (New York, NY: Alfred A. Knopf, 1967), 62; Rina Swentzell, "Conflicting Landscape Values: The Santa Clara Pueblo and Day School," *Places*, Vol. 7, No. 1 (1990): 18–27.

8. Kim Dovey, "Home: An Ordering Principle in Space," *Landscape*, Vol. 22, No. 2 (1978): 27–30.

9. Edward O. Wilson, *Biophilia* (Cambridge, MA: Harvard University Press, 1984).

10. Jay Appleton, *The Experience of Landscape* (New York, NY: John Wiley, 1975); R. Burton Litton, Jr., *Forest Landscape Description and Inventories: A Basis for Land Planning and Design PSW49* (Albany, CA: Pacific Southwest Research Station, Forest Service, U.S. Department of Agriculture, 1968).

11. Donlyn Lyndon and Charles W. Moore, *Chambers for a Memory Palace* (Cambridge, MA: The MIT Press, 1994).

12. Jane Jacobs, *The Death and Life of Great American Cities* (New York, NY: Random House, 1961).

13. Robert Sommer, *Personal Space: The Behavioral Basis of Design* (Englewood Cliffs, NJ: Prentice Hall, 1969); Robert Ardrey, *The Territorial Imperative: A Personal Inquiry into the Animal Origins of Property and Nations* (New York, NY: Atheneum, 1966); Edward T. Hall, *The Hidden Dimension* (Garden City, NY: Doubleday, 1966).

14. Rachel Carson, *Silent Spring* (Boston, MA: Houghton Mifflin, 1962).

15. Kevin Lynch, *The Image of the City* (Cambridge, MA: The MIT Press, 1960); W. R. Lethaby, *Architecture, Nature & Magic* (London, UK: Gerald Duckworth, 1956).

16. D. Geoffrey Hayward, "Home as an Environmental and Psychological Concept," *Landscape*, Vol. 20, No. 1 (1975): 2–9.

17. Dan Bilefsky, "Many Black New Yorkers Are Moving to the South," *The New York Times* (June 21, 2011): sec. NY Region, 7.

18. Robert Harbison, *Eccentric Spaces* (New York, NY: Avon Books, 1980), 26.

19. Seymour Wapner, et al., "Epilogue: Similarities and Differences Across Theories of Environment-Behavior Relations," in *Theoretical Perspectives in Environment-behavior Research: Underlying Assumptions, Research Problems, and Methodologies* (New York, NY: Springer, 2000), 294; Daniel E. Berlyne, *Aesthetics and Psychobiology* (New York NY: Appleton-Century-Crofts, 1971); Constance Perin, *Everything in Its Place: Social Order and Land Use in America* (Princeton, NJ: Princeton University Press, 1977); David Lowenthal and Marquita Riel, "The Nature of Perceived and Imagined Environments," *Environment and Behavior*, Vol. 4, No. 2 (June 1972): 189–207.

20. Kenneth Bayes, *The Therapeutic Effect of Environment on Emotionally Disturbed and Mentally Subnormal Children* (Old Woking, UK: Gresham Press, 1967).

21. Amos Rapoport, "On the Attributes of 'Tradition'," in Jean-Paul Bourdier and Nezar AlSayyad, eds., *Dwellings, Settlements, and Tradition: Cross-Cultural Perspectives*, International Association for the Study of Traditional Environments (Berkeley, CA: International Association for the Study of Traditional Environments, 1989), 77–105.

22. Yi-Fu Tuan, *Space and Place: The Perspective of Experience* (Minneapolis: University of Minnesota Press, 1977), 34–39; Kenneth Frampton, "Towards a Critical Regionalism: Six Points for an Architecture of Resistance," in Hal Foster, ed., *The Anti-Aesthetic: Essays on Postmodern Culture* (Seattle, WA: Bay Press, 1983), 16–30.

23. Amos Rapoport, "The Mutual Interaction of People and Their Built Environment: A Cross-Cultural Perspective," World Anthropology (presented at the International Congress of Anthropological and Ethnological Sciences, The Hague: Mouton, 1976), 22–23.

24. Amos Rapoport, *Human Aspects of Urban Form: Towards a Man-Environment Approach to Urban Form and Design*, Urban and Regional Planning Series, Vol. 15 (Oxford, UK: Pergamon Press, 1977), 7, 42, 110.

25. Susanne Langer, *Feeling and Form; a Theory of Art* (New York, NY: Scribner, 1953), 400.

26. Kenneth E. Boulding, *The Image: Knowledge in Life and Society* (Ann Arbor: University of Michigan Press, 1956).

27. Mircea Eliade, *The Sacred and the Profane; the Nature of Religion* (New York, NY: Harcourt, Brace, 1959).

28. Leo Marx, *The Machine in the Garden: Technology and the Pastoral Ideal in America* (New York, NY: Oxford University Press, 1964).

29. Guy Debord, *The Society of the Spectacle*, trans. by Donald Nicholson-Smith (New York, NY: Zone Books, 1995), 35–46.

30. Roderick Nash, *Wilderness and the American Mind* (New Haven, CT: Yale University Press, 1967).

31. Janet Abu-Lughod, "Disappearing Dichotomies: First World–Third World, Traditional–Modern," *Traditional Dwellings and Settlements Review*, Vol. 3, No. 2 (1992): 7–12; Charles J. Holahan, *Environment and Behavior: A Dynamic Perspective* (New York, NY: Plenum Press, 1978); Paul Oliver, "Handed Down Architecture: Tradition and Transmission," in Nezar AlSayyad and Jean-Paul Bourdier, eds., *Dwellings, Settlements, and Tradition: Cross-cultural Perspectives* (Lanham, MD: University Press of America, 1989), 53–75.

32. Edward C. Relph, *The Modern Urban Landscape: 1880 to the Present* (Baltimore, MD: The Johns Hopkins University Press, 1987).

33. Randolph T. Hester, Jr., "Reciprocal and Recombinant Geometries of Ecological Democracy," *Places*, Vol. 19, No. 1 (2007): 68–77.

34. Kenneth E. Boulding, *Three Faces of Power* (Newbury Park, CA: Sage Publications, Inc, 1989).

35. Francis Huxley, *The Way of the Sacred* (London, UK: Aldus Books, 1974).

36. Emile Durkheim, *The Elementary Forms of the Religious Life* (New York, NY: Free Press, 1965).

37. Shepard, *Man in the Landscape: A Historic View of the Esthetics of Nature*, 41; Harbison, *Eccentric Spaces*, 74.

38. Lethaby, *Architecture, Nature & Magic*, 113 and 132.

39. Amos Rapoport, *House Form and Culture* (Englewood Cliffs, NJ: Prentice-Hall, 1969), 22.

40. Community Development By Design, *Las Pulgas Canyon: An Evaluation of Site Suitability for Natural Open Space* (Berkeley, CA: Santa Monica Mountains Conservancy, 1990), 38–47; Bernice E. Johnston, *California's Gabrielino Indians* (Los Angeles, CA: Southwest Museum, 1962), 46; Bruce W. Miller, *The Gabrielino* (Los Osos, CA: Sand River Press, 1991).

41. Ian L. McHarg, *Design with Nature* (Garden City, NY: Natural History Press, 1969); Frederick R. Steiner, George F. Thompson, and Armando Carbonell, eds., *Nature and Cities: The Ecological Imperative in Urban Design and Planning* (Cambridge, MA: Lincoln Institute of Land Policy, 2016).

42. Rapoport, "On the Attributes of 'Tradition'."

43. Rapoport, *House Form and Culture*, 80; Florence C. Ladd, "Residential History: You Can Go Home Again," *Landscape*, Vol. 21, No. 2 (1977): 15–20; Langer, *Philosophy in a New Key*, 156–57.

44. David V. Canter, *The Psychology of Place* (London, UK: Architectural Press, 1977), 128.

45. Berlyne, *Aesthetics and Psychobiology*; Langer, *Philosophy in a New Key*, 158; Robert Coles, *Children of Crisis, Volume 2: Migrants, Sharecroppers, Mountaineers* (Boston, MA: Little, Brown and Company, 1971), 26; Tuan, *Space and Place*, 188; Frances Moore Lappé and Jeffrey Perkins, *You Have the Power: Choosing Courage in a Culture of Fear* (New York, NY: Jeremy Tarcher, 2005), 9, 85.

46. Quote from Joshua Meyrowitz, *No Sense of Place: The Impact of Electronic Media on Social Behavior* (New York, NY: Oxford University Press, 1985), 308; see, also, Marshall Berman, *All That Is Solid Melts into Air: The Experience of Modernity* (New York, NY: Viking Penguin, 1988), 20.

47. Martin Luther King, Jr., and James M. Washington, "Letter from a Birmingham Jail," in *I Have a Dream: Writings and Speeches That Changed the World* (San Francisco, CA: Harper, 1992), 83–100.

48. Belinda Hurmence, *My Folks Don't Want Me to Talk about Slavery: Twenty-one Oral Histories of Former North Carolina Slaves* (Winston-Salem, NC: John F. Blair, 1984).

49. Sandra Cisneros, *Woman Hollering Creek and Other Stories* (New York, NY: Random House, 1991), 85–113.

50. David Lowenthal and Hugh C. Prince, "Transcendental Experience," in Seymour Wapner, Saul B. Cohen, and Bernard Kaplan, eds., *Experiencing the Environment* (New York, NY: Plenum Press, 1976), 123.

51. Tuan, *Space and Place*, 54, 186; Harold M. Proshansky, Abbe K. Fabian, and Robert Kaminoff, "Place-identity: Physical World Socialization of the Self," *Journal of Environmental Psychology*, Vol. 3, No. 1 (1983): 57–83.

52. Gene Wilhelm, "Dooryard Gardens and Gardening in the Black Community of Brushy, Texas," *Geographical Review*, Vol. 65, No. 1 (1975): 73–92; doi:10.2307/213834.

53. Seonaid Mairi Robertson, *Rosegarden and Labyrinth: A Study in Art Education* (London, UK: Routledge & K. Paul, 1963), 48.

54. Clare Cooper Marcus, *The House as Symbol of Self* (Stroudsberg, PA: Dowden, Hutchinson & Ross, 1974); Clare Cooper Marcus, *House as a Mirror of Self: Exploring the Deeper Meaning of Home* (Berkeley, CA: Conari Press, 1995).

55. Rapoport, *Human Aspects of Urban Form*, 371.

56. Tuan, *Space and Place*, 20, 179.

57. William H. Ittelson, Karen A. Franck, and T. O'Hanlon, "The Nature of Environmental Experience," in Seymour Wapner, Saul B. Cohen, and Bernard Kaplan, eds., *Experiencing the Environment* (New York, NY: Plenum Press, 1976), 187–206.

58. Martin Luther King, Jr., "I've Been to the Mountaintop" (Mason Temple, Memphis, TN, April 3, 1968).

59. Frances Hodgson Burnett and Tasha Tudor, *The Secret Garden* (Philadelphia, PA: Lippincott, 1962); see, also, Martha A. Strawn, *Across the THRESHOLD of India: Art, Women, and Culture* (Staunton, VA: George F. Thompson Publishing, 2016).

60. Dovey, "Home," 27–30.

61. Sandra Cisneros, *The House on Mango Street* (New York, NY: Vintage Books, 2009), 5; Asuncion Horno-Delgado, ed., *Breaking Boundaries: Latina Writing and Critical Readings* (Amherst: University of Massachusetts Press, 1989).

62. Donald Appleyard, *Planning a Pluralist City: Conflicting Realities in Ciudad Guayana* (Cambridge, MA: The MIT Press, 2003), 65–67.

63. Henry Schaefer-Simmern, *The Unfolding of Artistic Activity: Its Basis, Processes, and Implications* (Berkeley: University of California Press, 1948), 9.

64. Christopher Grampp, *From Yard to Garden: The Domestication of America's Home Grounds* (Chicago, IL: Center for American Places, 2008).

65. Simon Nicholson, "Theory of Loose Parts: How Not to Cheat Children," *Landscape Architecture*, Vol. 61, No. 6 (1971): 30–34; Simon Nicholson and Barbara K. Schreiner, *Community Participation in City Decision Making* (Milton Keynes, UK: Open University Press, 1973).

66. Roger Hart, *Children's Experience of Place* (New York, NY: Irvington Publishers, 1979); Robin C. Moore, *Childhood's Domain: Play and Place in Child Development* (London, UK: Dover, 1986); Louise Chawla, "Childhood Place Attachments," in Irwin Altman and Setha M Low, eds., *Place Attachment* (New York, NY: Plenum Press, 1992), 63–86.

67. Yoshida Kenko, *Essays in Idleness* (New York, NY: Columbia University Press, 1967).

68. Gaston Bachelard, *The Poetics of Space* (Boston, MA: Beacon Press, 1994).

69. Florence C. Ladd, "Black Youths View their Environments: Some Views of Housing," *Journal of the American Planning Association*, Vol. 38, No. 2 (1972): 108–16; see, also, Alex Harris and Margaret Sartor, eds., *Dream of a House: The Passions and Preoccupations of Reynolds Price* (Staunton, VA: George F. Thompson Publishing, in association with the Center for Documentary Studies, 2017).

70. Shepard, *Man in the Landscape; a Historic View of the Esthetics of Nature*, 46.

71. Lowenthal and Prince, "Transcendental Experience," 120; Sigmund Freud, *A General Introduction to Psychoanalysis* (New York, NY: Boni and Liveright, 1920).

72. Christian Norberg-Schulz, *Existence, Space, and Architecture* (New York, NY: Praeger Publishers, 1971); Christian Norberg-Schulz, *The Concept of Dwelling: On the Way to Figurative Architecture* (New York, NY: Rizzoli, 1985).

73. Lowenthal and Prince, "Transcendental Experience."

74. Tuan, *Space and Place*, 202.

75. Donald Appleyard, *Inside vs. Outside: The Distortions of Distance* (Berkeley: Institute of Urban & Regional Development, University of California, 1979); Irwin Altman and Joachim F. Wohlwill, *Human Behavior and Environment: Advances in Theory and Research*, Vol. 1 (New York, NY: Plenum Press, 1976); Dean MacCannell, *The Tourist: A New Theory of the Leisure Class* (Berkeley: University of California Press, 1999).

76. Eleanor Roosevelt, "Do One Thing Every Day that Scares You"; www.quotationspage.com/quote/35592.

77. M. E. Hecht, "The Decline of the Grass Lawn Tradition in Tucson," *Landscape*, Vol. 19, No. 3 (1975): 3–10; Rachel Kaplan, "Patterns of Environmental Preference," *Environment and Behavior*, Vol. 9, No. 2 (1977): 195.

78. Bachelard, *The Poetics of Space*, 150.

79. Joseph Sonnenfeld, "Variable Values in Space and Landscape: An Inquiry into the Nature of Environmental Necessity," *Journal of Social Issues*, Vol. 22, No. 4 (1966): 71–82; John Tierney, "Grasping Risk in Life's Classroom," *The New York Times* (July 18, 2011): D1 and D3; Ellen Sandseter and Leif Kennair, "Children's Risky Play from an Evolutionary Perspective: The Anti-Phobic Effects of Thrilling Experiences," *Evolutionary Psychology*, Vol. 9, No. 2 (2011): 285–95.

80. Geoffrey Chaucer, *The Merchant's Prologue and Tale* (London, UK: Cambridge University Press, 2001; originally published in 1478); Jean-Francois Bastide, *The Little House: An Architectural Seduction* (New York, UK: Princeton Architectural Press, 1996).

81. Rapoport, *Human Aspects of Urban Form*, 142.

82. Jean Foreman, *Previews Book of Dream Houses: A Guide to the World's Finest Real Estate* (New York, NY: Harmony Books, 1978).

83. Michael Southworth, *City Learning: Children, Maps and Transit* (Berkeley: University of California, Center for Environmental Design Research, 1988).

84. Martin Heidegger, *Poetry, Language, Thought*, trans. by Albert Hofstadter (New York, NY: Harper & Row, 1971), 143–61; Frampton, "Towards a Critical Regionalism"; David Seamon, *Dwelling, Seeing and Building: Toward a Phenomenological Ecology* (Albany, NY: SUNY Press, 1993).

85. Jack J. Spector, *The Aesthetics of Freud: A Study in Psychoanalysis and Art* (New York, NY: McGraw-Hill, 1972), 100.

86. Anne W. Spirn, *The Language of Landscape* (New Haven, CT: Yale University Press, 1998); Derrick Jensen, *A Language Older Than Words* (New York, NY: Context Books, 2000); Estella Portillo, "Introduction," in Rios C. Herminio and Ignacio Romano Octavo, eds., *Chicanas En La Literatura y El Arte*, Vol. 1, El Grito 7 (Berkeley, CA: Quinto Sol Publications, 1973), 5.

87. Paul Krapfel, *Shifting: Nature's Way of Change* (Cottonwood, CA: Paul Krapfel, 1989).

88. Tuan, *Space and Place*, 74.

89. Kenneth H. Craik, "Appraising the Objectivity of Landscape Dimensions," in John V. Krutilla, ed., *Natural Environments: Studies in Theoretical and Applied Analysis* (Baltimore, MD: The Johns Hopkins University Press, 1972), 292–346.

90. Kevin Lynch, *Managing the Sense of a Region* (Cambridge, MA: The MIT Press, 1980).

91. Ernö Goldfinger, "The Sensation of Space," *Architectural Review*, Vol. 90, No.11 (1941): 129–31; David Lowenthal, "Finding Valued Landscapes," *Progress in Human Geography*, Vol. 2, No. 3 (1978): 373–418.

92. Kent C. Bloomer and Charles W. Moore, *Body, Memory and Architecture* (New Haven, CT: Yale University Press, 1977), 10; Geoffrey Scott, *The Architecture of Humanism: A Study in the History of Taste* (Gloucester, MA: P. Smith, 1965); Peter Smith, "The Pros and Cons of Subliminal Perception in the Built Environment.," *Ekistics*, Vol. 34, No. 204 (November 1972): 367–69.

93. Erich Fromm, "Value, Psychology, and Human Existence," in Abraham H. Maslow, ed., *New Knowledge in Human Values* (New York, NY: Harper & Row, 1959), 151–64; Ann Leone Philbrick, "The Ambiguist Despite Herself: How Space Nurtures and Subverts Identity in Colette's 'Le Toutounier'," *Modern Language Studies*, Vol. 11, No. 2 (April 1, 1981): 32–39; doi:10.2307/3194564.

94. Ernest K. Mundt, "Three Aspects of German Aesthetic Theory," *The Journal of Aesthetics and Art Criticism*, Vol. 17, No. 3 (1959): 287–310; Peter H. Kahn and Stephen R. Kellert, *Children and Nature: Psychological, Sociocultural, and Evolutionary Investigations* (Cambridge, MA: The MIT Press, 2002); Peter H. Kahn, Jr., *The Human Relationship with Nature: Development and Culture* (Cambridge, MA: The MIT Press, 2001); David W. Orr, *Ecological Literacy: Education and the Transition to a Postmodern World* (Albany: State University of New York Press, 1992).

95. Langer, *Philosophy in a New Key*, 260; Hadley Cantril, *The Pattern of Human Concerns* (New Brunswick, NJ: Rutgers University Press, 1966).

96. James E. Lovelock, *Gaia: A New Look at Life on Earth* (New York, NY: Oxford University Press, 1979).

97. Carolyn Merchant, *The Death of Nature: Women, Ecology and the Scientific Revolution* (San Francisco, CA: Harper & Row, 1980).

98. David Abram, *The Spell of the Sensuous: Perception and Language in a More-Than-Human World* (New York, NY: Pantheon Books, 1996).

99. Anthony Cavender, *Folk Medicine in Southern Appalachia* (Chapel Hill: University of North Carolina Press, 2003), 55–59; Robert Bushyhead, "Medicine Stories," in Barbara R. Duncan, ed., *Living Stories of the Cherokee* (Chapel Hill: University of North Carolina Press, 1998), 150–58.

100. David Seamon, "Different Worlds Coming Together: A Phenomenology of the Relationship as Portrayed in Doris Lessing's Diaries of Jane Sommers," in *Dwelling, Seeing, and Designing: Toward a Phenomenological Ecology* (Albany, NY: SUNY Press, 1993), 219–46; Lethaby, *Architecture, Nature & Magic*, 90.

101. Victoria Chanse, "Contexts and Complexities: A Case Study in Evolving Participatory Watershed Stewardship," *Landscape Journal*, Vol. 30, No. 1 (2011): 121–32.

102. Terry Tempest Williams, *An Unspoken Hunger: Stories from the Field* (New York, NY: Pantheon Books, 1994).

103. Milton Rokeach, *Beliefs, Attitudes, and Values; a Theory of Organization and Change* (San Francisco, CA: Jossey-Bass, 1968).

104. James Earl Hester, "The Legacy of a Former Sinner," *The State*, Vol. 45, No. 10 (1978): 24–25; Alister E. McGrath, *The Reenchantment of Nature: The Denial of Religion and the Ecological Crisis* (New York, NY: Doubleday, 2002).

105. Keith H Basso, *Wisdom Sits in Places: Landscape and Language Among the Western Apache* (Albuquerque: University of New Mexico Press, 1996).

106. Deborah Pellow, "Spaces That Teach: Attachment to the African Compound," in Setha M. Low and Irwin Altman, eds., *Place Attachment*, Vol. 12, Human Behavior and Environment (New York, NY: Plenum Press, 1992), 187–210.

107. Aldo Leopold, *A Sand County Almanac and Sketches Here and There* (New York, NY: Oxford University Press, 1949); Connie Barlow, "Because It Is My Religion," *Wild Earth*, Vol. 6, No. 3 (1996): 5–11; Wendell Berry, *A Continuous Harmony: Essays Cultural and Agricultural* (New York, NY: Harcourt Brace Jovanovich, 1972); Robert Scarfo, "Stewardship in the Twentieth Century," *Landscape Architectural Review*, Vol. 7, No. 2 (1986): 13–15.

108. Victoria Chanse and Randolph T. Hester, Jr., "Characterizing Volunteer Involvement in Wildlife Habitat Planning" (presented at the CELA 2002: GroundWork, Syracuse, NY: Council of Educators in Landscape Architecture, 2002), 39; Robert L. Thayer, Jr., *Gray World, Green Heart: Technology, Nature, and the Sustainable Landscape* (New York, NY: John Wiley, 1994).

109. John K. C. Liu, "A Continuing Dialogue on Local Wisdom in Participatory Design," in *Building Cultural Diversity through Participation* (presented at the The Third Annual Pacific Rim Participatory Community Design Conference, Taipei, Taiwan: National Taiwan University, 2001), 444–50; Grant Jones, *Voice of the Earth: Discovering Nature's Rules for Landscape Design* (Seattle, WA: Skookumchuck Press, 2011); Abraham H. Maslow, *New Knowledge in Human Values* (New York, NY: Harper, 1959); Frances Moore Lappé, *Democracy's Edge: Choosing to Save Our Country by Bringing Democracy to Life* (San Francisco, CA: Jossey-Bass, 2006); Wes Jackson, *Becoming Native to This Place* (Lexington, KY: University Press of Kentucky, 1994); Mary Evelyn Tucker, et al., *Buddhism and Ecology: The Interconnection of Dharma and Deeds* (Cambridge, MA: Harvard University Press, 1997).

110. Christina Greene, *Our Separate Ways: Women and the Black Freedom Movement in Durham, North Carolina* (Chapel Hill: University of North Carolina Press, 2005); Dolores Hayden, *The Power of Place: Urban Landscapes as Public History* (Cambridge, MA: The MIT Press, 1997), 178–87; Leslie Brown, *Upbuilding Black Durham: Gender, Class, and Black Community Development in the Jim Crow South* (Chapel Hill: University of North Carolina Press, 2008), 178–86.

111. Shepard, *Man in the Landscape; a Historic View of the Esthetics of Nature*, 40.

112. Ibid., 116.

113. Suiteki Kawai, "The Moment of Landscape: In the Sequential Experience of Pathways in Old Japanese Sacred Precincts" (Department of Landscape Architecture, University of California, Berkeley, 1993).

114. Thomas Carlyle, *The French Revolution: A History* (New York, NY: Modern Library, 1934), PT I, BK VII, CH 4.

115. Scott, *The Architecture of Humanism*, 36.

116. Bloomer and Moore, *Body, Memory and Architecture*.

117. Carl G. Jung, *Man and His Symbols* (London: Aldus Books, 1979), 94.

118. Joan Lowy, "Automation in the Air Dulls Pilots' Skill," *Herald-Sun* (August 31, 2011): A4.

119. Daniel B. Smith, "Is There an Ecological Unconscious?," *The New York Times Magazine* (January 31, 2010): MM36.

120. Roger S. Ulrich, "View through a Window May Influence Recovery from Surgery," *Science*, Vol. 224, No. 4647 (1984): 420–21; Clare Cooper Marcus and Marni Barnes, *Healing Gardens: Therapeutic Benefits and Design Recommendations* (New York, NY: John Wiley, 1999); Michael Hough, *City Form and Natural Process: Towards a New Urban Vernacular* (New York, NY: Van Nostrand Reinhold, 1984).

121. Michael Bernick and Robert Cervero, *Transit Villages in the 21st Century* (New York, NY: McGraw-Hill, 1997); Stephen Carr, et al., *Public Space* (London, UK: Cambridge University Press, 1992); Charles Flink and Robert M. Searns, *Greenways: A Guide to Planning, Design, and Development* (Washington, DC: Island Press, 1993).

122. Allan B. Jacobs, Elizabeth MacDonald, and Yodan Rofe, *The Boulevard Book: History, Evolution, Design of Multiway Boulevards* (Cambridge, MA: The MIT Press, 2003).

123. Katharine Alvord, *Divorce Your Car! Ending the Love Affair with the Automobile* (Gabriola Island, BC: New Society Publishers, 2000); Elizabeth Rosenthal, "Across Europe, Irking Drivers Is Urban Policy," *The New York Times* (June 27, 2011): A1, A8.

124. Frances Moore Lappé, *Liberation Ecology: Reframing Six Disempowering Ideas that Keep Us from Aligning With Nature—Even Our Own* (Cambridge, MA: Small Planet Media, 2010).

125. Hayden, *The Power of Place*; Abu-Lughod, "Disappearing Dichotomies."

126. Alexis de Tocqueville, et al., *Democracy in America* (New York, NY: Alfred A. Knopf, 1945; originally published in 1835).

127. Relph, *Place and Placelessness*; Edward Allen, ed., *The Responsive House* (Cambridge, MA: The MIT Press, 1975).

128. Robert D. Putnam, *Bowling Alone: The Collapse and Revival of American Community* (New York, NY: Simon & Schuster, 2000); Richard Sennett, *The Fall of Public Man* (New York, NY: Alfred A. Knopf, 1976).

129. Randolph T. Hester, Jr., "Life-cycle Stages of Participatory Democracy," in Organization of Urban Re's (OURS), ed., *Citizen Participation in Urban Governance: International Community Planning Forum Proceedings* (Taipei, Taiwan: Department of Urban Development, Taipei City Government, 2005), 558–80.

130. Allen, *The Responsive House*.

131. Cisneros, *The House on Mango Street*, 107.

132. Robert S. Ogilvie, "Recuiting, Training and Retaining Volunteers," in Randolph T. Hester, Jr. and Corrina Kweskin, eds., *Democratic Design in the Pacific Rim: Japan, Taiwan, and the United States* (Mendocino, CA: Ridge Times Press, 1999), 242–49; Randolph T. Hester, Jr., "The Place of Participation: An American View," in Randolph T. Hester, Jr. and Corrina Kweskin, eds., *Democratic Design in the Pacific Rim: Japan, Taiwan, and the United States* (Mendocino, CA: Ridge Times Press, 1999), 22–41.

133. Wilhelm, "Dooryard Gardens and Gardening in the Black Community of Brushy, Texas"; Yu-Ting Kuo, You-Jen Chen, and Ying-Feng Chen, *Four Communities, Five Factors* (Taipei, Taiwan: National Taiwan University, 2010).

134. Studs Terkel, *Working: People Talk about What They Do All Day and How They Feel about What They Do* (New York, NY: Pantheon Books, 1974); Robert N. Bellah, et al., *Habits of the Heart: Individualism and Commitment in American Life* (Berkeley: University of California Press, 1985).

135. Rapoport, *House Form and Culture*, 21; Lappé and Perkins, *You Have the Power*, 127.

136. Allan B. Jacobs, *Making City Planning Work* (Chicago, IL: American Society of Planning Officials, 1978).

137. Martha A. Ackelsberg, *Resisting Citizenship: Feminist Essays on Politics, Community, and Democracy* (New York, NY: Routledge, 2009), 29; Richard L. Mattson, "The Cultural Landscape of a Southern Black Community: East Wilson, North Carolina, 1890 to 1930," *Landscape Journal*, Vol. 11, No. 2 (1992): 144–59.

138. Karl Linn, *Building Commons and Community* (Oakland, CA: New Village Press, 2008); Donald Appleyard, *Liveable Streets* (Berkeley: University of California Press, 1981), 215–39; Richard Register, *Ecocity Berkeley: Building Cities for a Healthy Future* (Berkeley, CA: North Atlantic Books, 1987).

139. Marcia J. McNally, "Nature Big and Small," *Landscape Journal*, Vol. 30, No. 1 (2011): 19–34.

140. David Harvey, *The Condition of Postmodernity: An Enquiry into the Origins of Cultural Change* (Oxford, UK: Blackwell, 1989).

141. Manuel Castells, *The City and the Grassroots: A Cross-cultural Theory of Urban Social Movements* (Berkeley: University of California Press, 1983); Manuel Castells, *The Power of Identity, Vol. 2, The Information Age: Economy, Society and Culture* (Oxford, UK: Blackwell, 1997); Edgar Anderson, "Dump Heaps and the Origin of Agriculture," in *Plants, Man and Life* (Berkeley: University of California Press, 1967), 136–51; Clarissa T. Kimber, "Spatial Patterning in the Dooryard Gardens of Puerto Rico," *Geographical Review*, Vol. 63, No. 1 (1973): 6–26; Hecht, "The Decline of the Grass Lawn Tradition in Tucson"; Frederick J. Simoons, "Two Ethiopian Gardens," *Landscape*, Vol. 14, No. 2 (1965): 15–20; Wilhelm, "Dooryard Gardens and Gardening in the Black Community of Brushy, Texas."

142. James S. Duncan, Jr., "Landscape Taste as a Symbol of Group Identity: A Westchester County Village," *Geographical Review*, Vol. 63, No. 3 (1973): 334–55; Joan I. Nassauer, "Messy Ecosystems, Orderly Frames," *Landscape Journal*, Vol. 14, No. 2 (1995): 161.

143. Eliana Rivero, "From Immigrants to Ethnics: Cuban Writers in the U.S.," in Asuncion Horno-Delgado, ed., *Breaking Boundaries: Latina Writing and Critical Readings* (Amherst: University of Massachusetts Press, 1989), 189–200; Aberto Sandoval, "Dolores Prida's 'Coser y Cantar': Mapping the Dialectics of Ethnic Identity and Assimilation," in Ibid, 201–20; Shenglin Chang, *The Global Silicon Valley Home: Lives and Landscapes Within Taiwanese American Trans-Pacific Culture* (Stanford, CA: Stanford University Press, 2006); Gloria Anzaldua, "La Conciencia De La Mestiza: Toward a New Consciousness," in Estelle Freedman, ed., *The Essential Feminist Reader* (New York, NY: Modern Library, 2007); Willow Lung-Amam, "Landscapes of Difference: Race and Ethnic Diversity and the Changing Form of Suburbia" (Las Vegas, NV: Urban History Association, 2010); James T. Rojas, "The Enacted Environment: The Creation of 'Place' by Mexicans and Mexican Americans in East Los Angeles" (Cambridge, MA: The MIT Press, 1991).

144. Marjorie Agosín, *Mujeres De Humo* (Madrid, Spain: Torremozas, 1987).

145. Michael Rios, "Claiming Latino Space: Cultural Insurgency in the Public Realm," in Jeffrey Hou, ed., *Insurgent Public Space: Guerrilla Urbanism and the Remaking of Contemporary Cities* (New York, NY: Routledge, 2010); Leonie Sandercock, *Making the Invisible Visible: A Multicultural Planning History* (Berkeley: University of California Press, 1998); Margaret Crawford, "Contesting the Public Realm: Struggles over Public Space in Los Angeles," *Journal of Architectural Education*, Vol. 49, No. 1 (1995): 4–9; Setha Low, *Rethinking Urban Parks: Public Space & Cultural Diversity* (Austin: University of Texas Press, 2005); David Harvey, *Consciousness and the Urban Experience* (Oxford, UK: Blackwell, 1985).

146. Laura J. Lawson, *City Bountiful: A Century of Community Gardening in America* (Berkeley: University of California Press, 2005); Jonathan Leib, "The Witting Autobiography of Richmond Virginia: Arthur Ash, the Civil War, and Monument Avenues Racialized Landscape," in Richard Schein, ed., *Landscape and Race in the United States* (New York, NY: Routledge, 2006), 187–211.

147. Randolph T. Hester, Jr., Shenglin Chang, and Shih Wang, eds., *The Living Landscape: Reading Cultural Landscape Experiences in Taiwan and America* (Taipei, Taiwan: United Force Culture Enterprise Co., Ltd, 1999).

148. Randolph T. Hester, Jr. and Marcia McNally, *The Language of Wildlands Appreciation: A Literature Review of Descriptions and Values* (Berkeley: Department of Landscape Architecture, University of California, 1987), 50–52.

149. Susan Suntree, *Sacred Sites: The Secret History of Southern California* (Lincoln: University of Nebraska Press, 2010); Klara Kelley and Harris Francis, *Navajo Sacred Places* (Bloomington: Indiana University Press, 1994); Shenglin Chang and Willow Lung-Amam, "Born Glocal: Youth Identity and Suburban Spaces in the U.S. and Taiwan," *Amerasia Journal*, Vol. 36, No. 3 (2010): 29–51.

150. James Holston, *Insurgent Citizenship: Disjunctions of Democracy and Modernity in Brazil* (Princeton, NJ: Princeton University Press, 2008); John Friedmann, *The Prospect of Cities* (Minneapolis: University of Minnesota Press, 2002); Blaine Merker, "Taking Places: Rebar's Absurd Tactics in Generous Urbanism," in Jeffrey Hou, ed., *Insurgent Public Space: Guerrilla Urbanism and the Remaking of Contemporary Cities* (New York, NY: Routledge, 2010), 45–58; Rafi Segal, Eyal Weizman, and David Tartakover, *A Civilian Occupation: The Politics of Israeli Architecture* (Tel Aviv, Israel: VERSO, 2003); Derek H. Alderman, "Naming Streets for Martin Luther King, Jr.: No Easy Road," in Richard Schein, ed., *Landscape and Race in the United States* (New York, NY: Routledge, 2006), 213–36.

151. Herbert J. Gans, *Urban Villagers: Group and Class in the Life of Italian-Americans* (New York, NY: Free Press, 1962).

152. John Horton, *The Politics of Diversity: Immigration, Resistance, and Change in Monterey Park, California* (Philadelphia, PA: Temple University Press, 1995); Anastasia Loukaitou-Sideris and Tridib Banerjee, *Urban Design Downtown Poetics and Politics of Form* (Berkeley: University of California Press, 1998).

153. Clara Irazábal, "Ethnospaces," in Tridib Banerjee and Anastasia Loukaitou-Sideris, eds., *Companion to Urban Design* (New York, NY: Routledge, 2011).

154. Mark Abrahamson, *Urban Enclaves: Identity and Place in America* (New York, NY: St. Martin's Press, 1996); Edward Blakely and Gail Snyder, *Fortress America: Gated Communities in the United States* (Washington, DC: Brookings Institution Press, 1997); Willow Lung-Amam, *Trespassers?* (Berkeley: University of California Press, 2017).

155. David Lowenthal, *The Past Is a Foreign Country* (New York, NY: Cambridge University Press, 1985).

156. Kim Sorvig, "The Wilds of South Central," *Landscape Architecture*, Vol. 92, No. 4 (2002): 66.

157. Setha Low, *On the Plaza: The Politics of Public Space and Culture* (Austin: University of Texas Press, 2000).

158. David Lowenthal, "Age and Artifact: Dilemmas of Appreciation," in Donald W. Meining, ed., *Interpretation of Ordinary Landscapes: Geographical Essays* (New York, NY: Oxford University Press, 1979).

159. John K. C. Liu, "The Tawo House Building in the Face of Cultural Domination," in Randolph T. Hester, Jr. and Corrina Kweskin, eds., *Democratic Design in the Pacific Rim: Japan, Taiwan and the United States* (Mendocino, CA: Ridge Times Press, 1999), 64–79.

160. Michael Hough, *Out of Place: Restoring Identity to the Regional Landscape* (New Haven, CT: Yale University Press, 1992).

161. Horton, *The Politics of Diversity*.

162. Arthur M. Schlesinger, *The Disuniting of America: Reflections on a Multicultural Society* (New York, NY: W. W. Norton, 1998).

163. Janice Perlman, *Myth of Marginality: Urban Poverty and Politics in Rio De Janeiro* (Berkeley: University of California Press, 1980); Robert Sommer and Robert L. Thayer, Jr., "The Radicalization of Common Ground: People's Park, Berkeley," *Landscape Architecture*, Vol. 67, No. 6 (1977): 510–14.

164. Gans, *Urban Villagers*.

165. Paul Davidoff, "Advocacy and Pluralism in Planning," *Journal of the American Institute of Planners*, Vol. 31, No. 4 (1965):

331–38; Frances F. Piven, "Whom Does the Advocate Planner Serve?," *Social Policy*, Vol. 1, No. 1 (1970): 32–37.

166. Lawrence Susskind and Jeffrey L. Cruikshank, *Breaking the Impasse: Consensual Approaches to Resolving Public Disputes* (New York, NY: Basic Books, 1987); Lawrence Halprin, *The RSVP Cycles: Creative Processes in the Human Environment* (New York, NY: G. Braziller, 1970); Randolph T. Hester, Jr., *Planning Neighborhood Space with People* (New York, NY: Van Nostrand Reinhold Co, 1984); Daniel Iacofano, *Meeting of the Minds: A Guide to Successful Meeting Facilitation* (Berkeley, CA: MIG Communications, 2001); David de la Pena et al., eds., *Design as Democracy; Techniques for Collective Creativity* (Washington, DC: Island Press, 2017).

167. May T. Watts, "The Stylish House," in *Reading the Landscape of America* (New York, NY: Macmillan, 1975), 320–57.

168. Tuan, *Space and Place*, 58.

169. Robert L. Thayer, Jr., "Conspicuous Non-Consumption: The Symbolic Aesthetics of Solar Architecture," in *Proceedings of the Eleventh Annual Conference of the Environmental Design Research Association*, 1980, 118–29.

170. Vance Packard, *Status Seekers: An Exploration of Class Behavior in America and the Hidden Barriers that Affect You, Your Community, Your Future* (New York, NY: D. McKay, 1959); Wendell Berry, *The Unsettling of America: Culture and Agriculture* (San Francisco, CA: Sierra Club Books, 1977).

171. Simon Partner, *Assembled in Japan: Electrical Goods and the Making of the Japanese Consumer* (Berkeley: University of California Press, 2000).

172. Ernst F. Schumacher, *Small Is Beautiful: Economics as If People Mattered* (New York, NY: Harper & Row, 1973); United States, *Statistical Abstract of the United States, 1960*, 80th ed. (Washington, DC: U.S. Census Bureau, 1960); United States, *Statistical Abstract of the United States, 2000*, 120th ed. (Washington, DC: U.S. Census Bureau, 2000).

173. Hester, Jr., *Planning Neighborhood Space with People*, 38.

174. Ladd, "Black Youths View Their Environments."

175. Oscar Newman, *Community of Interest* (Garden City, NY: Anchor Press, 1980).

176. Joan I. Nassauer, *Placing Nature: Culture and Landscape Ecology* (Washington, DC: Island Press, 1997); Louise Mozingo, "The Aesthetics of Ecological Design: Seeing Science as Culture," *Landscape Journal*, Vol. 16, No. 1 (1997): 46–59.

177. Brian H. Walker and David A. Salt, *Resilience Thinking: Sustaining Ecosystems and People in a Changing World* (Washington, DC: Island Press, 2006), 139–151.

178. Milton Kotler, *Neighborhood Government: The Local Foundations of Political Life* (Indianapolis, IN: Bobbs-Merrill, 1969).

179. Nicole Ardoin, "Toward an Interdisciplinary Understanding of Place: Lessons for Environmental Education," *Canadian Journal of Environmental Education*, Vol. 11, No. 1 (2006): 112–26.

Step 6: Inhabiting the Sacred in the Everyday Landscape

1. Jan Wampler, *All their Own: People and the Places They Build* (Cambridge, MA: Schenkman Publishing Company, 1977); John B. Jackson, "The Westward-moving House," *Landscape*, Vol. 2, No. 3 (1953): 8–21; John R. Stilgoe, *Common Landscape of America, 1580–1845* (New Haven, CT: Yale University Press, 1983).

2. Elizabeth Murray, *Cultivating Sacred Space: Gardening for the Soul* (San Francisco, CA: Pomegranate Communications, 1997).

3. Sue Bender, *Everyday Sacred: A Woman's Journey Home* (San Francisco, CA: Harper, 1995).

4. Richard Louv, *Last Child in the Woods: Saving Our Children from Nature-Deficit Disorder* (Chapel Hill, NC: Algonquin Books, 2005).

5. Dawn Callan, *Awakening the Warrior Within: Secrets of Personal Safety and Inner Security* (Novato, CA: Nataraj Publishing, 1995).

6. Randolph T. Hester, Jr., *Neighborhood Space* (Stroudsburg, PA: Dowden, Hutchinson & Ross, 1975), 83–126.

7. Jane Jacobs, *Death and Life of the Great American Cities* (New York, NY: Random House, 1961), 103–05.

8. Henry David Thoreau, as quoted in Robert Blaisdell, ed., *Thoreau: A Book of Quotations* (Mineola, NY: Dover Publications, 2000), 33.

9. Randolph T. Hester, Jr., *Design for Ecological Democracy* (Cambridge, MA: The MIT Press, 2006), 363–85.

10. Sharon G. Danks, *Asphalt to Ecosystems: Design Ideas for Schoolyard Transformation* (Oakland, CA: New Village Press, 2010); Paul H. Gobster and R. Bruce Hull, *Restoring Nature: Perspectives from the Social Sciences and Humanities* (Washington, DC: Island Press, 2000).

11. Mark Francis, "The Everyday and the Personal: Six Garden Stories," in Mark Francis and Randolph T. Hester, Jr., eds., *The Meaning of Gardens: Idea, Place, and Action* (Cambridge, MA: The MIT Press, 1992), 106–215.

ACKNOWLEDGMENTS AND CREDITS

Acknowledgments

Support for the research for this book was generously provided by the Department of Landscape Architecture and Environmental Planning at the University of California, Berkeley, primarily through the Beatrix Farrand Fund.

Credits

Unless otherwise credited, all illustrations—charts, diagrams, drawings, maps, paintings, photographs, and plans—were made by Randolph Hester, Amber Nelson, or students and staff under their supervision at North Carolina State University, University of California, Berkeley, Community Development by Design, or SAVE, International. All illustrations are used by permission. Some drawings of sacred places are not credited per agreement to protect the privacy of participants.

The following figures are credited to the person listed.

Fig. 4. Jerry Blow.

Fig. 13. Marcia McNally.

Fig. 18. Billie Harper.

Fig. 22. Marcia McNally.

Fig. 32. John Syorey

Fig. 33. Will Hooker.

Figs. 44 and 45. Emily Smith.

Fig. 75. John Willis, from his book, *Mni Wiconi: Honoring the Water Protectors at Standing Rock and Everywhere in the Ongoing Struggle for Indigenous Sovereignty* (George F. Thompson Publishing, 2019).

Fig. 95. Patrick Waddell.

Fig. 96. Frederick R. Steiner.

Fig. 107. Will Hooker.

Fig. 113. Thom Sutfin.

Fig. 114. Yasuhiro Endoh.

Fig. 121. Marcia McNally.

Fig. 133. Jerry Blow.

Herewith the locations for the painting (frontispiece) and photographs that appear on the following pages:

2: Kyoto, Japan.

10: Beseeching the God, Sagino Mori Temple, Kyoto, Japan.

20: Manteo, North Carolina.

46: Fito's Place, Berkeley, California.

60: Colca Canyon, Peru.

88: Transport boat, Amazon River, Brazil.

116: Offering prayers to the Virgin, San Cristóbal Mountain, Santiago, Chile.

142: Organizing the dead, cemetery, La Paz, Bolivia.

172: Yodeling with Amber's grandfather, Bob Loper, Cody, Wyoming.

254: Drying soccer jersey and socks on a wire fence, Cabo Pantoja, Peru.

274: Ramona and her grandparents at low tide, Rio de Janeiro, Brazil.

ABOUT THE ESSAYIST

FREDERICK R. STEINER is Dean of the School of Design and Paley Professor at the University of Pennsylvania who previously, from 2001 to 2016, was Dean of the School of Architecture and Harry M. Rockwell Chair in Architecture at the University of Texas at Austin. A Fellow of both the American Society of Landscape Architects and American Academy in Rome, he has been a Fulbright-Hays research scholar at Wageningen University in the Netherlands, a visiting professor at Tsinghua University in Beijing, China, the past president of the Hill Country Conservancy, and the past chair of Envision Central Texas. His articles have appeared in *Environmental Management, Journal of the American Planning Association, Landscape and Urban Planning, Landscape Architecture,* and *Landscape Journal,* among many others, and his acclaimed books include *Nature and Cities: The Ecological Imperative in Urban Design and Planning* (Lincoln Institute of Land Policy, 2016), co-edited with George F. Thompson and Armando Carbonell, which was designated a Best Book of the Year in 2016 by the American Society of Landscape Architecture, *Design for a Vulnerable Planet* (Texas, 2011), *The Living Landscape* (Island Press, 2008), *Human Ecology* (Island Press, 2002; 2016), *Ecological Design and Planning* (John Wiley, 1997; 2007), co-edited with George F. Thompson, and *Soil Conservation in the United States: Policy and Planning* (Johns Hopkins, in association with the Center for American Places, 1990).

ABOUT THE AUTHORS

Randolph T. Hester, Jr. was born in 1944 in Danville, Virginia, and he grew up at Hesters Store, North Carolina. He completed his undergraduate degrees in landscape architecture and sociology at North Carolina State University and his graduate degree in landscape architecture at Harvard University. He has an Honorary Doctorate from Dalhousie University. Hester is Director of the Center for Ecological Democracy and Professor Emeritus of Landscape Architecture at the University of California, Berkeley. He practices landscape architecture in North Carolina and the East Asian-Australasian Flyway. His built work has won national awards, and he is credited with saving the black-faced spoonbill from extinction. His books document fifty years of innovation in community design, including *The Neighborhood Guide to the Thoroughfare Plan* (Wake Environment Publications, 1973), *A Citizens Guide to Local Government* (Goals for Raleigh/Wake, 1975), *Neighborhood Space* (Dowden, Hutchinson and Ross, 1975), *Community Design Primer* (Ridge Times Press, 1990), *The Meaning of Gardens* (The MIT Press, 1990), with Mark Francis, *Community Planning Method and Technique* (Gendaikikakushitsu Publishers, 1997), *A Theory for Building Community* (Yungliou Press, 1999), with Sheng Lin Chang, and *Design for Ecological Democracy* (The MIT Press, 2006). He resides in Durham, North Carolina.

Amber D. Nelson was born in 1982 in Rota, Spain, and she grew up somewhat nomadically in various places throughout the United States and Latin America. She completed her undergraduate degree in architecture at Columbia University and a dual master's degree in architecture and landscape architecture at the University of California, Berkeley. At UC, Berkeley, she taught the course "Landscape as Sacred Place" as well as other courses in environmental design. After teaching at Berkeley, she undertook an epic travel from Berkeley to Bahia, Brazil, by land, including by truck, boat, and bicycle, with the seventy-year-old Mestre Acordeon, a legendary capoeira master. Her professional focus is experiencing and promoting public sacred places through self-made landscapes and sustainable tourism. Currently, she is the South America manager for Context Travel, a B Corporation that specializes in the deep experience of place, led by academics in the field. When not traveling, she and her family reside in Rio de Janiero, Brazil. This is her first book.

ABOUT THE BOOK

Inhabiting the Sacred in Everyday Life: How to Design a Place that Touches Your Heart, Stirs You to Consecrate and Cultivate It as Home, Dwell Intentionally within It, Slay Monsters for It, and Let It Loose in Your Democracy was brought to publication in an edition of 1,000 softcover copies with gatefold flaps, with the generous support of the University of California, Berkeley. The text was set in Adobe Caslon Pro, the paper is Korean Matte Art, 150 gsm weight, and the book was professionally printed and bound by Dong-A Printing in Korea.

Publisher: George F. Thompson
Editorial and Research Assistant: Mikki Soroczak
Manuscript Editor: Purna Makaram
Book Design and Production: Ann Lowe and David Skolkin

Published in 2019. First softcover edition.
Printed in Korea on acid-free paper.

George F. Thompson Publishing, L.L.C.
217 Oak Ridge Circle
Staunton, VA 24401-3511, U.S.A.
www.gftbooks.com

27 26 25 24 23 22 21 20 19   1 2 3 4 5

The Library of Congress Preassigned Control Number is 2018953844.

ISBN: 978–1–938086–65–6